CAPITAL AND LABOR IN AMERICAN COPPER, *1845 – 1990*

WERTHEIM PUBLICATIONS IN INDUSTRIAL RELATIONS

Established in 1923 by the family of the late Jacob Wertheim "for the support of original research in the field of industrial cooperation."

An early view of the Anaconda Shaft and Headframe. (*Photo courtesy of C. Owen Smithers, Butte, Montana.*)

CAPITAL AND LABOR IN AMERICAN COPPER, *1845–1990*

LINKAGES BETWEEN PRODUCT AND LABOR MARKETS

George H. Hildebrand
Garth L. Mangum

Distributed by

HARVARD UNIVERSITY PRESS

Cambridge, Massachusetts

London, England

1992

This book is printed on acid-free paper, and its binding materials have
been chosen for strength and durability.

Library of Congress Cataloging-in-Publication Data

Hildebrand, George Herbert.
    Capital and labor in American copper, 1845-1990 : linkages between
product and labor markets / George H. Hildebrand and Garth L.
Mangum.
        p.   cm.—(Wertheim publications in industrial relations)
    Includes bibliographical references and index.
    ISBN 0-674-09481-6
    1. Industrial relations—United States—History.   2. Copper
industry and trade—United States—Employees—History.   3. Copper
industry and trade—United States—History.   I. Mangum, Garth L.
II. Title.   III. Series.
HD6976.M72U554 1991
331'.0422343'0973—dc20   91-18174
                                                          CIP

TP

To Florabelle and Marion,
for their patience and their support

FOREWORD

This volume is extraordinarily instructive to academics and practitioners alike. The linkages and interactions of local labor markets and specific global product markets over long periods of historical time—interlacing evolving technology (including geology) and public policies with the dynamics of business and labor organizations—create the framework for a penetrating understanding of economic and labor history.

The analysis of the United States copper story depicted on a century-and-a-half canvas stands in sharp contrast to much of current short-term labor-market research and admonitions urging competitive strategies on businesses in niche product markets. The long-term interaction and adjustment processes ongoing in institutional policies are today largely unseen or overlooked. Even the hysteresis view, which sees long-term decline as arising from the hardening of competitive arteries, needs to appreciate the productive interactions of labor and product markets and the consequences for competitive survival of adaptive businesses and unions.

Furthermore, this copper story underlines the difficulty, often the futility, of seeking to transfer prominent features of one industrial relations system (in this case the industry-wide wage uniformity of basic steel) to another (the copper industry) without an appreciation of the basic features of the two systems. Most notably, the lack of technological homogeneity in nonferrous or copper mining (attributable basically to geology), the character of competition among domestic producers in the two sectors, the contrasts in the skill-mix between steel and copper, and the forms of labor organization that emerged in the two industries, account for the failure to adapt steel patterns to copper in the environment of the 1970s and 1980s. Efforts to transfer institutions across national borders—as in U.S. designs for Japan after World War II, or many current aspirations for Eastern Europe—need to be subjected to comparable product-market and labor-market analysis.

With regard to the training of future academics and practitioners, the wisdom of this volume suggests that much of the analytics of current microeconomic or policy analysis contributes little to an understanding of business and labor organizations and their interactions. Nor do these disciplines provide the perspective to interpret the decisions and the course of long-term organizational history. This insightful account of the copper industry provides an indispensable yet often missing element in the education of those concerned with policymaking over time in the private institutions of our market economy.

The authors have very special qualifications for this study. George Hildebrand has published extensively on labor economics and wage determination. He has also served over many years as an arbitrator in labor-management disputes in the copper industry, among other sectors. Garth Mangum has written widely on labor markets and public policy and like his coauthor is an arbitrator in labor-management disputes. His familiarity with the communities of the copper region is lifelong. The authors bring both direct experience and considered reflection to their book, a fact that is reflected in the previous Wertheim Committee support of their publications.

John T. Dunlop

ACKNOWLEDGMENTS

Many people, some now gone, helped to instruct us in the intricacies of American mining. Others have been most helpful in other ways. Among them—and in no order of preference—are Gwen Luke, Wayne Holland, James H. Peterson, Camille Guth, John F. Boland, Jr., John Corbett, Vernon H. Jensen, Sylvain Schnaittacher, M. P. Scanlon, Les Presmyk, Jack Ladd, Larry Bench, Alex Lopez, Tom McWilliams, William J. Uren, Wayne H. Burt, Ralph Sievwright, Douglas Soutar, Mike Noto, Benjamin Aaron, James Speer, Robert Skiba, Larry Disera, Bob Jackson, Charles Daly, and Alexis Fernandez.

We are also much indebted to the unstinting help provided by the General Library and the Institute of Industrial Relations, Engineering, and Social Science Libraries at the University of California, Berkeley; and to the Martin P. Catherwood Library at Cornell University.

G.H.H.
G.L.M.

CONTENTS

TABLES

FIGURES

ILLUSTRATIONS

CAPITAL AND LABOR
IN AMERICAN
COPPER, *1845–1990*

CHAPTER 1

THE COPPER INDUSTRY AND
ITS INDUSTRIAL RELATIONS

THE STORY OF THE COPPER INDUSTRY in the United States is in many ways the story of most of our old-line, basic, "smokestack" industries. Forty years ago 125,000 people were employed; today the number is 25,000. Behind that bald statement lie countless quiet stories of individual and family displacement and community decline. While in some of its uses copper is still essential, in many others viable substitutes can do the job. And abundant supplies of copper are available internationally at competitive cost. Whereas the U.S. industry on the eve of the First World War produced nearly 60 percent of the world's copper, it now produces only 17 percent. Where it once exported one-third of its product, one-quarter of our copper is now imported. As recently as the 1950s, U.S. firms owned most of the foreign sources of supply; today, Japanese firms own rising proportions of domestic U.S. capacity, and the U.S. foreign properties long ago were nationalized.

Nevertheless, the industry's overall experience has not been negative, nor does its current status justify pessimism. The mid-1980s were a painful trial by fire, but copper rebounded to reach a historic high in profitability. Despite declining ore grades and a wage level four to five times that of its major international competitors, the firms of the U.S. copper industry have fought back to their status as the world's lowest-cost producers. Although the number of jobs in the industry has declined and wages have been cut during these traumatic years, in an economy of expanding service employment copper is still a high-wage island. Some communities threatened by closures have experienced resurgence because of an industry comeback. And copper's survival has not been the result of any government bailout, international agency assistance, or protectionist device. The industry, a major source of employment and economic strength in the communities where its production units are located, has saved itself through dogged determination and skillful internal investment, as well as a bit of luck in world affairs. From this experience of relative decline but stubborn persistence, we hope in this book to identify lessons that may be helpful not only to copper and other historic industries, but to newer industries as they in turn are buffeted in a competitive world.

Economic development ascends a staircase that generally climbs from subsistence levels of farming and fishing to factory production of the essential consumer products formerly made in the home or the workshop—textiles, clothing, and shoes—to the turning of available natural resources into intermediate products for more sophisticated goods.[1] On this third stairstep, along with steel, glass, oil, and petrochemicals, are copper and other basic metals. From there the staircase leads upward through basic and complex assembly, on to exotic materials and abstract services, and into realms we have yet to explore. In a hungry and aggressive world, at every step on the staircase there are those struggling upward, fighting for levels of income which appear inadequate to those on the higher steps but munificent to those below. The alternatives for the pioneers, which the United States has been, are to move up to higher steps or to stand and compete on familiar ones. The latter has been the choice of a leaner but more aggressive copper industry. Its fight and survival offer lessons to those on every step of the economic staircase.

But industry is not an impersonal abstraction, nor does it comprise only entrepreneurs or stockholders or managers. It is a personalized construct of all of these, as well as employees at all levels—suppliers of essential inputs and distributors of outputs—and the communities in which they live. The welfare of all is inextricably intertwined, yet each must look out for himself or herself while recognizing that interdependence. When all is said and done, there are only people, and an industrial enterprise has no raison d'être other than to serve them.

A business firm lives or dies by its ability to serve its product market. A by-product, and one of its societal justifications for existence, is the provision of employment opportunities. Since labor is a major input and usually the largest single cost, business survival also assumes that labor productivity will continue to rise rapidly enough to offset the increase in labor costs. Hence to understand an industry means to understand both its product markets and its labor markets.

It has often been said that the first principle of labor economics is that the demand for labor is a derived demand—derived from the demand for the product labor is employed to produce. Of course, production will not occur in the private-enterprise sector of an economy unless labor can be hired at a cost which, combined with all other factors of production, leaves a sufficient margin to make the enterprise an attractive outlet for investment. The skills available, as well as their costs, influence the production processes used. Yet the price at which the product can be sold constitutes but one blade of the labor-market scissors. The nature of the product or service predetermines within fairly strict limits the processes through which production can occur. Raw-material sources and market locations largely dictate where production will occur. Hence, one cannot understand a labor market without familiarity with the product market with which it interacts.

INTERACTIONS OF THE PRODUCT MARKET AND THE LABOR MARKET

The story we tell is the history of the U.S. copper industry from 1845 through 1990 from the vantage points of both its product market and its labor market. We laud the entrepreneurs who originated it, the managers who have directed it, and the labor leaders who have sought to protect its employees from both the harshness of its working environments and the occasional callousness of those whose focus is necessarily directed to output, costs, and profits. We also point out their errors resulting from poor judgment, lack of foresight, and too-frequent insistence on applying to unfamiliar situations policies and practices that worked well under very different circumstances. The industry is a small one, but it fills a critical niche in the national and world economy. The viability of the industry and the welfare of those involved in it are justification enough for a study. But our motivations are broader than that: there are lessons to be learned from its history.

On the product-market side, it is worth understanding the life cycle of industries. Why do they begin, expand, and deteriorate? Is there something inevitable about the cycle, as there is in the human life pattern? To what extent was the decline of American copper avoidable, given alternative policies? Could the course of events have been foreseen and altered? It will become evident that two great firms which once dominated the industry and now no longer even exist began their slide with attempts to diversify. It will also be shown that all of the firms outside nonferrous mining that bought into the industry at one point or another left licking their wounds. Despite that record, the firm which is currently number one in the industry has recently made a decision to diversify until copper becomes the source of only one-half its total revenues. Yet the firms which have survived and grown were firms committed to the industry for more than monetary reasons, willing to invest in themselves to protect and expand their historical bases. What are the lessons of all this in the age of mergers, acquisitions, and leveraged buyouts?

There are lessons for public policy. Here is an American industry that was hurt by the willingness of international agencies to finance the expansion of its international competitors during periods of worldwide overcapacity. Yet if its own government had heeded its appeals for protection, it would never have had the motivation to restructure and retool itself to become again a formidable competitive producer in the world market. Here is reassurance that a traditional U.S. industry can compete from its domestic base if it has the courage to put its money where its faith is.

On the labor-market side, this book is the completion of a long-delayed tale. Vernon Jensen's two impressive volumes, *Heritage of Conflict* and *Nonferrous Metals Industry Unionism, 1932–1954*, carried the story of employee organization in a chaotic industry from its start in the 1880s to the mid-1950s.[2] In essence, Jensen's studies covered the colorful and violent history of the Western Federation of Miners and its more prosaic successor, the Mine, Mill and Smelter Workers Union, which fell under communist control in the 1940s with disastrous consequences. Mine Mill was beset with costly and distracting legal battles long before its absorption into the United Steelworkers of America in 1967. What is the consequence of replacing a weak employee organization native to an industry with a strong one whose policies and procedures have been formed in the crucible of a quite different industry? What happens when wage policies established in an industry with a higher skill mix, a more oligopolistic market structure, and an absence of external competition are applied to an industry of lower-level skills which is already enmeshed in international competition? Mine Mill was a union of the semiskilled and unskilled in an industry whose skilled workers were craft unionists looking out for their own interests through preexisting organizations. How does a strong industrial union, accustomed to enrolling all skill levels within its ranks, create a bargaining coalition to encompass diverging interests while still presenting a united front? There is a strong case to be made for matching the scope of a union's claimed negotiating jurisdiction with the scope of the product market of the employers with which it bargains, particularly in a mass-production industry. But United Steelworkers went far beyond organizing all of the workers in its parent industry, to become in fact a multi-industry metal workers' union. Are such conglomerate unions viable?

Can pattern-bargaining practices which work in an industry of uniform technology and cost structures be imposed on another where geology largely dictates both technology and production costs, which in turn vary widely across competing firms? What does a union do when it discovers that the wages it has won for its members are five times those of its international competitors? Specifically, how does it respond when the engine of its wage escalation is not its triennial exercise of bargaining power, which it could moderate, but rather a cost-of-living allowance that is tied to the price level by a mechanism negotiated nearly twenty years before, without regard to productivity or the survival of the jobs of its members?

HOW ABOUT A ROAD MAP?

Be forewarned: this book tells a complex story and has a complex framework within which to enclose it. A road map—in fact, two of them—in this chapter will make the trail easier to follow. This section supplies a chapter outline. The following section provides a rationale for the book, the next a synopsis of our story, and the final section of Chapter 1 ties the copper experience into received theories of labor and product markets. The remaining chapters put meat and muscle on those skeletons.

Throughout, the emphasis of this book is product-market–labor-market interaction. But, in an extractive industry it is not enough to be conversant with product and labor markets. Geology, geography, and technology are powerful factors in determining both policy and result. Chapter 2 describes those factors as a basis for understanding all that follows.

Thereafter, the book is divided between the events of 1845–1945 and 1946–1990. The close of the Second World War is chosen as a watershed, for a number of reasons. Until then and for a while thereafter, U.S. firms dominated the world of copper. There was substantial foreign production, but American firms owned much of it. The close of the war marked the beginning of independent political and economic development for what had been vassal states. Forces were put in motion which would lead to expropriation. By 1945 all of the major copper-ore bodies since brought into production were known and had experienced some degree of extraction. Though there would later be drastic realignment, all of the copper-producing entities active in the world in 1990 at least had antecedents in the pre-1946 period. The same can be said of today's technology; some of it had not been applied much, but it was all known by 1945. In U.S. labor history, it was the stringencies of the Second World War that put economic power behind the political decision in the 1930s to foster collective bargaining. Given wartime controls, there was little meaningful collective bargaining in the copper industry before 1946. Which union was ultimately to represent most of the industry's employees was foretold by the politics of the immediate postwar period.

Chapters 3 to 9 alternate between product-market and labor-market considerations, divided between the two periods of time. Chapter 3 details the histories of the copper pioneers and the companies they created during the industry's first century. Chapter 4 describes product-related forces, as copper extraction begins on the shores of Lake Superior in 1845, and follows subsequent developments westward to what by 1945 had become a mighty industry. Chapter 5 then chronicles the emergence of unions and collective bargaining from the Western Federation of Miners and the Industrial Workers of the World to the International Union of Mine, Mill and Smelter Workers.

Chapter 6 follows the postwar experience of the U.S. copper producers, watching the death of the pioneers and their replacement by battered but successfully competitive youngsters. Chapter 7 parallels those company-by-company developments with a discussion of the world product market from 1946 to 1990, tracing the decline of a proud U.S. industry to the position of number two behind an emerging but largely underdeveloped country. Chapter 8 returns to the labor market, marking the slow demise of the Mine, Mill and Smelter Workers and the emergence of the United Steelworkers of America (USW) as the driving force in collective bargaining for the copper industry during the years 1946 to 1966. Chapter 9 brings the collective bargaining story forward to 1990, describing the creation of coalition bargaining, the rise of union power, the pursuit of industry-wide bargaining, the penalties of success, and the ensuing decline. Chapter 10 draws lessons from the century and a half of history and applies them to the current scene and to future expectations.

WHY ANOTHER BOOK?

There are at least ten significant books about the American copper industry, some of them very distinguished. Naturally, they vary greatly in subject matter and methodology according to the particular author's interests and objectives. Of these studies, two are concerned with the initial development of the industry on the Upper Michigan peninsula.[3] Another deals with the economics and specialized technology of the great porphyry mines of the Southwest.[4] Three deal with costs, prices, and competition in the industry as a whole.[5] Five present histories of the leading companies.[6] The aforementioned Jensen volumes document the fascinating and long-ignored story of labor and industrial relations, not only in copper but in the entire realm of nonferrous mining over six decades.

In undertaking our own study, we noted that all of the industry-wide studies were between twelve and thirty years old, preceding the most crucial years in the industry's history, and that they paid little attention to many of the individual companies whose activities had dominated the entire experience of American copper. More important, none of the three general studies included any discussion of unionism and labor relations, although these matters have been an integral part of the industry's story for more than a half-century. Finally, the sole scholarly treatment of labor and unionism ends in 1954. By its author's conscious choice (for which he had ample reason), neither the employer nor the product market is given extensive consideration. Accordingly, it appeared to us to be worthwhile to enlarge public knowledge of this old and still important industry.

First and foremost, there was a real need to incorporate unionism and industrial relations as a central part of an updated overall study of the copper industry. Second, the best way to accomplish that objective was to link these matters to the labor and product markets in copper, where the strategies and policies of both management and unions are shaped, tested, and modified. Third, with the foregoing approach we could bring the story of American copper up to date, at the same time widening its scope to incorporate new information and to include the vital, hitherto disregarded factor of labor.

The result of our efforts, then, is not a labor history as such, or a business history as such, or a corporate history as such, but an amalgam of them all. We present a synthesis of all three types of organizations and activities, including their reciprocal influences on one another and on the industry. It is the first time that this point of departure has been taken in a study of American copper.

Some may object that copper is too small an activity to justify an undertaking of this scope. When a single firm such as General Motors, for instance, can employ 350,000 individuals, why so much attention to an industry which never employed more than 150,000 and currently employs barely 25,000 people? The short answer is that size is neither the sole determinant nor even a necessary determinant of scholarly interest and importance.

Consider some of the questions the industry presents. Why did the United States lead world production for a full century when richer deposits existed elsewhere? Why did the relative real price of American copper fall substantially and persistently for more than five decades prior to 1946? Why did this downward trend flatten out thereafter, even as other countries were becoming powerful competitors? Why has it proved impossible to establish a working monopoly in U.S. copper? Why has the price of copper been so volatile throughout the history of the industry? What was the real significance of the introduction of open-pit mining at Bingham Canyon, Utah, in 1906? Is the introduction of leaching and electrowinning after 1980 likely to have an impact comparable to the open-pit, fine-grinding, and the flotation process? Why did the Anaconda Company—the greatest producer in the industry for fifty years—quit entirely in 1983? How is the domestic price of American copper influenced alike by trading on the London Metal Exchange and by the rate of production of CODELCO, the state mining enterprise of Chile?

On the labor side, there are just as many basic questions to challenge the investigator. For example, how did American copper acquire its strange and complex mixture of many craft unions and two competing industrial unions, while in basic steel—a far bigger industry—only a single large industrial union is to be found? Why should the membership and leadership of these diverse organizations in copper have displayed over the years such a strange amalgam of traditional Gompers-style business unionism, Lewis-style CIO industrial unionism, European revolutionary syndicalism, British and German evolutionary socialism, and even Stalinist communism?

Was it chance that caused the International Union of Mine, Mill and Smelter Workers in 1946 to reach out for one big union and centralized industry-wide bargaining? Why did these carefully formulated ambitions meet with complete failure? What captured the interest of the United Steelworkers of America in the nonferrous mining industry, and in copper in particular? Why were the attempts of the USW to raid the weak and almost bankrupt Mine Mill union almost completely unsuccessful? After years of conflict, what brought about the absorption of Mine Mill by the Steelworkers in 1967? After their years of noncooperation with Mine Mill, how was the USW able to weld together within the year a complex coalition with the craft unions? What was the outcome of its efforts to achieve industry-wide bargaining, first in nonferrous mining and then in copper alone? Failing that, how did the USW introduce pattern-following bargaining in copper after 1968, and why did this system collapse after 1980?

A SYNOPSIS OF THE ISSUES

Many influences have shaped the answers to these fundamental questions over the years. The results can be comprehended only through a reexamination of the history of the copper industry. And to the extent that the economic dimension has been predominant in shaping the experience of the industry, that dimension can best be grasped by reference to the actions, and the interactions, of the industry's product and labor markets. A synopsis of the events and issues to be discussed throughout the volume will provide another tour guide for the terrain ahead.

Two Divergent Industries

The Steelworkers brought with them to the copper industry a whole range of experience and expectations shaped in a quite different crucible; as we will discover, they and the copper industry suffered for it. For that reason it will be helpful to contrast some of the differences between the product and labor markets in these two very different industries.

Economic success in any industry requires a sustained ability to bring human talent together with machines, raw materials, and technology, to obtain a product that is acceptable in quality and can be made available at a competitive price. All of these components are encapsulated in the

dichotomy between capital and labor or, alternatively and more analyt-
ically, between product markets and labor markets. For an industry to
succeed, its product and labor markets must interact in ways consistent
with the prevailing requirements of price and quality imposed by the
buyers of its output. In the case of American copper, these buyers also have
ready access to a well-developed international market.

Industries differ in the requirements imposed by their product markets,
their labor markets, and their technologies. In some cases the pressures
that emerge will be very similar across firms in a given industry, while in
others these forces will be quite divergent in their impact. Throughout
most of its history, the basic steel industry has been characterized by
homogeneity of both technology and product across firms. Furthermore,
its labor force has also tended to be stable and homogeneous. In consequence, a stagnation characteristic of bilateral monopoly prevailed from
1946 to about 1970. Thereafter, product-market competition finally made
a breakthrough with surging imports, specialty producers, mini-mills, and
substitute products such as aluminum and prestressed concrete.

In these respects the differences between copper and steel have been
profound for more than a century. Geology had long ago determined that
the particular technology requisite to copper extraction, ore reduction,
and refining would differ sharply from one property to another. To illustrate, the deposits in the peninsula of Upper Michigan—or, for that
matter, Butte, Montana—called for meticulous vein mining deep underground; hoisting distances of up to 8,000 feet; and highly specialized
crushing procedures. By contrast, the southwestern porphyry mines permitted the use of open pits and immense power shovels, with consequent
nonselective mass-production mining. This sort of mining also requires
fine-grinding, flotation, and concentration—in short, specialized techniques appropriate to the ground. Moreover, the machines and equipment
needed for underground operations—air drills and mucking machines, for
example—differ totally from those employed in open-pit mining. The
coexistence of other metals of value is another complication of geology
that creates vast differences in production techniques, costs, and profit
potential.

On the labor side, too, there have always been sharp differences within
the copper industry, compared to the uniformity of skill requirements
within basic steel. Copper typically is found in remote and isolated places.
The location of such deposits has usually dictated the nearby placement of
ore-reduction activities such as crushing, concentration, and smelting.

Thus the setting is one in which the work force itself will be remote from contact with others. In copper, this characteristic has been combined with major ethnic differences across locations; for example, Indians and Hispanics in New Mexico and Arizona; a combination of Anglos and southeastern Europeans in Utah; and Irish, Cornish, and Slavs in Montana.

Ethnicity has not been the sole distinguishing factor for labor in copper. The differences in technology already noted have led to corresponding variations in skilled-labor requirements across the copper-mining regions. The great underground mines such as the Anaconda required skilled hardrock miners and timbermen, and a broad array of maintenance craftsmen. At the Ray underground mine in Arizona, where a specialized technique known as block caving was used, the miners had to possess additional skills required for that type of mining. By contrast, at the immense open-pit mine at Bingham Canyon, Utah, the traditional miners, muckers, and timbermen gave way to shovel operators, oilers, electricians, and railroad trainmen. Indeed the shift to open-pit mining, by introducing mechanization and mass production, brought about the predominance of semiskilled and unskilled jobs, and the introduction of some new skilled positions.

The upshot is that major differences have always prevailed among the copper producers, granted that increasing convergence toward standardization has been developing for three-quarters of a century.

In steel, by comparison, uniformity in technology, job structure, and labor requirements was achieved earlier and maintained longer. Moreover, uniformity in basic steel was accelerated by the success of the United Steelworkers in organizing the industry almost completely by 1946. Of special importance was the fact that the USW was an industrial union and that it achieved exclusive jurisdictional rights in the industry, a basic principle of the labor movement in the United States going back to the very beginnings of the American Federation of Labor as a means to prevent interunion competition exploitable by the employer.[7] By contrast, copper never had single-union representation. There were always craft unions, and, for a while at the turn of the century and again after the Second World War, dual industrial unions. Diversity and pluralism have been the rule in copper.

By the early 1950s a stable form of collective bargaining had been jointly established in basic steel, in which uniformity was given powerful further stimulus by a system of industry-wide bargaining through a multi-employer committee. With its advent the industry enjoyed a certain equilibrium in its labor relations, because it had to negotiate with only a single all-encompassing union, and above all because of the absence of disruptions (in those years) in its product market from competitive imports or from the entry of new domestic producers.

Steel was destined to lose those seeming advantages, beginning in the 1960s and accelerating during the 1970s, as rising imports, specialty firms, and mini-mills cut into the most profitable markets. Major innovations in processing also were introduced, which altered labor requirements. As a result, since the 1970s the firms in basic steel began to exhibit some of the same sharp differences in technical setups and cost structures that had prevailed in copper over a much longer period. At the same time, the wave of steel imports that began to gather force by 1970 imposed a cap on domestic prices. That also parallels, but with a time lag, the experience in copper, which has faced an import surplus since 1940 and competitive price ceilings in the world market for much longer.

From the standpoint of the labor market, a union that pursues uniformity in wages and benefits across firms in an industry that turns out an array of products can achieve its objective and even maintain it—at least for a time—if the requisite homogeneity prevails in labor, capital, and technical requirements, and in the product markets of the industry. Basic steel met these conditions for a brief three decades, then experienced drastic change. Dissolution of the pattern of interfirm uniformity in job structure, wages, and benefits followed. By contrast, copper has never had these conditions at any time down to the present day. In consequence, the carefully planned effort of the United Steelworkers to achieve uniformity throughout the nonferrous mining industry proved abortive from the outset in 1967, and impossible to preserve even in copper extraction and refining after temporary success with pattern-following bargaining for ten years.

Labor and Product Markets through Time: The Case of the Upper Michigan Peninsula

The history of the American copper industry begins with the opening of the Cliff Mine on the outer end of the Keeweenaw peninsula in 1845. Over the following thirty-five years Michigan was the dominant if not quite the only source of copper production. During this period the industry began to display certain significant characteristics that were to prevail throughout most of the subsequent history. One was a pronounced volatility of product price, the origin of which lies primarily in the technical nature of derived demand. Another trait was the appearance of a large number of producers, each operating under absentee corporate ownership, with Boston and New York as the main sources of capital and hence as centers of control. These two cities also constituted the principal product markets, where copper was sold in bars and ingots through brokers and agents.

Rapid expansion during the 1860s caused the number of companies to increase substantially, with much accompanying financial distress. It soon became evident that output tended to outrun domestic demand; that imports from Europe were a constant threat to price; that the demand was inelastic, so that small changes in output had a magnified reverse impact on price; that if price were to be kept at profitable levels, export dumping would be essential to eliminate domestic "surpluses." The solution called for joint control of sales and outputs—the so-called Lake Pool, which was established under the leadership of the Calumet and Hecla Mining Company in 1871. In this arrangement each producer was assigned an export quota, the effect of which was to reduce domestic supply and thereby to protect price. This system of price control lasted until 1884, when it was destroyed by the uncontrolled production of the new western mines.

In these years of Michigan dominance, American copper revealed another important characteristic: a strong and continuing growth of productivity in labor and capital that derived jointly from the deepening of mines, access to larger and richer ore bodies, improved methods of ore extraction and reduction, and—in the early 1880s—the arrival of a railroad in the district. From a lengthier perspective, this favorable trend in factor productivity was to continue right through to the end of the Second World War as the industry spread westward. The consequences, of course, were directly beneficial for both profit and wage potential.

Survival despite price volatility depended on keeping control of labor costs. An ample supply of labor was maintained, notwithstanding the isolation, by aggressive recruitment outside the area and nation and because of the difficulty of leaving the peninsula. The isolation, small geographic compass (the entire district covered only about 100 square miles), and company town settings aided and abetted resistance to unionism and collective bargaining. Wages and working conditions were set unilaterally by the employers, initially under free competition in the small labor market, and (after 1870 at least) under the guidance of the Lake Pool. Wages could fluctuate freely in response to copper prices, which, significantly, were linked directly to world prices. The Lake Pool thus was able to moderate the fluctuations deriving from abroad, but only by adjusting output and export quotas. At the end of this lengthy causal chain were the miners, who for many reasons lacked a self-help organization to advance their interests by a labor-market price-fixing device of their own.

Impact of the Westward Migration of the Industry

In 1881 the Copper Queen Mine began production in Bisbee, Arizona. One year later the Anaconda Mine was opened in Butte, Montana. These two vast underground properties were soon followed by several others, in the Clifton-Morenci, Globe-Miami, and Verde Valley districts of Arizona; in the large patchwork of mines around Butte; and, after the turn of the century, in the Bingham Canyon in Utah. Each of these new districts reproduced in form the dominant characteristics of Upper Michigan— large numbers of relatively small operators with absentee corporate own- ership and control, unstable prices, considerable financial distress, but (except for a limited time at Butte) management control of the labor supply and wage rates. None of the western mines ever established a counterpart of the Lake Pool or even made the attempt, except for an abortive unilateral effort byAnaconda to control price by limiting produc- tion during 1899–1902. It is unlikely that they could have done so with the diversity of locations and geologic conditions.

The new mining districts were scattered at great distances from each other, for the most part in remote places. The mine workers found self- organization difficult, and outside organizers had little access. The mine operators prescribed wages and working conditions unilaterally in each district. It was part of their policy to reduce standards with each major fall in price. It was also established policy to fight attempts at unionization with any and all weapons, and to break strikes by importing replacements, generally accompanied and protected by sheriff's deputies or state militia. Even the brief success of unionism in Butte was not a matter of economic bargaining power but of the competition for votes between two opposing "Copper King" candidates for the United States Senate. Other than that, there was no significant collective bargaining breakthrough until the com- bination of the National Labor Relations Act (NLRA) with the tight labor markets of the Second World War.

The miners themselves typically had no clear conception of their orga- nizational goal in those early years. Their strikes were either purely defensive—against wage cuts—or simply to obtain an immediate increase in pay. Either way, the more sophisticated notions of recognition by the employers, formal negotiations with those employers, and renewable long-term agreements as the outcome were seldom pursued. Instead, a strike constituted a temporary mobilization of strength until it was won or lost, usually the latter.

To be sure, the Western Federation of Miners had been formed in Butte as early as 1893, as a national union for production workers in nonferrous mining. In principle, the WFM espoused industrial rather than craft unionism and in essence endorsed the One Big Union concept. But over its brief two decades of existence it was crippled by weaknesses which were eventually to prove fatal. Its finances were always meager. It could not cope with the political and economic power of its determined adversaries, the mine operators. It was cut off from effective help from the American Federation of Labor by that organization's own frailties and by the opposition of craft unions competing for members within the same work force. And it had no umbrella of protective federal legislation.

Moreover, the WFM suffered from internal conflicts that prevented the organization from defining its own objectives in a consistent and unambiguous way. There were the classical trade unionists, some of whom were socialists who believed in self-organization on a permanent basis to gain recognition, formal collective bargaining, and permanent labor contracts. There was an influential syndicalist faction whose revolutionary outlook found expression in formation of the Industrial Workers of the World in 1905, while maintaining active dual membership in the WFM. This group had no interest in recognition for collective bargaining, given its opposition to and even contempt for permanent contracts that would imply acceptance of the legitimacy of the employers' role. As a result, the Western Federation of Miners was trapped in ideological warfare—from within by its own syndicalist members and from without by ruthless and destructive attacks of the IWW.

In 1906 the Utah Copper Company (later Kennecott) undertook what was to become the greatest innovation in copper history—open-pit mining. The immediate consequence was a transformation of the entire job structure in ore extraction and transport, in crushing and grinding, and in concentration and smelting. In essence, a group of traditional craft occupations involved in copper mining and smelting was converted to a collection of mechanized jobs of varying skills, in many ways reminiscent of factory employment. This development was of course potentially favorable to an industrial union such as the WFM and its 1916 successor, the

International Union of Mine, Mill and Smelter Workers, but was of no advantage because neither body had the political or economic strength to grasp the opportunity.

Before 1935, unionism in American copper was based on unrecognized locals. For production employees, these locals were affiliated with the WFM, or later with Mine Mill. For the crafts in maintenance and repair and local mine railroads, affiliation was with the appropriate national craft unions, which in turn were affiliated with the American Federation of Labor (AFL). As noted earlier, few of these locals were recognized by employers and able to engage in collective bargaining, although they did conduct strikes. The technological revolution wrought by the open-pit system, which in time did make copper mining into a mass-production industry, did not eliminate the need for the craft occupations. Nevertheless, if the WFM or Mine Mill had been able to exploit the opportunity conferred by the transition to mass production, these craft jobs might have been incorporated as well, as happened years later under rather different conditions in basic steel. Instead, the mixed bag of craft and industrial unions became the dubious legacy of the copper industry, to be made permanent at the time real organizing opportunity arrived in 1937, when the United States Supreme Court decided that the National Labor Relations Act (or Wagner Act) was constitutional.

How the Wagner Act Changed Market Relationships

With the introduction in 1935 of a federally guaranteed right to collective bargaining, the copper unions could petition for elections as bargaining agents, and upon winning could seek certification from the National Labor Relations Board (NLRB). With the same action the employers acquired the duty to bargain collectively in good faith. A vital part of the NLRB's assignment was the determination in each instance of the appropriate bargaining unit. In its discharge of this responsibility the NLRB had come under early attack from the AFL for allegedly favoring large, all-inclusive units—for instance, plant-wide rather than single-craft occupations. Obviously, the plant-wide units were the preference of the emerging industrial unions of the new CIO (until 1938 the Committee for Industrial Organization and thereafter the Congress of Industrial Organizations), which were just gearing up their organizational drive. Naturally, the old-line crafts of the AFL had no desire to be merged into large mixed units. To protect their representation claims they succeeded in persuading the board to adopt its "Globe doctrine," under which any clearly established craft was accorded the right to a representation election for its group alone before any plant-wide election could be held. Then, if the craft group voted for craft representation, such a unit would be certified for collective bargaining separately from the other occupations. Thus the very issue industrially oriented unionists had been bitterly complaining about within the AFL for years—what they saw as a divisive exclusiveness subject to employer "divide and conquer" tactics—could be perpetuated under the act by carving out craft groups in their own representation units. In consequence, they feared, industrial unionism would be stalled in the mass-production industries.

In that regard, the advantage lay with totally new industrial unions such as the Steelworkers and the Auto Workers, where neither craft nor industrial unions had any significant history. Because of copper's peculiar legacy of a large array of craft organizations alongside Mine Mill as an industrial union, the industry acquired a patchwork representation pattern under the NLRB's Globe approach. That is, on each property there would be separate representation units for each of the crafts in maintenance, repair, and railroad operations. In addition, there would be a production-worker unit for the machine operatives and unskilled laborers in the pit, the crushing plant, the concentrator, the smelter, and, where applicable, the refinery. The result, then, was multiple unionism on a very large scale, subdivided further by individual mine properties, even for multifacility firms.

It should be remarked that the NLRB had adopted its Globe doctrine to recognize and protect the principle of self-determination, which lay at the core of the National Labor Relations Act. However, the price for dedication to that principle was the weakening of another: the principle of bargaining effectiveness. In other words, in situations of factory unionism, self-determination by occupation tended to dissolve the common interests otherwise shared by employees in a single establishment. In the case at hand, Mine Mill as an industrial union found itself a relatively small organization surrounded by a large group of craft unions, hence unable to exert unitary control in the formulation and execution of collective bargaining strategy throughout the nonferrous mining industry.

For their part, the larger companies had long since achieved unified ownership or control in their respective districts: Calumet and Hecla in Michigan from 1923 on; Anaconda in Montana in 1910; Kennecott in Utah, Arizona, New Mexico, and Nevada by 1936; Phelps Dodge in other parts of Arizona in 1931; and ASARCO (American Smelting and

Refining Company) over custom and contract smelters and refineries in several locations from 1919 on. These developments meant that in each mining district where one of the giant firms conducted operations—with the single exception of ASARCO—one employer would confront a divided array of unions, each of them decentralized internally by property. In short, the industry now had a pluralistic and decentralized system of collective bargaining.

Two Errant Factors in the Copper Labor Market

At some point between 1936 and 1942, members of the U.S. Communist Party and their sympathizers penetrated and then took control of the national offices of Mine Mill. An early result of this takeover was the spread of sentiment within the union in favor of industry-wide bargaining and single-union representation throughout nonferrous mining. In no necessary sense were industrial unionism and industry-wide bargaining logically dependent on Marxist ideas. But within the Leninist version of Marxism there was harsh contempt for craft unionism and equally intense hostility to decentralized bargaining, with strong commitment to the One Big Union concept and therefore to a preference for collective bargaining on an industry-wide basis. The ultimate unexpressed goal was heightened class struggle, for which centralized wage-making was but a means. For the time being, therefore, the communist leadership in Mine Mill came to share the same immediate outlook as those traditional unionists who stood for industrial unionism and industry-wide bargaining as ends in themselves, but for entirely different reasons.

Another consequence of the Stalinist takeover of Mine Mill was that after the war ended the union joined the left-wing faction of the CIO. Soon the left-versus-right conflict within the industrial union federation broke into the open, with bitter attacks on Philip Murray (the CIO president) and his associates. These in turn led to a series of private trials conducted by the CIO, in which certain unions were charged with communist control and with following the party line to the neglect of trade-union interests. Accordingly, Mine Mill was so charged and tried. In February 1950 it was expelled from the CIO and began its lengthy decline and eventual absorption by Murray's United Steelworkers.

Expulsion opened the way for USW to undertake a raiding campaign aimed at capturing the Mine Mill locals and thereby taking over the role of bargaining representative for the production workers of the industry. Of collateral importance, these raids offered the potential of enhancing the Steelworkers' ambition to become the one union for all metal workers in the United States.[8]

Isolation, the need to defend itself against the raids, denial of access to the NLRB, and a series of federal prosecutions involving the communist leadership all took their toll on Mine Mill's never-strong finances. Yet the raids themselves proved to be an egregious failure, yielding only a few small bargaining units at Kennecott and Phelps Dodge.

More important, apart from the deep-seated ideological divisions separating Mine Mill and the USW, the two organizations shared a common vision for unionism in nonferrous mining—in essence, unitary control and representation in some form on an industry-wide basis. This outlook was, of course, precisely the ruling concept of the CIO and the unions which had created it and which it had created. Control of Mine Mill by communists obviously was a serious obstacle to any cooperation between the two organizations. Raiding had been unsuccessful. And the numerous craft unions of the industry remained secure and effective in their own right and not at all interested in grandiose visions of industry-wide collective bargaining.

During 1966–1967, this situation was to undergo seismic change. The Mine Mill leaders finally wriggled free from a decade of federal prosecutions deriving from the communist issue and some peculiar legislation of the time. Because raiding was no longer an option, the USW leadership decided to offer Mine Mill a merger on attractive terms that would absorb the smaller organization as part of the Steelworkers and provide jobs or retirement for Mine Mill officers and staff. Negotiations began during the summer of 1966, and by the following January an agreement had been reached, just in time for the 1967 round of collective bargaining.

The Goal of Unified and Centralized Wage-Setting

Contract expirations were due at the end of June 1967 in much of nonferrous and all of copper. At this point, to unify and centralize negotiations on the union side, the leaders of the USW had to overcome two formidable obstacles. They needed to enlist some twenty-five craft unions in support of the idea, which would overturn a tradition of many years' standing. That support was gained by the promise of much more effective bargaining on behalf of each craft's particular objectives if joint action were undertaken. Even more difficult, the USW leadership had to find a

way to compel the employers to bargain on a centralized basis, notwithstanding their stalwart opposition and the advantage conferred by the
long-established decentralized system of NLRB-certified bargaining units.
How could these legal sanctions be overcome?

The first step was getting all of the unions to join a coalition for
conducting negotiations, to be directed by a single Steelworkers spokesman. This central negotiating committee was then given exclusive control
over the decisions to strike, to settle, and to return to work on any
property. Other procedural rules required that all contracts were to bear
the same termination date, and that there was to be one master agreement
for each company, including all of its subsidiaries. Left open was whether
simultaneous negotiations for all companies could be achieved or whether
a pattern-following sequence should be undertaken for the companies in
successive order.

The demands of the unions emphasized the attainment of uniformity in
wages and benefits across the whole nonferrous industry—all metals and
all stages of production. The objective was not just equal pay for identical
jobs, but rather equal pay for *comparable* jobs across the industry. Moreover, each participating union could propose special demands to be approved by a joint conference before bargaining began. In this way any
union with a special interest or problem could be accommodated within an
industry-wide set of demands.

In what can best be described as a remarkably complex and difficult
achievement, the Steelworkers union assembled its coalition in the spring
of 1967. Letters were sent to each employer, declaring that the unions
were seeking company-wide master agreements, simultaneous expiration
dates, and wage uniformity (the last also described as "common economic
settlements"). The deadlock that quickly followed was soon transformed
into an industry-wide strike lasting more than eight months.

The ultimate outcome was a costly defeat for the unions and the employees they represented. The employers succeeded in blocking any bargaining on a coalition basis. Instead, the scope of every negotiation was
confined to the original boundaries of the certified bargaining units established long before by the NLRB. There was no master agreement for any
company, and no semblance of industry-wide wage uniformity was
achieved. Increases at the mines, smelters, and refineries were larger than
those agreed upon for the fabricating plants, regardless of comparability of
jobs. Increases in copper exceeded those in lead, zinc, and other branches
of metal mining. Instead of uniform expiration dates, there was an even

greater divergence among mine properties than among fabrication plants and across the various metals involved.

The failure of the coalition's 1967 attempt at industry-wide negotiations and settlements for the whole of nonferrous was followed by a retreat in the next round—1971—to a much narrower goal that was limited to copper only, and at that only to copper mining, smelting, and refining. Moreover, the negotiating method was changed by substitution of a version of pattern-following bargaining, used typically in automobiles and meat packing. In this strategy the coalition first selected the employer deemed most likely to agree to a settlement closest to the objectives. Once obtained, this settlement became *the* pattern. By accepting it, the chosen firm became the wage leader and was free of the threat of a strike. The coalition could then turn to the other producers, insisting upon acceptance of the pattern as a condition for settlement, accompanied by the threat of a strike against each of the holdouts at a time of the coalition's choosing. As the number of settlements increased, the pressure against the remaining holdouts mounted, and in a subtle way: a strike when all competitors are producing in an industry with a homogeneous product threatens an almost certain loss of market share and possible long-term loss of customers (unless a struck producer chooses to continue operations, as Phelps Dodge was to do in 1983).

Pattern following continued with three more negotiations after 1971, the last in 1980. In these nine years the coalition was able to advance toward wage uniformity with four successive settlements, each resting on a strictly enforced pattern. By 1980, however, the industry entered a seven-year depression in which cathode prices were to fall over 35 percent because of severe credit deflation during 1979–1982, which greatly reduced demand; and a large surge of imports from Chile and Peru (because of the substantial rise in the external value of the dollar in these years), which increased copper supply. Simultaneously, the automatic mechanism for adjusting wage rates to the cost of living (COLA) won by the coalition in the 1971 negotiations, moved inexorably upward by a cumulative 45 percent during the same period. By 1982, all of the producers were suffering large and increasing operating losses, causing them to cut back drastically on operations or to close down entirely.

In the months just before the 1983 negotiations were to begin, some of the companies began thinking seriously about demanding wage concessions from the unions, probably influenced by similar discussions between the Steelworkers and the basic steel industry. Then suddenly, without warning, Kennecott and the coalition made public a new agreement that contained no concessions—at least none of value except to Kennecott itself. With this coup the coalition lost no time in informing the other operators that the Kennecott agreement was to be the pattern for settlements throughout the industry, with no deviations. In short, pattern-following in copper was to be identified with complete inflexibility, despite the critical state of the industry's finances, and notwithstanding the fact that the USW was even then considering offering a dramatic wage cut in basic steel.

Finding themselves with no prospects for concessions from the union coalition and in dire economic circumstances, Phelps Dodge and Duval Corporation (the latter now part of Cyprus Minerals) decided to bargain hard for cuts, despite the Kennecott precedent—and, more significant, to continue operating if they were struck. This situation posed the first real threat to the pattern-following system. And although the coalition leadership seemed unaware of it at the time, the threat also carried mortal implications for the survival of collective bargaining at the two companies.

In any case, the strikes ensued and both firms took the drastic step of continuing operations, although initially on a reduced scale. By introduction of strikebreakers (replacements) and various protective measures, Phelps Dodge soon managed to build its production back to normal. The coalition persisted with the strike for two more years, without offering any concessions, and thereafter lost a series of decertification elections across its Arizona properties. In the outcome, therefore, a substantial portion of domestic copper production slipped out of union control, at the same time crippling the bargaining power of the unions at other companies and eliminating their ability to employ pattern-following in the future.

In meeting with disaster in 1983–1984, the USW coalition later came under severe criticism from the Steelworkers' top directorate for its stubborn insistence on a policy of no cuts regardless of extensive job losses and the undeniable financial predicament of the employers.[9] By 1985 the rift produced a change in coalition leadership, and with this change a drastic shift to a flexible approach in bargaining in 1986 and 1989–1990. Its essence was not to start from a predetermined pattern, but to let the facts and circumstances of the particular employer relative to the prevailing economic conditions serve as the ultimate guide. It was, in fact, a return to decentralized bargaining, but with retention of the coalition. Accordingly, the pattern concept was abandoned, just as it had been in basic steel in

1984. The company-by-company settlements of 1989 and 1990 were obviously interrelated but were not slavishly dictated.

JOINT WAGE-MAKING AFTER 1946

Lending structure and order to the extremely complex history of collective bargaining in American copper mining after 1946 are some penetrating and highly useful explanatory principles first developed by John T. Dunlop in 1954.[10] They require brief discussion before they can be applied to the case at hand.

The Job Cluster

One of the central problems in wage theory today, as Dunlop noted years ago in a judgment that still holds true, is to account for the formation of particular wage structures which emerge under the decisions of a particular wage-making authority, whether unilaterally by management or jointly with one or more unions. Equally important is the need to account for changes in wage structures through time. The place to begin the inquiry is with the job structure involved—or, more particularly, the job clusters into which jobs are actually grouped for administrative and negotiating purposes.

Dunlop defined a job cluster as "a stable group of job classifications or work assignments within a firm (wage determination unit)" linked together by technology, administrative organization of production, or custom, because they have "common wage-making characteristics."[11] As these influences change, the cluster may also change. Within a given cluster, the pay rates will be interdependent and therefore sensitive; certain of them will be key rates in the double sense that the other job rates will be subordinate and thus linked to them, and that they will be particular points of impact for external forces—movements in the price level, changes in the labor supply, or wage movements in comparable industries.[12]

In copper mining there is a job cluster for each of the maintenance and repair jobs—for example, maintenance machinist, helper, and apprentice; or electrician, helper, and apprentice. Beyond the skilled trades such as these, there are some largely mechanized production jobs of the factory type. These, too, can be highly skilled, semiskilled, or unskilled. For instance, jobs in the pit include power shovel operator, oiler, and laborer. Similar production job clusters are found in the crushing plant, the concentrator, and the smelter.

Another characteristic of the copper case is that each of the craft clusters is represented by a particular craft union, whereas the production-worker groups belong to the Steelworkers as an industrial union. In this environment of multiple unionism, the wage-setting authority is the employer on the property and the USW-led coalition. Since 1985, most of the Phelps Dodge and Cyprus Minerals properties no longer have had union representation, although they remain linked to the copper wage contour because they continue to compete in the same product market and for the same labor.

The Wage Contour

Dunlop devised the concept of the wage contour to refer to a group of employing firms which possess "common wage-making characteristics" because they are linked to one another by common product markets or a common labor-market organization.[13] The emphasis here is on the special sensitivities—product, labor source, or labor-market organization—that make such firms highly conscious of their interdependence. The result is a wage contour. More particularly, the contour embraces particular clusters of jobs or occupations, at a particular location, in a particular sector of industry. The firms that fall along this contour thus will share a given product market (local newspapers or hospitals, or transcontinental railroad freight services) and may either share a labor market or be scattered over the region or nation.

A decisive element in any wage contour is that the employers involved are *competitors in the same product market* (which in turn is a primary source of their interdependence), are faced by a common price structure, and therefore are especially sensitive to any differences in costs. That is why, when a union shares in the wage-setting authority through collective bargaining, it will insist that the employers recognize their own interdependence by "taking wages out of competition"—to use the classic formulation.[14] To the union this stance typically means uniformity of wages and benefits for comparable jobs in comparable clusters along the same wage contour. The same intent is conveyed by the expression "equal pay for equal work." Behind the equity terminology is the conviction that differences in comparable wage rates should not be permitted among competing firms, because such a differential will benefit only the least efficient producers while undermining the most efficient and the wages they could and might be willing to pay. Here, it will be obvious, is the genesis of the pattern concept.

In copper there are several wage contours—one for each of the crafts across firms and one for the production workers. Others exist for office employees and for technical experts such as metallurgists and mining engineers. Clearly, these contours are highly interdependent, though somewhat less so since the formation of the coalition in 1967. Nevertheless, the realities are still there. Any obscurity results from the internal resolution of conflicts over relative basic rates, and over increases in those rates, by bargaining within the coalition over formulation of contract demands and, often, again in agreeing to a settlement. Since 1983 matters have been complicated by the elimination of collective bargaining by two important producers who continue to share the same product market. They share the same wage contours, but have more freedom of action in labor matters. What we have in this situation might be termed interdependence without complete collective bargaining—a significant source of weakness to the unions.

The Key Bargain

Movements in the wage structure, where there is collective bargaining, will be linked to certain settlements that play a well-recognized initiating role that justifies terming them key bargains. That is, they provide a standard settlement for other bargains which follow. Several variants exist.[15] Thus one firm may be the price leader in an oligopolistic industry whose sellers practice what Joseph Schumpeter called co-respective competition, meaning that they recognize their mutual interdependence and, simultaneously, concede price leadership to a dominant firm. In basic steel for many years the former U.S. Steel Corporation was the price leader. After the corporation had reached a contract settlement with the United Steelworkers, it could make what it considered to be appropriate price adjustments in full confidence that its competitors would make parallel settlements and increase prices accordingly.

In copper, producers have had no lasting control over price since the collapse of the Michigan Lake Pool in 1884. They have been ruled by the COMEX (Commodity Exchange) price, which is itself closely tied competitively to the London Metal Exchange (LME) price and reflects the ever-present possibility of imports and exports as price-equilibrating forces. To be sure, until around 1978 the companies quoted a "producer's price" for copper of a certain grade and type, in return for which a client could have an assured place in the queue in times of extreme scarcity. Those quotes suggested an illusory stability and, therefore, market power, because the price so announced could not deviate significantly from COMEX and LME prices without inflows and outflows of copper that would compel change in the producer's own interest.

On the wage side before 1967, as we have seen, the copper industry operated under pluralistic and decentralized collective bargaining. Each of the many unions had its own job clusters and wage contours, but no organization was strong enough to enforce either wage leadership by a dominant firm or—as an alternative—industry-wide settlements. After the formation of the coalition, it became possible for the USW to impose pattern-following beginning in 1971, once the futility of attempting to impose industry-wide contracts on the whole of the nonferrous mining industry had become apparent. In pattern-following, the wage leadership exerted by the USW was sufficient to make Kennecott the wage leader, though obviously not the price leader, in copper. Thereafter, Kennecott and the coalition were able to negotiate the key bargain, which the unions would then extract from the other companies. On the labor side, the many separate contours continued to prevail, but they were now "coordinated" by the coalition *in camera* and then transmitted through the pattern to the other producers. Finally, wage linkage to a key bargain can also be established by winning common expiration dates for all contracts involving competing firms. Simultaneous dates permit simultaneous negotiations, which can establish common norms for settlements. Further, they allow the options of a joint strike or selective strikes to enforce wage leadership on a chosen producer.

All of these advantages the coalition of copper unions had, and have for the time being, at least partially lost. The implications of that loss were just beginning to emerge in the 1989 and 1990 negotiations. Subsequent chapters will detail the events which responded to these forces and speculate on where they are likely to lead.

CHAPTER 2

GEOGRAPHY, GEOLOGY, AND TECHNOLOGY

NEITHER THE PRODUCT MARKET nor the labor market of an extractive industry such as copper can be adequately understood without at least some familiarity with its geographic characteristics, its underlying geology, and the evolution of its technology. We consider these matters in turn in this chapter.

GEOGRAPHIC LOCATION

Copper, like almost any natural resource, is where you find it. Let us look now at the implications of the world geographic distribution of copper resources (Figure 2.1).

The Rim of Fire

Geologists call the circle of lands surrounding the Pacific Ocean the rim of fire, because of the evidence of extensive ore deposition through prehistoric and historic volcanic activity. Scrutiny of a relief map reveals a continuous chain of rugged mountains—the Andes—running northward

FIGURE 2.1 **Major World Copper Resources**

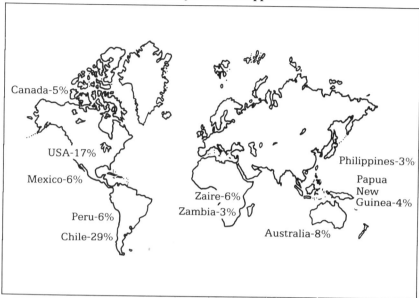

SOURCE: U.S. Congress, Office of Technology Assessment, *Copper: Technology and Competitiveness* (Washington, D.C.: Government Printing Office, September 1988), p. 10.

from the southern tip of Chile almost to the Panama Canal. Beginning with El Teniente in the heart of this great range, to the southeast of Santiago, Chile, we encounter the first of a series of vast copper deposits.[1] To the north are Potrerillos, Chuquicamata, the Southern Peru mines, and Cerro de Pasco.[2] Next is an extended interval ending at Cananea in far northern Mexico, where another important copper deposit is found in the high desert plateau beyond the north end of the Sierra Madre range.[3] Across the Arizona border many deposits appear, mostly in desert valleys rather than in the mountains themselves.

Proceeding farther north and somewhat to the east, one encounters the great Bingham Canyon Mine in the Oquirrh Mountains just west of Salt Lake City. These mountains are the first of the Basin and Range Province, the area between the Wasatch Range east of Salt Lake City and the Sierra Nevada, which has no outlet to the ocean. About 370 miles farther north, in the heart of the Rocky Mountains, is Butte, Montana, the site of probably the richest deposit of mineral ores, including copper, ever found. Beyond Butte there are a few minor deposits in British Columbia. Canada is a major producer, but the copper is mostly a by-product of the mining of other minerals, notably nickel and gold.[4] Continuing into Alaska, we reach the last noteworthy American copper site at the town of Kennicott, in the Wrangell range.[5] Beyond this point are the Aleutians and ultimately the Soviet Union.

As of today, only three other important deposits within the Pacific Rim need be cited—Bougainville Island, about 500 miles east of New Guinea; Copper Mountain, in western New Guinea; and Mount Isa, in western Queensland, Australia.[6] There are deposits of lesser commercial importance in the Philippines and Indonesia. Additional deposits no doubt exist in Southeast Asia, China, and the USSR, but they have never been developed for international trade and therefore are not relevant here.

An important observation may now be made: there is a much higher frequency of known copper deposits on the eastern rim of the Pacific Basin, mostly along the great mountain chain between southern Chile and southeastern Alaska, than anywhere else in the world. More than a random phenomenon, this perception is reinforced by the existence of a similar geographic pattern for the distribution of gold and silver ores.

It is known that there is a direct connection between mountain-range building and the deformations of the earth's crust, such as those deriving from the clash of the underlying continental plates. It seems reasonable to infer that tectonic movements in the past were an important factor in bringing about periods of volcanism that resulted in magmatic intrusions and upheavals. The same processes could have led to the release of copper-bearing solutions and gases from the mantle of the ancient earth, to give rise to the copper deposits of today.

Other Sources

A few copper deposits in Europe have been worked from time to time, but only those on the island of Cyprus, which gave the red metal its name, and the Rio Tinto in Spain have had substantial output historically. Having been mined since Roman times, Rio Tinto's rich ores have been exhausted, but techniques developed in the United States for extracting low-grade copper deposits have been sporadically applied there in recent years.[7] Commercial possibilities exist in Yugoslavia, Bulgaria, Poland, and Finland but would never be of a magnitude to be significant in world production.

The only meaningful competition to Western Hemisphere and Pacific copper is on the continent of Africa. Rich copper deposits in Zaire and Zambia have been known to the developed countries since Sir Henry Stanley's explorations in 1873–1875.[8] The surface copper was easily mined, but treatment and transportation of the ore were obstacles keeping those mines from significant production until the First World War. Begun under Belgian and British companies, the mines were nationalized by the new nations after the Second World War. Their ores are still comparatively rich by modern standards, but political instability has given their production an on-again off-again character.

Spatial Aspects of American Copper

Within the continental United States (excluding Alaska), three primary regions of copper deposition have emerged over millions of years: the Upper Michigan peninsula; the Butte district of southwestern Montana; and the contiguous western states of Arizona, New Mexico, Utah, and Nevada. The first major disconformity appears at once—the immense distance that separates the Michigan deposits from those of the American West. To underscore the point, it is approximately 1,140 miles from Houghton, Michigan, in the center of the peninsula, to Butte; it is 1,430 miles from Houghton to Santa Rita, New Mexico, and 1,630 miles from Houghton to Ajo, Arizona (Figure 2.2). Over the intervening expanse of more than a thousand miles between Houghton and these outer limits of the western mining region, there are no other significant known copper deposits. The result is a second major disconformity—no such deposit has ever been found in the Rocky Mountains except for Butte, although gold and silver properties have long been prominent in the region. Given the metallurgical affinity of those two metals for copper, the absence of the latter remains a puzzle. East of the Rockies, it should be added, are prairies, farmlands, and rolling hills, where copper is not usually found in mineable quantities until one reaches the small and remote Keeweenaw peninsula of Michigan.

In the 118 years since the Cliff Mine was developed in 1845 as Michigan's first copper property, the peninsula has produced 5.4 million short tons (1.08 billion pounds) of copper. From 1845 until the beginning of copper mining at the Copper Queen Mine in Arizona in 1881, the Lake Copper of the several Michigan mines was the only domestic source of supply. Given the extreme isolation of the peninsula mines from the western group that began emerging in the 1880s, one must conclude that the primal forces that created the extensive Michigan ore bodies had a range of operation limited to that district.

If we turn now to the western properties, they present peculiar disconformities of their own, as Figure 2.2 shows. Consider first the swarm of mines in central and southern Arizona and western New Mexico. Here we

FIGURE 2.2 Copper Ore Deposits in the Western United States

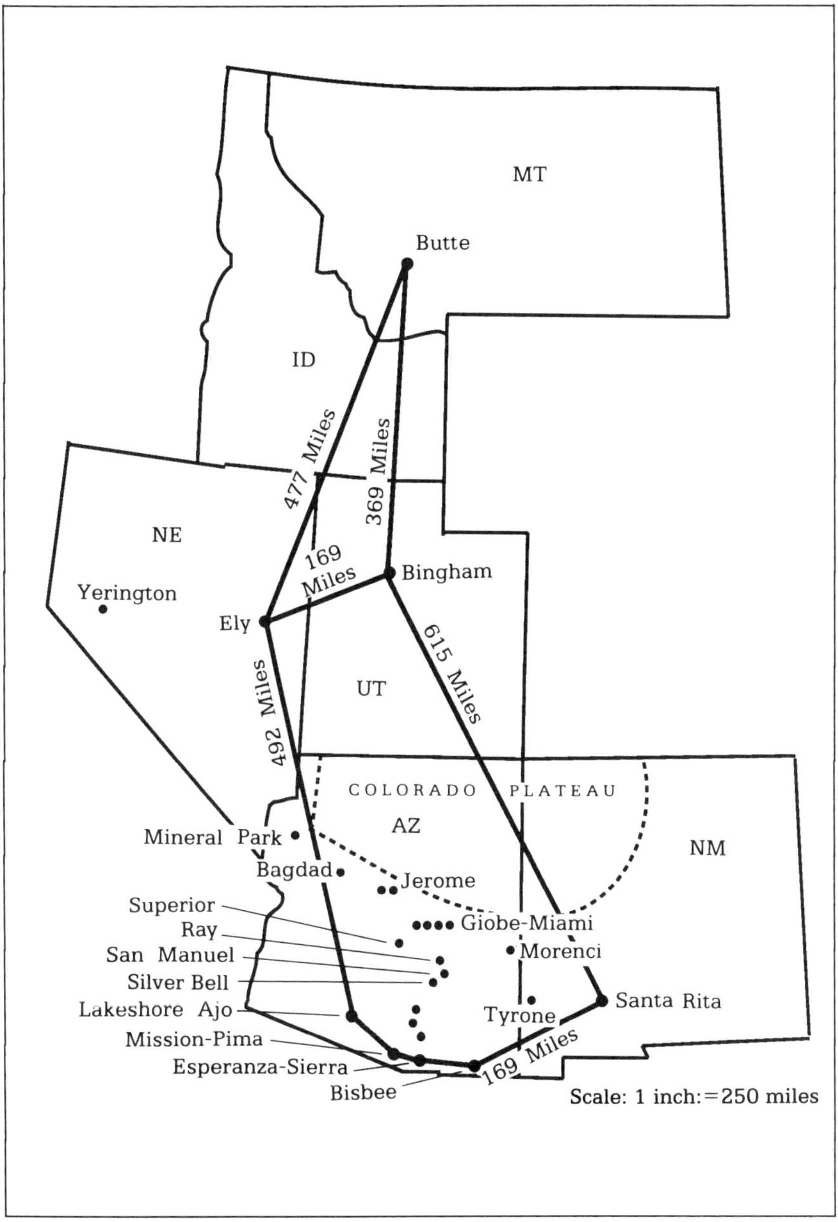

SOURCE: Adapted from *National Geographic Atlas of the World* (1975); and Charles A. Anderson, "Arizona and Adjacent New Mexico," in John D. Ridge, ed., *Ore Deposits of the United States, 1933–1967* (New York: American Institute of Mining, Metallurgical, and Petroleum Engineers, 1968), vol. 2, p. 1165.

find twenty-two deposits, of which all but five are being worked today. Many of them lie in mountainous territory, for example, Morenci, Superior, and Globe-Miami. The others, such as San Manuel and Mission-Pima, are found in desert valleys between ranges.

Second, observe the envelope curve that embraces all of the western deposits except Yerington, in western Nevada. It takes the shape of a Chinese spoon—wide and flat at the bottom (south), and narrowing to a point at its northern end. This is the joint effect of the high-density cluster in southern Arizona and New Mexico, and the far-distant scattering, relative to the lower nucleus, of the deposits at Bingham, Utah; Butte, Montana; and Ely, Nevada. There could be several causes for this low-density diffusion northward, but surely one of them must involve the special geological circumstances that created Butte, "the richest hill on earth."

Finally, the swarming of deposits in the southern part of the region suggests the operation of some special geological factor in the three outlying properties to the north, promoting their dispersion in some way. Alternatively, the explanation may rest on a common factor that produced a concentration of deposits in the south, through influences not present in the north.

Although our interest here concerns the spatial distribution of mineable copper ores, the industry as a whole includes the fabrication of copper products as well. The geographic distribution of the "factory" branch of the industry is discussed at length in other chapters, in particular those involved in recent labor-management relations. Here it need only be noted that the economic influence of weight losses on the location of ore-processing activities is largely eliminated after the smelting stage. In consequence, fabricating plants need not be close to the mines, and in fact have been strongly drawn to major industrial centers around the country, probably because of the advantages of proximity to final buyers of copper products.

GEOLOGICAL CHARACTERISTICS OF THE
AMERICAN DEPOSITS

Figure 2.3 identifies some of the characteristics of each of the world's principal copper deposits. We discuss here only those of the United States but, in so doing, define terms to make the world deposits interpretable.

FIGURE 2.3 Characteristics of Important Copper-Producing Areas in the Market Economy Countries

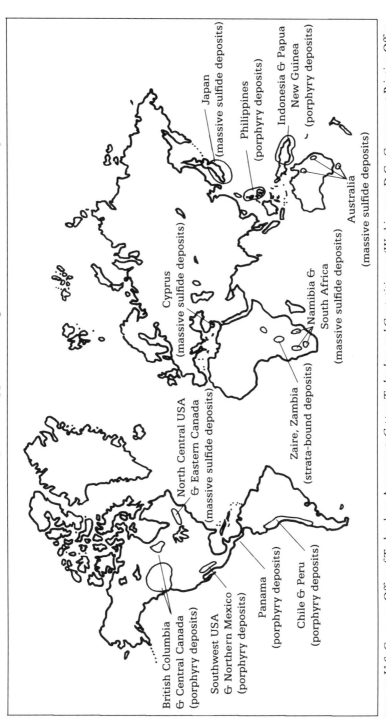

SOURCE: U.S. Congress, Office of Technology Assessment, *Copper: Technology and Competitiveness* (Washington, D.C.: Government Printing Office, September 1988), p. 93.

The Upper Michigan Peninsula

The Keeweenaw peninsula extends northeastward and then eastward like a slightly bent forefinger, pointing into Lake Superior from a base on the isolated segment of Michigan situated on top of the state of Wisconsin. Underlying the peninsula is the Keeweenaw fault, a strip of exposed lava that extends outward from Ironwood at the base to its outer terminus at Keeweenaw Point. Along this strip lies the native copper district, which extends for about 36 miles at a width of about 3 miles.[9] The strip passes through the middle of the peninsula, beginning directly south of the town of Ontonagon and ending about 7 miles northeast of Calumet.

Writing in 1966, Walter S. White of the U.S. Geological Survey stated that the native copper deposits of Michigan are found in stratified formations composed of amygdaloid and conglomerate beds.[10] The amygdaloid host rock represents congealed lava of magmatic or volcanic origin, while the conglomerate is derived from ancient streambeds. The copper itself is found in small to large grains, in nodules, and in masses of up to 400 tons. Typically, it is located in irregular and discontinuous fractures, in fissures, or in cavities. The location of these ore bodies has been controlled by accompanying folding and faulting, and by the permeability of the host rocks. Mining has been conducted to vertical depths of 5,500 feet, at shaft distances of up to 9,000 feet. Many deposits have been found close to the surface. The host rock strata show little evidence of intrusive bodies or dikes.

The evidence indicates that the Michigan ores were epigenetic; that is, they were formed after the deposition of the amygdaloid and conglomerate strata in which they occur. In origin, the copper solutions are now believed to be "down dip," White says, deriving from the bottom of a syncline beneath Lake Superior to the east and extending upward into the peninsula to the west. Under the pressure of a presumed massive intrusion of igneous rock or, instead, of lavas undergoing metamorphosis at depth, the solutions were forced upward to form deposits at receptive places in the host rocks. Both explanations have replaced an older one that accounted for the copper depositions by a supposed lateral and downward (supergenetic) circulation of meteoric water deriving from the earth's atmosphere in ancient times.

The lava hypothesis requires no assumption of a gigantic igneous intrusion, for which there is little evidence. It holds that as the lava was crushed and metamorphosed by the intense forces operating at the bottom of the syncline—presumably a spasm of volcanism—water that was driven by pressure from the voids and interstices of the lava-flow tops dissolved the copper surrounding it. The resulting copper solutions were then forced upward (hypogenesis) to become deposits in the cavities, fissures, and fractures of the overlying strata. On this view, the beds must have been deposited before the copper itself—and there is important evidence that they were.

This theory comports with evidence that the copper deposits were related to deformations in the host rocks, and that they followed most if not all of the periods of volcanism occurring along the peninsula. Finally, it also meets the requirement—imposed by other geological evidence—that the source and processes for the formation of the copper deposits were entirely regional in their scope. Still, a weakness remains and it is a serious one: this explanation calls for the presence of a huge volume of water, whose availability has yet to be demonstrated.[11]

Important questions persist concerning the origin of the Michigan copper deposits, although there is a good measure of agreement that they derived from ascending solutions, that the attendant forces were regional in extent, and that these forces derived from heat and pressure at great depth. No agreement exists regarding the period in geological time when copper deposition occurred, although the rocks of the peninsula are said to be from the late Precambrian era (about 600 million years ago).

Butte, Montana

The small city of Butte can lay persuasive historic claim to being the nation's greatest mining camp. It began life during an 1864 gold rush.[12] By 1867 the gold deposits were worked out, but silver was discovered in the same year. In 1882, while driving a crosscut at the 300-foot level of the Anaconda Mine, Marcus Daly found a rich vein of chalcocite, a copper sulfide known colloquially as copper glance. Thus began Butte's greatest boom, which was to last another eight decades. Its base lay in copper, but copper was only part of the story; for the ground below the town's barren hills was also to pour forth huge quantities of zinc, manganese, lead, and arsenic, along with 645 million ounces of silver and 2.5 million ounces of gold. Still, it was copper that became king, for in the years from 1880 through 1964 the many mines of Butte yielded 16.2 billion pounds of copper (8.1 million short tons).[13] By contrast, the Michigan mines produced only 5.4 million short tons over a much longer period.

Geologists believe today that the origin of Butte's enormous natural wealth began with three enormous tectonic blocks in western Montana; a central mass underlying the town itself; a north block of Precambrian age; and a south block, also of Precambrian age, that consists of archean rock, gneiss, schist, and granite. The central block is the source of the treasure trove that lay under Butte. Within that great block at its apex is a wedge-shaped mass known as the Boulder batholith, a massive intrusion of igneous rock that burst upward through the older formations in late Cretaceous times, about 70–78 million years ago. The batholith is composed of quartz monzonite, which serves as the host rock for the many Butte ores. Actually, this rock mass is thought to be a composite of several intrusives—a mafic (magnesium and iron) group and a granodiorite (a granular igneous rock) group on both the north and south sides. The batholith extends about 70 miles northeast on its long axis and varies between 15 and 30 miles in width. Butte itself is about two-thirds of the way south, along the western edge of the main formation. To the west there are eight "islands" of the same host rock, rising from a sea of other formations, some of which are the same age.[14]

In his pioneering studies for the Anaconda Company, Reno H. Sales in 1913 described the Butte metals as constituting three zones: the central, where rich copper ores are found, free of zinc and manganese; the intermediate, where copper dominates but is accompanied by zinc; and the peripheral, where there is no copper of commercial grade. Sales called the inner zone and the nearby islands the Copper Front.

Mineralization at Butte has taken place in two separate vein systems. The Anaconda consists of five main veins and twelve to fifteen smaller ones, all running east and west, and converging downward toward the west. The main veins end in the heart of the district but reappear much farther east. These veins, together with clusters of closely adjacent fractures known as horsetail ore bodies, constitute what Sales called Main Stage mineralization. At much greater depths, different minerals and different rock structures are encountered that are older than those in the Main Stage.

The other group is known as the Blue Vein system. The veins strike northeast through the center of the district and later begin to merge at deep levels with those of the Anaconda group. In Sales's opinion, the Anaconda group is the older. It is also the richer, with lengths of up to 5 miles, depths of 4,500 feet, widths averaging 20 to 30 feet, and at some locations chalcocite bonanzas of even 100 feet.[15]

As with the ores of the Michigan peninsula, the original deposition of the copper-bearing solutions is believed to be hypogenetic, with some lateral flows in the western areas. After many years of study, Sales argued in 1954 that as the molten batholith rose from its magmatic source and began crystallizing, a "cupola" emerged out of the main body and penetrated the solid granite above. Dikes rising from the primary mass also broke into the hard granite, cooled and solidified, and thereby isolated the magmatic cupola, which remained liquid while solidification proceeded downward within the batholith itself. This flow top thus became a natural site for the accumulation and concentration of water, sulfur, and the ore metals. In turn, penetration of the upper granite by the dikes altered its internal cooling stresses and weakened the whole structure. The result was the formation of the fractures of the Anaconda vein system. As further cooling occurred, mineralization followed.[16]

As noted earlier, Sales and his colleagues referred to this hypogene migration of the metal solutions as the Main Stage in the process of mineralization and vein formation. In their view, as the solutions ascended they deposited bornite and chalcocite (both rich copper sulfides); enargite, which contains arsenic as well as copper; and chalcopyrite, which includes iron as well as sulfur and is much less rich (34.6 percent when pure). In any case, the dominance of the copper sulfides links the Butte deposits to the other great ore bodies in the United States.

The Western Porphyries

"Porphyry copper" is regarded by geologists as an inexact term which wrongly suggests that the host rocks involved in this large group of copper deposits have a common nature, including a peculiar crystalline structure. Probably the description was quickly accepted because the early great mines at Bingham, Ely, and Morenci all did have copper-bearing porphyry rock. Then the expression was applied to the many other copper deposits in Nevada, Arizona, and New Mexico, where the host rocks were entirely different (for instance, schists, silicated limestones, and volcanic rock). Other variations are dependent upon processes of deposition, nature of mineralization, and times of formation of these ore bodies.[17]

In any event, Arthur B. Parsons has provided a useful list of the common characteristics of these copper deposits that elides the foregoing differences and thus makes the term still useful for technical classification.

(1) The deposits are so extensive that they can be mined efficiently only at large scale, through underground block caving or open pits.

(2) The distribution of the copper minerals within the ore bodies is sufficiently uniform to make mining in bulk more efficient than the classical selective process.

(3) The genesis of the ore has involved the intrusion of igneous rock, either porphyry or closely related other rocks, which suggests that deep, slow-cooling rock masses supplied the heat and energy to make available the metals involved.

(4) The upper layers of copper ore have been concentrated by the process of natural leaching known as *secondary enrichment*.

(5) The dimensions of the ore body depend on two factors: the geological fact that ore grade declines with both lateral extension and increase of depth, and the economic fact that prevailing price and extraction costs will set the limits of mineable ore at any given time.

(6) In all of these mines, the ore typically is a low-grade sulfide (not exceeding 3 percent), hence requires fine grinding and concentration before smelting.[18]

In comparison with the small and far-distant mining districts of Butte and Upper Michigan, the western porphyries are very numerous in the region below the Colorado Plateau, which runs across Arizona and into central New Mexico, where it turns north. North of the line of this plateau are three other porphyry mines, separated by distances of more than a hundred miles—Yerington, Nevada, on the west; Ely, Nevada, on the eastern Nevada border; and Bingham Canyon, Utah, on the east.

Charles A. Anderson of the U.S. Geological Survey refers to the region south and west of the Colorado Plateau as the Basin and Range Province. Here the main group of porphyry copper mines is located.[19] The region consists of huge mountain blocks bounded by faults. No Paleozoic ores occur. The central and pervasive geological characteristic of the province is the massive extent of the intrusion of igneous rocks—in stocks (minor batholiths), sills, and dikes that made their appearance between the late Cretaceous period (as in Butte) and the early Tertiary age, between 80 and 40 million years ago.

Table 2.1 provides information concerning the types of intrusive rocks and their estimated ages at several important mining locations. Note the prominence of monzonite and porphyry rocks in these locations; also that the age range of these intrusive rocks extends from 45 million years (Bingham) to 163 million years (Bisbee), with considerable concentration at 56 to 72 million years. Finally, Ely and Bingham, both of which are in

TABLE 2.1   **Dominant intrusive rocks at leading porphyry mines in the West, and their estimated ages**

Location	Rock type	Estimated age[a] (millions of years)
Ajo	Quartz-orthoclase pegmatite	63
Bagdad	Quartz monzonite	71
Bingham	Biotite-augite monzonite porphyry	45
Bisbee	Granite	163
Ely	Monzonite	122
Esperanza	Phlogopite-sericite	63
	Muscovite-quartz veinlet	61
Globe-Miami	Quartz monzonite, granite	60
	Granite porphyry	64
Mineral Park	Quartz monzonite	72
Mission-Pima	Granodiorite, quartz	56
	Monzonite porphyry	60
Ray	Porphyry	63
San Manuel	Altered granodiorite porphyry	67
Santa Rita (Chino)	Granodiorite porphyry	63
Silver Bell	Alaskite, quartz monzonite	63
	Mineralized quartz monzonite	67

SOURCE: Charles A. Anderson, "Arizona and Adjacent New Mexico," in John D. Ridge, ed., *Ore Deposits of the United States, 1933–1967*, vol. 2, p. 1169.

[a] Range only, between oldest and youngest rocks, for each location.

distant and anomalous locations compared with the others, fall well out-side the modal age range, with Ely at 122 million years and Bingham Canyon at only 45 million years. Both can be classed as porphyries.

For more than sixty years geologists have contended that intrusive rocks of the monzonite-porphyry type have "invariably accompanied" the disseminated copper deposits and thus were connected with their origin.[20] This suspected linkage has been reinforced by findings at Ajo that support an almost continuous transition from "late magmatic alteration of the Cornelia quartz monzonite to the final stage of shattering of the crystallized rock, allowing the permeation of mineralizing solutions to begin."[21]

The formations of these several ore bodies, while varying in some re-spects, show common traits. To illustrate, chalcopyrite and pyrite were the main hypogene source, chalcocite and covellite the dominant supergene sulfides. At Bingham canyon, mining started with supergene chalcocite, then worked downward into lower-grade sulfide ores at depth. The profile was similar at Ely. In a general way, Morenci experienced the same history; here, however, was a strong case of secondary enrichment of lower-grade ores, yielding an upper chalcocite layer of 50 to 1,000 feet in thickness. At the Lavender pit in Bisbee, a similar blanket of chalcocite was formed, ranging between 50 and 400 feet in thickness, with hypogene sulfides well below. By contrast, mining at Ajo began with oxide ores embedded in quartz monzonite and deriving from below, and again the lower-grade sulfides were encountered as mining advanced. At Santa Rita (Chino), chalcocite with pyrite was found in the enriched layers, with chalcopyrite as the principal ore. San Manuel displayed characteristics similar to Ajo— supergene oxide and sulfide ores at the top, with hypogene copper sulfide below as the main source.

A word is necessary at this point concerning the formation of chalcocite layers through the process of secondary enrichment, because these layers are such an obvious and important feature of the geological history of the porphyry deposits. Long after the intrusion and solidification of the igneous rock, erosion gradually wore away the cap and exposed the underlying original ore mass. The action of groundwater and oxygen in the air slowly transformed the copper sulfides at the surface into copper sulfate ($CuSO_4$). This blue vitreol solution then percolated downward into the mass. As long as oxygen is available, the solution grows ever richer in copper content. When the oxygen is exhausted, the copper sulfide solution reacts with the chalcopyrite and pyrite within the mass to produce chalcocite (Cu_2S), the richest of the copper sulfides (80 percent pure). Over long periods of time the chalcocite layer gradually moves downward, thickening as it goes.[22]

One residual question concerns the forces that determined the location of the porphyry copper deposits. In 1946 H. A. Schmitt observed that most deposits occur along a major rift within the Wasatch-Jerome "orogen," a term for a mountain mass that moves in unison. This particular mass intersects what geologists call the Texas lineament, which extends from southern California to the Rio Grande embayment in Texas. Within this region is a complex system of faults that in turn reflects ancient tectonic movements.[23] Here, then, was the natural locus for magmatic intrusions.[24] Intense fracturing and shattering is common to all of these deposits, with fracturing the central element in their formation. The causes of these phenomena are still unknown.

Today there is general agreement that the deposits are closely associated with magma. Yet the question remains, Why the substantial clustering of these particular deposits? One theory says that the metals are located within broad zones of the earth's crust and mantle, and are derived from the original meteoric material. Copper is among the metals at deep levels, while gold and silver are at the intermediate level. Within this context, it has been suggested, tectonic movements and geosutures could have released the deeper metals and the igneous rock, while orogens could have conveyed them upward as mineral solutions, to become deposits.

Another possibility is that the monzonite magmas were peculiarly hospitable to supplying copper for hypogenetic deposition, or at the least to providing a favorable structural environment for that deposition.[25] Perhaps the orogen and fault system typical of the Colorado Plateau accounts for the release of these monzonitic magmas in these particular locations, which in return produced the intrusions through which the original copper solutions could rise to form the deposits.

Credits for Coproducts and By-Products

A geological phenomenon of significance to the copper industry is the coexistence of copper with other metals of value—notably gold, silver, lead, nickel, zinc, cobalt, and molybdenum. Because those metals are removed along with the copper ore, they add no extraction costs while producing added revenues. They do add to processing costs beyond the mining stage, but they can make a considerable financial difference. The harvesting of copper, which might be uneconomic in isolation, can be turned into a profitable enterprise when the costs of production are shared among a combination of metals of various prices.

As Table 2.2 indicates, Canada is the winner in this coproducts and by-products credit sweepstakes. Such credits, on the average, cover 70 percent of Canadian copper-production costs. In fact, in 1980, by-products credits not only covered all Canadian production costs, but by themselves were a 6 percent profit source. With the exception of the huge Bingham Canyon open-pit mine, a significant producer of gold and molybdenum as well as copper, the U.S. mines are not well positioned in the by-products credit race; these credits contribute only a 12 percent average reduction in production costs. Moreover, the pursuit of by-products prevents the use of the lower-cost solvent extraction and electrowinning (SX-EW) technology discussed in the next section. It is for this reason that the Arizona copper mines have emphasized SX-EW as the focus of their cost-cutting efforts,

TABLE 2.2 Coproducts and by-products credits for major copper-producing countries, 1975, 1980, 1984

Country	Credits (percentage of production costs) in—		
	1975	1980	1984
Zambia	3	10	10
Zaire	19	57	35
South Africa/Namibia	15	57	42
Australia	26	65	36
Papua New Guinea	51	84	64
Philippines	23	43	40
Indonesia	23	48	30
Canada	76	106	69
United States	10	31	12
Mexico	69	70	65
Chile	10	26	19
Peru	54	68	49
Sweden	—	93	89
Average	31	54	40

SOURCE: Kenji Takeuchi, John E. Strongman, Shunichi Maeda, and C. Suan Tan, *The World Copper Industry: Its Changing Structure and Future Prospects* (Washington, D.C.: World Bank, 1987), p. 61.

whereas the owners of the Bingham Canyon Mine have concentrated on savings in materials handling so as to preserve by-products profits.

Declining Yields

A familiar result of the interaction of geology, economics, and technology is the declining yield of copper mining over time. Declining yield refers to the percentage of the volume of ore mined that becomes marketable copper at the end of the production sequence. It is to be expected that those in pursuit of profits from the mining and processing of copper would attack the richest ores first, moving on to the next-richest as the richest are exhausted. Therefore, yields will decline over time unless new ores are discovered to delay the process.

As richer deposits have been exhausted over time, technological methods have been developed to profitably harvest ores of lower copper content. Figure 2.4 illustrates this process for the United States. Pre-1906 average yields would have been much higher if data were available to show them. That date marks the development of techniques for mining porphyry copper. The peaks in the early 1920s and the early 1930s mark

FIGURE 2.4 **Average Yield of Copper Mined**
in the United States

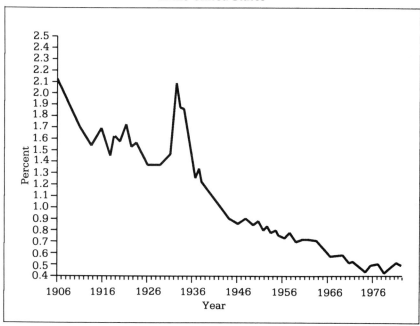

SOURCE: U.S. Department of the Interior, Bureau of Mines.

another related phenomenon: the closing of marginal properties during severe depressions. The yields of the 1980s would have been essentially unchanged from those of the 1970s except for the familiar closure of marginal properties in 1982–1985.

A CENTURY OF TECHNOLOGICAL CHANGE

Table 2.3 identifies each of the major U.S. copper mines and gives other significant data, including their roles in the history of technological change in the industry.

The Period of Underground Mining

Before open-pit operations began at Bingham Canyon in 1906, American copper was mined underground. The ore had to be broken in place, transferred to tram cars, moved to a hoisting shaft or exit adit, taken to the

TABLE 2.3 Principal copper mines in the United States[a]

Owning company and name of mine	Location	Type of mine	Year opened	Year closed	Remarks
Anaconda Company					
Butte Mines	Butte, Montana	U, P	1882	1983	E. and W. Berkeley Pits reopened 1986.
Carr Fork	Tooele, Utah	N	N	1981	
Twin Buttes (ANAMAX)	Pima County, Arizona	P	1971	A	Acquired by Cyprus Minerals.
Yerington	Yerington, Nevada	P	1954	N	
Appalachian Sulfides, Inc.					
Ore Knob	Ashe County, North Carolina	N	1958	N	
ASARCO, Inc.					
Mission	Sahuarita, Arizona	P	1962	A	
Sacaton	Sacaton, Arizona	P	1972	1984	
San Xavier	Sahuarita, Arizona	P	1974	A	
Silver Bell	Silver Bell, Arizona	P	1954	A	Converted to leaching 1982.
Bagdad Copper Corporation					
Old Dick	Bagdad, Arizona	P	1937	A	Acquired by Cyprus Minerals.
Banner Mining Company					
Banner and Miser's Chest	Lordsburg, New Mexico	N	N	N	Acquired by Pima Minerals.
Mineral Hill, Daisy	Pima County, Arizona	P	N	N	
Palo Verde	Pima County, Arizona	N	N	N	
Calumet and Hecla Consolidated Mining Company					
Ahmeek	Lake Superior County, Michigan	U	N	1967	All properties closed by strike August 19, 1967
Allouez	Lake Superior County, Michigan	U	1859	1967	
Calumet	Lake Superior County, Michigan	U	1866	1967	

Name	Location		Start	End	Notes
Centennial	Lake Superior County, Michigan	U	1896	1967	
Hecla	Lake Superior County, Michigan	U	1866	1967	
Oscola	Lake Superior County, Michigan	U	1873	1967	
Tamarack Mining	Lake Superior County, Michigan	U	1881	N	
Calera Mining Company					
Blackbird	Blackbird, Idaho	N	1858	N	
Calumet and Arizona					Acquired by Phelps Dodge 1931.
Irish Mag	Bisbee, Arizona	U	1902	1917	
New Cornelia	Ajo, Arizona	P	1917	1984	
Castle Dome Mining Company					
Castle Dome	Pinto Valley, Arizona	P	1943	1953	Owned by Miami Copper. Now owned by Pinto Valley (Magma).
Consolidated Coppermines Corporation					
Ruth Pit Extension	Ely, Nevada	P	1926	N	
Tripp Pit	Ely, Nevada	P	1926	N	
Veteran Pit	Ely, Nevada	P	1926	N	
Copper Cities Mining Company					
Copper Cities	Miami, Arizona	P	1954	N	Owned by Miami Copper.
Coronado Copper and Zinc Company					
Republic and Mammoth	Cochise County, Arizona	N	1950	N	
Duval Corporation					
Battle Mountain	Lander County, Nevada	N	1967	N	
Copper Canyon	Lander County, Nevada	N	1967	N	Acquired by Cyprus Minerals.

TABLE 2.3 (continued)

Owning company and name of mine	Location	Type of mine	Year opened	Year closed	Remarks
Esperanza	Pima County, Arizona	P	1959	A	
Ithaca Peak	Mineral Park, Arizona	P	1964	C	
Sierrita	Pima County, Arizona	P	1970	A	Acquired by ASARCO from ANAMAX Mining.
Eisenhower Mining Company					
Eisenhower	Pima County, Arizona	P	1978	A	
Howe Sound Company					
Holden	Lake Chelan, Washington	N	N	N	
Idarado Mining Company					
Treasury Tunnel Mines	San Miguel County, Colorado	N	1948	N	
Inspiration Consolidated Copper Company					Acquired by Cyprus Minerals 1988.
Christmas	Gila County, Arizona	U	N	C	
Inspiration	Globe-Miami, Arizona	U, P, L	1915	A	
Isle Royale Copper Company					
Isle Royale	Lake Superior County, Michigan	N	N	N	
Kennecott Copper Corporation					Acquired by RTZ Minerals 1988.
Alaska Group	Kennicott, Alaska	U	1910	1938	
Chino Division	Santa Rita, New Mexico	U, P	1910	A	Sold 1986 to Phelps Dodge.

Nevada Consolidated Division	Ely, Nevada	P	1908	1984	Sold 1986 to ASARCO.
Ray Mines Division	Ray, Arizona	U, P	1910	A	Owns Pinto Valley Mining.
Utah Copper Division	Bingham Canyon, Utah	P	1906	A	
Magma Copper Company					
San Manuel	San Manuel, Arizona	U, L	1957	A	Reopened 1990.
Superior	Superior, Arizona	U	1910	1982	
Miami Copper Company					Also founded Castle Dome and Copper Cities. Leaching by Pinto Valley.
Miami	Miami, Arizona	U, L	1910	A	
Noranda Lakeshore Mines, Inc.					
Lakeshore	Casa Grande, Arizona	U, L	1974	A	Acquired by Cyprus Minerals 1987.
Old Dominion Copper and Smelting Company					
Old Dominion	Globe, Arizona	U	1885	1941	Formed by Adolph Lewisohn; later sold to Phelps Dodge officials.
Phelps Dodge Corporation					
Copper Queen	Bisbee, Arizona	U, P, L	1881	L	Temporarily closed.
Metcalf	Morenci, Arizona	P	1974	1984	By acquisition of Detroit Copper and Arizona Copper.
Morenci	Bisbee, Arizona	U, P, L	1874	A	
New Cornelia	Ajo, Arizona	P	1917	C	By acquisition of Calumet and Arizona Copper.

TABLE 2.3 (continued)

Owning company and name of mine	Location	Type of mine	Year opened	Year closed	Remarks
Tyrone	Tyrone, New Mexico	P, L	1916	A	Closed 1921; reopened 1969.
Pima Mining Company					
Pima	Pima County, Arizona	P	1957	A	Now owned by ASARCO.
Pittsburgh and Boston Company					
Cliff	Lake Superior County, Michigan	U	1845	N	
Copper Harbor	Lake Superior County, Michigan	U	1844	N	
Quincy Mining Company					
Quincy	Lake Superior County, Michigan	U	185?	N	
Tennessee Copper Company					
Copper Hill	Polk County, Tennessee	N	1962	N	
United Verde Copper Company					
United Verde	Jerome, Arizona	U	1883	1953	Acquired by Phelps Dodge about 1935.
United Verde Extension Mining Company					
Little Daisy	Jerome, Arizona	U	1915	1938	
UV Industries, Inc.					
Continental	Piños Altos, New Mexico	P	N	1982	

Vermont Copper Company Elizabeth	Orange County, Vermont	N	N	N
White Pine Company White Pine	Lake Superior County, Michigan	U	N	A

SOURCE: U.S. Department of the Interior, Bureau of Mines, *Minerals Yearbook*, various issues; U.S. Congress, Office of Technology Assessment, *Copper: Technology and Competitiveness* (Washington, D.C.: Government Printing Office, September 1988), pp. 110–111; Robert G. Cleland, *A History of Phelps Dodge, 1834–1950* (New York: Knopf, 1952), pp. 3–5; Ira B. Joralemon, *Copper: The Encompassing Story of Mankind's First Metal* (Berkeley: Howell-North, 1973), pp. 255–256; Arthur B. Parsons, *The Porphyry Coppers* (New York: American Institute of Mining and Petroleum Engineers, 1933); Arthur B. Parsons, *Porphyry Coppers in 1956* (New York: American Institute of Mining, Metallurgical, and Petroleum Engineers, 1957).

[a] A = active; C = closed; L = leaching; N = no information; P = open-pit mine; U = underground mine.

surface, and then reduced, smelted, and refined. The technology required was dictated by these elemental necessities. Much of it—shaft sinking, tunneling, and stoping—had a history of some three centuries, largely originating in England and Germany. What followed with the emergence and development of American copper production was largely an accretion of minor modifications, augmented here and there by significant innovations. Technological change in this period was evolutionary and cumulative, not revolutionary.[26]

These small changes are countless and can be noted only briefly. For explosives, black powder gave way to nitroglycerin. Hand drilling yielded to air, water, and hammer drills. Cornish pumps were replaced by electric pumps distributed to various stations. Horse whims and windlasses were succeeded by steam and then electric hoists. Square sets and other forms of timbering were developed as rock support in unstable ground.[27] When large mines such as the Copper Queen and the Anaconda appeared in the early 1880s, the technique of finding ore bodies, blocking them out, and planning extraction became highly sophisticated. Actual mining usually involved stopes as a working chamber for drilling and blasting out the ore. The tasks called for skill because underground operations were expensive. The miner had to select the richest and softest ore and remove it without the dilution of grade that occurs when waste rock and ore of lower grade are included.

Animal-drawn or man-pushed railcars trammed the ore from the stopes to the hoisting shaft. In time, electric power was introduced through locomotives that could haul trains of larger cars. At the hoisting point, cages were used to lift the loaded cars to the surface. Later these gave way to skips, which were moving bins for hoisting the ore to the surface for automatic dumping into a tipple. As underground operations were perfected, drift and haulage tunnels eventually reached standard-gauge railroad dimensions.

Economical handling of the ore required removal of as much dross material as possible, as early as possible. At the surface, the ore had to be crushed so that as much non-ore-bearing material as possible could be eliminated and the valuable ores concentrated as a proportion of the total material handled at the downstream stages of copper processing. Before the 1870s, crushing was accomplished with sledgehammers, then with mechanical jigs and stamp mills. By the end of the century, jaw and gyratory crushers and ball mills were introduced to permit the fine grinding that was essential to the effective separation of lead, zinc, and copper from sulfide ores.

The first device for separating the mineral particles was the riffled shaking table, whose best-known version was the Wilfley table. Before its appearance around 1875, hand sorting, hand shoveling, stirring, and settling were the only ways to extract these metals. The shaking table was a notable step forward in separation by gravity concentration, because it added speed and efficiency to the process—in short, it expanded mill capacity. In turn the economic threshold was lowered to allow exploitation of lower-grade ores—a step toward what Julihn calls "nonselective" mass-production mining.[28]

Fine grinding was soon improved by other innovations such as Chilean mills, cone crushers, and rod and ball mills. Mechanical rake classifiers were added to the sequence, to sort out oversized pieces for a second trip through the circuit. Thickener tanks were introduced to permit the recovery of slime concentrates from waste mill water.[29]

During the underground period in American copper history, gravity concentration supplied the concentrates for smelting. Initially smelting involved a Welsh process that employed heat to extract copper, first by roasting the ore, then by smelting it in a reverberatory furnace to obtain copper matte, and finally by burning the matte together with green poles—all to remove slag, iron, sulfur, and oxygen. At the time a type of cupola furnace was used as an early version of the Bessemer process.[30]

One of the most important innovations, which came late in the period of underground mining, was block caving as a technique for ore extraction. It was first used in iron mining. In 1906 it was introduced at the Ohio mine of the Boston Consolidated Copper and Gold Mining Company, adjacent to what was to become Daniel C. Jackling's Utah Copper mine in Bingham Canyon. Louis S. Cates, later Jackling's associate and after that president of Phelps Dodge, was the innovator. Together with Felix McDonald, he developed block caving as a means to speed up output at a time when cash was low. Cates employed the same technique at the Ray Mine in 1911, while McDonald introduced it at Inspiration in the same year.[31]

In principle, block caving marked the beginning of nonselective mass-production mining underground—as it were, an extension of the older Comstock idea of using the richer ore streaks to cover the added costs of extracting lower-grade adjoining ores, while at the same time spreading the common overhead costs over more units of final mine product. In this way the unit total cost per pound of copper could be cut enough to absorb the higher direct cost of extracting the poorer-quality ore.

Block caving requires a large and relatively uniform ore body, intersected by joint and fracture planes that cause the ore to break up as the technique proceeds. The first step is the driving of a haulage level below the block. Next, a system of transfer raises is bored upward from this level, ending in a series of "grizzlys" or grill-covered openings. These raises serve as ore passes to convey the broken ore down to pockets for ore storage at the haulage level, where it is subsequently transferred to dump cars for moving the ore in skips to the surface.

The next step is the driving upward, into the block itself, of a series of extraction raises. Then the base of the block is undercut to induce its disintegration as the ore breaks up under its own weight and the block progressively collapses.

Block caving provided the way for underground properties to mine low-grade porphyry ores efficiently, by permitting their extraction in large volume yet at low unit cost. Put alternatively, caving increased the productivity of both capital and labor. In turn, several underground properties could compete more effectively against the many open-pit mines that appeared after 1906. Eventually, however, the extraction of the richer ores and the cost competition from surface mining reduced the viability of all types of underground copper mining. Wartime prices carried underground mines through the Second World War. But by 1946 only 42 percent of U.S. copper production was emanating from the few mines such as the Anaconda at Butte and the Copper Queen and Magma Superior in Arizona that could produce ore rich enough to justify the underground costs.[32] By the end of 1990 only Magma's San Manuel Mine and its recently reopened Superior Mine, along with White Pine in Michigan, were still operating underground. All the rest had been closed or converted to open-pit mining.

The Period of Open-Pit Mining

The basic principle of the open pit is simple: use power shovels to excavate a vertical series of terraces or benches along the slope of the exposed ore body after the overburden has been removed. The ore then moves in trains of dump cars along the same terraces to the primary crusher. As the mine develops, the benches so cut take the form of a downward spiral toward the bottom of the pit.

The power shovel dates from the late 1860s, when it was devised for construction of the first transcontinental railroad. After a visit to the Mesabi iron mines in early 1906, Daniel Jackling and Robert C. Gemmell of the Utah Copper Company immediately recognized that the humble steam shovel was the basic key to mining cheap ores in volume. By spring of 1906, Utah Copper began using these machines in Bingham Canyon.[33]

The next innovation that nurtured exploitation of porphyry ores, the flotation method of separation and concentration, did not arrive until almost a decade later. Flotation replaces gravity with a chemical process for separating the particles of copper sulfide from the other minerals and waste. Although an early patent for a version of the principle had been granted in 1886 to Mrs. William Everson, a mineralogist, flotation did not come into use in the United States until 1912, and then only in an experimental and unsuccessful way. In fact, the first large-scale use of the idea was at Inspiration, in about 1915.[34] Thus Jackling's original success did not depend on flotation; he used Wilfley tables and vanners for gravity concentration. In fact, Utah Copper did not adopt flotation until about 1920.

Flotation rests on differences in the surface properties of various mineral particles. When chalcopyrite or chalcocite—two common copper minerals—are placed in a trough filled with water to which a minute amount of oil has been added, these particles have a special affinity for the oil. Agitation of the water introduces air into the mixture, forming surface bubbles coated with oil, to which the particles attach themselves. This natural selectivity, as Parsons terms it, is the basis for separation by flotation. The copper-bearing bubbles can be floated off, collected, pumped to vacuum filters, and there dried out to become copper concentrate, ready for smelting.[35] Although flotation fitted perfectly into mass-production mining, it did not become widely used until after 1920, when technical problems had been resolved and patent litigation overcome.

In the transition from underground to open-pit mining, the basic technology from initial extraction through electrolytic refining remained fixed. Change was incremental or accretionary. Power shovels moved from steam to electric or diesel, while dipper capacity steadily increased. Rail operations in the pit and to the crushing plant underwent a similar evolution of motive power and load capacity. Prior to the Second World War, rail was almost the only means of haulage. But rail equipment became scarce during the war and some mines shifted to trucks. The latter proved more flexible, and as their capacity increased to as much as 170 tons, more and more mines abandoned rail haulage. Today moving belts and even slurry pipelines are used in ore haulage at Bingham Canyon and also at Morenci. Still, the large volume requirements at Kennecott have led recently to a reconsideration of the place of railcars in these operations.

Within smelters, two major innovations appeared around 1910—the

Pierce-Smith converter and the Cottrell precipitator. The converter is a special version of the Bessemer process that greatly increases furnace capacity at this stage of smelting, while use of magnesite brick for lining the device has given much longer life than the earlier acid converters. Moreover, its much greater effectiveness in burning out impurities permitted the elimination of preliminary roasting. Now the concentrates could go directly into the reverberatory matte furnace for removal of slag, followed by ladle transfer to the converters for heating and air blowing. Then the resulting blister copper could be sent to the anode furnace, where reformed gases now had replaced green poles for removing oxygen to obtain anode copper. The precipitator has two purposes: reduction of air pollution arising from smelting, and recovery of copper particles from flue dust in stack gases.

The transition to mass-production mining was the joint consummation of many diverse improvements, most of them small and cumulative. But a few represented major intrusions into long-established routines. Among the first of these breakthroughs was the early recognition on the Comstock lode, about 1876, that the richer veins could help pay for the exploitation of the lower-grade ores, whose recovery and reduction in turn could be financed by spreading the fixed or overhead costs of pumping, hoisting, supervision, and mill capacity over more units of final product (in this case, silver).[36] Another such intrusion—the Wilfley table and the vanner (for recovering copper from fines)—was the decisive element in favor of gravity separation. Separation in turn required fine grinding, which was accomplished first by the Chilean mill, a device with three standing, linked, and revolving crushing wheels known as mullers, moving on steel tracks. Finally, there was the steam shovel, which allowed ore to be broken in place in massive volumes.

All of these innovations lay at hand conceptually when Jackling and his associates began working experimentally at the Copperton mill in Bingham Canyon in 1899, testing porphyry samples for ore grade and recovery potential, and trying out methods of crushing, grinding, and concentrating the ore.[37] All that was needed was an act of creative synthesis by which all of the elements of mass-production mining could be combined for practical use.[38] This last decisive advance was achieved by Jackling and his colleague Gemmell in the Jackling-Gemmell Report of September 1899, a document that quickly became famous in the annals of American copper mining. Like many intellectual breakthroughs, their concept seems obvious once stated. Yet initially it was almost laughed out of the court of informed engineering opinion. The industry was to be revolutionized by the simple idea that initial high fixed costs, which were insupportable at low levels of production, could become infinitesimal if spread over a large enough output. By 1906 the great Utah mine finally began production, soon to prove beyond all doubt the economic feasibility of surface mining of the disseminated porphyry ores.

Figure 2.5 illustrates these traditional stages of copper production, which still prevail. The joint impact of this impressive class of mining innovations and the large group of cumulative improvements was a persistent and substantial increase in labor and capital productivity in copper mining and ore reduction. It shows up strongly in the long-term real (deflated) price of copper, which—depending on the measure—fell between a third and a half on average between 1885–1914 and 1919–1957, despite the fact that the average ore grade in the industry was declining rather sharply, from 3.0 percent to only 0.8 percent during 1919–1957.[39] Despite wild price gyrations, copper prices in real terms were never— during the next thirty years—to rise above the highs of that period.

Modern Innovations

Other than the volume of materials handling possible, there were no further innovations in the post–World War II period insofar as extracting ore from the mines was concerned. For sulfide ore there have been only gradual improvements in the handling of ores in preparation for smelting. The changes in the handling of oxide ores have been more dramatic, although the processes involved have a long history.[40]

Milling and smelting. For both types of ores, semiautogenous grinding has been introduced into the milling of concentrates. The new process, simply put, reduces the ore to powder by using rock-on-rock collision. This technology does not allow complete replacement of the less efficient ball- and-rod milling processes, however, since it can only be successfully applied on certain types of rock.

In smelting, the previously abandoned roasting process is now being reconsidered by some operations as a way of reducing sulfur emissions—a vital concern now in response to stringent environmental protection laws. A smelting innovation of the past twenty years has been the Outokumpu flash furnace developed in Finland. It depends on the spontaneous combustion of sulfur contained in the copper concentrate and oxygen, whereas traditional furnaces rely on external sources of heat to smelt copper. While

FIGURE 2.5 Principal Stages of the Copper Production Process

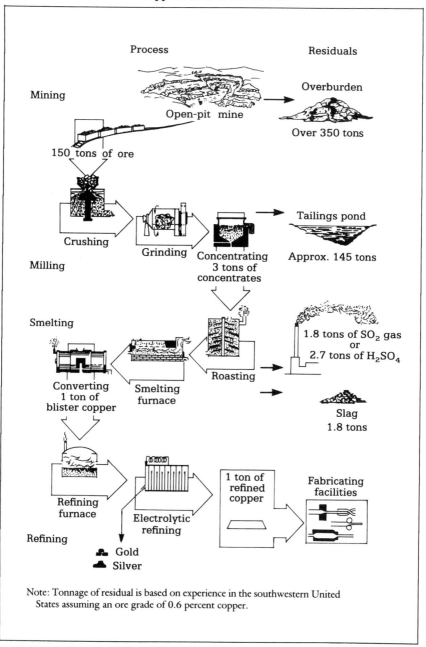

Note: Tonnage of residual is based on experience in the southwestern United States assuming an ore grade of 0.6 percent copper.

SOURCE: U.S. Congress, Office of Technology Assessment, *Copper: Technology and Competitiveness* (Washington, D.C.: Government Printing Office, September 1988), p. 8.

the flash furnace uses the concentrate's own content of sulfur in creating the heat needed for smelting, traditional furnaces burn off and emit some of the sulfur in the form of SO_2. With the costly and strongly enforced environmental standards concerning SO_2 emissions, the flash furnace's comparatively clean treatment of concentrates allows the emissions from the smelting process to meet primary pollution standards. Unfortunately, secondary standards cannot be reliably met by the use of a flash furnace, so new pollution control devices must be forthcoming to meet these restrictions.

From the smelter the molten copper-bearing matte is poured into a tilted converter; there oxygen, blown in through the sides via tuyeres, facilitates release of the remaining iron and sulfur from the matte and leaves almost pure copper. This blister copper is reheated in an anode furnace and poured on a casting wheel in 750-pound slabs for later refining. Impurities contained in the smelter copper at this point are predominantly precious metals.

At the refinery, the anodes are given a sulfuric acid bath. Sheets are placed between the anodes, where, through the process of electrolysis, copper coming off the anodes is collected on the starter sheets and taken out of the bath as cathodes, holding 100 to 200 pounds of refined copper. The impurities removed in this final process are collected at the bottom and are often sent to other refineries specializing in the recovery of precious metals.

Leaching and precipitation. For oxide ores, and to a lesser degree sulfide ores, it is possible to avoid the expensive melting and concentration stages through leaching and precipitation. Although the process has been known since the turn of the century, it has come into extensive use only with the cost-cutting drive of recent years. Figure 2.6 compares this hydrometallurgical approach with the traditional pyrometallurgical approach already described. The basic component for leaching of both underground and open-pit oxide output is sulfuric acid. In underground mines, one method calls for block caving to break up and pile the ore, which is then saturated with sulfuric acid. The other involves drilling bore holes into the ore body from the surface. This procedure permits the injection of sulfuric acid while the ore is still in place, after which the solution is collected in vats below and then pumped to the surface. The chemical reaction between the copper oxide and the acid creates copper sulfate ($CuSO_4$). The only difference in treating open-pit oxide ore output is the materials handling. Open-pit oxides are hauled out of the pit as in normal stripping procedure

FIGURE 2.6 Flow Sheet for Copper Production

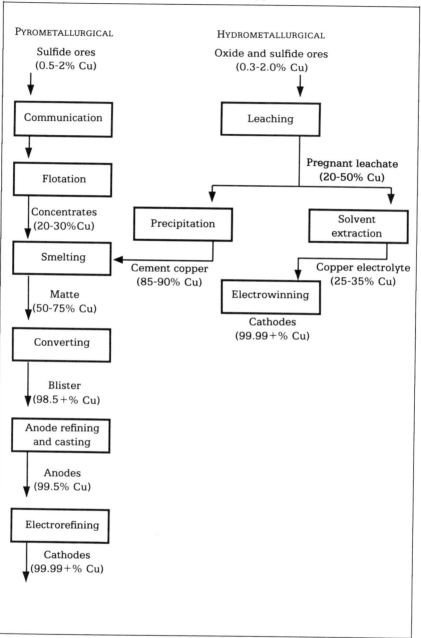

PYROMETALLURGICAL

Sulfide ores
(0.5-2% Cu)

HYDROMETALLURGICAL

Oxide and sulfide ores
(0.3-2.0% Cu)

Communication

Leaching

Flotation

Pregnant leachate
(20-50% Cu)

Concentrates
(20-30%Cu)

Precipitation

Solvent
extraction

Smelting

Cement copper
(85-90% Cu)

Copper electrolyte
(25-35% Cu)

Matte
(50-75% Cu)

Electrowinning

Converting

Cathodes
(99.99+% Cu)

Blister
(98.5+% Cu)

Anode refining
and casting

Anodes
(99.5% Cu)

Electrorefining

Cathodes
(99.99+% Cu)

SOURCE: U.S. Congress, Office of Technology Assessment, *Copper: Technology and Competitiveness* (Washington, D.C.: Government Printing Office, September 1988), p. 9.

and deposited in leaching dumps separated by ore grade; then, like the underground output, they are leached with sulfuric acid. Because the amount of copper recovered in this process is dependent on the strength of the sulfuric acid, the level of copper recovery sought depends on the price relation between copper and sulfuric acid. High copper prices and low sulfuric acid prices are the strongest combination for more committed effort toward high copper recovery levels through the leaching process.

After leaching, the drainage of copper sulfate must be recovered and further purified. This can be accomplished by either cementation or electrowinning. The less expensive process, cementation, is normally applied to low-grade ores, while the more costly, but more complete, electrowinning process is usually reserved for higher-grade processing.

In cementation, where the copper sulfate passes in solution over iron, the strong affinity of iron for sulfur overpowers the affinity of copper for sulfur, breaking their bonds and freeing the copper. The copper is precipitated from the solution and leaves what is called cement copper, fairly impure and suitable at this point only for use in low-quality brass. Additional refining of cement copper will purify it to usable quality. As a matter of fact, cement copper is sometimes further purified through the use of electrowinning, the second precipitation option.

Making use of high-voltage electric current, the copper solutions begin an electrolytic process in tanks. Via the polarization of electrical charges, the copper is drawn from its solution to starter sheets, where it collects at a much higher level of purity. In this way anode copper becomes cathode copper of much better quality. Electrowinning, while it has higher power costs, has relatively low labor costs, an important distinction considering the relatively high U.S. wage rates. The process is generally applicable only to the 13 percent of U.S. copper production which comes from oxide ores. The leaching and precipitation system is wasteful in that, while sulfide ores boast a recovery rate of somewhere around 95 percent, for oxide ore recovery rates fall in the 45–55 percent range.

Solvent extraction and electrowinning. While the leaching and precipitation processes are usually applied only to oxide ores, innovations in technology have made feasible the processing of otherwise uneconomical ores by several variants of solvent extraction. The basic SX-EW process can be applied to sulfide, oxide, and mixed sulfide-oxide ores through pretreatment of these ores. SX-EW also makes viable the recovery of copper from lower-grade ores and mine solutions that have traditionally been considered waste.

SX-EW depends on the transfer of ions between a copper-bearing aqueous solution, with copper extracted through application of sulfuric acid, and an organic reagent solution in which hydrogen and copper ions are traded. Through a subsequent settling process, aqueous and organic phases are separated and thus the copper is separated from many of its natural impurities. After extraction is accomplished through the work of the sulfuric acid and the organic reagent, the copper is carried in a solution of organic reagent to a stripping process, where another interaction between the organic reagent and the sulfuric acid strips the copper from the reagent and carries it in highly concentrated form to the electrowinning cells. There the copper is collected on starter sheets and removed as copper cathodes.

Thus, although few new processes for copper mining, smelting, or refining have emerged within the last forty years, intensified use of long-neglected technologies has had a strong impact on the costs of copper production, as will become clear in subsequent chapters.

CHAPTER 3

EMERGENCE OF THE
COPPER INDUSTRY

THE PRODUCT MARKET is an abstract concept representing the reality of flesh-and-blood buyers and sellers organized in a variety of production and consumption units. The interactions between buyers and sellers, and between employers and employees, will be more significant when viewed against the historical background of the companies and unions in the copper industry.

BEGINNINGS OF THE INDUSTRY

During 1840–1841 Douglas Houghton, state geologist of Michigan, reported the existence of a "mineral district" some 105 miles in length and 12 to 25 miles in width on the Keeweenaw peninsula of Upper Michigan.[1] Surface deposits of pure copper had long been known to the Indians of the region, but no systematic mining had ever been undertaken. This situation was to change dramatically when the Pittsburgh and Boston Company began development of the Cliff Mine in 1845 on a bluff over the Eagle River on the outer (eastern) end of the Keeweenaw.[2] Within three years, the Minesota Mine was opened at the southwestern end of the

Alexander Agassiz (1835–1910). The first of the U.S. Copper Kings, Agassiz was the founder of Calumet and Hecla Mining Company, a major innovator and outstanding manager, and a distinguished naturalist. (*Photo courtesy of the archives of Harvard University.*)

Marcus Daly (1841–1900). A pioneer hard-rock miner who found the great vein of chalcocite in the Anaconda mine at Butte, Montana, in 1882. He went on to form the original Anaconda Mining Company, which developed the mine at Butte, built the smelter at Anaconda, and the refinery at Great Falls. (*Photo courtesy of the World Museum of Mining and C. Owen Smithers, Butte, Montana.*)

The Anaconda Copper Mine and Mill at Butte, Montana, about 1887. The
entrance adit and tipple can be seen at the lower left of the six stacks of the smelter.
(*Photo courtesy of C. Owen Smithers, Butte, Montana.*)

peninsula in the Ontonagon area, and the Quincy Mine in the middle of the district near Portage Lake. By the end of the decade twenty-five companies were in operation, but only the Cliff and the Minesota mines proved to be highly profitable.

Both properties required selective vein mining, performed when the copper occurs in pure (native) form in regularly distributed patterns. Copper ore was also found on the peninsula in amygdaloid form, as "almonds," nuggets and/or masses scattered through the ore body. Extraction of these ores did not begin until 1856, on the Quincy and Pewabic properties.[3]

In the early 1860s Edwin J. Hulbert, a civil engineer, began a careful examination of the surface deposits around Portage Lake, in the middle of the peninsula. In 1864 he staked out the locations for what would eventually become the Calumet and Hecla properties. By a fortunate combination of chance and adroit use of the magnetic needle, Hulbert found the fabulously rich conglomerate lode, a breccia formation in which pure copper serves as the cement to hold sand and pebbles tightly together.[4]

Financing Hulbert was an astute blue-blooded Boston capitalist named Quincy Adams Shaw; as president of the Huron Mining Company, he had earlier employed Hulbert as his superintendent. Fate had also decreed that Shaw become a brother-in-law of Alexander Agassiz, a fellow Bostonian and son of the great geologist and zoologist Louis Agassiz. A naturalist himself, Alexander was already familiar with the Keeweenaw region. Together Shaw, Hulbert, and Agassiz were to develop the originally separate Calumet and Hecla companies.[5]

CALUMET AND HECLA MINING COMPANY

Early in 1866 Hulbert began mining a cramped open cut at the Calumet. Within a few months he found himself in deep trouble. The cut could not be enlarged and gave access only to the surface ore. His method of crushing was ineffective with the hard siliceous conglomerate, and his smelting facility was inappropriate. The resulting low metallurgical efficiency dictated high treatment costs, which in turn necessitated extreme selectivity in the choice of ores for processing. Only those with a very rich copper content could be used.[6] In other words, too much valuable ore had to be rejected.

Accordingly, Shaw sent Alexander Agassiz out to the Calumet to investigate. By March 1867 Agassiz had replaced Hulbert as superintendent.[7] Soon he had introduced a new type of steam-powered stamp mill, a better smelter, and a system of sharply descending drifts for getting at the ore bodies. Within two years both properties had begun to pay their way. In February 1870 the two boards agreed to merge under the name Calumet and Hecla Mining Company. On May 1, 1871, the board of directors of the merged company held its first meeting. Half a century later the original investment of $2 million had yielded a total of $152 million in cumulative dividends.[8] And by 1949 this great property had produced an aggregate of 1,636,000 short tons of copper from the two original mines, not large by Anaconda or Kennecott standards, but still very impressive.

At the time of its formation C & H was already the dominant property on the peninsula—or the Lake region, as it is also called. The area was virtually the sole domestic source of copper, a dominance that was not to be threatened until the opening of the Copper Queen Mine in Arizona in 1881 and the Anaconda in Montana in 1882.

C & H is a classic example of the underground mining typical of the period. It developed a system of shafts to penetrate downward into the ore body, with the declivity of the shaft conforming to the slope of the ore panel itself to the maximum feasible depth, below which vertical shafts were sunk. Lengthy drifts were run off these shafts at successive levels, with overhead stopes opened along the drifts to give access to the ore. Crosscuts between drifts increased the possibilities for breaking the ore in place within the stopes at a given level. Much timbering was required, particularly with increases in depth, to stabilize the hanging walls and provide roof supports in the stopes. At the outset, the actual ore-breaking was done via hand drilling, typically by three-man teams, in what was known as the double-jack method. The ore was then hand-shoveled into small tram cars on rails, which were pushed by hand to the hoisting cages.[9]

As president of C & H, Agassiz followed a farsighted policy. Its key elements called for buying the best equipment available, building for production capacity well ahead of current demand, and offering complete receptivity to innovations in all areas as developments came along.[10] In these ways the company gained flexibility in production and kept ahead in the endless struggle to bring down average cost, to increase the rate of recovery from the ore, and thereby to offset insofar as possible the inevitable downtrend in average ore grade. Countless incremental improvements were made over the years in explosives, drills and bits, hoisting equipment, ore transportation, crushing, and the concentration or "dressing" of ore before smelting.

During Agassiz's tenure, C & H built smelters at Hubbell, Michigan, near the mine site, and at Black Rock, near Buffalo, New York. The company did not get into fabrication until many years later, perhaps because its Lake copper was the highest quality available and could readily be sold as raw material. As early as 1904 C & H experimented unsuccessfully with a flotation process using bulk oil. By 1918 it had introduced the standard form of oil flotation.

For two decades C & H struggled with two problems affecting the economic efficiency of its mining operation: how to improve the rate of metallic recovery per ton of ore mined, and how to reduce the rate of metallic loss in waste tailings. These are not the same, although they work toward the same end.

The first step toward finer grinding came with the use of Chilean mills, introduced about 1908. By finer grinding, copper particles could be freed from the hard conglomerate and captured in part with use of the Wilfley table, which employs vibration to exploit the differences in specific gravity and thus to separate the copper fines—at least in part—from other minerals and waste rock. The second step came with the introduction of the ball mill a few years later.[11] This device consists of a revolving cylinder containing steel balls, which are mixed with the ore to break it down to a much greater extent than gyratory or jaw crushers can. As noted, the Wilfley table relies on gravity separation. When the company adopted the flotation cell system in 1918, it substituted what its long-time metallurgist, C. Harry Benedict, felicitously termed concentration upside down— meaning that the copper particles could be floated to the surface, to attach themselves to the oil bubbles on top of the liquid mixture. In essence, better grinding now yielded higher copper recovery per ton.[12]

Working in the same direction was C & H's adoption of the aqueous ammonia process for ore benefication through a special form of solvent extraction. Experimentation had begun in 1912. By 1915 a reclamation plant had been built to extract copper from the enormous stock of tailings accumulated at Lake Linden for almost half a century. The process employs aqueous ammonia, rather than acid, in a closed circuit made up of several steps: dissolving the copper in the solvent to obtain cupric ammonium carbonate; boiling out and recovering the ammonia for recycling, leaving the copper oxide as a precipitate; and reducing the copper oxide to obtain pure copper.[13] Once again the result is a gain in metallic recovery, this time from waste that still contains economically significant amounts of copper. Between 1915 and 1949, Benedict says that 417.9 million pounds of copper were extracted from 37.2 million tons of tailing sands, for a cumulative profit of $31.4 million.[14]

By 1920 C & H was a property in decline, both in extent of ore reserves and in ore grade. Resort to solvent extraction from old tailings staved off the downturn for several decades, but come it inevitably did.

Another offset to decline—again a symptom of that very process—was a massive consolidation of several peninsula mines in 1923. The purpose was to gain savings by combining hitherto separate facilities—in short, to make more efficient use of fixed capital such as railroads, smelters, reclamation plants, and electrolytic refineries. In this way, the Allouez (1859), Osceola (1873), Ahmeek (1880), and Centennial (1896) properties were absorbed by the original C & H to create the Calumet and Hecla Consolidated Copper Company.[15] Over the next two decades other mines were added as well. During the war years (1942–1946 inclusive) C & H mined 152.5 million pounds of copper—not a great deal relative to the other companies of the Big Five (Anaconda, ASARCO, Kennecott, and Phelps Dodge), but on its own terms very significant as well as comparable to the company's average annual output during its first decade when it was the dominant American producer.[16]

Today the Calumet and Hecla is virtually forgotten. In February 1968 it became a subsidiary through merger with Universal Oil Products Company.[17] Its mines had been closed since August 21, 1967, by a strike led by the United Steelworkers, which was attempting to impose centralized collective bargaining on the entire nonferrous industry. The new owners of C & H quickly announced their intent to close down all mining operations if an early settlement could not be reached. The threat went unheeded. Early in March they shut down the properties, at the cost of a thousand jobs.[18] Thus ended a mining operation that had enjoyed success on the Keeweenaw peninsula for nearly a century.

ANACONDA COMPANY

In October 1875 two obscure miners from Saint Lawrence County in upstate New York, Michael and Edward Hickey, filed a claim on a quartz outcropping on what was soon to become famous as "the richest hill on earth"—Butte, Montana. They called their claim the Anaconda.

The Hickey brothers were not entering virgin territory. Butte had been a riproaring placer mining camp, producing $90 million in gold between 1862 and 1868.[19] By the latter year the easily available placer gold was gone, miners began drifting away, and a town of thousands dwindled to no more than a hundred. But the hardier remnant went underground after silver, and by 1875 the population was back up to four hundred. Even though the presence of copper was no secret, the red metal was no more than a nuisance to those pursuing noble metals. Numerous rich silver mines were already in production when the Hickeys filed their claim.

To finance the necessary assessment work, the Hickey brothers sold a one-third interest to a silver miner named Marcus Daly for $15,000, also giving him an option to buy the entire property. This undeveloped silver claim marked the beginning of the most extensive underground copper mine ever found, an event comparable in importance only to the discovery of the C & H ore body in 1864.[20]

Daly had come to the United States from Ireland in 1856, as a boy of fifteen. After a stint at dockwork, he headed for San Francisco and then for Virginia City, Nevada, and its great Comstock lode. There he became a skilled hard-rock miner and a friend of George Hearst, later a senator. Keenly intelligent, Daly had the outgoing personality of the traditional Irishman. When he decided to try to finance the purchase of the whole Anaconda claim, Daly first approached the Walker brothers, two financiers in Salt Lake City whom he had helped earlier with the Alice silver mine in Butte. The Walkers declined, and Daly then turned to George Hearst in San Francisco.[21]

Since 1870 Hearst had belonged to a three-man mining syndicate whose other members were James Ben Ali Haggin and Lloyd H. Tevis. The trio had made a lot of money. Its real leader, Haggin, was favorably impressed by Daly. As a result, a decision was made to buy the Anaconda for $70,000, and to include Daly by awarding him a one-quarter share and the task of developing the property. Daly proceeded to sink a 300-foot shaft, then drive a crosscut that soon struck a massive clump of chalcocite, a copper sulfide of high metallic sheen and great richness.[22] Daly was now in ore—but it was copper, not silver.

This was traditional underground vein mining. The art calls for following the vein system and mining it very selectively to keep the ore grade rich enough to be profitable at the prevailing levels of cost and price. Daly lost no time in widening and deepening his exploratory drifts, in the course of which he found that the width of the main vein varied, incredibly, between

50 and 100 feet, with an average ore grade of 55 percent. In 1883 he built a concentrator and smelter at Anaconda, 26 miles to the west, where water was adequate and smelter fumes would not be a problem.[23] At this time the Daly group also bought the Saint Lawrence and Never Sweat claims, and timber lands at Bonner, Montana. In 1889 a serious fire compelled the rebuilding of the Anaconda facilities, which thereafter were known as the Washoe Copper Company.

In January 1891 the four partners formed the Anaconda Mining Company, whose capitalization was increased by the end of the year to $25 million.[24] A year later the new firm built an electrolytic refinery in nearby Great Falls. In June 1895 the Anaconda Copper Mining Company took over, merging three groups of properties. By this time the syndicate had already extracted 707 million pounds of copper, along with 18.6 million ounces of silver and 83,349 ounces of gold.[25] Daly described his policy in much the same fashion as Alexander Agassiz would have done for the Calumet and Hecla: "The policy of the Company has been not so much to realize immediate returns as to try to lay the foundation for a long life of activity and usefulness."[26] Daly spoke these words as superintendent, for Haggin had been elected president of the new company. Four years later Daly was to replace him, but a year after that he would be dead from diabetes at the age of fifty-nine.

Once started in 1895, and driven by Daly's outstanding talents for mining, the new Anaconda Company began a systematic study of the Butte vein structures, so that an efficient plan could be developed to coordinate operations at the large number of separate properties now under common control. The electrolytic refinery was built; recovery of sulfuric acid from stack gases was begun; leaching of tailings was started; and production of cement copper through ion interchange on iron scrap was initiated.[27] Also, in 1894 Daly had completed the building of the Butte, Anaconda, and Pacific Railway, a 20-mile line to connect the mines with the smelter.

In the year that Daly replaced Haggin as president, moves were afoot to bring about a giant consolidation of separate interests, including Anaconda itself. The concept had originated with Albert C. Burrage, who headed the group in control of the Butte and Boston and Boston and Montana interests in Butte. The real promoters of the idea, however, were Henry H. Rogers and William G. Rockefeller, who had large interests in all of these properties and were close associates of the first John D. Rockefeller. They were successful in interesting Marcus Daly as well. On

April 27, 1899, the Amalgamated Copper Company was formed as a holding company to take over ownership of all the participating interests through an exchange of stock. Rogers became president and assumed the task of coordinating the management of the underlying operating companies.[28]

Rogers, Rockefeller, and Daly had three motives in forming the Amalgamated: they saw big potential economies in a massive consolidation of the many separate properties on "the Hill." They also saw a chance to control the price of copper by creating a selling pool, a popular idea among businessmen in highly competitive industries in those days. And they saw dire need for a common front to withstand the depredations of one F. Augustus Heinze, who had arrived in Butte in 1889 possessed of a mining degree from Columbia University, to work as a surveyor in the Boston and Montana mine.[29] Before long, Heinze had begun attacking the big mines in court, stealing their ores as well when the opportunity arose.

Heinze had intelligence and ambition, and was unhampered by the conventions imposed by any routine deference to business ethics. His objective was to get rich, like the neighboring Copper Kings. His first step was a careful study of the Butte vein system, to lay the basis for a series of "Apex suits." In this way he could seek injunctions to stop operations at adjoining properties while his claim to extralateral rights was tested. Long a tradition in western mining law, the Apex principle holds that if the cap or top of a main vein can be shown to emerge on a particular claim, then the owner automatically enjoys "extralateral rights" to cross his vertical sidelines to follow up and mine the vein in an adjacent property. By searching out vein caps that showed signs of constituting an apex and picking up the claims on which these caps were located from the patchwork of which Butte was composed, Heinze slowly laid the groundwork for some 110 suits filed between 1895 and 1906.[30] Naturally, the liveliest controversies arose, and not by chance, where some of the Amalgamated's richest properties were adjacent to Heinze's claims. Adroitly manipulating a pair of notoriously crooked judges, Heinze's tactic was to apply for an injunction to stop the other party from mining while his claim was being adjudicated. In the meantime, he would have his miners break through the sideline into the other property to pluck out the richest ore in sight. All of these moves were accompanied by some carefully chosen populist rhetoric that was well received in the streets but provided no comfort to the Amalgamated leadership.

After ten years of this sort of thing, including litigation that cost the company millions, the directors of the Amalgamated decided that it would be easier to negotiate a settlement and pay off Heinze. To conduct the negotiations they chose John D. Ryan, who had become president of Anaconda in 1905. In February 1906 Ryan obtained an agreement. It cost the company $10.5 million. The only solace for the directors beyond ridding themselves of Heinze was the later knowledge that he soon dissipated his new fortune in mining and banking ventures.[31]

In 1909 Rogers died. Because of the Amalgamated's unpopularity, augmented by Heinze's incessant hostile propaganda, it seemed prudent to transfer Ryan to the task of liquidating the holding company. In the process, the capitalization of Anaconda copper was increased fivefold, to $150 million. Then, through exchanges of stock, Anaconda took title to seven underlying properties held by Amalgamated. The last step was to buy up Senator William A. Clark's two mines and smelter at Butte. Anaconda itself was now a holding company as well as the operating company, and in 1915 Amalgamated was liquidated. Anaconda controlled the Hill at last.[32]

The new president of the company was Cornelius F. Kelley, whose father had been a friend of Marcus Daly. Kelley evidently decided, upon taking office in 1918 (Ryan became chairman), that Anaconda required additional ore reserves if it was to remain viable. But all of the geological evidence indicated that Butte had no significant new ore bodies to offer. Besides, the Anaconda was now a deep underground mine, touching 4,000 feet. It was becoming increasingly expensive to operate, with its traditional stoping system and heavy timbering, particularly against the growing competition of the newer open-pit mines in Utah, New Mexico, and Arizona. The inference was clear. Anaconda had to go beyond Butte to make its future secure.

The first step had already been taken in 1913, when the company engaged William Braden, a distinguished mining engineer, to find it a copper mine in Chile. He located a good one—the Potrerillos—which Anaconda bought and in 1916 turned over to its subsidiary, the Andes Copper Mining Company, for development. Louis D. Ricketts, a mining expert with the stature of John Hays Hammond, was appointed to run the operation after Wilbur Jurden, its very able engineer of construction, had the property ready to operate. Potrerillos is of particular interest in that Anaconda had to develop it as an underground mine by reason of its very high "stripping ratio" (the ratio of overburden tonnage to ore tonnage), which imposed a level of production costs that foreclosed use of open-cut mining.[33] Accordingly, Anaconda elected a compromise solution: block caving in place of stope mining for the underground operation. This choice allowed access to mass-production techniques even with underground extraction.

The next step outward from Butte came on March 15, 1923, when Anaconda bought Chile Copper Company from the Guggenheim brothers for $77 million. This purchase gave the company ownership of Chuquicamata, which had the largest known copper ore body in the world and which was to become the largest open-pit mine ever developed, over 2 miles in length and located on a ridge at 9,400 feet in the Andes. By all odds, this acquisition of what was initially estimated as a reserve of 1 billion tons of porphyry ore of at least 1 percent grade seemed to assure Anaconda a long-term future in copper mining.[34]

In 1929 the company made its last foreign purchase, the old Greene Cananea Mine at Cananea, Mexico, in which it had already acquired a substantial interest in 1907. This property contained several productive mines and continued to be profitable through World War II.[35]

Another important development during the early years of Kelley's tenure was a decision in 1922 to achieve vertical integration for Anaconda, by the purchase of American Brass Company, which had seven fabricating plants scattered through the Brass Valley district of Connecticut and beyond into the Middle West and Canada. In 1929 this move was followed by the formation of Anaconda Wire and Cable Company, in behalf of which several specialty producers were acquired.[36] The cable company thus had eight production plants, ranging from Pawtucket, Rhode Island, to Orange, California. The two moves reflected a conviction that greater returns on investment could be gained if all stages of production, from the mine through the fabricating plant, were controlled by a single management—a version of the principle of increasing economies with size. A variation of this principle had already proved correct in the development of the open-pit porphyry mines after 1900. But it is unlikely that vertical integration has contributed significantly to the earning power of the copper companies. They are always free to sell their copper directly into the New York or London market; any fabricator, subsidiary or not, is equally free to buy copper on the open market at the going price. If there is any gain from vertical control, it must lie in internal technical economies that are far from obvious, or in special pricing arrangements for intrafirm transactions.

As the years passed, Anaconda became both an international concern and a diversified metals conglomerate. In 1946, for example, the company produced 3.7 million ounces of silver, 30,000 ounces of gold, 1.47 million pounds of molydenum, 1.55 million pounds of cadmium, 4,883 tons of arsenic, 15.6 million pounds of lead, 1.5 million pounds of zinc, and 111,397 tons of manganese. Beyond this huge array of metals, Anaconda also turned out 67.3 million board feet of lumber from the forest lands acquired by Daly years before, to provide timber for the mine.

Of the Big Five American copper companies in 1946, Anaconda unquestionably was the most diversified. Furthermore, it was the largest producer of copper itself—742 million pounds as against 594 million pounds for its nearest rival, Kennecott (data for both concerns include output from mines owned in Chile).[37]

As of 1946, therefore, Anaconda seemingly confronted an optimistic future, initially expressed by an ambitious project for redevelopment of its historic base in Butte and acquisition of new properties elsewhere. The realities of the next thirty years were to prove quite the contrary.

AMERICAN SMELTING AND REFINING COMPANY (ASARCO)

If by "copper producer" one means a copper-mining firm, then clearly ASARCO was not one of the Big Five in 1946, when it owned only three small copper mines in the United States. But copper production includes much more than mining. Beyond ore extraction, and depending on the reduction technique, there are several other phases of processing: crushing and grinding, concentrating, smelting, and refining. As an alternative, ore leaching, in place or in heaps, eliminates concentrating and smelting, but the anode copper obtained in solution must still be refined to yield copper cathodes.

ASARCO's role in American copper production has always been that of a smelter and refiner. In 1946, for example, it turned out 502 million pounds of copper (including properties owned abroad), placing it close to Kennecott, the number two processor that year, although at the time it owned not a single large mine in the United States.

The decision of ASARCO to concentrate on processing rather than on mining was taken many years ago, along with a larger decision to smelt and refine the whole array of nonferrous metals. In 1946 it was the biggest gold processor of them all (782,657 ounces), probably the largest silver processor in the world (47.7 million ounces), the largest lead processor (771 million pounds), and the largest zinc processor (248.4 million pounds).[38] If we set aside its foreign operations, ASARCO obtained the bulk of these metals either through smelting for other producers on toll or through tied operation—for instance, the Garfield, Utah, smelter which served Kennecott—in which other concerns provided ASARCO with smelter feed under long-term contracts.

One more ASARCO peculiarity remains. The company came under the control of Meyer Guggenheim and his seven sons in April 1901 and remained under the family's control until the last Guggenheim left the company in 1941. Control by the Guggenheims made ASARCO part of the most expansive undertaking for mine development ever seen—an American-based endeavor that, starting in 1905, produced four vast copper mines in the United States, another in Alaska, one in Mexico, and three outstanding properties in Chile. The role of ASARCO as a firm was minor in all this, although it provided much of the money as well as the experts and the executive talent, and smelting and refining facilities. Not least in this remarkable record of achievement was the formation of Kennecott Copper Corporation in 1915.

The history of ASARCO actually begins in 1848 with Meyer Guggenheim, who at the age of twenty was brought to the United States by his father. The family settled in Philadelphia. Meyer started work as a tailor, then sold coffee essence, then manufactured stove polish and bluing, then got into general merchandising. These activities were followed by that rarest of occasions, a successful railroad deal with Jay Gould—one that yielded $300,000.[39]

Meyer's coup financed a partnership in the lace business. A few years later Guggenheim bought out his partner and in 1881 formed M. Guggenheim's Sons, a family business whose first holding was the lace concern. Each of the sons was a partner, while Meyer guaranteed the firm's expenses.[40] At this point Guggenheim was approached by a Philadelphia friend, Charles H. Graham, for a loan to finance the development of two silver claims in Leadville, Colorado. Graham's two partners could not pay up their shares. With characteristic acumen, Guggenheim denied the loan but offered to buy out the partners and carry Graham's own share free of interest. For an expenditure of $5,000 he obtained a half-interest in the A. Y. Corman and Minnie Corman claims. He hired a mining engineer and arranged to dewater the shaft. Mining began, and within a short time a bonanza was struck. Meyer Guggenheim became a multimillionaire. More important, he became a mining magnate. His next step was to slash smelting costs by building his own reduction works in Pueblo, with four of his sons as equal partners.[41] After passage of an American tariff denying importation of lead and silver ores from Mexico, two of the sons, Daniel and Murry Guggenheim, became interested in building smelters south of the border. Two plants followed in 1892, and the family also acquired its first copper mine. In 1894 the brothers built a copper refinery at Perth Amboy, New Jersey. The family was now thoroughly engaged in the mining, smelting, and refining of silver, lead, and copper.[42]

In 1899 the Guggenheims formed, as a subsidiary of M. Guggenheim's Sons, the Guggenheim Exploration Company ("Guggenex"), to search for potentially profitable mines throughout the world, purchase them, develop them, and then invite public participation in them.[43] As the ablest and most entrepreneurial of the seven brothers, Daniel Guggenheim became president. Guggenex, financed by the parent firm, became the instrument through which the family engaged in mine development in the American Southwest, Chile, the Congo, and Angola.

ASARCO had an independent beginning on April 4, 1899, at the hands of the same Henry H. Rogers who had brought into being the Amalgamated Copper Company, to take over Anaconda at almost the same time. The guiding idea was identical: create a holding company to pool the interests of a group of independent and competing firms in the same line of business, in this case the smelting and refining of lead and silver ores. Rogers was joined in the ASARCO venture by Adolph and Leonard Lewisohn of the Miami Copper Company (Arizona), who also had copper interests in Michigan, Montana, and Tennessee, and a copper refinery in Perth Amboy. In addition, J. Pierpont Morgan had an indirect involvement. Rogers made a strong effort to bring in the Guggenheims, but they were not interested unless they could have full control. The upshot was that ASARCO took over seventeen companies, one partnership, fifteen smelters, five refineries, and two mines.[44]

From the outset ASARCO was a shaky proposition, burdened with debt and overcapitalization, labor disputes, excess inventories, and the formidable competition of the Guggenheims. Early in 1900 Rogers reluctantly renewed negotiations with the Guggenheims, offering $35 million in ASARCO stock for all of their business assets. Daniel Guggenheim saw an opportunity to drive a hard bargain. He demanded majority control and $45.2 million in ASARCO stock, in exchange for the assets of M. Guggenheim's Sons, $6 million in cash, and provision of two-thirds of

ASARCO's needed working capital. He added a teaser: all of Guggenex, if ASARCO would put all seven brothers on its board. Rogers turned this last proposal down, so the deal was made without the exploration company and with only five sons on the board. Thus on April 8, 1901, ASARCO became a Guggenheim company.[45]

Daniel had achieved his basic goal: effective market control of the nonferrous smelting and refining business in the United States. Meanwhile, the family could continue to use Guggenex to develop new mines to add substantially to its enormous fortune—directly by selling them and indirectly by tying them to long-term contracts to smelt and refine their ores at ASARCO smelters and refineries.

Daniel Guggenheim followed certain characteristic policies throughout his fifteen-year career as head of ASARCO and Guggenex: (1) hire the ablest experts available; (2) establish a strong position in copper, as the most profitable of the nonferrous metals; (3) make large capital investments only in depressed times; (4) protect ASARCO's smelting and refining interests in all financial arrangements with outside mining interests; and (5) confine ASARCO primarily to smelting and refining, not mining.

Following the takeover of control of ASARCO, Daniel Guggenheim initiated a vigorous program of expansion. Both the U.S. Zinc Company and Federal Mining and Smelting Company were acquired. In 1905 American Smelters Securities Company was established as a subsidiary to finance ASARCO's capital needs. Smelters were purchased in Everett and Tacoma, Washington; Selby, California; and Alton, Illinois. A refinery was built in Tacoma, and the largest copper smelter in the world was constructed at Garfield, Utah. The company also built a smelter in Mexico, where it had acquired five mines.[46]

Daniel's three greatest undertakings all involved the development of large copper mines. They are basic to the history of the American copper industry, but they involve ASARCO only tangentially; their financing was accomplished through Guggenex and the members of the family personally, while ASARCO's ancillary role was to provide professional personnel in some cases and smelting and refining services in others. Because the development of some of these mines was linked directly to the formation of Kennecott Copper Corporation in 1915, we will mention them only briefly in connection with ASARCO.

First, Daniel Guggenheim financed William Braden, a notable mining engineer who had been with ASARCO, to undertake explorations in

Chile.[47] This proved to be one of the best moves he ever made, for it was Braden who explored the Teniente Crater at 10,000 feet in the Andes Mountains southeast of Santiago, and subsequently established one of the great copper mines of the world. Braden had formed Braden Copper Company in 1904. Three years later Guggenex took $500,000 in the new company's bonds. By 1909 the Guggenheims had control, by providing $4 million in working capital. Conceding that they had exacted "stiff terms," A. B. Parsons, an outstanding mining expert, added that "they did advance money when no one else had the nerve to do it."[48] They also sent in their mining expert, Pope Yeatman, to serve as consulting engineer at El Teniente.

Yeatman faced a real challenge. The deposit was deep in the high mountains, with a top elevation of 10,132 feet and a depth below that level of over 1,000 feet. The only feasible way to mine the property was from *below*—by driving haulage adits into the mountain, with raises to reach upward into the ore.

El Teniente proved to be a very profitable exercise in mine development for the Guggenheims, given the mine's large reserves and the high level of its ore grade (114 million tons and 2.5 percent, in January 1916). But the family made its wealth far more from *developing* than from *operating* mines. Accordingly, El Teniente was sold in 1915 to the newly organized Kennecott Copper Corporation, which in its early years was itself a Guggenheim company, but ultimately would become independent.[49]

Daniel Guggenheim's success at Braden was followed by an even greater one in 1911, when he acquired control of Chuquicamata in northeastern Chile, today the greatest of the world's copper mines.

This property has a history that extends back to Inca times, before the Spanish conquest in 1536. In 1910 Albert C. Burrage, the Boston capitalist who originally had conceived the Amalgamated Copper Company, learned about Chuquicamata and acquired two options to buy the property. The risks of development were large, for the deposit lay high in the Andes, at the 9,400-foot level. Below was the Atacama Desert, one of the driest and most barren in the world. Access would be both difficult and expensive if this remote property were to be exploited at all.

Meanwhile, Yeatman was having his own investigation of Chuquicamata made for the Guggenheims. As matters turned out, Burrage and Daniel Guggenheim reached an agreement under which the Guggenheims would acquire a majority interest. Guggenex would take over the options; Burrage would retain a minority interest. In January 1912, Chile

The Washoe Smelter, Anaconda, Montana. This large reduction works was built in Anaconda in the late 1890's after the first one was destroyed by fire in 1888 and the second proved to be too small. The view is to the southwest. (*Photo courtesy of C. Owen Smithers, Butte, Montana.*)

Daniel Guggenheim (1856–1930). Guggenheim began his career as head of ASARCO in 1901. He financed and developed more important copper mines than any other individual: four in Alaska; Ely, Nevada; Bingham Canyon, Utah; Ray, Arizona; Chino, New Mexico; and Potrerillos, El Teniente, and Chuquicamata in Chile. (*Photo courtesy of John R. Corbett of ASARCO.*)

Daniel Cowan Jackling (1869–1956). Greatest of the copper magnates, Jackling founded the Utah Copper Company (Kennecott) and was responsible for the first successful exploitation of low-grade southwestern ore, through large-scale open-pit mining at Bingham Canyon. He also developed mines at Ely, Nevada; Ray, Arizona; and Chino, New Mexico. (*Photo courtesy of the American Mining Congress.*)

Exploration Company was formed to become the operating company. In July 1913, Chile Copper Company was organized to become sole owner of Chile Exploration, with Daniel Guggenheim as president. At this time ore reserves were "assumed" to be 150 million tons at 2.4 percent in grade. Chile Copper was given an initial capitalization of $95 million, to which $15 million in bonds was soon added, to be taken up by the Guggenheims and their friends. By May 1915, Yeatman was estimating the mine's reserves at 303 million tons, with 400 million tons indicated as "certain."[50] By 1957, under Anaconda's control and after forty years of mining, the ore reserve at Chuquicamata was fixed at 1 billion tons.

In 1923 the Guggenheims reluctantly sold majority control of this enormous property to Anaconda for $77 million, following this step in 1929 by selling their remaining minority share for approximately $82.5 million. Even at a total of close to $160 million, Anaconda got a remarkable bargain.[51]

But Daniel Guggenheim had not finished compiling his lengthy record of mining achievements.

One of the outstanding elements in that record was his early financing of Daniel C. Jackling, founder of the Utah Copper Company, who was known as the father of the porphyries for his notable pioneering in finding a way to recover copper profitably from low-grade and widely disseminated ore bodies.

Jackling had been working at Bingham Canyon, about 25 miles southwest of Salt Lake City, since 1898. He had developed a passionate faith in porphyry ores and by 1903 had obtained financing for a small mill at Copperton, a few miles below the mine site. Promising tests at Copperton confirmed the values established by mine sampling;[52] they showed the probable rate of copper recovery on a large scale; and they demonstrated the effectiveness of crushing and concentrating machines. The problem was how to raise the large amount of capital required to get into production. Jackling decided the answer lay with the Guggenheims.

Through an intermediary he persuaded Daniel Guggenheim to have the project thoroughly inspected. John Hays Hammond, the Guggenheims' top consulting engineer, sent in Seeley W. Mudd, another Guggenheim expert, who assigned Henry Krumb to make an extensive study of the property. Krumb's report was quite favorable and indicated an ore reserve of 40 million tons.[53]

The upshot was that Guggenheim and Jackling reached an agreement that assured the development of America's greatest open-pit copper mine:

(1) Guggenex was to underwrite a $3 million bond issue for Utah Copper Company; (2) American Smelters Securities was to buy $4.6 million in Utah Copper shares; and (3) ASARCO received a long-term contract to smelt the company's ore at about $7 per ton. With this contract ASARCO was able to build the Garfield smelter, largest in the world. In addition, Guggenex provided Utah Copper with the services of John Hays Hammond, who soon became its managing director, with Pope Yeatman as his associate and A. Chester Beatty as consulting engineer.[54]

It should be emphasized that, apart from ASARCO's special support role, the Guggenheims never shared the management of Utah Copper. Jackling alone ran the company.[55] Still, an extensive association between Jackling and the Guggenheims was to manifest itself in three other important situations. One involved Nevada Consolidated Copper Company, at Ely, in eastern Nevada. Since 1902 this property had been under development by Mark L. Requa and his associates, who had organized the White Pine Copper Company. In 1904 Requa established the Nevada Consolidated Copper Company, with W. Hinkle Smith as president and William Boyce Thompson as a director.[56] Two years later an ASARCO scout, George E. Gunn, visited the district, was much impressed, and picked up some options.[57] His friend Thompson then organized the Cumberland-Ely Copper Company to pick up and exploit Gunn's options. Probably through Gunn, the Guggenheims were persuaded to buy an interest via Guggenex, despite a negative opinion from Beatty, their engineer.[58] By 1910, after a careful study by Krumb, and acting through Guggenex, the brothers bought control of Nevada Consolidated, absorbed Cumberland-Ely for $7.6 million, and sent in Yeatman to direct construction of a smelter and other facilities. According to an enigmatic observation of Parsons, the Guggenheims then "forced" Utah Copper to take control of Nevada Consolidated—probably through their financial influence.[59]

In any case, ASARCO's Baltimore refinery got Nevada's business, while Utah Copper and Guggenex obtained a mine with high-grade ore but limited reserves. By 1915 Jackling had taken over its active management, and the property became a division of Utah Copper.[60]

The Jackling-Guggenheim association was reasserted at Chino Mines, Santa Rita, New Mexico, and again at Ray, Arizona, with Ray Consolidated Copper Company. At Chino a company had been created in 1899 by Rogers, Rockefeller, Burrage, and Daly. Seeking to engage in vein mining, it had overlooked the porphyry ore that Jackling was soon to exploit so successfully at Bingham Canyon. Nonetheless, Burrage continued to be attracted to the proposition, especially after a favorable report by John M. Sully that in 1906 recommended open-pit mining with steam shovels. By 1909 Hayden-Stone had decided to finance Chino Copper Company, after bringing Jackling to Santa Rita for an examination of the property. Jackling's reaction was favorable. Before long he was managing Chino as well.[61]

Apparently the Guggenheims provided no explicit financing for Jackling at Chino, but they did exert their "influence," as Isaac Marcosson tactfully describes their role; for Chino Copper from the start sent its ore to ASARCO's smelter at El Paso and its concentrates to ASARCO smelters at Baltimore and Perth Amboy. At the bottom of this influence were the family's large holdings of Utah Copper and Nevada Consolidated securities, and the strategic position of ASARCO's Garfield smelter in the rapidly growing Bingham Canyon complex.

This pattern was repeated at Ray, Arizona, with the Ray Consolidated Copper Company. Philip Wiseman, who had assisted Krumb with his decisive assay research at Bingham Canyon, managed to convince Seeley Mudd, the Guggenheim mining engineer, that Ray had the characteristics of, and therefore the potential for, another Utah Copper. In 1906 the two men took out an option on Ray and shortly afterward incorporated the Ray Company.[62] The fact that porphyry copper was involved quickly captured Jackling's interest. The prospect also appealed to Charles M. MacNeill and Spencer Penrose, who had originally staked Jackling at Copperton. While they were buying an interest at Ray, Wiseman was selling his own shares to Bernard M. Baruch, counsel to the Guggenheims— suggesting that they too might wish to become involved. By 1910 Jackling was managing this property also. He brought Louis S. Cates, future president of Phelps Dodge, down from Bingham to take over at Ray.[63] Cates's first problem was fundamental—the choice of mining method. The overburden was too thick to make an open cut profitable. Accordingly, Cates chose block caving, which he had seen used in diamond mining in South Africa. The result was an underground mine that employed a new extraction technique capable of producing 8,000 tons or more of ore per day.[64]

At the same time, the company elected to build a concentrator at Winkelman, Arizona, and apparently made plans for a smelter nearby. How serious was its intent is not known. What is known is that ultimately ASARCO built the smelter, at nearby Hayden, after some hard bargaining between Jackling and the Guggenheims.[65] Quite possibly Jackling bluffed his way through the negotiations, for he was never keen about operating a smelter. In any case, the Hayden smelter was open by 1912 and the Ray Company no longer had to ship its concentrates to ASARCO at El Paso. Significantly, it did send its copper anodes from Hayden to ASARCO at Baltimore for refining.

It is a long way from Ray, Arizona, to Cordova on the south coast of Alaska, but both places were part of the worldwide business empire that Daniel Guggenheim was building between 1900 and 1915. The Alaska portion of this complicated history belongs primarily to the emergence of Kennecott Copper as a Guggenheim enterprise. But ASARCO also played a role, and it must be mentioned here.

In 1900 a graduate in mining engineering at Columbia University named Stephen Birch found himself in Valdez, Alaska, where he learned about a copper deposit known as the Bonanza lode.[66] The find was in the remote Wrangell Range, near the Kennicott (original spelling) glacier, 200 miles inland through magnificent virgin country. Birch inspected the site, found a fantastically rich outcrop of copper glance, with incredible ore values of 70 to 75 percent. Birch acquired an option, then spent the next five years trying to raise money to develop the claim. In 1905 he did succeed in interesting J. Pierpont Morgan, no mean feat. But Morgan wanted expert opinion, which put him in contact with "Mr. Dan" Guggenheim. Always prudent, Guggenheim sent Pope Yeatman to Alaska for a personal and independent examination. Yeatman was strongly favorable, so the Guggenheims decided to invest.

Because it was a vast undertaking for those days, three investment banking houses—Morgan, Havemeyer, and Kuhn, Loeb (Jacob Schiff)—joined with M. Guggenheim's Sons (now Guggenheim Brothers) to raise the capital. In 1906 the Alaska Syndicate was formed.[67] The Guggenheims were to put up one-third of the money and to provide engineering and administrative services through ASARCO. Kennecott Mines Company was formed to conduct operations, with Birch as president.

Physically, the task was immense. The Guggenheims had to create the Alaska Steamship Company merely to establish regular contact between Alaska and the continental United States. Next, they had to prepare the port of Cordova to handle large tonnages. After this, they had to build a 196-mile railroad—part of it portable to permit crossing a glacier—to the town of Kennicott. Called the Copper River and Northwestern, the railroad cost $26 million. Silas Eccles of ASARCO took on the presidency of the line. Originally the syndicate had hoped to build a branch line to gain access to coal reserves needed for smelting and for railroad fuel, and to the Chugach forest for mine timber. These efforts were blocked by Secretary of the Interior Gifford Pinchot, with the consequence that only ore concentrating could be conducted at Cordova, while the concentrates had to be sent to the ASARCO smelter at Tacoma for reduction.[68]

By 1909 the Bonanza Mine was in production, but the railroad was not completed until March 1911. The first train out carried ore worth $250,000; by May 1915, a train of twenty-five cars hauled $345,000 in ore.[69] By 1914 the Mother Lode, Jumbo, and Erie mines were also in production. Both the Bonanza and Jumbo employed 16,000-foot aerial tramways to move their ore to the railroad.

In 1915 Daniel Guggenheim decided that the time had come to begin consolidating all of the family's copper properties in a single company. Thus Kennecott Mines Company became Kennecott Copper Corporation. In turn, KCC acquired the Beatson Copper Company, 25 percent of Utah Copper's stock, 98.5 percent of Braden Copper, the Copper River and Northwestern Railway, and the Alaska Steamship Company.[70] The combined assets of the company stood at $160 million. In the coming years it would acquire all of Utah Copper, along with Utah's affiliates—Nevada Consolidated, Chino, and Ray mines. For the time being, ASARCO itself would continue to emphasize the smelting and refining of nonferrous ores, maintaining a separate identity except for operation of the Garfield smelter for KCC's Utah concentrates.

In 1919 Daniel Guggenheim retired, and his brother Simon took his place.[71] Over the next decade ASARCO continued to develop into a more diversified company. As early as 1915 it had entered into vertical integration on the side of finished products by constructing a brass and copper rolling mill at Baltimore. In 1923 it added a rod and bare-wire plant. In 1927 it gained control of General Cable Company, to which it turned over its Baltimore wire and rolling mill in exchange for stock. A year later it bought a substantial interest in Revere Copper and Brass Company. Finally, in 1932 it acquired Federated Metals Corporation, which gave it entry into the secondary scrap market for nonferrous metals.[72]

During this same period ASARCO continued to buy interests in foreign mines, although not on the huge scale of 1905–1915. Its most important investment was a 40 percent interest in Mount Isa Mines Company of Australia, in 1930; it provided capital and expertise to develop this important property, which produced lead, zinc, copper, and silver. Then in 1936 ASARCO exercised a joint option on Big Bell Mines, a low-grade gold property in Australia, and also bought a minority interest in Kirkland Gold Mines in Canada. Its final mining acquisition of these years came in 1943 with the purchase of Ozark Mine and Smelting, a lead-zinc property in Missouri.[73]

By 1946 ASARCO had $217 million in total assets, had earned a net profit of $15.7 million, and was producing nineteen metals or minerals. Its properties included eight mines in the United States, fifteen in Mexico, and eight in other foreign countries; four copper smelters in the United States and two in Mexico; six lead smelters in the United States and two in Mexico; one zinc smelter in the United States and another in Mexico. In addition, ASARCO operated three copper refineries, four lead refineries, and two zinc refineries in the United States, and one lead refinery and a zinc refinery in Mexico.[74]

Despite ASARCO's world dominance in nonferrous smelting and refining by 1946, it treated no ores from Calumet and Hecla, Anaconda, or Phelps Dodge. Only Kennecott of the Big Five provided it with business, and then only for its Utah and Ray mines divisions. In short, ASARCO had to depend for its smelter feed on its own mines, on toll smelting from some of the sixteen small American copper companies, and on custom smelting from other mining ventures.

KENNECOTT COPPER CORPORATION

When Daniel Guggenheim incorporated Kennecott Copper on April 29, 1915, with Stephen Birch as president, his purpose was to put all of the Guggenheims' copper-mining properties in one basket. This consolidation included exchange of the family's shares in Braden Copper (El Teniente and Fortuna mines), in Kennecott Mines Company (Bonanza, Mother Lode, Jumbo, and Erie mines), in Nevada Consolidated (with holdings in Ely, Chino, and Ray), and in Utah Copper (Bingham Canyon and holdings also at Ely, Chino, and Ray). Thus four main corporate groups were turned over to the new company, all of them funneled through the Guggenheims. Nevertheless, the formation of KCC did not mean that it or the Guggenheims had majority control of Utah Copper. The new Kennecott was an investment rather than an operating company, as far as Utah was concerned. Jackling was still the real chief, although the Guggenheims continued to exert much influence.

Upon incorporation KCC received 25 percent of Utah stock (404,504

Bench mining at Bingham Canyon in 1977. The ore is blasted down, then moved to trucks by means of power shovels. (*Photo courtesy of Kennecott Corporation and Alexis C. Fernandez.*)

"The Richest Hole on Earth": Kennecott's open-pit copper mine at Bingham Canyon in 1981. The mine is still operating today, but conveyor belts, trucks, and slurry pipelines have replaced the railroad in the pit. (*Photo courtesy of Kennecott Corporation and Alexis C. Fernandez.*)

Louis Shattuck Cates (1881–1959). A major innovator and outstanding mining executive, Cates introduced underground block-caving at Boston Consolidated Mine in Bingham Canyon and then at Ray. He became Daniel Jackling's right-hand man and chief executive at Utah Copper. President of Phelps Dodge Corporation from 1930 to 1947, he also founded the open-pit mine at Morenci. (*Photo courtesy of the American Mining Congress and Phelps Dodge Corporation.*)

James Douglas, M.D. (1837–1918). Douglas was a talented Canadian metallurgist who took Phelps Dodge into copper mining in 1880 with the purchase of Detroit Copper Company (Morenci) and a portion of the Copper Queen property in Bisbee, Arizona. (*Photo courtesy of the American Mining Congress.*)

shares) from Guggenex, which also turned over all of the stock of the Copper River and Northwestern Railway, 53 percent of the stock of Alaska Steamship Company, and 98.5 percent of Braden Copper Company.[75] By 1923 KCC had built up its Utah shares to 77 percent, which gave it de facto control. In 1926 Nevada Consolidated, 43 percent owned by Utah, absorbed Ray Consolidated, which had already absorbed Chino Mines in 1924. The final step came on November 10, 1936, when KCC acquired all of the Utah company's assets.[76] In 1949 KCC created its Western Mining Division, which included the Utah Mines Division, the Nevada Mines Division, the Chino Mines Division, and the Ray Mines Division. Braden Copper continued to operate as a wholly owned subsidiary, but the Alaska mines and railroad had been closed down in 1938.

Because we have already told much of Kennecott's history in connection with ASARCO, we need recount only a few highlights here.

Let us look first at Jackling's magnificent achievement at Bingham Canyon, which changed the character of copper mining all over the world.

Daniel Cowan Jackling was born on a Missouri farm in 1869. After taking a degree in metallurgy and engineering at the School of Mines in Rolla, where he taught for two years, he headed west to Cripple Creek, Colorado. There he worked as a chemist and metallurgist and became friends with MacNeill and Penrose. From 1896 to 1900 he directed a metallurgical plant for a gold mine at Mercur, Utah. In this job he became acquainted with Captain Joseph R. DeLamar, the owner, and thereby learned about the Bingham Canyon copper ore.

Back in 1887, Colonel Enos A. Wall had visited Bingham and had begun filing claims on areas of evident copper mineralization there. In search of capital, Wall in 1895 persuaded DeLamar to buy an option on his holdings. While Jackling was learning about the metallurgy of the Bingham ores at the Mercur mill, DeLamar had received a negative report on copper prospects at Bingham from Hartwig Cohen, his consulting engineer.[77] Then in 1899 Cohen's successor, Victor M. Clement, estimated the ore value at 2.25 percent on average, adding that it "offers exceptional facilities for cheap mining, either by quarrying or caving." Acting for DeLamar, Clement offered Wall $50,000 for a one-quarter interest, with an option to buy an additional half for $250,000.[78] The deal enabled Jackling and Clement to begin mine development in 1899, with Jackling running tests at the mill. According to John Hays Hammond, Clement already had recommended at this early date that the mine be worked by steam shovels that would "terrace down" the mountain by open-cut mining.[79] Doubtless Jackling was eagerly receptive to this idea, for his mind had already grasped the basic need for high-volume production if the property were to be made profitable.

Eventually DeLamar lost faith in the project and let Jackling have the one-quarter interest.[80] At this time (1902) Jackling was working for MacNeill and Penrose once more, having left Mercur in 1901. In January 1903 Wall finally gave Cohen a "free" option for two-thirds of Wall's remaining three-fourths of his claims.[81] Jackling's job now was to persuade MacNeill and Penrose to buy out Wall. With his usual enthusiasm, he told MacNeill that he had "without any exception, the greatest opportunity in the world and that he just had to get in on it."[82]

MacNeill was somewhat distracted at the time by a strike of the Western Federation of Miners at his Cripple Creek properties, but he did listen. Finally he decided to send in an expert, F. H. Minard, to investigate. The ensuing report was a tepid endorsement. On June 1, 1903, MacNeill, Penrose, and the latter's brother, R. A. F. Penrose, a professor of economic geology at the University of Chicago, left for Salt Lake City. They used a horse and wagon to make the difficult trip out to visit the Wall property. After looking things over, Richard Penrose declared that Jackling was right in his appraisal, adding that Minard, mistakenly believing that the mine site was intended to be the location of a concentrator, had needlessly been put off by the lack of water. That evening at dinner MacNeill and Penrose agreed to put up the money. Utah Copper was launched at last.[83]

The key to understanding what Jackling was about to do was his conviction that low-grade porphyry ore could be mined profitably if there were enough of it and if there were room in which to engage in large-scale mining. In this type of ore, known as chalcopyrite, the copper particles are tiny and are scattered throughout the rock—"finely and widely disseminated." In vein mining, by contrast, the vein is typically a small part of the surrounding "country rock," and the metallic content is contained within the vein as nuggets, strips, stringers, and wires. By *selecting* the vein ore, the miner gets a high ore grade by discarding the rest. But in porphyry mining, *all* of the ore in sight is collected, *nonselectively*. How, then, could Jackling mine ore whose grade was at best 2 percent, and yet make money?

The next element in the imaginative synthesis that undoubtedly guided Jackling's thinking was an awareness that if one were to double the daily throughput of porphyry ore, it would require less than a doubling of the fixed facilities for mining—the town site and housing, the railroad, the power shovels, the crushing plant, the concentrator, and the smelter. In short, in these situations there exist latent economies of scale in which the physical returns from production can be made to increase by relatively more than the added investment in fixed plant. Jackling called this "mass-production mining." It involves the same principle that Henry Ford applied to the factory and Samuel Insull to the central electric station and power distribution. In essence, the fixed costs can be lowered by spreading them over more units of output.

The final element in Jackling's thinking was the idea of "beneficiating" or concentrating the ore after it comes from the mine. The purpose is to improve the ore grade to be treated at the smelter, essentially by eliminating as much waste rock as is efficiently possible. Crushing and fine-grinding frees the copper particles as much as possible, which in turn increases the potential recovery rate of copper from the ore.[84] The crushed ore pulp must then be concentrated. In Jackling's early phase with Utah Copper, Wilfley tables and vanners (shaking tables) were used, both of which employed differences in specific gravity to separate the copper particles from the other materials. By 1911 the technique of concentration was advanced even more dramatically by introduction of the flotation process in Australia. In 1912 the process was initiated at Butte, and by 1920 at Utah Copper. Flotation is accomplished by exploiting differences in the surface properties of the particles by immersing them in water in a large trough or cell to which oil or other reagents are added in minute amounts. Air is blown in from below and the pulp is mechanically agitated.[85] A froth of bubbles, coated by a film of oil, attracts the copper sulfide particles *upward*, separating them from the residue or gangue. The froth is floated off to the next cell below, where the process is repeated seriatim.

The end result is a fine material that, after drying, may hold 20 to 40 percent copper. In this way, the original ore, with a grade of, say, 0.5 to 1.5 percent, can be concentrated twentyfold or more for smelter treatment. And thus did Jackling, in the space of a decade, make Bingham Canyon what was soon to become the most productive copper mine in the United States. Since Jackling continued to run the Utah properties until 1942, he was at hand to witness this consummation of his vision for porphyry mining.

During the 1920s important changes took place. Introduction of the froth form of flotation raised the copper recovery ratio from 61 to 85 percent. In 1923 electric power shovels were adopted, followed by electrification of the mine railroad.[86] In May 1929 Kennecott entered into vertical integration by buying the Chase companies, which gave it four manufacturing subsidiaries later known as Chase Brass and Copper Company. By 1938 the four Alaska mines had been worked out and the railroad was abandoned. In 1944 Alaska Steamship Company was sold.

After Daniel Guggenheim's retirement in 1919, Kennecott gradually ceased to be a Guggenheim enterprise. The family itself, with its huge block of shares, gradually took on the characteristics of absentee owners. Kennecott Copper Corporation had gained a 77 percent controlling interest in Jackling's Utah Copper Company. Dissolving that company as an entity, Kennecott created in its stead the Utah Copper Division. With its takeover of the Utah Copper properties, Kennecott gained not only the Bingham Mine in Utah, but also the Nevada properties near Ely, the Ray Mine in Arizona, and the Chino in New Mexico. These were to become Kennecott's mainstay in copper mining. While the Bingham Mine is touted as being the first to use large-scale open-pit mining methods, the Ray Mine, under the leadership of Louis Cates within the Jackling organization, was the first to develop fully the block-caving techniques that were later emulated both at home and abroad by Ray's neighbor, Inspiration, and mines in Chile and northern Rhodesia.

Kennecott, historically, was well placed to respond to national and economic conditions. To endure the Great Depression, Kennecott looked to its low-cost producing facilities. Closing Ray for most of the period, reducing output at Bingham, and operating only sporadically at Chino and Nevada, Kennecott depended on its El Teniente Mine in Chile for maximum output and minimum cost of production. Kennecott's astute management allowed the company to pay dividends in all but two of the depression years. The dividends paid in 1937 were reported to have been greater than the total domestic payroll for that year. During the war the Braden Mine and another investment, the Chase companies, combined efforts to produce cartridge casings while they were in high demand. Kennecott's Chase subsidiary became one of the principal manufacturers of this wartime product. It was also during World War II that Kennecott passed Anaconda to become the world's leading primary copper producer.

Between 1941 and 1945 Kennecott produced 5.8 billion pounds of copper, of which roughly two-thirds came from its American mines. As of 1946, it had a net income of $23 million, total assets of $460 million, and no funded debt. The company had open-pit porphyry mines at Bingham; Ruth, Nevada; and Santa Rita, New Mexico; along with an underground mine at Ray, Arizona, and another, El Teniente, in Chile.[87] By 1940 total ore reserves were 1 billion tons of 1.1 percent copper.[88]

PHELPS DODGE CORPORATION

Of the five largest American copper companies in 1946, Phelps Dodge (PD) was easily the oldest, for the corporation of that date was a lineal descendant of a saddlery dealer, Anson Greene Phelps, of Hartford, Connecticut, who began his business career in about 1800.[89] Before long he was dealing in cotton exports and importing iron, copper, and tin. After 1812 he established himself in New York City. In 1828 one of his daughters married William E. Dodge, a dry-goods merchant in the city.[90] A year later another daughter married a young merchant, D. Willis James. In 1834 Anson Phelps formed two partnerships—Phelps, Dodge and Company in New York, and Phelps, James and Company in London. The business grew rapidly. Before long it had developed the Ansonia Brass and Copper Company, the largest brass producer in the country and a pioneer in Connecticut's Brass Valley district. With Phelps's death in 1853, Dodge steered Phelps Dodge into coal, iron mining, and timber in the Scranton region of Pennsylvania. With these investments, he used PD to promote the building of the Erie, Lackawanna, and Jersey Central railroads. Nevertheless, PD was still strictly an eastern enterprise. How did it ever become involved in Arizona copper?

In the early 1860s the Clifton-Morenci district in Arizona was opened up for mining largely through the efforts of Robert Metcalf, who developed the Longfellow claim along Chase Creek. In 1875 a man named William Church formed the Detroit Copper Mining Company by bringing together a group of claims in the district. Church soon found that he required a new smelter in a better location, and means for bringing water from a distant source on Eagle Creek. The need for capital took him east in 1880, where he called unannounced on William E. Dodge. Dodge was readily interested in the prospect, but wanted a competent inspection beforehand. For this task he chose a young metallurgist, Dr. James Douglas.

Douglas was a Canadian of Scottish descent who had studied for the ministry in Edinburgh, turned to medicine at Laval University in Montreal, then finally found his *métier* in geology and chemistry. As coinventor of the Hunt-Douglas process for electrolytic refining of copper, he landed at a refinery in Phoenixville, Pennsylvania, where he first learned about the

Copper Queen Mine in Bisbee, Arizona. In 1881 Douglas was consulted by Phelps Dodge regarding the advisability of building a copper smelter on an island in Long Island Sound, which brought him into contact with William E. Dodge. Douglas' verdict on the smelter project was negative. More important, it was rendered only days after Church's unexpected visit to Dodge. The upshot was that Dodge sent Douglas out to Morenci to look over the Detroit property. His trip also took him to Bisbee. Both camps strongly impressed him, with the result that Dodge and his partner, D. Willis James, decided to advance Church $30,000 for a block of Detroit Copper shares.[91] PD now had its first stake in Arizona.

Douglas' visit to Bisbee led him to take an option on the Atlanta claim, which was adjacent to the new Copper Queen property. PD took over this option, then spent $70,000 over the next two years in a futile search for ore. With much effort, Douglas persuaded the disillusioned partners to put up a final $15,000 to finance his sinking of a vertical shaft. In July 1884 a bonanza lode was found at 200 feet. At about this same time the Copper Queen group had drifted east into the same ore body. To avoid a likely Apex suit, PD bought the Copper Queen and in August 1885 formed the Copper Queen Consolidated Mining Company.[92] Phelps Dodge and Company de facto had become an Arizona enterprise. And in the Copper Queen, Dodge and James had acquired one of the most extensive underground copper mines. During 1885 to 1908 alone, it produced 730 million pounds of copper, paying out $30 million in dividends.[93]

In the early years operations were concentrated near the surface on the rich oxide ores of 20–25 percent grade. Then rich sulfide ore was found deeper down. These ores sustained production until the end of underground operations (except for leaching) in 1976.

The remote location of Bisbee in 1885 soon drew the partners into the railroad business. Their first venture, the Arizona and Southeastern, established a western connection with the Santa Fe and the Southern Pacific at Fairbank and Benson, Arizona, respectively. This line was then extended east to Douglas, where the Douglas smelter was located. In 1903 it was extended farther east to El Paso for the dual purpose of attracting ores for toll smelting to Douglas and (incidentally) adding bargaining leverage against the Southern Pacific and the Santa Fe. Next, the partners acquired the El Paso and Northeastern, which extended to Dawson, New Mexico, where the coal deposits of their Stag Cañon Fuel Company were located. A branch was acquired from Lordsburg, New Mexico, to Clifton, Arizona, to connect the Detroit Copper properties via the Southern Pacific. Finally, in 1910, the Benson branch was completed to Tucson, with extension to Los Angeles a serious prospect. At this point the partners controlled a 1,200-mile system, the El Paso and Southwestern, which was eventually sold to the Southern Pacific in 1924 for approximately $64 million.[94]

Railroading was not the primary interest of Dodge and James, however. It was an activity forced on them, so to speak, to permit the growth of their mining business.

In 1895 their mining interests were enlarged by acquisition of what was to become the Moctezuma branch of Phelps Dodge and Company in Nacozari, Sonora, Mexico. The seller was M. Guggenheim's Sons. The purchase was made on the reliable advice of Louis D. Ricketts, who became manager of the branch. A railroad was then built from Nacozari north to Douglas, to provide access to the smelter.[95]

Following the death of both principals, the seventy-year partnership was dissolved. In 1908 Phelps, Dodge and Company became a business corporation, with James Douglas as president. The eastern mercantile and metals business was sold off, while the Arizona, New Mexico, and Mexico properties—except for the railroads—were turned over to the new concern. The present Phelps Dodge Corporation was formed later, in 1917.[96]

Also in 1917, the Bisbee and Jerome labor deportations occurred. Those unhappy events are discussed elsewhere, because the present chapter is concerned with the economic development of the copper industry (its labor relations are a topic substantial enough to be considered on its own).

In 1921 PD acquired the Arizona Copper Company, which had operated in the Morenci district since the early 1880s, mostly under the direction of a very capable Scot by the name of James Colquhoun. This property was of enormous importance to PD because it gave title to the Clay ore body, a mass of 450 million tons of gray porphyry lying on both sides of Chase Creek above Morenci. The deposit had been known since 1914. By 1942 it had become the Morenci pit, second only to Bingham in the United States.[97]

Walter Douglas—son of James Douglas—retired as president in 1929, after holding the post since 1916. His successor was Louis Shattuck Cates, a graduate of the Massachusetts Institute of Technology, who had been superintendent at the Boston Consolidated in Bingham Canyon when that property was acquired by Utah Copper in 1910. Cates went on to manage the Ray Mine for Jackling, then later was brought back by Jackling to run Utah's entire operation at Bingham.

Cates was an exceptional mining executive and PD gave him ample chance to prove it. His first accomplishment came within two years: the introduction of vertical integration. Nichols Copper Company had been acquired just before his arrival, because it had developed a special process for the electrolytic treatment of copper that yielded cathodes of unusual purity and effected the separate recovery of gold and silver. Accordingly, in 1930 Cates built a new refinery at Laurel Hill, New York, to put the process to work. That same year, PD bought National Electric Products Corporation, which controlled wire and cable plants at Habirshaw (Yonkers), New York, and Fort Wayne, Indiana. Phelps Dodge Copper Products was formed in 1938 to manage all manufacturing operations, while Phelps Dodge Refining assumed responsibility for the plants at Laurel Hill and El Paso.[98]

Cates's next move came in 1931, a very depressed year, when the company acquired Calumet and Arizona Mining Company. The C & A had developed the very rich Irish Mag Mine in Bisbee in the late 1890s and had operated it profitably until the depression in 1930. It also owned the New Cornelia property at Ajo, which was rich in ore but handicapped by difficult processing problems. By 1931 C & A was rich in reserves but poor in cash, while for PD the problem was the opposite. So a deal was struck that gave PD almost complete ownership in Bisbee, a smelter in Douglas, and a large open-pit porphyry mine at Ajo, with a direct railroad connection to the SP. Thus Phelps Dodge was ready when wartime copper needs asserted themselves.

The achievement for which Louis Cates will be best remembered is his leadership in the creation of the Morenci open-pit mine and reduction works, a project similar in magnitude to the development of Bingham Canyon between 1905 and 1910 by his long-time friend Daniel Jackling.

Cates's goal was to create a mining and reduction complex that both technically and economically would be appropriate to exploit the huge ore body acquired with Arizona Copper Company in 1921. PD had been running tests on treatment of this ore between 1928 and 1931. Simultaneously, it had undertaken an extensive drilling program to evaluate the size, configuration, and average value of the deposit. Assessment of the results of these investigations led to two major conclusions: (1) that an open-pit mine economically would be substantially preferable to underground block caving, or "timberless" mining; (2) that the entire Morenci operation would have to be replaced with new facilities for crushing, milling, smelting, and ore transport.

The onset of the Great Depression compelled PD to shelve the project until mid-1937, while operations at Morenci were shut down. Work was finally started with Wilbur Jurden, loaned by Anaconda, as chief engineer to design the project. Jurden located the facilities for ore treatment downhill from the mine, in an arrangement that was ideal because it would take advantage of gravity and everything could be placed from scratch. The pit initially was to be a mile across and 1,800 feet deep, requiring removal of 50 million tons of overburden. Planned capacity was to be 27,000 tons of ore per day, but in 1941 it was increased to 45,000 tons at the instigation of the federal government. Final cost involved $42 million for PD and $26 million for the government. By 1942 the huge complex was in operation, at just the right time given the urgent wartime requirements.[99]

In some respects Morenci was the apotheosis of open-pit porphyry mining as Jackling had envisaged it some forty years earlier. It is unique in that it was conceived and built as a unit, on the basis of the latest technology, and without merging old facilities with new ones. By contrast, Bingham Canyon was older as a layout and had developed with the accretions of years. Both mines were founded on the same principles: massive non-selective stripping of the ore, from benches cut into the sides of the pit; gyratory crushers and ball mills for crushing and grinding; flotation for concentrating the ore; and the three-stage smelting process (reverberatory, converter, and anode furnaces) for processing anode copper. The anode bars were sent to El Paso for refining.

A look at Morenci shows a vast agglomeration of diverse mining activities, tied together by many miles of railroad, in a neat and well-ordered complex. As soon as it came onstream in 1942, it was obvious that it was to be the centerpiece of all PD operations. It remains so to this day. But Morenci may prove to be the last of the country's great open-pit copper mines; the future eventually may belong to Chile.

Cates saw PD through the years of World War II and retired in 1947. The figures for the company's operations in 1946 will help relate it to the four other major producers. In that year PD refined 409 million pounds of copper, including toll and custom accounts—well below 742 million pounds for Anaconda and 594 million for Kennecott, but an impressive total nonetheless. In addition, the company refined 1.96 million ounces of silver, 60,745 ounces of gold, and 350,000 tons of coal. Net income for the year stood at $14.9 million, which yielded a return of 11.7 percent on capital stock. Total assets were $206.7 million, and true to its Scottish heritage, it had no funded debt. Over the war years 1941–1945, PD refined 2.956 billion pounds of copper.[100]

Except for its Nacozari operation, Phelps Dodge has always confined its production activities to the continental United States. Moreover, its existence has always been based on copper. Its gold and silver output are mine by-products, while its coal production at Dawson, New Mexico (Stag Cañon branch), existed only to provide fuel to its own railroads and to the Southern Pacific for its steam locomotives. Furthermore, Morenci was the core of the company's copper production by 1946. To be sure, the Copper Queen branch at Bisbee and Douglas was for many years the primary source of its wealth and income, but by the 1940s it had begun to lose relative position and its future was limited. Ajo (New Cornelia branch) by contrast had become a steady and profitable producer by war's end, whereas Tyrone (Burro Canyon) had closed down in 1918 and was not to be reopened until 1969.

OTHER PROMINENT PRODUCERS

From 1915 on the Big Five accounted for more than 80 percent of American copper output. But several other important properties require mention too.

Miami Copper Company

In the area lying between the towns of Superior and Globe, in the Superstition Mountains of Arizona, four major operations were established, three of them shortly after 1900. One of them, the Miami Copper Company, was organized in 1908 by Adolph and Samuel Lewisohn, in its first years as a traditional underground mine. After 1925 its rich ores were approaching exhaustion. The choice was whether to invest in an attempt to exploit an adjacent low-grade porphyry ore body by underground extraction, or to abandon the property. By ingenious introduction of a new technique known as high tower block-caving, with extraction raises and undercutting, the Miami management was able to earn excellent returns for another two decades. Meanwhile, in 1941 Miami organized the Castle Dome Copper Company as a subsidiary that in 1943 inaugurated an open-pit mine just west of Miami, in Pinto Valley. At the time this mine was viewed as a short-lived wartime venture, and it actually was closed in 1953. Subsequently acquired and redeveloped by Cities Service, it was later bought by Magma Copper Company, which has continued leaching operations there to the present time.[101]

Newmont and Magma

The Newmont Mining Corporation and the Magma Copper Company were the creations of William Boyce Thompson.[102] It was Thompson's father who, with the Butte copper boom of the 1880s, first began to invest in mining after his Butte contracting business became successful. As a result of his father's prosperity, young Thompson was able to attend prestigious schools such as Phillips Exeter and the Columbia University School of Mines. With this education behind him, he returned to Montana to work in the management of his father's various mining interests before heading off to Wall Street and making a name for himself in the investment community.

Thompson's clientele consisted mostly of people interested in copper-mining investments. Thompson teamed up with George Gunn, a prospector he had become acquainted with during his stint in mine management. While Thompson dealt with the investors, Gunn sought suitable mining ventures in the western United States. Able to lay first claim to such lucrative porphyry deposits as the Metcalf in Arizona and those in Ely, Nevada—and developing Newmont's best mine, Magma—Thompson became quite successful and through his ventures met many of the day's premier mining engineers. With them Thompson combined mining knowledge and investor funds to create a number of profitable ventures in copper mining.

Thompson formed Magma Copper Company in 1910 through purchase of an older silver mine at Superior, Arizona, for $130,000. Henry Krumb of Utah Copper fame had recommended the property to Thompson. Superior was a classic case of underground vein mining, following two main stalks down almost to 5,000 feet. Unstable ground required use of square sets and backfilling for support, a costly technique that was justified only by the high values of the bornite deposit at hand. Through 1972 the mine produced almost $1.5 billion in copper, gold, and silver.[103]

By 1921 Thompson had compiled a sizable personal fortune through his investments and his involvement in some of the leading mines of the day, including Magma. In preparation for retirement he created the Newmont Corporation to handle his investments, combining the names of his Montana beginnings and his New York residence. Newmont was, in fact, a company with a diversified portfolio including sulfur and oil, but with copper predominant. Copper investments in addition to Magma were in Kennecott, Chile Copper Company, and Anglo-American Corporation of South Africa.

After Thompson did retire, his attorney, Charles F. Ayers, and geologist Fred Searls, Jr., worked as a team to guide Newmont through the next thirty-two years. Although it sold its Chile Copper Company investment in Chuquicamata to Anaconda, Newmont expanded in copper by investing in four other mining companies during the late 1920s. Two of these had no long-term implications for the company. For the first time, however, Newmont accepted management responsibilities along with its 50 percent interest in O'Okiep in Namibia and 30 percent interest in Tsumeb in South Africa. These two mines were Newmont's true "gold mines," earning at least as much as all other Newmont investments combined.

While O'Okiep and Tsumeb were booming, conflict and dissension in the boardroom were holding back Newmont progress on other fronts. With younger executives looking to promote new projects, with Searls committed to finding many small projects requiring only partial Newmont investment, and with the old guard fighting to retain its cautious 1930s strategies, Magma, in which Newmont had a controlling 15 percent interest, was being starved.[104]

Inspiration Consolidated Copper Company

So highly appreciated were his talents that Henry Krumb was also successful in persuading Boyce Thompson in 1908 to buy certain claims in the Miami, Arizona, area, which by 1911 became the Inspiration Consolidated Copper Company (now owned by Cyprus Minerals Corporation). Its property surrounds Miami Copper on both its east and west sides. Soon after it was formed, Inspiration acquired Live Oak Development Company, partly through the help of John Ryan of Anaconda. Louis Ricketts was brought in to plan the mill and concentrator, which included installation of the first large flotation plant in the United States. Again helped by Anaconda financing, Inspiration was able to obtain a new smelter, built by an Anaconda subsidiary, the International Smelting Company. Although its ore was of the porphyry type, Inspiration's initial mining plan called for a form of underground block caving originally employed at the Ohio Mine in Bingham Canyon.[105] Three-quarters of a century after the formation of the company, it is still active, now as a large open-pit mine with its own refinery and rod mill, also owned by Cyprus Minerals.

CHAPTER 4

THE COPPER MARKET TO THE
END OF WORLD WAR II

IN LINE WITH THE CONCEPT of the demand for labor as derived from the demand for the product thereof, the product-market history of copper is a necessary component of the dual drama of business enterprise and labor organization. This chapter traces the shifting position of the United States in world production over the period 1870 to 1946 and the long-term decline of the American copper export surplus.

THE DEMAND FOR COPPER

Copper has long been used for cookware, ornaments, and military hardware. Modern usage began with the addition of copper sheeting for roofs and sheathing for ship hulls, as well as for brass clocks, piping, and valves. The real breakthrough came with electrification, beginning around 1880 with Faraday's discovery of electromagnetism and Edison's practical inventions. Copper's qualities of conductivity, durability, and cheapness made it the metal of choice for motors, generators, wiring, cable, switchgear, and for telephone and telegraph systems. The growth of automobile manufacturing added automotive wiring and radiation to the list, which was soon augmented by household electrical appliances and high-tension power production and distribution components.

The key to understanding the patterns of demand for copper, however, is recognition that it is primarily an industrial good. For instance, in the pre-1946 period traced in this chapter, studies by the Federal Trade Commission reported that in both 1920 and 1940 capital goods accounted for 71.2 percent and 71.8 percent respectively of copper consumption, whereas consumer goods (automobiles, refrigerators, radios, and the like) represented only 8.9 percent of consumption in 1920 and 13.5 percent in 1940.[1]

Copper is used almost entirely as an intermediate good, bought by firms engaged in further production to serve the final demand for the products of industry. Thus the demand for copper has two major components. One involves the rate of *replacement* of copper embodied in existing fixed capital, such as electrical machines, cables, wiring, and tubing. This kind of demand is normally quite steady because it is tied to long-run depreciation policies. But copper demand has a second component—the rate of expansion of *additions* to fixed capital over the entire economy, or net capital formation. Changes in this rate are closely geared to movements in the final demand for the products of industry—that is, to overall business fluctuations. Inherently, final demand does not change at a steady rate. The rate itself increases, decreases, and in recessions may turn negative.

To illustrate, if final demand shifts upward from a 2 percent annual rate of advance to 4 percent, this doubling effect will exert powerful upward leverage on the total demand for copper because of the doubling of the rate of additions to fixed capital called forth by the jump in final demand. In business contractions, this leverage—often called the magnification of changes in the derived demand for intermediate goods—works in reverse. Accordingly, the notorious short-term instability of the demand for copper flows jointly from the instability of final demand itself and from the role of copper as an intermediate good.

This inherent volatility in the industry did not become obvious until after 1918. Probably the explanation is that over the preceding decades the rapid introduction of electrification in buildings, houses, manufacturing, and transportation so dominated the expansion of copper demand from its initially very small base that overall fluctuations in the economy counted for little.

Within thirty-five years after the industry had gotten its start in 1845, the electric lamp and the electric motor had been invented, bringing into being the manufacture of electrical machinery and equipment, cable and wire, along with the whole electrical utility industry. These basic innovations opened up a large array of uses for copper. Per capita annual consumption rose rapidly with the popular spread of electrification from the 1880s on. A 5.8 percent average annual increase in industrial output in the United States, Western Europe, and to a lesser degree Japan over the years 1890 to 1918 was the source of a corresponding 5.8 percent annual increase in world copper output (Figure 4.1).

The end of military hostilities in 1918 was followed by a sharp and deep economic depression in most of the countries involved. There followed a period of industrial expansion, including new uses for copper in automobile radiators and wiring, household electrical appliances, and high-tension power production and distribution. In response, the compound

FIGURE 4.1 World Copper Mine Production

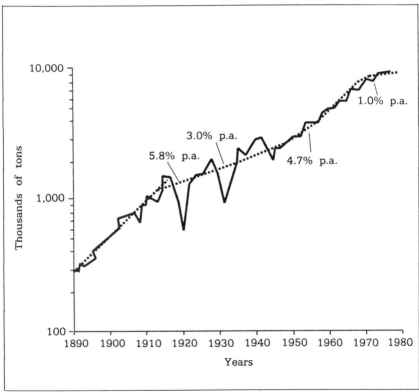

SOURCE: Kenji Takeuchi, John E. Strongman, Shunichi Maeda, and C. Suan Tan, *The World Copper Industry: Its Changing Structure and Future Prospects* (Washington, D.C.: World Bank, 1987), p. 9.

rate of annual increase in copper demand was 8.4 percent between 1922 and 1929.

Thereafter, a new long-term influence was added to the increasingly cyclic pattern of copper demand. U.S. per capita consumption of copper reached its peak in 1929, at 20.9 pounds. This consumption represented a gain of 77.1 percent over 1912, with almost all of it caused by recovery from the contraction of 1919–1921. After 1929, furthermore, per capita consumption fell sharply below this peak and remained there until 1941, when the soaring demand for munitions completely distorted the figures.[2] In the first full peacetime year, 1946, consumption per head quickly fell back to only 19.8 pounds, which was almost exactly equivalent to 1940 and just below the 20.9 pounds recorded in 1929.[3] For the "normal" years of 1922–1929 together, average consumption per head was 16.8 pounds. This maturation of copper consumption was to become increasingly apparent in the years after 1946.

The combination of cyclic and trend movements reduced copper consumption from nearly 2 million tons in 1929 to less than 900,000 tons in 1932. Indeed, the 1929 level was not regained until 1937. Moreover, copper consumption expanded only moderately with World War II, because civilian use almost ceased and industrial production was curtailed. Accordingly, the United States became the primary producer and user, in its role as the "arsenal of democracy."

The U.S. term for copper demand is "apparent consumption," measured indirectly as the residual remaining after net exports and net additions to inventory (if positive) are deducted from the sum of primary production plus reused scrap. From 1908 through 1946 apparent consumption rose from 270,000 short tons to 1.8 million, a 6.8-fold increase for a compound annual rate of 5.1 percent. Instead of a smooth trend, however, large surges in demand occurred during 1908–1918, 1922–1929, and 1932–1942. The last period represented recovery from the depths of the depression and the initial upswing in demand at the beginning of the Second World War, which peaked at 2.4 million short tons in 1942 before drifting down to the 1946 figure.

U.S. SUPPLY

Over the long run, of course, world demand and world supply must be approximately equal. What is significant for our story is where the supply came from. In 1870 U.S. output was 14,112 short tons. By 1946 the total reached over 1 million tons, a 71-fold increase. Yet production in 1946 was actually no larger than in 1929. For the sixteen years that followed 1929, copper showed no sustained growth apart from three war years. On the contrary, the Great Depression dragged output down to only 225,000 tons in 1933, equivalent to the level of 1896.

If we break this production series into segments that correspond to the principal turning points in the history of the industry, we can gain significant insight into that history. During the decade of the 1870s, the Upper Michigan properties were the only important source of American production. Between 1881 and 1905, a series of major underground mines emerged in Arizona—the Copper Queen, the Longfellow in the Morenci district, the Irish Mag, the Old Dominion, the United Verde, and the Moctezuma, which supplied concentrates to Douglas from just over the border in Mexico. Moreover, the Butte district in Montana had started copper production at the Anaconda in 1882, followed by several other mines there soon after.[4]

Utah Copper began operations in 1906, to be followed within a decade by Nevada Consolidated, Ray, Miami, Inspiration, Chino, Magma, the United Verde Extension, and the four Kennicott[5] mines in Alaska. In 1917 the New Cornelia was in production at Ajo, Arizona, and one year later Phelps Dodge opened its Tyrone Mine in New Mexico. Thereafter the list of major properties remained stable through the end of World War II.

Accordingly, there are five significant reference segments for isolating growth rates over the period. They are 1870–1880 (the Michigan period); 1881–1905 (the emergence of Arizona and Montana); 1906–1918 (the opening of the porphyry period);[6] 1922–1929 (the recession and recovery after World War I); and 1933–1946 (the Great Depression and World War II). A tabulation of the figures appears in Table 4.1. It should be noted that the contraction years of 1919–1921 and 1930–1932 have been excluded because our concern here is with rates of growth. No attempt has been made to fit growth curves to minimize the deviations; these did not become significant until after 1918.

Between 1870 and 1929 sustained and substantial increases in physical output occurred as the periods succeeded each other, with 1922–1929 attaining the maximum at 75,193 short tons per year. Thereafter the prolonged depression and the rapid contraction in postwar 1946 sharply flattened the annual rate of increase compared with the earlier period. Worth remarking is that the rates of average annual increase show a jump

TABLE 4.1 U.S. copper output, selected periods, 1870–1946[a]

Period	Change in output over period (short tons)	Average change per year (short tons)	Compound annual rate of increase (percent)
1870–1880	16,128	1,613	7.8
1881–1905	408,552	17,023	11.0
1906–1918	495,364	41,280	6.3
1922–1929	526,357	75,193	11.2
1933–1946	375,000	28,846	7.8

SOURCE: U.S. Federal Trade Commission, *Report on the Copper Industry*, Part 1, "The Copper Industry of the United States and International Copper Cartels" (Washington, D.C.: Government Printing Office, 1947), pp. 30–31; year 1946 from U.S. Department of the Interior, Bureau of Mines, *Minerals Yearbook, 1946* (Washington, D.C.: Government Printing Office, 1948), p. 459.

[a] Smelter production; excludes scrap recovery and withdrawals from inventory.

of 10.5-fold for the Arizona-Montana period over the Michigan period; that the porphyry period advanced only 2.4 times over its immediate predecessor; and 1922–1929 increased only 1.8 times the porphyry years. Clearly, the rate of average annual increase in output showed the greatest advance in the Arizona-Montana years. Equally clearly, the rate of expansion began slowing after 1905, declining absolutely after 1929.

If we look at compound rates of annual growth, all periods together ranged from a low of 6.3 percent (1906–1918) to a high of 11.2 percent in 1922–1929. This last figure is somewhat inflated, because 1922 was a relatively depressed year. More important, all of these relative rates of annual increase are unusually high. They are also well sustained over the entire seventy-six years. Clearly, the Arizona-Montana period stands out: for twenty-four years it yielded a compound annual growth rate of 11.0 percent, reflecting the opening of a fabulous series of mines and a collateral soaring of demand as the age of electrification got under way.

Plotting annual outputs on semilogarithmic paper reveals two salient features: (1) an almost unbroken and incredibly steep series of increases from 1870 through 1912; and (2) two very steep declines—1919–1921 and 1930–1933—that for the first time indicated the severe instability of the American copper industry (Figure 4.2). Both declines were followed by sharp expansions, but both peaks barely exceeded output in 1929. What emerges is the conclusion that the industry had achieved its highest relative rate of increase by 1912. Thereafter it entered a period of

FIGURE 4.2 Smelter Production in the U.S., 1870–1946

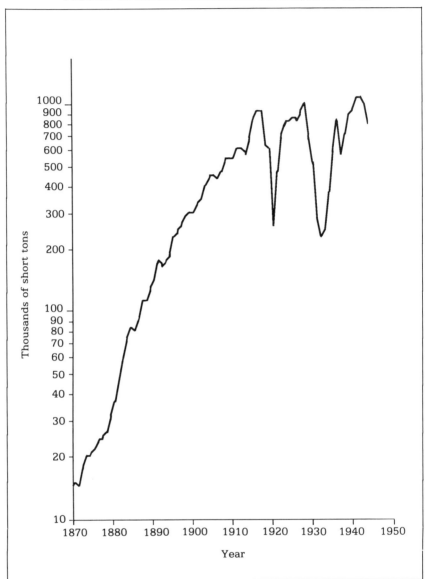

SOURCE: U.S. Federal Trade Commission, *Report on the Copper Industry, Part 1*, "The Copper Industry of the United States and International Copper Cartels" (Washington, D.C.: Government Printing Office, 1947), pp. 30–31; 1945–1946 from U.S. Department of the Interior, Bureau of Mines, *Minerals Yearbook, 1948* (Washington, D.C.: Government Printing Office, 1949).

instability and high volatility, with a much slower rate of long-run growth. Behind this later behavior were wartime surges of demand and two major economic contractions, as well as the post-1929 decline in per capita copper consumption.

In examining trends in American copper production, we should consider changes in the relative position of the United States in world output (Table 4.2). During the Michigan period (1870–1880), the United States contributed 15 percent of the world total, while Spain and Portugal, the main European sources, also accounted for 15 percent of the total. In those years Chile accounted for 36 percent, mostly derived from the predecessor mines of El Teniente and Chuquicamata.[7]

From that beginning, the American share of world production surged upward to 57 percent during 1911–1915. Between the 1870s and 1911–1915, Chile's output collapsed to 4 percent; Spain and Portugal's from 15 to 5 percent. In the latter period Canada reached 4 percent to begin her emergence as a leading producer.

After 1911–1915, the American share fell rather sharply until World War II, when it rose moderately and then dropped to 30 percent by 1951–1955. As the earlier data show, this declining share (except during 1931–1935) does not represent an absolute drop in production. Rather, it reflects the enormous cumulative impact from the development of the Katanga mines in Zaire after 1920, and the Zambian properties (Roan Antelope, Rhokana, Mufulira, N'Dola, N'Changa, and Rhodesian Selection Trust).[8] Thus by 1931–1935 Africa contributed 18 percent of the world total, compared to 23 percent for the United States. The redevelopment of the great Chilean mines, starting around 1915, restored that nation's output to about one-sixth of the world total. In the 1930s and after, Canada began producing about 10 percent of that total. In other words, geographic competition began asserting itself strongly after 1920, cutting deeply into the relative share of the United States in world copper output.

The next problem to consider involves changes in the American import-export position over the years before 1946. The record of both imports and exports of American copper after 1900 reveals an irregular series of sharp spikes and deep troughs. The two world wars, the steep contraction of 1919–1921, and the Great Depression starting in 1929 account for these movements and point once more to the magnification of shifts in derived demand characteristics of copper as an intermediate good when major changes in total demand occur.

TABLE 4.2 **Copper-mine production by country or region, 1900–1950**

	Percentage of world total				
Country or region	1900	1920	1929	1938	1950
United States	55.7	57.4	46.5	25.2	32.7
Canada	1.7	3.8	5.8	12.9	9.5
North America	57.4	61.2	52.2	38.1	42.2
Australia	4.7	2.8	0.7	1.0	0.6
Other industrial	12.2	11.4	10.1	9.0	4.2
Industrial total	74.3	75.4	63.0	48.1	47.0
Zambia	0.0	0.3	0.3	12.6	11.8
Zaire	0.0	2.0	7.0	6.2	7.0
Other Africa	1.4	0.6	1.1	1.1	1.9
Africa total	1.4	2.8	8.5	19.9	20.6
Chile	5.3	10.2	16.5	17.5	14.4
Peru	1.7	3.6	2.9	1.9	1.2
Mexico	4.5	5.2	4.4	2.1	2.4
Other Latin America	0.4	2.1	1.1	0.8	1.0
Latin America total	11.9	21.1	24.9	22.2	19.0
Philippines	0.0	0.0	0.0	0.2	0.4
Papua New Guinea	0.0	0.0	0.0	0.0	0.0
Other developing Asia	0.0	0.0	0.4	0.4	0.3
Asia and Oceania total	0.0	0.0	0.4	0.6	0.7
Southern Europe	10.9	0.3	1.4	4.0	3.2
Developing total	24.2	24.2	35.1	46.8	43.6
Industrial plus developing	98.6	99.6	98.1	94.9	90.6
East European nonmarket	1.4	0.4	1.9	5.1	9.4
World total	100.0	100.0	100.0	100.0	100.0

SOURCE: Kenji Takeuchi, John E. Strongman, Shunichi Maeda, and C. Suan Tan, *The World Copper Industry: Its Changing Structure and Future Prospects* (Washington, D.C.: World Bank, 1987), p. 17.

From the beginning of the present century, exports have represented a substantial share of primary smelter production (which excludes scrap, inventory drawdowns, and exports less imports). During the peacetime years of 1908–1913, the export share of American production ranged between 70.3 percent (1908) and 75.7 percent in 1913. For the peacetime period of 1922–1929, exports peaked at 78.1 percent of output in 1922, falling to a low of 68.3 percent in 1924.[9]

For the two peace periods cited, it is of interest to consider the net impact of the export surplus on total available copper supply. For 1908 and 1913, the export surpluses were 33.1 percent and 30.7 percent respectively, relative to all domestic copper supply.[10] In 1922–1929 net exports swung between 9.4 percent (1922) and 12.1 percent (1924), for a very sharp drop in little more than a decade. During the war years the export surplus shrank significantly, whereas total domestic supply increased substantially. During World War II the export surplus turned negative beginning in 1940, reaching −721,000 short tons by 1945. In short, the United States had become dependent on an import surplus to meet its surging wartime demand for copper.

The downshift in the ratio of net exports to total domestic supply shows up clearly during the peacetime years after World War I and even more strongly during World War II. At the same time, domestic copper supply showed a diminishing elasticity of response to increases in domestic and world demand. Between 1915 and 1918 supply rose 40.3 percent, against only 15.7 percent from 1940 to the peak year 1943.

As a copper exporter, the United States reached its peak in 1928, at 561,000 short tons (Figure 4.3). Thereafter exports showed a strongly declining profile through 1945. In sharp contrast, imports rose dramatically from 1908 through 1929, collapsed through 1933, then soared through 1945. Imports, it seems, were gradually replacing domestic production for meeting long-term increases in domestic demand. The transition was a subtle one, concealed as it was by impressive discoveries and achievements in mine production and scrap recovery all through the years from 1900 to 1945. Yet the underlying evidence is clear: in 1929 import and export tonnages were in exact balance, at 487,000 short tons. The export surplus was never to regain its earlier volume; after 1939 it turned decisively negative right through 1946.

Behind the behavior of the figures for output and exports after 1900 are three basic changes in trend. The first is a slackening in the rate of growth in domestic copper output, indicated by the fundamental turning point in 1912. The second is the long-run decline in the export surplus, which asserted itself by the mid-twenties. Finally, there is the development of extensive new copper deposits overseas, beginning with the Chilean mines during 1912–1920, then the vast properties in Zaire, Zambia, and South Africa in the 1930s. Because these mines could be worked more profitably

FIGURE 4.3 Imports and Exports of Copper, United States, 1908-1945

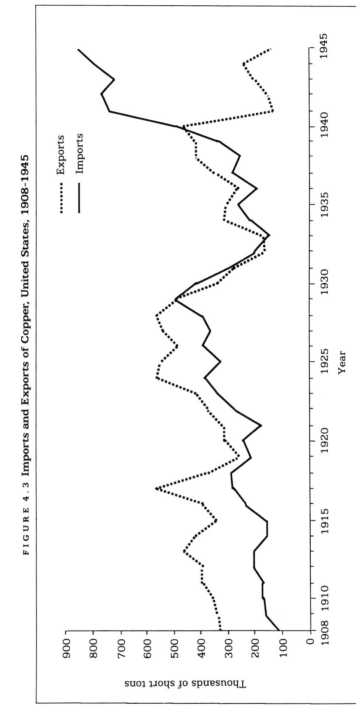

SOURCE: Data provided by U.S. Tariff Commission, published in U.S. Federal Trade Commission, *Report on the Copper Industry, Part 1*, "The Copper Industry of the United States and International Copper Cartels" (Washington, D.C.: Government Printing Office, 1947), p. 66; 1945 from U.S. Department of the Interior, Bureau of Mines, *Minerals Yearbook, 1945* (Washington, D.C.: Government Printing Office, 1947).

with their richer ores and lower labor costs, they attracted fresh capital that created an alternative to increased development in the United States. In consequence, no major mines made their appearance in this country between 1915 and 1946. We may infer that the prospective rate of return from such investments was too low to attract the necessary capital.

Although U.S. copper consumption increased 6.8-fold during 1908–1946, the total quantity of copper supplied by U.S. production during those years increased only 2.12-fold, or at a compound annual rate of 2 percent. What was happening over these years was a gradual encroachment of consumption on available home supply. Domestic consumption was outrunning domestic production, except for the depression periods of 1919–1921 and 1930–1932. Over the long run, the excess of supply over demand was preserved (although it continued to shrink) through declining net exports. But in 1940–1941 total copper demand finally overtook supply. The United States became a net importer, and a substantial one at that. During 1942 to 1945 the import surplus averaged 560,750 short tons yearly. This volume sustained an average annual rate of consumption of 2.24 million short tons.

Inflated wartime demand lay back of the data for the 1940s. On the supply side, the apparent inelasticity of response in domestic production actually reflected the ease with which imports could be obtained from Canada and Latin America, and at the same time the difficulties of finding and/or exploiting new domestic copper deposits in a comparatively short period.[11]

PRICES AND COMPETITION

The Evolution of Pricing Systems

Because the pricing of copper has always been complicated, a few basic distinctions are required. One concerns the difference between quoted prices and prices created in *bourse trading*. A quoted price is named, usually by the seller, on a take-it-or-leave-it basis: the seller is the price-maker and the buyer the price-taker. This method is sometimes called *administrative pricing*. Typically there is no negotiation between buyer and seller, although this is not to say that quoted prices are entirely or even substantially isolated from competitive forces.

In bourse trading, buyers and sellers meet to agree upon a market-clearing price for copper of a given grade and shape. Prices determined this way are flexible and are backed by copper stored and available in warehouses. The buyers participate in the price-making as well as the sellers. And the sales contracts entered into can involve "spot" (immediate) or future deliveries for specified dates.

Until the formation of the New York Commodity Exchange (COMEX) in May 1929, there had been no organized competitive market of the bourse type in this country, although the London Metal Exchange (LME) had long served this purpose for Europe. Before COMEX, transactions were conducted in a variety of ways: (1) sales of mine concentrates to custom smelters and refineries, (2) sales of refined copper of specified grade and form by refineries to wholesale merchant dealers and fabricators; (3) sales of refined copper by mining companies direct to dealers and independent fabricators; (4) sales of refined copper by mining companies to fabricating subsidiaries mostly acquired in the 1920s; and (5) sales of refined copper by mines, refiners, and dealers for export.

Except for transactions through COMEX, these categories of price-making were of the quoted type, usually for future delivery. Thus all can be viewed as various forms of producers' prices. The most important category was the U.S. producers' price, which, except during serious price swings, was uniform among sellers because listed terms were known and freely circulated among traders.[12] The leading mines preferred the quotation system, because they believed it dampened price fluctuations. These they considered undesirable because sharp upswings would encourage commodity substitution against copper, while declines could take price below long-run cost of production. Collaterally, these companies were averse to COMEX because it promoted futures trading, which was thought to increase price volatility.[13] The claim was ill founded, as it turned out. Trading in futures is a way of stabilizing the value of inventories through hedging transactions. It also smooths out price fluctuations, rather than exacerbating them. The impersonal system merely denied the producers a false sense of control of their own selling price.

Critics of the producers' price-setting system have contended that it led to quasi-monopolistic prices, to rigidity of prices, and, through rigidity, to surpluses and shortages because the markets could not clear; and that with shortages the system led to rationing of buyers to the advantage of sellers. In any event, the producer-price system was maintained until 1978, when it was formally abandoned. Thereafter the COMEX quotations became the measuring rod for prices.[14] Some producers today quote their prices as a fixed markup over the COMEX figures.

The Behavior of Prices, 1870–1946

The average nominal price of copper per pound moved from 21.2 cents in 1870 to 13.9 cents in 1946. This moderate decline conceals several sharp upswings and downswings over the intervening seventy-five years, although the trend of copper to become ever cheaper is unambiguous. The peak price for the entire period was quickly reached in 1872, at 35.6 cents per pound. Thereafter the price dropped sharply but irregularly to a low of 9.5 cents in 1894. A similarly irregular advance then got under way, topping at 29.2 cents in 1917. With the postwar slump, the price fell to 12.7 cents in 1921. A moderate recovery brought the price to 18.2 cents by 1929, followed by the steepest fall of the whole period, to an all-time low of 5.7 cents in 1932. Recovery to 13.3 cents in 1937 gave way to a controlled price of 11.9 cents during the war.[15]

The extent and frequency of these price movements underscores the extraordinary volatility of copper prices throughout their lengthy early history. At the same time, the very fact of this instability puts in serious question any contention that the American branch of the industry was controlled by a cartel or was an instance of de facto monopoly exerted by the price leadership of some of the large producers. To be sure, administrative or quoted pricing prevailed throughout these years. Yet from the start, the drift of the nominal price was persistently downward, with many intervening fluctuations. The rigid prices often noted for steel, oil, and automobiles were never evident in copper, except in periods of government control.

The other significant fact about the price of copper during this long period is that when deflated to real terms, it shows a rather strong and persistent declining tendency. This movement is evident in Figure 4.4, where nominal prices have been deflated by the implicit price index for gross national product, or GNP (1958 = 100). For 1890–1894 the average real price per pound was 5.0 cents, while the average real price during 1940–1945, the end of the period, was only 2.28 cents, a rather substantial decline of 54.4 percent over the fifty-five years. When these annual observations are fitted to a least-squares trend to bring out the central tendency by reducing the influence of the extreme values, the average annual rate of decrease in the real price of copper becomes 1.31 percent per year.[16]

The profile of the real price of copper over these years shows four distinct upward surges: 1895–1899, 1904–1907, 1914–1916, and 1932–1937. There is no easy explanation for the first two of these swings,

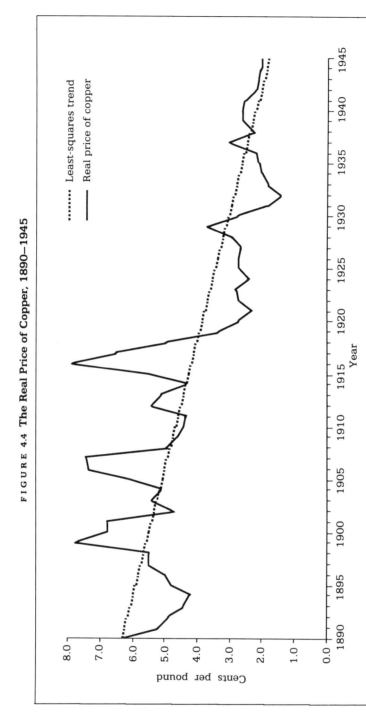

FIGURE 4.4 The Real Price of Copper, 1890–1945

SOURCE: Nominal prices deflated by the implicit price index for GNP (1985 = 100). U.S. Bureau of the Census, *Historical Statistics of the United States, Colonial Times to 1970* (Washington, D.C.: Government Printing Office, 1975), part 1, sec. F, p. 224.

but the third obviously is linked to the First World War, while the fourth reflects the intermediate recovery phase of the Great Depression.

What is much more important is the persistent downtrend in real price over the entire period. If we bear in mind that the implicit price deflator for GNP is the most sensitive and most extensive measure available, it is reasonable to conclude that the terms of trade increasingly favored a fixed basket of GNP goods in exchange for a pound of copper—more copper per unit of GNP goods, and fewer GNP goods per pound of copper. Another way to view this development is to say that the economic efficiency of the resource inputs applied to the production of copper was consistently improving over the same lengthy period. There is no simple explanation for the increasing relative efficiency of copper production. During the earlier years, however, the opening of a series of very rich mines, accompanied by the effects of an increasing scale of production, undoubtedly were contributing factors. After the turn of the century, the successful exploitation of the low-grade porphyry deposits and the rapid introduction of block caving and open-pit mining also certainly were major influences.

With the end of the Second World War, the great period of expansion for American copper came to an end. As Figure 4.5 shows, the overall trend of the real price broke away from the long period of substantial decline to turn flat for the next forty years. Further consideration of the reasons for this change must be deferred until Chapter 7. Here let us note only that the real price of copper showed considerable instability, in particular with substantial jumps in 1953–1956, 1961–1971, 1973–1974, and 1979–1980. Certainly the Korean and Vietnamese conflicts were a factor, although of themselves they do not constitute a sufficient explanation.

Attempts at Price Control

During the 1860s Michigan production expanded rapidly with the discovery of the great Calumet lode. For many properties, financial difficulties were acute because prices were both low and unstable. In 1869 Congress enacted a special 5 percent tariff to help the industry. The following year copper producers met in New York City and agreed to create the Lake Pool to remove "surplus" copper from the domestic market. By dumping enough excess copper in foreign markets, they hoped to sustain the U.S. price. When the Calumet and Hecla Mining Company was formed in early

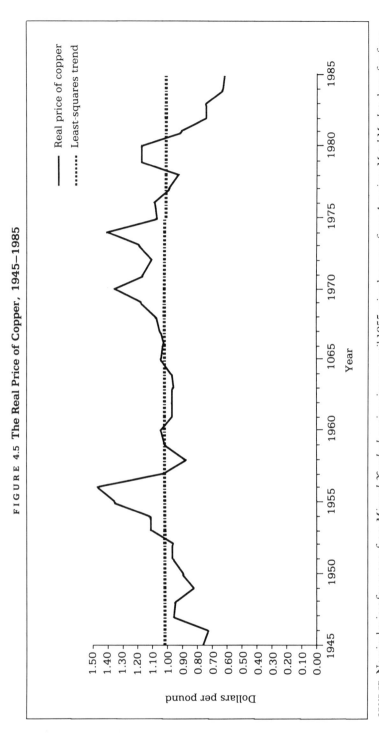

FIGURE 4.5 The Real Price of Copper, 1945–1985

SOURCE: Nominal prices for copper from *Minerals Yearbook*, various issues; until 1955 price data were from *American Metal Market*, thereafter from quotations for delivered electrolytic to U.S. destinations. Implicit price deflators for GNP (1982=100) from U.S. Department of Commerce, Bureau of Economic Analysis, *The National Income and Product Accounts of the United States, 1929-82* (September 1986), table 7.4.

1871, it instantly became the dominant producer with 65 percent of total output. Under its leadership the smaller firms in the pool were assigned designated quantities to export, the total of which ranged from 50 to 100 percent of the C & H export tonnage. As a result, between 1870 and 1884 the U.S. domestic price regularly commanded a premium over the import price, with the control of exports as the instrument to protect the premium. According to William B. Gates, Jr., the pool may also have engaged in the restriction of output, but this is not certain.[17]

By 1884 new production from Arizona and Montana had rendered the pool ineffective. The response of C & H was aggressive price cutting, at times accompanied by deliberately increased production, designed to push the price low enough to force the western mines to suspend output. This period of cutthroat competition led Channing Clapp of C & H to reflect seriously on the advantages of combination, noting in passing that "our French friends . . . [are] very anxious to have us unite with them."[18]

Not surprisingly, in October 1887 M. Secrétan, director of the largest fabricator in Europe, obtained the cooperation of three large French banks to finance long-term purchase contracts to buy the entire outputs of large producers around the world, at a guaranteed price of 13.5 cents a pound. The contracts also called for limitations on production. C & H accepted a contract, along with other important Michigan producers, bringing all Lake copper into the selling pool. By mid-1888 Secrétan's group, together with a cooperating syndicate, claimed control of 80 percent of world copper output.[19]

The consequences of the Secrétan corner were predictable: prices rose over 20 percent, sales declined, output jumped, and scrap recovery increased. So great was the flood of additional copper that by early 1889 the combination was making ten-year purchase contracts and attempting to obtain agreements to restrain output by 20 percent. These measures would have transformed the buyers' pool into a production cartel as well. Then Secrétan's supporting bank failed, and the creditor banks began frantically to unload their copper holdings. The market was demoralized as prices fell more than 20 percent. At this point Anaconda stepped in to insist on an orderly liquidation of stocks, under threat of flooding the market itself.[20]

The Secrétan experience exposed the Achilles' heel of all such corners: the ability of producers and traders outside the combination to undercut the artificial price by increasing output while simultaneously reducing consumption.

The next major attempt at price manipulation was initiated in 1899 by William G. Rockefeller, brother of John D. and a major investor in Anaconda; Henry H. Rogers, who had founded the American Smelting and Refining Company as a merger to control price; and a Boston broker, Thomas W. Lawson. The original plan was to bring about a giant inter-regional combination for the purpose of controlling mine production at Butte and in Upper Michigan. Calumet and Hecla seems to have had no official part in the plan. The initial goal was to form the Amalgamated Copper Company to take control of Anaconda and the mines operated by the Butte and Boston and Boston and Montana groups. These complex deals brought Leonard Lewisohn—a New York copper dealer who also was involved with the Old Dominion Mine in Arizona—and his associate R. S. Bigelow into the combination. Together Lewisohn and Bigelow controlled several mines in Michigan and Montana and thus were entirely familiar with pools and price manipulation.[21]

With the founding of Amalgamated in the fall of 1899, Rogers appointed Lewisohn as selling agent, but removed him within a year over a personal dispute.[22] At this point the group dominated 20 percent of world production. Starting in early 1899, it began restricting output, building an inventory of 93 million pounds by the end of 1900—which soared to 210 million pounds by the end of 1901. Prices rose from 12.4 cents in 1898 to 17.8 cents the following year, then held at 16.5 cents during 1900 and 1901. In 1902 the price collapsed by more than 25 percent. Rogers' ambitions had ended in failure for the usual reasons: Amalgamated was unable to control domestic, let alone world, supply; output and imports increased; scrap recovery expanded; exports fell. At no time thereafter was the domestic price of copper effectively manipulated upward by a private combination of producers unaided by a national government.[23]

On the contrary, from 1902 on, intervention in the U.S. domestic copper market was an affair of the federal government. It occurred first with World War I price controls when the ceiling price was set in 1917 at 23.5 cents per pound. In June 1918 the ceiling was lifted to 26 cents.[24] With the end of the war, inventories began to pile up and prices dropped sharply. By 1921 copper had fallen to 12.7 cents a pound. Meanwhile, in 1918 Congress had passed the Webb-Pomerene Act, which made legal the formation of export associations (cartels) through which producers could allocate sales among themselves to permit the orderly liquidation of excess stocks through sales abroad. To this end the industry formed the United Metals Selling Company in 1919, which took title to 50,000 tons of copper in the government reserve. Early in 1921 the Copper Export Association was formed to absorb 200,000 tons, against which $40 million was borrowed to pay off cash-starved producers.

These export associations must have had some short-run influence on domestic and foreign prices. But except for the period April 1929 through April 1930, it could not have been significant. Indeed, undercutting by outsiders and nonmembers was a continuous problem throughout the 1920s.[25] Perhaps the lack of success of these associations helps to explain the adoption of a 4-cent per pound import duty on copper in the Smoot-Hawley Tariff Act of June 1932. Instead of maintaining export prices through promotion of centrally controlled sales, the emphasis of government intervention shifted to raising the import price of copper.

In April 1934 the new approach—that of raising the domestic price—was taken still further, when the code for nonferrous metals was adopted under the National Industrial Recovery Act of 1933. Domestic sales quotas were created; users agreed to buy copper only through these quotas; and minimum prices could be imposed if "destructive price cutting" were to occur. The code succumbed when the U.S. Supreme Court killed the NIRA in May 1935.[26]

With World War II, government intervention returned. The import duty of 1932 was suspended. A price ceiling, with administrative allocation of copper supplies, was adopted at the level of 11.9 cents. Producers were encouraged to expand output. Marginal mines were paid a premium to cover costs in excess of the uniform ceiling. Those controls remained in effect until early 1946. Prices thereupon began to advance, averaging 13.9 cents for the whole year.

Competition or Monopoly?

The Lake Pools in the 1860s and 1870s were the most important and most effective attempt of domestic producers to control prices, precisely because of the dominance of the Michigan mines in the American market and the limited extent of import competition at the time. These producers had exclusive control of a comparatively small production site—the peninsula deposits, which embraced only 100 square miles. They were well organized; access to the market could be denied indirectly to new domestic producers. In 1869 foreign producers also were blocked when Congress helpfully imposed an import duty on copper. Not until the 1880s was the Michigan combination finally broken—by the spectacular series of new mines opened in Arizona and Montana. Unhampered access to new deposits was the obvious means for the pool's destruction.

The Secrétan corner, of course, was another private attempt to control price. But it was foreign and it was temporary. Without the enormous financial resources required to achieve the necessary control over worldwide production, it was doomed to fail. The Amalgamated Copper undertaking was an even more futile venture. It could not even control American production, let alone world production.

What remained in the price control field were government interventions (price ceilings and allocations in the two world wars), the export associations sponsored by the Webb-Pomerene Act, tariff duties, and the nonferrous code under the National Recovery Administration. The wartime controls flowed from the conviction that direct government regulation of price and materials allocations was the most efficient way to support modern warfare. To the extent that it is effective, this approach temporarily eliminates the competitive market.

As for the export associations and the NRA codes, both were government-sponsored devices in the service of the same end: to introduce a floor below which prices could not fall, instead of ceilings above which they could not rise. For extreme conditions of deflation, where markets are distressed by large amounts of excess supplies, there is the real possibility that short-run prices can fall below long-run costs of production and long-run demand. If the condition persists, business failures and the destruction of needed long-run production capacity can follow.

Such was the rationale for the formation of the copper export associations and the NRA code. It was also the technical justification for the production controls and price-raising schemes of the Agricultural Adjustment Act of 1933. To sum up, there is an economic case for these forms of government intervention *for the short-run circumstances existing at the time.* The real problem is that these circumstances eventually change, while pressures to keep the anticompetitive controls grow ever greater. This process did take place in American agriculture, but not in American copper. Yet there remain those who doubt that copper is a fully competitive industry, despite the absence for many decades of demonstrated private collusory activity.

In 1947 the Federal Trade Commission found it

difficult to see how a really independent and truly competitive open market can exist with three companies, Anaconda, Phelps Dodge and Kennecott, producing more than 80 percent of the primary copper, and with foreign copper barred from competition by the 4 cent duty. Furthermore, the fabricators integrated with the "big three" have first call on the copper produced by their mining operations.[27]

The implication is that size of firm provides the market dominance that can emerge, regardless of absolute firm size, when the number of sellers is few—in short, oligopoly.

In copper the number of sellers has never been small, even at the time of the Lake Pools. Arrayed in descending order of size by sales or output, the American copper firms have always presented a lopsided statistical distribution, with three or four leaders followed by a long tail of smaller firms, a total of twenty to twenty-five in the present century. This pattern, indeed, was exactly the one that defeated Rogers and Amalgamated in 1901. Rogers' reckless attempt has not been repeated since that time, for the only way to control price in this situation is either to acquire and combine all of the competition in a superfirm—which would have been impossible under the antitrust laws—or to form a cartel under central direction, with enforcement powers—also a ready target for civil and criminal prosecution under antitrust laws.

There were other forces that represented a continuing threat to private price fixing and price manipulation: increased imports from abroad, and the entry of new producers at home. Competition through commodity substitution of other metals for copper might also have been a factor, but technological developments of that kind did not become important until after World War II.

Imports began to gain in significance after 1915 with the development of the great Andean mines, followed over the next two decades by the opening of major deposits in Canada and Africa. Although American copper interests controlled the Andean mines, they did not dominate the other branches of foreign production in those years. Severe import competition would have held the American price to a margin equivalent to the COMEX price plus unit transportation costs, except for temporary circumstances. Furthermore, new firms could be, and in fact were, formed in the United States to develop new deposits. Here again was a source of supply that was beyond control by putative domestic monopolists.

It might still be contended that, absent any formal attempt at control, there would exist corespective competition (Schumpeter), in which no single large firm dares to change price for fear of reaction by its other large rivals (matching any cut but refusing to match a rise), while the numerous smaller producers would also hold prices steady for self-protection.[28] This reasoning applies, however, to cases of true oligopoly or fewness of sellers, which has not been true of copper even back to the Lake Pools. In short, the number of firms in American copper has always been too large to provide the stability that price rigidity requires. Empirically, too, copper prices have always changed frequently, even under the quotation system. There is no "normal price" to which all the producers adhere regardless of changes in the market.

Instead of price stability, there has been all of the price volatility to be expected with very low short-run elasticities of demand and supply. Industrial users cannot easily substitute for copper, and copper producers cannot vary rates of production by much. As a result, major shifts of demand will produce large changes in price, to ration scarce supply, while major shifts in supply will also have large effects on price. Thus a sharp fall in price does not appreciably increase sales because substitution is feasible only for longer periods.

To summarize, the price of copper showed a great deal of short-run flexibility between 1880 and 1946, except when price ceilings were imposed. At the same time, long-run nominal price represented a rare case of a declining trend in a major commodity. Finally, the deflated real price of copper during these years revealed a strongly declining trend, as technological and organizational improvements were introduced and passed through to buyers. Output rose with demand over the years, meaning that improvements in capacity were forthcoming as needed.[29]

None of these characteristics was at variance with what one might expect from a competitive industry. At the same time, the obvious traits of a monopoloid market structure—short-run price rigidity, long-run upward trends in nominal and real prices, persistent supernormal profits, stagnant technology, and lethargic management—were not lasting features of the industry over the many decades after 1880.

CHAPTER 5

THE ROOTS OF COPPER
INDUSTRY UNIONISM

THE CRITICAL FACTOR driving the American labor market in copper during the post–World War II period was the grafting onto the industry of a wage structure and pattern of work rules designed for another industry characterized by markedly different labor-market and product-market forces. To understand this occurrence and its economic consequences—a story told in Chapters 8 and 9—it is first necessary to understand the origin and the weaknesses of the Mine, Mill and Smelter Workers Union. Why was one of the three historic industrial unions within the American Federation of Labor, with roots going back about seventy-five years, swallowed by the CIO-originated United Steelworkers of America, only one-fourth its age?

INDUSTRIAL RELATIONS

Chapter 3 has traced the emergence of a copper industry in the United States. The historic union within the industry, however, had deeper roots. The more explosive industrial relations that accompanied the search for precious metals established the pattern which was the heritage of copper unionism.[1]

As long as employers were the lucky ones and employees the unlucky among the wave of prospectors who rushed to California in the 1850s and then washed backward through the mountains of the West during the decades that followed, there was little incentive for labor organization. Panning and placer mining required little capital and limited skill. One could pick up and move on, hoping for better luck tomorrow. The lure was always the mother lode from which the showings had washed. Ultimately, of course, the surface showings in a given area were exhausted and then it was necessary to abandon the site or go underground. When the choice was to move on, the high mobility of labor made the establishment and maintenance of a stable union impossible. When the choice was to go underground, a different dynamic emerged. Vernon Jensen begins his chronicle of the Western Federation of Miners with this potent statement:

> Men who have gone into the bowels of the earth to seek and toil for metals, precious and base, and those who have milled, smelted, and refined the ores, have given us a magnificent history. Parts of it are as fine, noble, and useful as the metals themselves. Other parts are as dark and foreboding as the deep recesses from which men have taken the valuable ores appear to nonminers. Much of it shows the cankering effect which metals have had on some men. The history is a story of human life in all its reaches and manifestations. Many of the episodes took place in the turbulent West, usually in camps and towns created solely by the activity of the mine and mill, without the moderating effect that people engaged in more sedentary economic pursuits give to the communities in which they reside. Even when mines were found near established communities based on other economic activity, the influence of mining on them was often pervasive and certainly unmistakable. In any event, every metal-producing center is marked by the selfsame telltale characteristics.
>
> The struggles of the hard-rock miner, the millman, and the smelterman, within the bowels of the earth, within the mill where the ores are crushed, and within the smelter where the metal is removed from the waste rock, and among themselves and with their employers reveal many heroic men. With them are also found those molded, not to say deformed, by the earth's wickedness and hardness. The rough-and-ready frontier-like conditions, so prevalent in the distant and isolated areas where mining and smelting have usually been undertaken, were highly formative.[2]

For underground mining it was no longer the lucky and the unlucky; it was capital and labor. New sets of skills were necessary. Ore had to be separated from rock with minimum expensive handling of dross. Except for the richest ores, machinery was needed to grind and crush the ore for transport to a smelter where the precious metals could be removed from the base. Mining engineers were required to keep the overburdening mountains from caving in on the hapless miners. Silver ore was generally found mixed with lead, copper, and zinc in either sulfide or oxide ores, which demanded more complex mining and smelting. Financiers who might never see a mine or meet a miner were essential to amass the capital to purchase machinery and to pay wages during the elongated process from exploration to pay dirt. Hired managers were necessary to represent the absentee wealthy or the anonymous stockholders. Miners, mill men, and smelter workers were no longer working temporarily for a grubstake before moving on to a new prospecting venture. They had become permanent, subordinate wage workers in an emergent industry. Their bosses were no longer simply the lucky ones among their peers but strangers, constrained to respond to the "bottom line" of impersonal financial systems unacquainted (and therefore unconcerned) with the exigencies or the dangers inherent in the extraction of wealth from the earth. The independence of the traditional miners (differentiated from the newly wealthy primarily by luck) was later diluted by the aggressive recruitment of immigrant workers, both to increase the production volume needed to support the investments and to promote docility among the work force. Later, the development of surface mining reduced the dangers but intensified the capital requirements, while doing nothing to diminish the social distance between management and labor.

The same dual incentives of mutual benefit and wage protection underlay the largely independent and sporadic emergence of local unions throughout the mining areas of Nevada, Utah, Idaho, Montana, and Colorado during the last third of the nineteenth century.[3] In the absence of any kind of insurance system or health care provisions for the miners and their families, the benefit objective fostered the most enduring concern. Nothing more seems to have emerged, however, than mechanisms for the collection of contributions or assessments to help meet the costs of accidents, illness, or death.[4]

The principal economic objective of these early local unions was a more sporadic one. Like most emerging labor organizations, the miners were faced with the need to take wages out of competition. But here the thrust was more often to protect customary wage rates against cuts than to pursue and win higher wages.[5]

As long as mines were locally and personally owned, and used labor-intensive production methods, ores which would not support customary pay rates could be ignored. Profit margins might narrow or mines temporarily close when the market price would not support costs at the customary wage rate. But absentee corporate owners had greater fixed costs and continuing dividend expectations to carry. Expansion of the mining industry brought new competitive pressures. With monetization of the economy came financial power and fluctuating market prices. Since most other costs were fixed, wages were an obvious point of attack to maintain profitability. Technological change, attraction of cheap labor, and wage cuts were the combined response to price pressures. The miners of the era did not generally resist technology, possibly because it was rudimentary and because it often reduced their physical exertion and risks. But they did attack personally and violently the Chinese and the groups of scab labor and strikebreakers brought into mining camps by employers during strikes, although they ignored or accepted individual migrants. They organized primarily against wage cuts.

From the Comstock lode of Nevada in the 1860s to Leadville, Colorado, in the 1880s, from the Coeur d'Alenes of Idaho and back to Cripple Creek, Colorado, in the 1890s, followed by the more general Colorado "labor war" at the turn of the century, the scenario for precious-metals mining was always similar.[6] Formal labor-management agreements did not exist. The accepted wage rate would be something like $4.00 per day, with the number of underground hours varying but eight the pursued objective. Pressed by market prices, the employer would cut the rate to $3.50 or even $3.00 per day. The employees then would organize and refuse to work for less than the customary rate.

The standard wage or the depression rate might be as much as $1.00 per day less at certain times and places, but the pattern was unvarying. The employers would hire "detective agencies" to recruit laborers from far away, bring them in by rail, use their own growing political power to have company or detective agency personnel deputized and the state militia called out when necessary to guard the strikebreakers. Violence would break out from both sides. With superior firepower in the hands of management, economic pressure ultimately would force the miners to surrender. Because of the superior skills of the experienced miners, they would be rehired at prestrike rates and the imported labor would be displaced. Leaders among the strikers would be identified, sometimes deported from the community, and often blackballed throughout the industry. Market pressures would ease and, with the need to restore employer-employee relations and productivity, the customary rate would be restored until the next recurrence. Meanwhile, the early unions were also pursuing legislation to establish the eight-hour day underground.[7]

FEDERATION

The mine-owner policy of driving from their camps strike leaders and those assumed to be most prone to union organization had the perverse result of assuring the spread of union experience and encouraging links among independent local unions. More substantively, few miners accumulated any significant savings. Strikers would quickly be starved out without contributions from those working at other mines. Few of the local unions maintained a formal structure with consistent dues payment and regular meetings during periods of no disputes with employers. Although working miners appear to have been reasonably generous with their striking or locked-out compatriots, there was no formal machinery for collecting and transferring moneys between the independent local unions. Taking wages out of competition was a first principle of unionism. Otherwise, it was held, competition would drive all wages to the lowest paid within the product market. Control of the labor market also required a closed shop and some method of orderly transfer of experienced miners from one local union to another, so that they would not become a source of skilled help willing to work below the established scale.[8] All of these forces drove the independent local unions emerging in camps throughout the West toward formal affiliation.

Western Federation of Miners

Thus is was that in May 1893 forty representatives from fifteen miners' unions met for five days in Butte, Montana, to establish the Western Federation of Miners.[9] Their objectives were pay compatible with the dangers of their employment; pay in lawful money, spendable wherever the miner rather than the employer chose; safe and healthy workplaces guaranteed by law as well as by appropriate equipment and employer policies; abolition of employer-paid armed forces, convict labor, and child labor; repeal of conspiracy laws; employment preference for union members; and education for miners' children.

It was a time of serious depression and widespread unemployment. The new and unstable organization lacked the resources to help any of its affiliates or to mount a substantial organizing effort. It also lacked experienced leadership. In 1896 at Leadville, Colorado, the WFM for the first time entered as a body into a strike action.[10] The depression rate of $3.00 a day was cut to $2.50. The Leadville miners struck, with WFM support. The mine owners imported strikebreakers. In the ensuing violence four union miners were killed. The mines reopened under military protection and the strike was broken.

Obviously, more than the miners' resources were needed. Hoping to obtain funds, organizers, and/or pressure on the users of mined products, the WFM in 1896 affiliated with the American Federation of Labor.[11] However, the fifteen-year-old "House of Labor" was itself strapped for resources and the scattered reaches of the West were not high among its priorities. When petitioned for support of strikes in Colorado and Idaho, the AFL circularized its constituent national and local unions for financial and moral assistance. The response was meager in both respects. Correspondence from AFL president Samuel Gompers to WFM president Edward Boyce advised patient negotiation with employers at the very time when violence was escalating on both sides in the mining camps.[12] Miners were replying to company guards with gun battles and dynamiting of company facilities.[13] Boyce replied that there were more effective means than strikes to win industrial conflicts, declaring himself disposed to "get out and fight with the sword or use the ballot with intelligence."[14] Disillusioned, the 1898 WFM convention formally voted to withdraw from the AFL.[15]

Western disenchantment with the AFL was not limited to the miners. Therefore, western locals of a number of other national unions as well as several independent local ones, state federations of labor, and city trade and labor councils, responded to a WFM call to meet in 1898 to form the Western Labor Union.[16] In 1902 the WLU established an office in Chicago and changed its name to the American Labor Union, seeking to position itself as an alternative to the AFL.[17] Even though the moral support was greater, financial assistance was no more forthcoming from the regional federation than it had been from the national federation. For the Western Federation of Miners, the WLU/ALU was only an added burden, because the WFM was the major underwriter of the attempted broader western and national body.

The Wobblies (Industrial Workers of the World)

At the same time as the miners were trying to extend their organization for mutual support, the mine owners were organizing on a statewide basis, concurrently with a national open-shop movement of all employers.[18] In their case, they did not share financial resources, only communication on blacklists of union activists and political pressure on elected officials. The concerted antagonism of the employers, their superior political as well as economic power, and their ability to obtain the frequent intervention of governmental power on their behalf were radicalizing forces among the miners. Looking back on the labor situation of the western mines from the vantage point of thirty years later, objective historians were to describe it as "class war on a grand scale."[19] The strife that spread across Colorado in 1903–1904, including a declaration of martial law, was to become known historically as the Colorado labor wars.[20]

The modest initial program of the WFM to secure fair compensation and safe working conditions through education, organization, legislation, and arbitration gave way to declarations against capitalism and the advocacy of socialism, to be accomplished by violence if necessary. Yet the struggling union lacked the resources to carry out these threats. The skills of its members were too easily replaceable. Neither they nor their union could withstand the income loss for a period long enough to win employer concessions. The occasional tepid attempts of AFL affiliates to organize craft workers around the mines, and the Western Federation's residual antagonism from the earlier lack of AFL support, caused the WFM to deride the federation as a lackey of the capitalist class, its most generous sin being "perpetuation of outgrown, artificial craft divisions which only kept the workers pitted against one another, thus weakening their resistance to capitalist tyranny.[21] Yet practically every WFM strike was being lost, and the cooperation and assistance of some broader labor body was considered essential.

Establishment of the American Labor Union office in Chicago did serve the purpose of giving the WFM contact with other disaffected and dissatisfied units of the budding organized labor movement. There emerged an informal meeting in January 1905 of representatives of the United Brewery Workers, the United Brotherhood of Railway Employees, the United Metal Workers—each a fledgling national industrial union—a few local unions, the Socialist Party, the Socialist Labor Party, and the Socialist Trade and Labor Alliance.[22]

A manifesto was drawn up stressing the increasingly united front of employers' associations that exercised brutal force, injunctions, and military power to crush any show of labor organization. Machines were displacing labor, it was said, while growing concentration in ownership of the tools of production was sharpening class antagonisms and sinking otherwise proud workers into the status of wage slaves. At the same time, the manifesto argued, the artificial division along craft lines was diminishing the already weak power of workers to resist. Trade monopolies were being formed with excessive initiation fees, and union men were scabbing on one another. Workers, ignorant of their potential political power, were as divided at the ballot box as they were on the picket line. The AFL was seen as hindering the growth of class consciousness and fostering the erroneous doctrine of harmony of interest between employee and employer. Said the manifesto:

> Previous efforts for the betterment of the working class have proven abortive because limited in scope and disconnected in action. Universal economic evils afflicting the working class can be eradicated only by a universal working class movement . . . of one great industrial union embracing all industries . . . founded on the class struggle . . . with recognition of the irrepressible conflict between the capitalist class and the working class.[23]

The manifesto was circulated as widely as possible to local and national unions throughout the country. All who agreed with its premises were invited to a formal convention in Chicago in June 1905 to organize implementation of those principles.

Some forty labor organizations responded. The only national unions to join were the Western Federation of Miners, Eugene Debs's United Brotherhood of Railway Employees, the United Metal Workers International Union, the United Brotherhood of Carpenters and Joiners, the Metal Polishers and Buffers Union, the International Musicians' Union, and the Hotel and Restaurant Workers.[24] The rest were local bodies, either independent or not authorized to represent their nationals. Of the national unions, only the Hotel and Restaurant Workers was at the time an AFL affiliate, though many of the local unions were. A number of those in attendance were sent as observers, without power to bind their organizations. Among the rest, voting power was distributed by organization membership. Of the 51,000 total available votes, the WFM held 27,000 and the American Labor Union (of which the WFM was the largest

affiliate) had 16,750. The United Metal Workers had 3,000 votes, and the
United Brotherhood of Railway Employees 2,087. Both were also affiliates of the ALU. The Socialist Trade and Labor Alliance was awarded
1,450 votes, leaving less than 1,000 votes for all others in attendance.[25]
The American Labor Union, the Socialist Trade and Labor Alliance, and
the United Metal Workers were all in an advanced stage of disintegration.
Hence, the WFM was the only stable labor organization of any substance
involved.

All that united the delegates was a commitment to industrial unionism, a
preference for socialism, and an opposition to the AFL. They were sharply
divided over whether to "bore from within" the existing trade unions or to
advocate withdrawal into One Big Union; whether to pursue "pure and
simple" trade unionism dedicated to improvement in wages, hours, and
working conditions or to push for political reform; whether to maintain
ideological purity at all costs or to indulge in pragmatic pursuit of short-
run, concrete goals.[26] All of those issues were left hanging at the end of the
first convention—but from it emerged the Industrial Workers of the
World.

The history of the IWW, and WFM's involvement in it, might have been
quite different if Charles H. Moyer, the WFM president (after Boyce
became a mine owner), along with William D. Haywood, WFM secretary,
and George A. Pettibone, a Denver small-businessman and former Idaho
miners' union leader, had not been kidnapped from Colorado in early
1906 and spirited off to Idaho to be tried for the murder of ex-Idaho
Governor Frank Steunenberg.[27] One Harry Orchard, a shadowy figure
who vacillated between union involvement and employment as a detective
agency labor spy, had confessed to planting the bomb which killed Steunenberg, but the issue was whether he had been instructed to do so by the
WFM leadership.[28]

By the time Clarence Darrow, in one of the famous trials of labor
history, won the freedom of Haywood and Pettibone late in 1907, with
charges against Moyer finally being dropped, the IWW had undertaken
and lost a number of strikes.[29] The second IWW convention had been
marked by warring between the Socialist Party and the Socialist Labor
Party, charges and countercharges among IWW leaders over the handling
of the limited treasury, and withdrawal of a number of earlier affiliates.[30]
The WFM had been the most influential labor body at the formative 1905
IWW convention, and Moyer and Haywood had been its most influential
representatives. After declining to be president, Moyer had been elected to

CHAS. MOYER, Denver, Colo.

Charles H. Moyer (187?–1929). A pioneer labor leader in Western mining, Moyer began as a smelterman for Homestake Mining in Lead, South Dakota. In 1902 he succeeded Edward Boyce as president of the Western Federation of Miners (WFM). In this post he was an early advocate of industrial unionism and a firm believer in collective bargaining and long-term agreements. Bitter strikes in Cripple Creek and Telluride, Colorado, broken by the state militia, turned Moyer into a socialist for a time, but without changing his view of unionism. In 1905 he helped found the Industrial Workers of the World (IWW), with WFM as an affiliate. As a result of disputes with revolutionary syndicalists in the IWW, he took the WFM out of the IWW and later back to the AFL. Attacks by the wobblies caused dissolution of the WFM in 1914 and formation of the Mine Mill Union in 1916. Moyer was its first president until his ouster in 1926. (*Photo courtesy of Cassandra M. Volpe, Archivist, University of Colorado.*)

Encounter on a street corner in Butte, in 1920. On the far left is Cornelius F. Kelley, president and later chairman of Anaconda; next is John D. Ryan, probably the best chief executive the company ever had; next is J. Bruce Kremer, a prominent Butte attorney and member of the Democratic National Committee from 1908; and last, Senator William Andrews Clark, major mining operator in Butte and Arizona, and historic adversary of Marcus Daly. These four dapper gentlemen were attending a convention of bankers in Butte. (*Photo courtesy of C. Owen Smithers, Butte, Montana.*)

the IWW executive board. Without the two leaders there was limited continuity of WFM representation between the first and second IWW conventions. Therefore, the WFM was a less stabilizing influence than it might otherwise have been when a divisive split arose within the IWW, in which the more revolutionary and less bargaining-oriented faction prevailed.[31] Since WFM delegates were found on both sides of the IWW squabble, the divisiveness carried over into the 1907 WFM convention, with the union coming close to a split itself.[32]

Upon his release from prison, Moyer attempted to heal the IWW rupture, but WFM intervention was rejected by those who had won the IWW leadership. Under the ideology of the new directors, all of the officers of the WFM, the United Mine Workers, the Brewery Workers, and the Lithographers would have had to resign. Even more, these unions would have had to repudiate all contracts with employers and all check-off systems in order to remain in the IWW.[33] Thereupon Moyer, whose interests were turning in the more conservative direction of business unionism, led the 1908 WFM convention into a withdrawal from the IWW. While Moyer was in prison, a split had occurred between Haywood and himself. Having become radicalized, Haywood cast his lot with the IWW and ultimately left the country to die in the Soviet Union.[34]

Challenged by the WFM's drift toward "pure and simple" trade unionism, the IWW launched a long-range policy of infiltrating WFM locals, seeking to capture the politically militant among them. A letter to that effect later fell into Moyer's hands.[35] Meanwhile, the two organizations found themselves in conflict in a number of strike situations, with the WFM increasingly seeking recognition and written agreements with employers and the IWW disdaining such conservative relationships. Employers hired detectives to infiltrate both groups and use them against each other. To the IWW, the WFM with its new conservatism was no different from the "labor fakirs" of the AFL and therefore an appropriate target for enmity.

While the WFM, as an industrial union, claimed jurisdiction over all "workers in and around the mines," the IWW sought to enlist all workers in the mining towns, including those in stores, banks, telegraph offices, and newspapers. Class, not product, industry, or organization was the only criterion for membership. Accordingly, the IWW came into more direct conflict with craft unions such as the printers than did the WFM. Since the IWW and WFM jurisdictional claims were not coextensive, the IWW had incentive to attempt to enroll WFM members in its broader, class-oriented organizations. In cases when the WFM and IWW were pursuing the same employers, the IWW sometimes called a strike first to take credit for militancy and then refused to compromise when employers were willing to grant concessions to the somewhat more acceptable WFM.[36] The IWW still disdained contractual relations with employers. While still with the WFM, Haywood had bragged: "We have not got an agreement existing with any mine manager, superintendent, or operator at the present time. We have got a minimum scale of wages and the eight hour day, and we did not have a legislative lobby to accomplish it."[37] As secretary of the IWW, he could reinforce that philosophy, whereas the WFM under Moyer would have welcomed the stability of a collective bargaining agreement. Some employers expressed themselves as willing to negotiate with the WFM locals but not with the IWW, further setting the two labor organizations at odds. And these enticingly dangled contractual agreements remained as elusive as ever.

Vernon Jensen concludes his chapter on the IWW with the sentence, "Paradoxically, the IWW frequently were found effectively accomplishing a result which the employers desired—the destruction of WFM unions."[38] Moyer's continuance until 1924 at the head of the less ideological union ensured that the two organizations remained bitter enemies until the IWW's disappearance from the industrial scene, destroyed as an employee organization by its opposition to U.S. involvement in World War I.

Reaffiliation

Having broken with the IWW, the WFM abandoned its ambitions for a restructuring of society. The WFM leaders as individuals did not necessarily abandon their preference for socialism; however, their advocacy appears to have been more a reaction to what they viewed as an unholy alliance between employers and governments than an ideological commitment to public ownership of industry. Lacking the political power to effect a change of government, the WFM became focused solely on traditional objectives—wages, hours, and working conditions. Indeed, without Haywood, the entire WFM leadership took on a more conservative cast. The more militant and radical individuals maintained dual membership in the WFM and the IWW, which led to continued local dissension. But the WFM after 1908 largely confined its political action to pursuit of the eight-hour day and to limitation on the use of state militias in labor disputes.

The WFM continued to hunger for support from others within the labor movement. The Western Labor Union, American Labor Union, and IWW efforts had all proved abortive because their alliances were with those who were even weaker than themselves. Some movement back and forth between metal mines and coal mines was occurring, and the WFM and the United Mine Workers of America recognized each others' membership cards.[39] The UMW leadership was sympathetic to the hard-rock miners and responded more generously than any other union to the WFM appeal for funds to support the Idaho trials of its leaders. Yet there was no ambition to extend the union's jurisdiction outside coal mining. The UMW and the United Brewery Workers, as the only two substantial industrial unions, were gaining more influence within the AFL. The WFM was also beginning to extend its organizing efforts to miners outside the West, such as in the copper mines of Michigan, lead mines of Missouri, iron mines of Minnesota, and to smelter workers in other states. In the process it overextended its minimal organizing staff and never had the means to service those it enlisted.

When Moyer returned actively to the presidency of the WFM in 1908, he initiated an exchange of fraternal convention delegations between the WFM and the UMW. By 1910 the UMW was recommending to the executive council of the AFL the reaffiliation of the WFM and the establishment of a special mining department for both organizations. The proposed WFM jurisdiction (as cited in Jensen's *Heritage of Conflict*) was all work in the "metalliferous and mineral mining industries" except coal mining, including "all underground and surface wage-workers in said industries, also all of those employed in mills, smelters, refineries and other reduction works which treat the product of said mines" (p. 240). This sweeping jurisdictional claim aroused the immediate opposition of the craft unions, especially the Machinists and the Steam Engineers, who claimed jurisdiction over these crafts in the mining camps. Some WFM units, notably the strongest locals in Butte, resisted reaffiliation for fear they might be restrained from exercising their jurisdictional ambitions. Gompers recommended to both sides that the WFM be allowed to affiliate, but let time and negotiation settle the jurisdictional issue. Only the threat of the UMW to withdraw from the federation brought the AFL's reluctant acceptance of WFM in 1911.

On the surface, the jurisdictional issue was left unsettled. The WFM never aggressively pursued the enlistment of craft workers but continued as a union of semiskilled miners and smelter workers, ultimately engaging in coalition bargaining with the craft unions. By 1911, therefore, the WFM was back in the House of Labor, one of three significant industrial unions within an organization dominated by crafts, and at a time when socialist political leanings were not that unusual among unionists. Nevertheless, these events had at least three troublesome implications for the future: (1) the WFM and its successors could never become true industrial unions because of the mining and milling employees outside their occupational scope; (2) the crafts would be guaranteed status as independent bargaining units once the National Labor Relations Act was in force after 1935; and (3) the pattern of multiple unionism with decentralized local bargaining was locked in for an interminable future.

ORGANIZATION

The AFL endorsement may have been heartwarming, but it made no difference in the WFM's persistent defeats by the employers. New discoveries of precious metals declined at about the same time that the development of electricity and the acceleration of industrialization were expanding the demand for the base metal, copper. We have already seen that the Michigan copper range was the only important U.S. source before electrification, beginning as early as 1845; however, other copper deposits were known and could be developed as demand warranted. Silver mines at Bingham and Butte were transformed into predominantly copper mines simultaneous with electrification during 1881–1906, as also happened sporadically in smaller properties in Nevada. The rich copper deposits of Arizona were developed during the same period. Initially, copper mining used the same selective techniques as did mining of precious metals; that is, the restricted higher-valued deposits of ore were followed wherever they led. As the richer deposits were exhausted, different technologies and mining methods were required to move and process massive amounts of dross material to capture small amounts of pay dirt. First underground block caving and then aboveground open-pit mining became economically essential after the turn of the century.

   The new methods required much greater capital investment and a different skill mix for labor. If anything, craft requirements were expanded, whereas the numbers and skills required of hard-rock miners were lessened. The WFM suffered the handicaps of being an industrial union before government support made that organizational form viable. At the same time, the alliances between mine owners and the local and state political figures who used deputized company guards and detective agencies along with state militias did not change. The union's limited treasury was constantly drained for strike benefits; no major strike was won before the 1930s.

Even before its reaffiliation with the AFL, the WFM had hesitantly begun to expand its jurisdiction beyond the western mines. Organizing the Missouri lead mines was a defensive measure.[40] As a doorway to the vast surplus labor reserves of the nonindustrial South, the Missouri mines were a training and recruiting ground for strikebreakers for the western properties. Of course, this apparently inexhaustible labor supply also thwarted organizational efforts.

The major obstacle confronted by WFM organizers in the Minnesota iron mines was language and national origin. Eighty-five percent of the employees were foreign born, primarily in Finland, Italy, and the Slavic countries.[41] Living and working conditions were poor, but the organizers could not communicate with the non-English-speaking workers and the employing subsidiaries of the steel companies were effective in playing the nationalities against one another. Disastrous strikes in 1907 and 1913–1914 seriously tainted the image of the WFM in the region. It was finally the Steelworkers Organizing Committee (SWOC) in the 1930s which, backed by federal legislation, finally brought unionization to the iron mines, in both Minnesota and Alabama.

Chapter 3 traced the development of the U.S. copper industry in a geographic sequence from Michigan to Arizona to Montana to Utah. The history of industrial relations in the industry followed quite another sequence. The difference was the union's roots in precious metals.[42] The copper properties in Montana and Utah began as sources of silver and related metals, with copper production evolving later. The seedbeds of mining unionism were the silver and gold mines of Nevada, northern Idaho, and Colorado, in none of which copper ever became important. Miners from those sites found their way to Butte and to Park City, Eureka, and Bingham in Utah. There they established bases for unionism which were inherited as Butte and Bingham became copper operations. By contrast, the Michigan mines lacked a history of precious metals. Mining in Arizona began with silver, but the isolation of the Arizona territory, the remote location of the mines, the harsh desert conditions, and the lasting resistance of its Indian tribes made the area an unusually hostile environment for unionism, which was later imported into the state from a copper rather than a precious-metals base.

Montana as a Copper Producer

The Butte Miners' Union No. 1 became the largest local in the WFM in part because Butte was home to the biggest copper-mining operation in the nation. For peculiar political reasons, it was the wealthiest and financially the most generous local in the national union.

In Chapter 3 we traced the company history of Butte's transition from gold to silver to copper. There we introduced Marcus Daly, Frederick Augustus (Fritz) Heinze, and Senator William A. Clark, but we did not note their political competition, which was to have an indirect yet strong influence on the history of the Western Federation of Miners. Following Montana's acceptance into statehood in 1889, Clark, owner of two highly profitable mines, wanted to become a United States senator, a position filled in that era through appointment by the state legislature.[43] During the 1893 legislative session, Daly of the Anaconda Copper Mining Company used his influence to block such an appointment. Daly wanted Anaconda, his smelter city, to become the state capital. Clark retaliated in an 1894 referendum by successfully backing Helena. (Between them he and Daly spent nearly $3 million, or $56 for each vote cast.) In 1899, through generous bribes, Clark finally purchased the legislative appointment, but Daly persuaded the Senate not to seat him. Clark and Heinze, previously enemies, united to fight Daly. Heinze's political motive was to protect the tenure in office of his bought and paid-for district judge, William Clancy, who was providing him with favorable decisions in his apex suits and contested mining claims.

In that setting Daly, Clark, and Heinze needed all of the votes they could get. In Butte, Montana's area of largest population, that meant the miners' votes. The seeds of unionization had been brought to Butte by the gold and silver miners from Nevada and Idaho. With expansion of the copper industry, those seeds sprouted into three separate WFM locals—one of miners, one of mill and smelter men, and one of engineers—each concentrated in a different area of the Butte complex. Rather than experiencing the familiar violent employer opposition, labor organization was now welcomed by the Copper Kings as a means of marshaling political support. All of the mining companies were united with their employees too in their championship of free coinage of silver, another reason for catering to the labor vote.

The silver-tongued Heinze positioned himself as champion of the working man against the monopolist trust, a war cry made more plausible by the merger of Anaconda with Amalgamated. To win allegiance, the Clark and Heinze companies granted the miners their long-sought eight-hour day with no cut in pay.[44] Amalgamated resisted, but could not afford to stay far behind in the contest. Pitched battles often raged underground, with Heinze employees persistently breaking through into Amalgamated properties to abscond with the rich ores.

Full employment at relatively high wages gave the Butte locals the numbers and the means to assist other struggling WFM locals. But the competition among employers for the political loyalties of their employees also divided the loyalties of the union members. That schism would ultimately destroy the Butte locals and almost bankrupt the parent union.

The three-way employer competition for worker votes had corrupted both the Republican and Democratic parties. The populist goal of free silver coinage had been pursued in Montana through the People's Party, which also endorsed labor's goals of the eight-hour day, abolition of child labor, workplace health and safety laws, and free public education. As the free silver issue faded after the defeat of William Jennings Bryan in 1896, the People's Party became the labor party under the Montana Federation of Labor and emerged as the Socialist Party of Montana in 1902. Thereafter, the Butte WFM members were divided among the Democratic Party and opposing conservative and progressive factions within the Socialist Party.[45]

The other dimension dividing union loyalties was ideology. During the period that the Butte miners were being coddled by their employers, most of them did not share the radicalism of their union brothers in other states, who were being bludgeoned by the harsh combination of employer power and governmental authority. Their "socialist" party advocated a variety of reforms but limited its public-ownership advocacy to public utilities. The Butte locals opposed affiliation with the AFL—but because of jurisdictional conflicts with the AFL craft unions, not because of any contempt for AFL conservatism. The majority of Butte miners were in opposition to the development of the Western Labor Union, the American Labor Union, and, finally, the IWW. Their goals involved wages, hours, and working conditions, all of which they felt able to win. Despite a militant business unionism, their prevailing view was strongly antisyndicalist.

The political war of the Copper Kings was to last a decade and a half. The truce with labor died in the process. First, Clark made his peace with Anaconda, allegedly in return for a promise not to oppose the Senate confirmation he finally won. When in 1903 Judge Clancy handed down a particularly grievous decision, Amalgamated flexed its muscles by shutting down and throwing 15,000 wage earners out of work.[46] With winter coming on, the situation was sufficiently desperate for the governor to call a December special session of the legislature, which met all of the company's demands. Perceiving defeat, Heinze sold out to Amalgamated and left the state.

Without Clark and Heinze, the union lost its balance-of-power position. The locals were soon split between conservatives who, recognizing their lack of bargaining power, resolved to be as cooperative with the company as possible, and progressives who wanted to fight on at any cost. The progressives were furious in 1907, when the conservative leadership signed a five-year contract with Amalgamated for a wage that would vary with copper prices. At the next WFM convention they accused their conservative colleagues of having violated the historical WFM policy against any time-bound contractual agreement with an employer.[47] The contract, already signed, was allowed to stand.

Butte delegates were among the leaders in accomplishing the 1908 withdrawal of the WFM from the IWW. The IWW resolved to infiltrate, capture, or disrupt the Montana WFM locals, capitalizing on their inherent disunity. Soon they were prominent within the progressive wings of both the union and the Socialist Party, which provided the Butte city administration from 1912 to 1915. During that period IWW members became so internally disruptive that they were purged from the party in 1913.[48]

Amalgamated fought the Socialist Party by frequently discharging socialists and by refusing to allow the miners time off to vote. It manipulated union elections by making voting day a holiday and then using its influence on behalf of conservative candidates. The conservative leaders rewarded the company in 1912 by extending the existing price-linked contract, which had resulted in no wage increase since 1907. Nor did the contract contain health and safety provisions, despite the fact that job conditions were deteriorating.[49]

During the same year the company discharged 500 miners for their socialist political affiliation, while the union refused to take retaliatory action. The company had played "divide and conquer" by discharging primarily Finns, whom the predominant Irish were not anxious to support. All of the Butte mining companies followed up with the introduction of a "rustling card" system. To be considered for employment at any mine, an application had to be filled out at a company employment office. References were checked and, if the investigation proved satisfactory, the applicant was given a card authorizing him to look for work. If found undesirable, he was frozen out of consideration for employment. Upon being hired, he surrendered the card; so if he was laid off he had to go through the same process again. If his previous employer labeled him a troublemaker, he could not get another card. When the progressives put through a referendum to strike about this blacklisting process, the conservative leaders merely ignored it.

Throughout this growing internal strife, president Moyer of the WFM supported the conservative faction, but its members did not reciprocate. The Butte locals opposed reaffiliation with the AFL and ran opponents to Moyer at WFM conventions.[50] As the largest concentration of membership in the WFM, the Butte locals opposed further assessments to meet the financial needs of the united body and demanded repayment of loans they had made to the WFM during the Idaho trials.

The strife between conservatives and progressives within the Butte locals came to a head in a dispute over the conduct of the June 1914 election within the Butte Miners' Union.[51] When the progressives' demand for use of voting machines rather than printed ballots was refused, they boycotted the election. The result was the reelection of what was characterized as "the company slate." Instead of the usual parade on Miners Union Day, a legal holiday in Butte, a mob raided, wrecked, and pillaged the union hall. An insurgent-dominated referendum the following day voted 6,348 to 243 to leave the WFM and AFL and to form a new, unaffiliated organization of the same name. When Moyer arrived a few days later in an attempt to quell the revolt, few showed up for his talk at the wrecked meeting hall. While he was speaking, an armed crowd estimated at 150 attacked the hall. One man was killed; Moyer and his supporters fled via the fire escape. The mob then dynamited the hall.[52] Moyer attributed the rebellion to the IWW, estimating its membership as 600. The IWW disclaimed responsibility, stating that its adherents in Butte numbered no more than 100 and could have succeeded only by exploiting latent discontent.

By the first of August, the new Butte Miners' Union had signed up 500 members but had not yet been recognized by the mining companies. Amalgamated chose that moment to lay off 2,000 workers, blaming the severe depression in the copper market consequent to the outbreak of war in Europe. When the committees from the new local union began to show up at the mine entrances examining cards to enforce a closed shop, the company and leading Butte businessmen informed the governor that an insurrection was in progress and demanded that the National Guard be sent to restore order. Although the sheriff agreed, the socialist mayor protested the action. When a company employment office was damaged by dynamite early one Sunday morning, the governor responded with the National Guard and martial law.[53] The insurgent leaders were jailed until their sentences were voided by the Montana Supreme Court a few months later. A blacklist of union supporters was circulated and many left the area. With the continuing mining depression, a nonunion job was preferable to no job. Those who were allowed back returned to work.

Except for the small engineers' local, the WFM was dead in Montana. Not until after the passage of the National Labor Relations Act in 1935 would its successor, the Mine, Mill and Smelter Workers Union, be able to revive industrial unionism in the state. But labor unrest did not disappear in the interim. The AFL craft unions survived. The unaffiliated local union continued, but the combination of company gunmen and the rustling card left it powerless. Rising profits and prices, without accompanying wage increases, provided tinder that was set off by a mine explosion and fire in June 1917 killing 164 men. IWW organizers hurried in to revive the moribund independent miners' union, leading close to 12,000 miners into a strike joined by the AFL crafts.[54] Federal mediators persuaded the crafts to return to work shortly, but with no concessions from the employers, the miners remained out until September and then returned to work accompanied by malingering and low productivity.

Local vigilantes responded by lynching an IWW organizer.[55] Federal troops moved in to protect copper production. Concerted governmental pressures gradually throttled the IWW nationally. Failure of an IWW-called 1918 general strike throughout the West, including Butte, essentially marked the end of miners' unionism in Montana until its revival in the 1930s.

Utah

The Utah story is a shorter one. There simply was no significant copper-mining unionism in the state until the Second World War. The territory's silver and lead mines were developed primarily by prospecting soldiers before and during the Civil War. The Mormon population was devoted to community rather than individual interests, with the development of an agricultural base the first priority.[56] Some of the early Mormon leaders were active in mining developments and some Mormon labor was available to the mines on a temporary basis. As miners' pay over the years became more attractive than subsistence agriculture, some of the local population began to divide their time between jobs and farms. Few had the long-run interest to devote themselves to union organization. Unionism rose and declined according to the ebb and flow of veterans from the mining camps of surrounding states, but never took firm root. Furthermore, the Utah mines tended to be small with direct contact between owners and employers and a minimum of absentee ownership. The eight-hour day underground was guaranteed by law when the territory became a state in 1896, removing one traditional labor-management issue from controversy. There were at least fifteen WFM locals in the Utah precious-metal mines at the turn of the century, but no sign of labor ferment.[57]

The existing organized camps were all small and not adjacent to the Bingham Canyon property when the absentee-owned Utah Copper Company arrived on the scene in 1903. Daniel Jackling's approach to labor organization was total opposition, which he manifested by simply ignoring it. The open-pit expansion occurred simultaneously with the flood tide of immigration from southern Europe. The bulk of the mine labor required was unskilled. Local labor was not available for rapid recruitment even if it had been preferred. The steam shovel operators, railroad men, and skilled maintenance people had their own AFL craft unions. Greek and Slav immigrants without local ties became the majority of the copper mine, mill, and smelter work force. WFM locals emerged among them but were powerless. For unlike an underground mine, which might fill with water or face the threat of fire during a long strike, an open pit could easily be shut down to wait out a strike.

Periodically, and to no avail, Bingham miners requested wage increases. In one instance in 1909, 300 Greeks demanded a 50-cent-per-day increase in their $1.75 wage, and a one-hour cut in their ten-hour day. Ignored for over a month, they finally walked out. They subsequently went back to work with a 25-cent increase for the ten hours. When shortly afterward a young Greek was shot by a company guard for stealing coal, the community applauded.[58] In 1912 the WFM and the AFL craft unions combined to demand a 50-cent-per-day pay increase. The company ignored the unions but posted notice of a 25-cent increase. Thereupon all but the railroad brotherhoods struck. The company's response, with the support of the sheriff, was to import gunmen. A group of more than 500 Greek miners offered to go back to work at the existing rate if the company would simply eliminate the Greek "labor czar" to whom they had to pay tribute and whose store they had to patronize in order to retain their jobs. The company replied that it was paying the individual a salary for the legitimate task of obtaining Greek workers for the mine.

Accosted by newspaper reporters, Jackling refused to discuss the labor situation. When they asked about the importation of gunmen, he responded that the strike was caused by outside agitators from whom the company must protect itself. The company was going to resume operations, if that required "throwing out all the union men and replacing them with nonunion men."[59] When the Nevada group struck in sympathy with the Utah miners, the company refused arbitration. It resumed production with Italian strikebreakers and gradually returning miners, the deputized gunmen dealing forcefully with any interference.

Over the succeeding years there were periodic waves of IWW agitation but no further effective union organization in the Utah copper industry. The 1930s and the Wagner Act brought some resurgence of unionization in the precious-metal mines but not among the employees of Utah Copper or ASARCO. That awaited World War II and the support of the War Labor Board.

Michigan

The Michigan copper range was never successfully organized. The impenetrable defenses of the employers were isolation and paternalism. The WFM made sporadic efforts from 1904 to 1914, in part at the instigation of the Montana employers, who resented the competition of copper mined at lower wage rates. However, there was no preexisting base of precious-metal mining and no interacting flow of miners from the western mines.

The Michigan copper range was on the Keeweenaw peninsula, extending into Lake Superior in Upper Michigan. In this physically isolated region, housing had to be provided and food stored for the long, severe winters. The Calumet and Hecla Company established the towns and either built the housing or allowed workers to build their own homes on company land.[60] The company owned the stores and built the schools, churches, and other public buildings, including the armory for the local militia. It provided the electricity, gathered the garbage, and employed the public servants. On election day the polls were supervised by company officials; voters had to verbally request either Democratic or Republican ballots. Even employees of the independent mines relied on the Calumet and Hecla community infrastructure. The company was also aggressive in the organized importation of labor directly from Europe to offset labor shortages the isolated location might have engendered.[61]

This paternalism inevitably generated some discontent. Sporadic spontaneous strikes occurred between the Civil War and the end of the century, but except for a few brief and ineffective appearances of the Knights of Labor, there was no apparent connection to any labor organization. The weight of law and militia was readily available when management called; strikes were brief, except for a three-week shutdown in 1872.[62]

A slowing of immigration tightened the labor market after 1905. An independent local union was formed at about that time; it affiliated with the WFM but disappeared within two years. WFM organizers appeared again in 1909 to point out that Montana miners were averaging $3.87 for an eight-hour day and those in Arizona $3.40, compared to Michigan's $2.36 for ten or eleven hours. By 1912 five WFM locals had been established, but progress continued to be slow until Calumet and Hecla introduced the one-man drill, which threatened both job security and job safety. Even though the union tried to postpone strike action until its strength had increased, the internal pressures proved too great and a strike was called in July 1913.

In a fashion typical of an earlier period in the West, the company hired a detective agency and the county sheriff deputized 1,700 of their men. At the sheriff's behest, the governor also sent in the entire Michigan National Guard and the company hired and imported nearly 3,000 strikebreakers. Supportive visitations by labor notables such as Mother Jones, John Mitchell, John L. Lewis, and Clarence Darrow were of no avail.[63] Throughout, the company refused any discussion with WFM leaders or any attempt at mediative intercession. There were shootings, all by the deputies. WFM president Moyer was shot and loaded onto a train out of town without treatment for his wounds. Seventy-two persons, mostly children, were killed in a panicked stampede at a Christmas party when someone yelled "fire." The drain in strike relief funds was more than the WFM could support in the deepening depression and in the absence of Montana income. By April 1914 the strike was called off. The company unilaterally introduced the eight-hour day but ignored all other demands. By the end of the First World War, miners' average daily wages were $5.62 in Arizona, $5.03 in Montana, and $3.76 in Michigan—but nothing else had changed. The Michigan copper range retained its nonunion status until the passage of the National Labor Relations Act in 1935 put the federal government's weight on the union side of the scale.[64]

Arizona

With its forbidding terrain and fierce Apaches, Arizona was slower to develop its minerals than surrounding regions. Such tough silver-mining towns as Tombstone are lurid in history but their operations were relatively small. Although "snowbird" miners from Utah, Idaho, Nevada, and Montana sometimes wintered in Arizona, they did not bring unionization with them and they did not stay. Much of the common labor in the Arizona mines was Mexican, Indian, and non-English speaking. For all of these reasons, union organizing efforts followed rather than preceded the opening of copper mines. The copper-mining companies were powerful and well financed from the beginning instead of growing from small independently owned mines. So the opposition to unionism was formidable from the start. The first significant labor dispute occurred in 1903, when the territorial legislature passed an eight-hour law which the employers ignored.[65] The miners at Morenci struck to enforce the law, even though no organized local union existed. Paradoxically, the state militia and federal troops were called out to put down the strike.

As the largest copper employer, Phelps Dodge effectively kept the union out by paying the union scale and strictly observing the eight-hour law, at the same time chasing out union organizers and discharging union members. When the WFM opened an office in Bisbee, the three companies there began laying off large numbers of workers. A strike was called, and the union was simply ignored until it called off the abortive effort after nearly a year. Other experiences were similar. For instance, when the WFM called a strike against three operating companies in the Clifton-Metcalf-Morenci district in 1912, the companies merely shut down and refused to talk with the union. Only after four months of idleness during which the price of copper rose and their losses began to mount did the companies condescend to discuss the issues. Even then they did so only upon the agreement of the WFM to leave the scene so that the strikes could be settled with the State Federation of Labor, through the intervention of the United States Conciliation Service, for a 67-cent-per-day increase.[66]

This and other failures of the WFM, its inability to provide strike benefits, and criticisms of Moyer from other mining camps all damaged the union's credibility. There was apparently some desire for organization but no faith in the WFM as the vehicle. The copper companies remained adamantly opposed to unionization, discharging any who came to be known as union sympathizers.

After 1907 the IWW was a divisive influence in WFM organizing attempts in Arizona. In addition, the companies were able to play off the Mexican and Anglo workers against each other and to run their own slates of officers in local union elections as a few such locals became established. Mining depressions in 1908 and 1914 were further impediments. A liberal Democrat who was the state's first governor from 1912 to 1916 was helpful to the WFM cause but was defeated by a more corporation-oriented Republican after 1916, just as impending war was generating copper demand and providing a more conducive setting for organizing. It was during 1916 that the International Union of Mine, Mill and Smelter Workers was formed, perhaps in the hope of leaving behind the aura of radicalism. It was also in 1916 that the IWW convention allotted several thousand dollars to a special fund for organizing Arizona's copper miners.[67] The attack was launched both by infiltrating and capturing Mine Mill locals and by establishing dual union competition.

The opposition of the IWW to the war and the overreaction of the government to that opposition reflected unfavorably on all Arizona labor unions. Wartime copper demand was creating economic conditions favorable to the unions, but each time Mine Mill began to organize or made demands, IWW representatives would appear on the scene to try to take control. Officers of AFL unions began to suspect the companies of paying the expenses of the "wobblies," as the IWW members were known, to bring the unions into disrepute. A Loyalty League sponsored by the companies and armed by the War Department was put in place to harass the IWW but did not discriminate between wobblies and other trade unionists. The Mine Mill constitution required authorization of the international union to call a strike, but under the circumstances a strike call by the IWW could result in an unauthorized work stoppage, beyond the control of the Mine Mill locals. When this occurred in Jerome in 1917, 104 participants were rounded up by businessmen and other citizens. Sixty-seven who could not prove that they were not members of the IWW were placed in railroad cars and shipped to Needles, California, where they were released to find their way back through the desert.[68]

In another strike attributed to the IWW in Bisbee a short time later, a posse of 1,200 citizens led by the local sheriff rounded up all miners not at work, held them incommunicado at a baseball park for a time, then loaded them into boxcars and left them stranded in the New Mexico desert, 174 miles away, without food or water. They were given refuge, bare rations, but no shoes at an army camp at Columbus, New Mexico, where they remained separated from their families from July through September.[69] The dragnet was indiscriminate, and businessmen as well as AFL and IWW members were included in the deportation. Thereafter, identification slips were issued to workers, and all strangers were denied entrance to the town.

Disruption of wartime copper production brought a presidential mediation commission to Arizona. It settled the strikes but could not alleviate the basic issues. Short-term gains were made in both organization and wages, then were lost to widespread blacklisting and postwar depression. In Arizona, too, copper unionism was dead until the Wagner Act and the Second World War.

NEAR OBLIVION

The combination of the 1914 mining recession, the IWW strife, and the disruptions of the Butte membership largely immobilized the WFM. With the flow of funds from Butte reduced to a trickle and fewer employed miners to pay dues elsewhere, the union was no longer able to support its far-flung organizing efforts, which were also hampered by the competition of the IWW. The WFM was forced to reduce its staff of organizers markedly and was unable to provide financial support in the Arizona strikes.

Merger with the United Mine Workers had occasionally been discussed on both sides since UMW's advocacy of WFM reaffiliation with the AFL in 1908. In 1914 the WFM made overtures that resulted in a meeting in Butte between representatives of the two unions.[70] Unfortunately, the UMW thereby witnessed the chaos in the largest WFM local. The coal miners' union responded that within its primary jurisdiction were 300,000 unorganized coal miners whose product was in direct competition with union-mined coal: self-preservation required addressing all available resources to organizing the unorganized within their own industry. The WFM membership numbered only 17,000 of an estimated 200,000 metal miners scattered over a vast territory, to which the UMW would be required to allocate resources in case of a merger. Therefore, the parallel mining union's overtures were reluctantly refused. Practically speaking, the short and stormy life of the Western Federation of Miners was over.

To all these external troubles were added internal unrest centering in Arizona and growing opposition to Moyer's leadership. Moyer retained his office by a vote of 4,510 to 2,784 in 1916, but both the Arizona and Montana votes were against him. It was this same convention that attempted to lay the radical past to rest by changing the union's name to the International Union of Mine, Mill and Smelter Workers (IUMMSW). It also replaced the militant class struggle preamble it had adopted in 1907 with a more pragmatic one:

> We, the workers in the metal industry are united for the purpose of increasing wages, shortening hours, and improving working conditions by removing or providing as far as may be [sic], the dangers incident to the work, eliminating as far as possible, dust, smoke, gases, and poisonous fumes from the mine, mill and smelter; to prevent the imposition of excessive tasks; to aid all organizations of working people in securing a larger measure of justice, and to labor for the enactment of legislation that will protect the life and limb of the workers, conserve their health, improve social conditions and promote the general well-being of the toilers.[71]

The next convention in 1917 added for the first time the explicit objective of negotiating contracts with employers. Though not raised in status to the preamble of the union's constitution, the checkoff of union dues also began appearing among the organization's declared objectives.

Even the rising copper demand, first from war in Europe and then from U.S. involvement, was not enough to lift the union out of its moribund condition. Many Mine Mill leaders were opposed to U.S. participation in the European war but swung to the side of patriotism once war was declared. The numerous Irish miners, many of whom had fled their native land to escape British conscription, were not as easily mollified.[72]

As in Arizona, throughout the union's jurisdiction the virulent IWW opposition to the war reflected unfavorably on the new Mine, Mill and Smelter Workers Union, which was not separated from the IWW in the public mind or in the press. The strikes, which were frequent in mining states throughout the war, were considered unpatriotic and disruptive of the war effort, and the mix of economic and political issues was impossible to disentangle. Paradoxically, with Woodrow Wilson's support of collective bargaining in general, Mine Mill locals were organized or expanded in various parts of the East and the South, but there was no significant growth in the union's traditional western jurisdiction.[73]

Peace in the world did not bring peace to the IUMMSW. Red-baiting of the IWW reflected indiscriminately on the Mine Mill union as well. Postwar wage cuts fomented strikes, which were then won by the employers, who imported replacements and refused to rehire union members. The postwar depression of 1921 further decimated the union ranks. Paradoxically, IWW membership rose during this period, while Mine Mill membership declined further.

The old-time miners with their roots in precious metals were disappearing from the scene. Copper mining and smelting now dominated metal mining. These were mass-production industries manned by semiskilled and unskilled workers who increasingly were immigrants—Mexicans in Arizona and southern Europeans elsewhere. Montana had largely been lost to the union; Michigan, Utah, and Arizona had never been successfully organized. These were the centers of the copper industry. No conventions were held in 1922 or 1924. Moyer and his colleagues resigned in 1924.[74] At the 1927, 1928, 1929, and 1930 conventions only six or seven locals were represented. Such was the condition of the once militant metal miner's union on the eve of the New Deal.

REINVIGORATION

The National Industrial Recovery Act (NIRA) was the spark which reignited unionism in the nonferrous mining industry. Not that the moribund union had any meaningful voice in the formulation of the codes of fair competition for the industry. Only three significant local unions remained by 1933, all in Montana and consisting of engineers, smelter men, and refinery workers, not miners.[75] They had no voice that could be heard in Washington. But the voice of Washington could be heard in the mining camps, promising protection for organized labor. The charter of the Butte Miners' Union No. 1 was held by its secretary—a one-man local. Thomas H. Brown, newly elected president of the Mine, Mill and Smelter Workers Union, was in Washington to represent the union in the NIRA code-making process; but the union lacked the clout for him to be influential.[76]

It was the NIRA recognition of legal rights for organized labor that sparked hope among the miners. Within a few weeks 3,500 had signed up with the union in Butte alone. Without any signs of recovery for the industry or expansion of employment opportunities, similar though less dramatic stirrings were felt in the lead, silver, and copper mines of Utah; the gold and silver mines of Idaho; the iron mines of Alabama; the lead mines of Missouri, Oklahoma, and Kansas; the copper and zinc mines of Tennessee; and by the smelter workers in Illinois and Pennsylvania.[77]

With the organization almost totally moribund, new leadership had to be selected and relations with employers established. With government support, the latter was easier than the former. In addition to the inevitable clashes of personal ambition, there remained the historic division between radical and conservative objectives. The IWW was no longer on the scene as an organization, but the same sentiments remained among a substantial body of old-time members and their sons. Communism became a source of controversy among the leadership, most of whom were opposed to its infiltration, but the rank and file proved to be more tolerant about its revived and familiar militancy. A sign of this at the 1934 convention was the return from the conservative 1916 constitution preamble to the historical class-struggle declaration of 1907.

Along with the internal struggles and external battles with employers, another conflict was brewing within the AFL. Settlement of a successful strike against Anaconda Copper in 1934 was accomplished on the union side at the national level by the AFL Metal Trades Department on behalf of its constituent unions. Within Mine Mill there was much dissatisfaction over the terms of settlement and because it had been imposed by John P. Frey, head of the Metal Trades Department, without the consent of the Mine Mill workers. As organizational efforts intensified, jurisdictional clashes were emerging between the craft unions and the industrially oriented Mine Mill.[78]

The issue had arisen on a broader scale at the 1934 AFL convention. In 1935 Mine Mill charges of jurisdictional transgressions before the AFL executive council added fuel to an already smoldering fire. Continuing the fraternal alliance of 1910, John L. Lewis of the UMW championed the Mine Mill cause unsuccessfully at both the 1934 and 1935 AFL conventions.[79] Mine Mill thereupon became one of the eight charter members of the new Committee for Industrial Organization. At the time Mine Mill confessed to having only 17,000 dues paying members among its claimed 30,000.[80] Nevertheless, during this period it was successful in solidifying its Montana membership and in organizing the brass manufacturing areas of Connecticut, also dominated by Anaconda Copper.

The first flush of reinvigoration stalled when the United States Supreme Court in 1935 found the National Industrial Recovery Act to be unconstitutional. Few companies had followed Anaconda's lead in recognizing Mine Mill, most remaining adamantly opposed. Matters changed drastically in 1937, when the U.S. Supreme Court upheld the constitutionality of the National Labor Relations Act and thereby put the federal government squarely behind collective bargaining.

The basic weakness of Mine Mill was that it had been an industrial union of semiskilled workers in an era in which only skilled workers had any bargaining power. Now it was finding that government sponsorship of collective bargaining was not enough. A stable union leadership and a substantial demand for labor were also essential. Little progress could be made until economic recovery had followed the outbreak of war in Europe. The production of the nonferrous metals industry was essential to national defense. The Montana membership was solidified, some Utah and Michigan locals were added to the union's ranks, and Arizona was successfully organized, as were the Alabama iron mines and the smelters and refineries of the American Smelting and Refining Company (ASARCO), which were scattered outside traditional mining areas.

Despite the rush to hire workers and meet production demands, management opposition to unionism did not simply melt. For example, the union for years had tried to organize the tri-state lead-mining district of Oklahoma, Kansas, and Missouri. Following a strike in 1935, ten years of NLRA litigation involving antiunion violence, company unions, and collusive dual unionism with the AFL crafts all were required to bring the area under Mine Mill representation.[81] Early success was achieved in the iron mines of Alabama. In Utah, Mine Mill was able to revive unionism in the underground mines but because of intraunion conflict lost out to a supposedly independent employees' association at the Bingham Mine and smelting complex. The Arizona copper companies had also read the NLRA portent of government preference for collective bargaining and had taken refuge in company unions. Rivalry between Mine Mill and the AFL craft unions, railroad brotherhoods, and the Metal Trades Department—along with internal strife among Mine Mill organizers—led to a long, slogging effort before Mine Mill was able to represent most of the semiskilled mine and smelter employees in the state. ASARCO smelters and refineries outside the traditional mining areas were picked off one by one through NLRB elections after the beginning of the war. An organizing drive followed by NLRB elections in 1939 disestablished a company union in Michigan and resulted in Mine Mill certification. By 1941 the smaller Michigan mines were operating under union contracts. But it took until 1942, after two more NLRB elections and state and federal government concessions on copper price controls, before a union contract was successfully negotiated with Calumet and Hecla.[82] By war's end, Mine Mill membership had reached 92,000, peaking at 114,000 in 1948.[83]

COMMUNIST INFILTRATION

Even at its time of hard-won triumph, Mine Mill manifested a death wish that was eventually to do it in. It was not emergence and rise to dominance of the historical radical influences within Mine Mill that finally led to its expulsion from the "House of Labor" in 1950. That particular radical tradition was syndicalism—by now a dead issue. Those who initially rose to power with the revitalization of the union after 1933 were all political conservatives. But they were untried and inexperienced. After several years of divisive struggle limited to personality issues and local jealousies, Reid Robinson of Butte rose to the presidency in 1936 to join a bitterly divided national leadership.[84] He and those who remained or came into office with him were conservative business unionists. Initially he fought vigorously against the signs of communist influence emerging within Mine Mill, as occurred in many other industrial unions during the economic debacle of the 1930s. Yet for reasons which have never been satisfactorily explained, he began in the late thirties to hire known communists as organizers and internal union staff. In that, too, he was not unique. John L. Lewis had used communists as effective organizers for the CIO, although he was careful to keep them out of his own United Mine Workers, where they might have threatened his power base.[85]

Robinson made no such positive use of communist organizers. It may be that, as an unsophisticated miner on the CIO executive board, Robinson was simply enticed away by selective exposure to the "fleshpots" of the nation's capitol. At any rate, the union, which had throughout its history housed radicalism within its ranks and now appeared to have little if any remaining, was to have its national leadership gradually and surreptitiously captured by communist influence from the outside. All that the past history of radicalism now contributed was a reluctance to make political views a factor in consideration for union office. Merger with the National Association of Die Casting Workers in 1944 added a further source of communist influence.[86] The majority of the executive board remained conservative, but perceived the issue as one of staff outsiders against traditional miners, rather than of left versus right. Robinson and his staff were able to color the criticisms as attempts to sow disunity and interfere with the war effort. Gradually, because the right wing was never able to unite and organize itself as effectively as the left, enough executive board members were replaced to give Robinson a 7–5 majority as president.[87]

Mine Mill came out of the war period strengthened economically but bitterly divided in its leadership. Its situation was not appreciably different from that of a number of other CIO unions. With wage and price controls, little collective bargaining had been necessary; organization had been almost automatic. The war effort had been the common concern of anti-communist and communist alike. Now aggressive collective bargaining would be necessary to catch up on wages and keep up with inflation. National opinion was shifting against organizations tainted by communism. Unions without that taint were willing to raid those so besmirched. Mine Mill locals, repelled by their national leadership situation, began to secede; between forty-two and fifty locals with 26,000 to 35,000 members did so by 1947.[88] Robinson resigned in 1946, to be replaced by his executive assistant, Maurice Travis, who himself had communist affiliations.

CHAPTER 6

CHANGING INDUSTRY

STRUCTURE, 1946–1990

THE FIRMS IN THE U.S. copper industry emerged from World War II with every appearance of strength and vitality. Yet the apparently most powerful of them were to disappear over the next forty-five years, and none was to escape unscathed from the rigors they would all confront. It is worth examining individually the corporate experience of each of the major U.S. companies during the postwar period, before turning to the product-market forces which buffeted them and the interacting industrial relations developments which nearly brought the industry to its knees.

ANACONDA

In retrospect, Anaconda's aggressiveness ended with the death of its chief executive officer, John D. Ryan, in 1933. By that time he had paid off the company's long-term debt, purchased the remaining shares of the Chuquicamata, Portrerillos, and Greene Cananea mines, and positioned the company for survival during the lean years of the Great Depression. Ryan's successor, Cornelius F. Kelley, who was to head the firm for the next thirty years, perceived it as a static entity and did little beyond attempting to

148

maintain the status quo. Anaconda's output did not increase during the high-demand period of World War II. A Yerington, Nevada, mine was purchased in 1951, but only to offset Butte's diminishing production, not to expand. In the late 1950s block caving was tried at Butte, along with open-pit mining at the Berkeley Mine, again only to maintain output— but neither proved profitable.[1]

Throughout most of Anaconda's history it had been a diversified, non-ferrous producer of silver, gold, lead, zinc, manganese, and copper. Since 1921 its leaders had deliberated over the desirability of entering the aluminum market. By the time that thirty-year debate had ended with a positive decision in 1951, the window of opportunity had effectively been closed by Alcoa, Reynolds, and Kaiser. The wartime government aid available to the aluminum industry had also been forfeited through Anaconda's indecision. Nevertheless, the company moved ahead with a large-scale effort.

The ill-timed move into aluminum started with the takeover of an undercapitalized reduction works. The drain on resources for this capital-intensive undertaking came at a time when needed modernization of antiquated mining operations and development of the Berkeley pit were also claiming a great deal of Anaconda's available capital. The rapidly expanding financial requirements sent the company scurrying back to its stockholders in search of an $85 million increase in capital in 1957.

Anaconda's venture into aluminum production may have been the beginning of its demise. The many trade-offs and compromises that were required to finance and facilitate the company's entrance into an already substantially closed aluminum market left its copper operations financially unattended during times of opportunity in that industry. Those efforts also left Anaconda economically unstable and ill prepared to handle the events that were to come in the 1960s and 1970s.

Having gone into the depression in a strong, largely debt-free position, but failing to respond to the increased copper demand brought about by the war, Anaconda missed a number of opportunities to capitalize on benefits available in copper, meanwhile throwing good money after bad in a losing battle for recognition in the aluminum business. Equally harmful to the long-run interests of the company was the fact that the managerial floundering drew its attention away from Chilean politics. Signs that Chuquicamata, by far Anaconda's premier copper-producing property, was headed down the path toward expropriation were becoming easily recognizable in the 1960s. As Anaconda and Kennecott continued to reap enormous profits from their Chilean investments, Chilean citizens became resentful of the limited benefits they were deriving from the foreign sale of their domestic mineral resources.[2] Pressure on government officials to retain more of the copper profits in Chilean coffers intensified as copper prices rose. Chile's political machinery responded by levying increasingly heavy taxes on sales made by the foreign producers. Tax increases were not enough for the Chilean people, however—or perhaps more accurately, for aspiring Chilean politicians. The ultimate action in Chile's effort to capture more of the monies reaped from copper export was taken by President Salvador Allende upon his inauguration in 1971.

The Chilean properties were of substantially different magnitudes in relation to the total operations of Kennecott and Anaconda—11 percent of copper production for the former and 75 percent for the latter. Nevertheless, differences in managerial foresight and response to changing government policies also contributed to the fact that the Chilean expropriation was devastating to the very foundation of Anaconda, whereas Kennecott was only lightly damaged. At the first signs of imminent government takeover, Kennecott put into effect policies to minimize the impact. Chileans were brought into management to build good will. At the same time, after concluding that expropriation could not be avoided, the company put a halt to any further investment in the Chilean holdings. A plan was implemented that responded to Chile's demands for expanded production without further capital outlays by Kennecott. Ultimately, the Chilean government compensated Kennecott for the sale of its 51 percent interest in the El Teniente operation.

In contrast, Anaconda, falsely secure in its relationships with the Chilean government and blinded to a substantial degree by its own arrogance, either did not recognize or simply ignored the warning signs. Continuing to pour time, money, and manpower into the Chuquicamata operation and another Chilean property called the El Salvador, Anaconda became increasingly indentured to the will of the Chilean government. The company took no precautions; it brought no Chileans into management, continued to invest its own funds in the expansion demanded by the Chilean government, and even guaranteed a sizable Export-Import Bank loan. The heavy funding and indebtedness that Anaconda had undertaken left it almost helpless when the fateful day of expropriation came. Compensation was not grasped when it was first available; thereafter it was uncertain, delayed, and, at the last, minimal. In a single great blow, the loss of its properties in Chile cost Anaconda 30 percent of its net worth. With the Chilean mines gone and its U.S. properties in continuing decline, the firm became desperate to acquire compensating ore reserves. It purchased and expanded the large but low-grade Twin Buttes deposit in Arizona.[3] That operation not only proved to be inadequate to offset the Latin American production losses but, once in operation, was unprofitable as well.

The lack of foresight demonstrated by Anaconda's top management in Chile and the failure to make Twin Buttes profitable led to the dismissal of C. Jay Parkinson, who had taken on leadership of the company in 1968. He was a Salt Lake City lawyer whose perceived abrasiveness and arrogance were charged with hastening the downfall of relations with the Chilean government. Replacing Parkinson was John B. M. Place, a Chase Manhattan banker who took on the formidable task of rebalancing the company's debt-equity ratio, which had gone out of control during the Parkinson reign. Neither Parkinson nor Place had a mining background; finance had become the dominant consideration. The loss of the Chilean properties, while a disaster for Parkinson, was one of the few hopes for Place, in that it provided years of total freedom from the corporate income tax.

Early in his tenure, Place trimmed the fat from Anaconda's operations by terminating nearly one-half of the headquarters staff and selling off many of the company's unprofitable U.S. ventures, including $117 million of timberland. The final settlement with the government of Chile left nearly 15 percent of Anaconda's assets with little present value because of the distance and uncertainty of payoff, and the small size of the future cash flow. The company's only significant foreign copper investment was in Iran. Its long-mined base property at Butte was running out of profitable ore. Though still the second largest copper company in total assets, this one-time copper-mining giant found, once the dust had settled, that its only remaining profitable operations were in brass and wire.

Anaconda's final chapter began with the struggle to resist a takeover by the Crane Company, which had interests in brass. To thwart that attempt, Anaconda purchased Crane's faltering competitor, Walworth Company, in 1975. That strategy only delayed the acquisition effort and, through an arrangement with Crane's parent, Atlantic Richfield Corporation (ARCO), the takeover of Anaconda was finally accomplished in 1981. Yet its performance was not substantially improved under ARCO management. And ARCO soon suffered the fate of other oil companies which had become involved in mining: in 1983 it totally closed its Montana

A head-on view of the Washoe Smelter. This view, which looks westward, indicates the large scale of the reduction works. Taken in the early twenties. (*Photo courtesy C. Owen Smithers, Butte, Montana.*)

The Marcus Daly monument at Butte. Superintendent of the Anaconda Mine until 1900, Daly was backed by Senator George Hearst and James Ben Ali Haggin. He introduced a pioneering system of medical insurance and a bank. (*Photo courtesy of the American Heritage Center, University of Wyoming, and Dr. Charles C. Daly.*)

operations after having lost $750 million. The impact was, of course, devastating for Butte and the surrounding area, for which the company and its predecessors had provided the economic base for more than a century.

Subsequently, what had been Anaconda's Butte properties were purchased by Washington Contractors, a construction company that commenced operations in one of the Berkeley pits under the name Montana Mineral Resources.[4] The timing could not have been better. Having purchased the mine for $12 million when copper prices were below 60 cents per pound, the new owner earned $40 million in six months by extracting and concentrating the ore before shipping it to Japan for refining.[5] At the close of 1989, the fortunate company exulted at having paid profit-sharing checks to its 320 nonunion employees (whose base pay was only $6 an hour) every quarter since mid-1987.[6] Important as they were to the local economy and those employed, in historical perspective the employment and payroll were minor and of little comfort in the long saga of labor organization.

KENNECOTT

Kennecott's leadership policy progressed with one chief executive officer instructing the next until tragedy struck at the top in 1949. E. T. Stannard, CEO since 1940, boarded a commercial plane with his understudy, Arthur D. Storke, intending to visit a Canadian mining venture. Both met their deaths with the explosion of a bomb placed by a greedy husband in the luggage of a well-insured wife, also on board.[7] With that blast Kennecott was left with no immediate successor and its board scrambled to bring in someone from outside. Thus came the appointment of Charles R. Cox, head of United States Steel's Carnegie-Illinois unit, a corporate genealogy that became significant in the jurisdictional competition between the Mine, Mill and Smelter Workers and the United Steelworkers over the next few years.

Cox, whose tenure lasted from 1950 to 1962, brought with him a new, if not more prosperous, era. Because of its unique relationship with the Guggenheims and ASARCO, Kennecott had been slower than Anaconda and Phelps Dodge in moving toward vertical integration. The outsider, Cox, immediately resolved to break Kennecott away from its reliance on ASARCO for smelting capacity. From his first board meeting, Cox sought to buy ASARCO's Garfield smelter, which had processed the Bingham Canyon ore since 1906. He began by constructing Kennecott's own refinery at the same locality. In 1959, Kennecott succeeded in acquiring the giant Garfield smelter, after threatening to build its own smelter at the site. (Since Garfield's main throughput came from the Bingham Mine, a Kennecott smelter would have left ASARCO's virtually idle.)

The 1950s also saw the construction of a refinery in Baltimore, primarily to process South American ores. In addition, Kennecott built a smelter near ASARCO's Hayden, Arizona, plant to handle feedstocks from its Ray Mine that historically had been processed at the ASARCO facility. Because ASARCO had sufficient throughput from other mining concerns in the area, the two Arizona smelters were able to coexist. Kennecott also continued vertical integration by getting into copper fabrication, as its rivals had done twenty years before, but that venture was not successful.

In addition to the breakaway from the Guggenheims and ASARCO, Cox attempted relatively unsuccessful diversification and exploration strategies. To diversify, Kennecott first entered a joint venture with the Quebec Iron and Titanium Corporation. The project took ten years to reach the break-even point and another five to show significant profits. Passive diversification involved the company in large purchases of stock in Anglo-American, the South African mining combine, Kaiser Aluminum (where Kennecott's holdings became second only to those of the Kaiser family), and joint oil explorations with Continental Oil Company. Like Phelps Dodge, Kennecott found oil exploration not worth the investment; like Newmont, it sold its Anglo-American interest by 1952. After unsuccessful attempts to develop less expensive mining and processing methods for the Quebec operation, Kennecott became discouraged with the venture. Turning its attention from diversification to integration, the corporation purchased Okonite, a leading manufacturer of underground cable. The government was to take a hand in this relationship, however, for the Antitrust Division of the Justice Department filed suit, forcing Kennecott to sell at a loss in 1965.

A driving force behind Kennecott's diversification attempts may have been its accumulated cash from the Chilean reimbursement, augmented by substantial cash flow from its still very profitable U.S. operations. These profits could have been increased by spending the money to buy the same cost-cutting technology it was to introduce at its Ray, Chino, and Bingham properties twenty years later, at much higher cost. But with production costs well below world copper prices already, there seems to have been little incentive to do so. Instead, in 1966, with nearly $200 million in excess cash, Kennecott began negotiations for the purchase of Peabody Coal Company, the largest independent company in the coal industry.[8] Despite the strong promise of nuclear power at the time, Kennecott saw coal as a profitable long-run answer to increased energy demand in a world of declining resources. Furthermore, Peabody was primarily engaged in fulfilling long-term contracts with electric utilities, a source of steady cash flow at stable prices to offset the volatility of the copper price and income structure.

As usual, expectation and reality proved to be quite different. With its investment in Peabody, Kennecott had diversified into another capital-intensive industry and thus divided its eggs between two financially demanding baskets. The condition of Peabody at the time of the lengthy negotiations with Kennecott was an omen of things to come. Because of buying out two independent coal producers, Peabody was in trouble with the Justice Department. After eventually being forced to sell some of its key Illinois mines, Peabody shareholders were in a position to accept the Kennecott merger and did so in January 1968, a year and a half after the proposal was made public. The total price paid by Kennecott, including production royalties, was estimated at $621.5 million—a shock to stockholders, who had calculated the market value at $475 million.

Within four months of Kennecott's acquisition of Peabody, the Federal Trade Commission made good its promise to fight the merger, holding that Kennecott was in violation of the Clayton Antitrust Act on grounds of restraint of trade. Undaunted, Kennecott believed its own attorneys, who thought the antitrust suit would not be upheld in the courts. In consequence, Kennecott launched a sizable investment plan for the modernization of Peabody. Having sold half of its Kaiser Aluminum holdings to finance the coal purchase, Kennecott sold the other half to finance further investment in Peabody. A large part of the costs of modernization were incurred to comply with the increasingly stringent government safety standards being applied to underground mining operations.

An unexpectedly poor operating performance at Peabody crushed dividend hopes. Prior to the Kennecott purchase, Peabody profits were reported at $28 million; after the acquisition, Peabody fell into red ink. The long-term utility contracts which had been attractions soon became detriments. Tied to those contracts, the coal-mining company could not take advantage of rising energy prices or adequately offset rising production costs. Coupled with the fact that coal output per manhour was decreasing industry-wide during that period, the profit prospects at Peabody were bleak. Before acquisition of the coal company, Kennecott's gross margin had averaged 33 percent; the 1970 gross margin dropped to 26 percent. By national standards this was highly respectable, but not unusual for the volatile copper industry. Moreover, Kennecott had now been replaced by Phelps Dodge as the highest profit maker in the industry. Ultimately, the diversification sought through the Peabody acquisition served to increase the company's risks rather than reduce them.

Kennecott's dilemma over what to do with Peabody was laid to rest by the refusal of the United States Supreme Court on April 2, 1974, to review the antitrust case. The court thus upheld the FTC ruling, which gave Kennecott one year to divest itself of the coal properties. By means of legal and tactical maneuvers, Kennecott delayed its final divestiture and in 1977 sold its Peabody operation to a holding company headed by Newmont Mining Corporation.[9] The Peabody acquisition was undeniably a strategic error, antitrust aside; but no one has yet adequately explained why federal authorities found the combination of coal and copper production to be anticompetitive.

Meantime, while its attempts at diversification were failing, Kennecott was investing in exploration. Estimates of exploration expenditures totaled over a million dollars for the decade of the 1960s, an amount thought to be equal to the combined total spent by all of its competitors.[10] Kennecott geologists explored many parts of the world but focused mainly on the North American continent. Limiting the success of the exploration activities was the fact that the company's experience had been restricted to open-pit mining. Thus it refused to consider any properties requiring underground mining. Geologists were instructed not to waste time and money on exploratory drilling below 1,500 feet. As a result, little of value was developed. Phelps Dodge subsequently proved Kennecott to have been overly cautious, by developing and profiting from the Arizona properties the larger company had rejected.

With the problems Kennecott faced in the 1970s with El Teniente and Peabody, its financial commitment to exploration dwindled. Expenditures shrank to the point where it was spending less, when adjusted for corporate size, than some of the smallest firms in the industry. Although the nationalization of El Teniente and the divestiture of Peabody left Kennecott feeling somewhat stripped of natural resources, as of 1974 it was still the world's largest independent producer of primary copper, all of it U.S. based. It is ironic that, despite the millions of dollars spent on exploration during the 1950s and 1960s, Kennecott retained its leadership position solely through the continued production of its Jackling-developed porphyry properties.

With the gain of over a billion dollars from the Peabody divestiture, its nominal value swollen by inflation, and the profits reaped from the escalation during the 1960s and 1970s of the price of gold, an important by-product of the Bingham Canyon Mine, Kennecott was faced with a high liquidity ratio and thus a growing threat of corporate takeover. To forestall a raid, Kennecott invested over half of its liquid excess, $567 million, in purchase of the Carborundum Corporation in late 1977.[11] This acquisition, however, did not stop Curtiss-Wright Corporation from attempting a takeover of the giant copper firm. Kennecott staved off this raid at high cost to both companies, then retaliated two years later when it tendered a $164 million counterbid for the aerospace company.[12] After battles in both court and boardroom, Kennecott withdrew its offer and agreed to a settlement that won them the one-time Curtiss-Wright holding, Dorr-Oliver. Watching all of this financial manipulation were insiders, who could see alternative uses in mine improvement, and the unions, who were continuing to pursue wage and benefit improvements for their members.

Kennecott was not to be an independent entity for much longer. Standard Oil of Ohio, fat with profits from its Alaskan North Slope oil venture, was looking to diversify in an effort to reduce its liquidity, much as Kennecott had attempted to do with Peabody and Carborundum. But at the time neither SOHIO nor Kennecott was aware that the American copper industry was on the brink of disaster. Although copper prices the year before were at an all-time peak of approximately a dollar a pound, the year of the SOHIO purchase, 1981, saw copper prices fall a full 20 cents, followed by a further decline to an average of 61 cents a pound by 1985.

SOHIO bought Kennecott shares at $35.12, although they had been selling at only $27.15 before the merger announcement. Having paid $1.7 billion, SOHIO encountered a $59 million loss from its copper operations in its first six months. A total of $600 million was ultimately lost before the Bingham complex was temporarily closed in 1985.

SOHIO was a wholly owned subsidiary of British Petroleum. Despite several succeeding years of continuing losses at Kennecott Copper, BP allowed SOHIO to announce its intention to retain and modernize the Bingham Canyon property, to return it to its earlier status as one of the world's lowest-cost copper facilities. Drastic cuts in labor costs were made a prerequisite of a plan to invest approximately $400 million in the facility.

Earlier, Kennecott had sold a one-third interest in its Chino, New Mexico, property to the Mitsubishi Corporation. Now to obtain funds for the Bingham modernization, SOHIO sold its remaining two-thirds interest in Chino to Phelps Dodge Corporation for $93 million and its Ray, Arizona, property to ASARCO for $72 million. A number of secondary concerns acquired in the Kennecott purchase were also sold, and the Nevada mines were closed permanently for lack of mineable ore.

Because of its gold, silver, and molybdenum by-products, the Bingham operation did not lend itself to SX-EW technology. Therefore, the essence of the modernization was a streamlining of materials handling, a proposal Kennecott engineers had had on hold all during the diversification era. The $400 million was spent primarily to replace the railroad ore haulage with belt transmission and a slurry pipeline, and to construct a new concentrator.

In the midst of the modernization effort, British Petroleum resolved to replace the SOHIO management with executives more directly responsive to the parent company. In the process, Kennecott acquired a new name— BP Minerals America—but retained most of its existing management.[13] The historic Kennecott name was not to fade that easily. At the close of 1988 came the announcement that the mining and related operations of BP Minerals were being sold to generate cash to respond to British government orders that British Petroleum recover most of the large block of its stock owned by the government of Kuwait.[14]

The new owner of the Bingham Canyon property was RTZ (Rio Tinto Zinc), Ltd., the British company that had come into existence in the nineteenth century to reopen the historic Roman copper mining operations at Rio Tinto, Spain.[15] One of the world's largest metal-mining firms, RTZ today produces copper, aluminum, iron ore, lead, molybdenum, tin, zinc, gold, and silver. It also produces coal, oil, uranium, and industrial chemicals and is the owner of U.S. Borax and Chemical Corporation. It suffered from its oil and gas involvement in the North Sea but maintained its base in copper with a 30 percent interest in the Chilean Escondida Mine and a 49 percent interest in Bougainville.[16] With smaller-scale copper operations in Canada, South Africa, Portugal, and Australia, RTZ promises to become the world's largest privately owned miner of copper.

In addition to its practice of leaving existing management in place whenever possible, RTZ restored to the single-property operation two historic names and called it the Kennecott Utah Copper Company. The new owner was so pleased with the first-year profits from its acquisition that it authorized expenditure of an additional $227 million for further concentrator and related improvements.[17] With that addition, a facility which in 1970 employed 8,000 people and as recently as 1982 produced 170,000 tons while employing 4,800 people, will now with 2,400 people produce each year 270,000 tons of refined copper, 350,000 ounces of gold, 2.5 million ounces of silver, and 12 million pounds of molybdenum. The target production cost for the 1986–1989 modernization was 52 cents per pound, a 75 percent reduction from the premodernization status in constant dollar terms and a 350 percent improvement in labor productivity compared to 1980.[18] Rumor has it that the production-cost target was surpassed during the first year of production, some suggesting cost figures of less than 45 cents. That same first year, 1989, RTZ discovered that for an investment of $3.7 billion it had purchased a single property (now known as the Kennecott Corporation) which produced one-third of the total profits of its worldwide operations.[19] It is ironic that the nearly $400 million one-year profit from the Bingham Canyon property approximated the entire cost of the modernization which, along with labor concessions and favorable prices, had made it possible.

PHELPS DODGE

The first ten years after World War II proved highly profitable for Phelps Dodge. In 1947 the company purchased the last holdout of the Bisbee deposits, the Shattuck-Denn Mining Company, and dividends increased nearly fourfold over those of the war years.[20] The 1950s and early 1960s found Phelps Dodge investing in other copper companies, including a northern Rhodesia copper venture operated by AMAX Corporation, as well as in oil and zinc. But after disappointing joint ventures with Cyprus, a copper producer, and Carter and Continental, both oil companies, Phelps Dodge absented itself from the oil exploration scene.

Phelps Dodge also found the financial demands of the aluminum industry to be more than it cared to bear. Avoiding the smelting and reduction of aluminum, Phelps Dodge set to collaborating with Billitor, a subsidiary of Royal Dutch Petroleum, and Conalco, a subsidiary of Alusuisse. By means of a Phelps Dodge loan, an agreement was funded whereby Billitor would provide alumina to Conalco for processing and Conalco would in turn send the processed aluminum to fabricating facilities provided through either acquisition or construction by Phelps Dodge. By 1970, PD had seventeen such plants; but when it perceived the large additional investments required, it chose to bow out, trading its fabricating facilities to Conalco for a 40 percent holding in that company. PD's remaining interest, coupled with its original loan to the aluminum venture, later created a $100 million cash-flow problem when its copper interests demanded further investment. Ultimately this situation led the company to sell its Conalco interest in the late 1970s.

An exceedingly profitable venture for Phelps Dodge arose in 1954 when the company, in conjunction with ASARCO, took a one-sixth interest in a mine development in southern Peru. Although the equity portion of the investment did not begin to pay off until 1966, the project totally paid back the loans and maintained an annual dividend to PD from 1966 to 1971 of about $7 million a year, almost 100 percent of the investment. Because of subsequent development at the nearby ore body, Cuajone, dividends were again plowed into the new venture. This development required no further funds from Phelps Dodge, and the company acquired a 15 percent holding in the new mine as well. During the 1960s Phelps Dodge also invested in and supplied managerial expertise to a number of copper-fabricating facilities abroad. Although dividends were reinvested in the various interests, PD did receive valuable remuneration for its management input.

In 1968, under the leadership of George B. Munroe, Phelps Dodge reopened its old Tyrone, New Mexico, property as an open pit, and began development of the Metcalf Mine at Morenci. While Metcalf was meant to fill the void left by the depleted Bisbee property, which ultimately was closed except for leaching in 1975, Tyrone was developed as a growth mine. As a sign of the times, PD also made its entry into the uranium market by acquiring Western Nuclear in 1970.

With the seventies came growing concern and activity on the environmental front. Smelters were closed at Ajo and Morenci. The Douglas smelter was PD's big polluter and its most difficult environmental issue.[21] Since ore from Tyrone was to be processed at the old Douglas smelter, the new environmental laws became a severe problem, forcing Phelps Dodge to come up with alternative plans for handling the Tyrone ore. With a ready water supply on nearby Phelps Dodge–owned land, the new Hidalgo smelter was built in southwest New Mexico to serve Tyrone. Using the Finnish Outokumpu method of flash smelting, the company put in place smelter production that was well within the limits of state and federal air-quality standards. With extensions granted through the support of the Arizona state government, the Douglas smelter remained operating with some modifications until its final closure in January 1987. By that time the company had spent $250 million in an unsuccessful effort to bring its four smelters into compliance with air-pollution standards.

Prior to its closure, the Douglas smelter was used to process ore from Morenci and toll process ore from the Cyprus Sierrita Mine near Tucson. Abandonment of the smelting activity left 300 workers unemployed and dried up over $4 million in payroll and other millions in taxes. Since the closure left Phelps Dodge with only one operating smelter, the company had to rely on toll smelting of its excess ores. Increased reliance on the SX-EW processes, which require no smelting, has eliminated that problem, however.

The impact of the costs for pollution control came at the worst possible time for Phelps Dodge. With copper prices plunging in 1981–1984, the company's losses were staggering. Nevertheless, its management resolved to make the requisite investments to retain its new position as the nation's largest copper producer and to do so at the world's lowest costs. PD historically had been an acquisitions-oriented company, expanding by purchase of already discovered properties from financially desperate sellers. Throughout the late 1960s and early 1970s it had also increased its exploration budget from $2 million to nearly $9 million per year, which resulted in substantial investments in Australia and South Africa.[22] Traditionally, Phelps Dodge had been financially self-sustaining, never seeking additional financing from its stockholders and rarely resorting to borrowing. At this point the company changed its policy under the pressure of costly pollution controls, mounting losses, the need to cut costs, and the growing threat of takeover.

As a final step to stem its growing losses, Phelps Dodge stopped all mining temporarily in April 1982. The later aggressive collective bargaining tactics described in Chapter 9 occurred in this setting. The company next launched a diversification drive to bring its investments outside the copper industry to near-equality with those within it.[23] It expanded its mining activities in other nations. At the same time, it introduced and enlarged SX-EW production and undertook major modernization efforts at Tyrone and Morenci.[24] When SOHIO announced its willingness to sell Kennecott's Arizona and New Mexico interests, PD purchased for $93 million a two-thirds interest in the Chino complex, including its smelter, then invested heavily in an SX-EW operation for its new acquisition. Solvent extraction was introduced at Morenci at about the same time.

With these and other improvements, Phelps Dodge in one decade had invested over $1.4 billion, taking its long-term debt from zero to $606 million.[25] In the process, it became the largest U.S. copper producer, with an announced goal of reducing its copper production costs to 50 cents a pound, a target subsequently achieved.

All of this was perfectly if fortuitously timed for the 1986 run-up in copper prices. By 1985 the company's operations were again in the black. By 1987 its dividends had been restored, it was reducing its debt, and it was buying back stock. Profits set company records in both 1988 and 1989 before dropping back modestly in early 1990. Even then, they were sufficient to support the announcement of an additional $365 million outlay for further cost-cutting developments.[26] On the world copper scene, it today shares ownership at Morenci with Sumitomo (15 percent) and at Chino with Mitsubishi (33 percent), owns 16 percent of Southern Peru Copper, has smaller copper interests in South Africa and Chile, and has a feasibility study under way for a major new mine in the latter country.

ASARCO

The American Smelting and Refining Company, which changed its name to ASARCO in 1962–1963, emerged from the Second World War as the world's largest custom smelter and refiner, involved in the processing of at least twenty-five metals in addition to copper.[27] At that point it owned a lead refinery in Omaha, a silver smelter in Selby, California, and a Nevada forge, as well as copper smelters in Garfield, Utah; Hayden, Arizona; and Tacoma, Washington; and refineries in Baltimore and El Paso. Via its Guggenheim heritage, it was involved in precious-metals mining in Australia, Peru, and Mexico. It was the largest employer in Mexico with its silver-mining interests there, and it had smelting interests in the Philippines. Furthermore, ASARCO was forward integrated to a degree through its interests in Revere Copper, General Cable, and Federated Metals.

Whatever output fluctuations might occur elsewhere, ASARCO had been secure in its domestic operations primarily because it handled all of Kennecott's Bingham Canyon smelting requirements. When Kennecott decided in 1950 to integrate vertically, ASARCO's smelting future was at risk. If Kennecott built its own smelter in lieu of relying on ASARCO's Garfield smelter, that unit would lack sufficient throughput for economic operation and would become a multimillion-dollar albatross. In Arizona there were enough alternative users of ASARCO's smelting capacity that the building of a Kennecott smelter at Hayden would not be devastating.

Fortunately for ASARCO, it was able to negotiate sale of the Garfield smelter to Kennecott. The experience, however, dramatized the custom smelter's vulnerability to lost feedstock and the potential long-range benefits of having its own uninterrupted and stable base of concentrate supply. Therefore, the company began looking for promising mining ventures within reasonable distance of its smelting and refining facilities. It purchased the Silver Bell ore body in Arizona in the 1950s and opened the Mission and Sacaton mines in the 1960s. The Silver Bell and Sacaton properties were closed when copper prices fell during the 1980s. Still, ASARCO was not dissuaded from paying $72 million for Kennecott's Ray facilities when they became available in 1986, an investment it was able to recoup threefold by the close of 1988.[28] It also purchased Kennecott's Missouri lead mines to accompany its own mine, smelter, and refinery there. Earlier it had added smelters for silver and lead in Helena, Montana, and Amarillo, Texas, as well as silver mines in Idaho.

Like most companies in the copper industry, ASARCO began losing money in the early 1980s and did not recover until 1987.[29] Nevertheless, it undertook an aggressive cost-cutting program to assure its long-run viability, investing as well in the expansion and modernization of its Mission and Ray properties, and in 1989 buying into the rejuvenation of the old Anaconda Mine at Butte. As of 1990, ASARCO remains the leading smelter and refiner of copper in the world; it is also fifth in the United States in copper production, as well as first in the world in silver production.

CYPRUS MINERALS

The company which stands number two in the U.S. copper industry in 1990, Cyprus Minerals, was not even listed as an also-ran in 1946. Its beginnings were in 1912, when Seeley W. Mudd and Philip Wiseman (who, with Daniel Jackling, had developed the Ray properties in Arizona) sent a young engineer named C. Godfry Gunther to investigate the possibility of renewing production at the ancient Roman mines on the island of Cyprus.[30] Gunther spent the rest of his life trying to bring that operation to profitable production. Alcoholic and broke, he was removed from its management by his benefactors just as success was on the horizon in

1922.[31] Still, it was 1936 before the Mediterranean mine had paid back its debts and had begun paying dividends.

Controlling interest in the Cyprus Minerals Corporation remained with the Mudd family. By the end of the Second World War, large cash flows and sizable profits were being generated, and Cyprus went looking for diversification. It invested in Peruvian iron ore in 1952 and Australian iron ore in 1961. Its first investment in domestic copper mining came with the Pima ore body in Arizona in 1955, followed by the Bagdad (Old Dick) and two other smaller mines, also in Arizona, shortly thereafter. When its Peruvian iron-ore operations were expropriated in 1975, Cyprus determined to sell its Australian holdings as well, making copper the company's bread and butter once again.

Cyprus was acquired by Standard Oil Company of Indiana (later AMOCO) as part of the oil industry's drive for diversification, then was spun off in 1985. In the interim it had spread into coal in Colorado, Kentucky, Pennsylvania, Utah, and Wyoming; gold in Australia; molybdenum in Arizona and Idaho; talc in Montana and Alabama; and calcium carbonate, kaolin, and barite in the southeastern United States. Once again on its own, it moved strongly into copper and gold. In copper it acquired the Esperanza-Sierrita operation and the Mineral Park Mine in Arizona from the Duval Corporation.[32] It added the Lakeshore and Twin Buttes mines in Arizona and the Piños Altos property in New Mexico. While most of its gold-mining expansion in the United States focused on Nevada, Cyprus chose to open a major gold operation in Arizona with the Copperstone Mine.[33] It later added beryllium in Texas and talc in Vermont and Spain. In 1988 it bought from Newmont Mining Corporation the Foote Minerals Company, a producer of lithium in the southeastern United States.[34] All of this was capped later in the same year by purchase of the entire properties of the Inspiration Resources Company for $125 million in cash.[35]

In Chapter 3 we described the origin of the one mine owned by Inspiration Consolidated. Until the 1960s its owners—which included Anaconda with 27 percent—had been happy with their high return on the mining investment alone.[36] With the copper boom and high prices of the 1960s, the company undertook vertical integration by bringing on line in 1968 a new electrolytic refinery and rod mill, and added to the smelter it had acquired from ASARCO.

Until 1973 Inspiration had maintained a close association with Anaconda, even maintaining its offices in Anaconda's headquarters building in New York City. That association ended when Anaconda moved out in

1973 and later abandoned its copper activities. To avoid a takeover attempt by the Crane Company in 1974, which had threatened Anaconda as
well, Inspiration created and sold a new issue of stock to Hudson Bay
Mining and Smelting Company of Canada, which diluted Anaconda's
interest. Subsequently, Inspiration Copper became a subsidiary of Inspiration Resources Company, along with a variety of Canadian mining and
U.S. agribusiness and equipment-leasing operations.[37] Only Inspiration's
Arizona properties were purchased by Cyprus. These consisted of an open-
pit copper mine, two concentrators, an acid plant, an SX-EW plant, a
smelter, and a rod mill, to which Cyprus announced plans in 1989 to add a
refinery.[38] Thus, although by 1989 Phelps Dodge was first in U.S. copper
production with output for the year of 1 billion pounds of copper, Cyprus
was a close second, with 731 million pounds. These operations contributed to the company's highest-ever earnings during that year.[39]

That Cyprus as a new and powerful factor in copper had implications for
collective bargaining soon became apparent. In its purchase of the Inspiration properties, Cyprus inherited union contracts which it refused to
recognize on the grounds that it had bought the facilities, but not the
company which had signed the labor agreement.[40] We shall discuss the
aftermath of this development in Chapter 9.

MAGMA AND NEWMONT

During 1946–1955 Magma Copper's mine at Superior, Arizona, was
equipped with failing and aging machinery—a mine badly in need of
funding for repair and modernization. A. J. McNab, then Magma's president, saw that for a relatively small additional investment Magma's copper
output could be increased from 35 million to 50 million pounds annu-
ally.[41] Increased production threatened the life span of the mine, however.
McNab took the advice of Wesley P. Goss, who was involved with Newmont in the O'Okiep development in South Africa, and sought to attain
both the expansion of Magma's original mine at Superior and the acquisition of a replacement property. The replacement came to be San Manuel,
about 60 miles south of the Superior deposit. It had been offered to
Magma and turned down in 1941, but when exploratory drill holes found
1 percent copper content, Magma's interest was captured. A thorough
examination of the property began in 1945. In 1952 financing was secured
through the Reconstruction Finance Corporation to supplement Newmont's subscribed amount and public stock sale. Production at San Man-

uel started in 1956, but did not turn a profit until 1960 because the timber supports were inadequate for the stresses of the unusually deep underground mine. In time the problem was resolved and San Manuel became one of the most productive underground mines using the block-caving method.

During the deliberations and infighting over Magma in the 1940s and 1950s, Newmont was also pursuing a project known as the Sherritt Gordon copper-nickel mine in Manitoba, Canada.[42] Here, for a $27 million investment, Newmont would eventually gain a 40 percent interest. In contrast to Magma—which faced problems of large-scale mining—the Manitoba project was wrestling with metallurgical obstacles. Fred Searls, the American geologist whom we have met before, found the problems at Manitoba challenging to his personal interests and gave important support to the project. But even when the Manitoba ore problem was largely resolved, the mine still was not a major profit maker compared to San Manuel. Although it required an investment of over $100 million, the San Manuel operation reaped about fifteen times the profits of its rival in Manitoba.

The year 1953 marked a turning point in Newmont policy when Plato Malozemoff, the man in charge of the Sherritt Gordon project, became Newmont's president, whereupon Searls became chairman of the board. Malozemoff's goal was to reshape Newmont from its role as an investment company into the parent of a number of viable minerals producers to be managed by Newmont personnel. While issues of finance were handled at the New York office, operational questions of the various mining companies were dealt with by each firm's general manager. Disillusioned by the seemingly poor potential of its Hudson Bay Mining operation, Newmont began eliminating its interests in that investment. It took up a 29 percent interest in the South African Palabora project and a 10 percent interest in the Cuajone project in Southern Peru—both copper properties. The 1950s, even with these moves, were not good years for Newmont. The South African and Peruvian investments would not pay off until much later.

After San Manuel began to make money, Newmont's attitude toward Magma changed. Magma's success was impressive, but the provisions of its RFC loan blocked payment of dividends. Profits to the company were being plowed back without direct monetary benefit to the stockholders, which included Newmont. To remedy this situation, Newmont took over 80 percent of Magma's outstanding stock. Once antitrust questions were resolved, Newmont took over the remaining 20 percent of Magma in

1969, to become at last the parent company that Newmont's founder, W. Boyce Thompson, had created nearly sixty years before.

Next, Magma bought a deposit adjacent to San Manuel known as the Kalamazoo. This purchase provided the company with a large ore reserve. With Newmont's acquisition, San Manuel's capacity was doubled and forward integration was accomplished in 1971.

During the 1970s approximately 50 percent of Newmont profits came from Magma and from Southern Peru Copper, with over two-thirds of its total return coming from the various copper holdings. Newmont was also rapidly investing in specialty materials such as vanadium, lithium, and ferroalloys, as well as staples such as oil, cement, and zinc. It was a coventurer in the purchase of Peabody Coal from Kennecott. Then in the 1980s it was caught up in the Nevada gold rush and eventually, through its Newmont Gold subsidiary, rose to become the second-largest gold producer in North America.[43]

In this context, the decline in copper price and the consequent losses of the 1980s became increasingly troubling to the parent company.[44] When Magma's deficit reached $40 million per year, Newmont spun it off as an independent company by distributing its shares to the Newmont stockholders in March 1987. Newmont also turned over Pinto Valley Copper Corporation to Magma, and $150 million of Magma's $350 million debt to the parent company was forgiven.

Magma thereupon borrowed an additional $300 million to modernize and install a new flash furnace in its smelter, expand its refinery, implement a new mining plan in its underground mine, and undertake SX-EW recovery, both in an underground in situ leaching facility and by heap leaching at the surface. These occurrences took place on the eve of the sharp upturn in copper price trends. With the combination of the cost reduction, estimated at 28 cents per pound for the SX-EW operations, and skyrocketing prices, Magma was earning nearly as much per quarter for itself in late 1988 as it had been losing per year for its parent. Continuing with record profits in 1989, it came full circle in 1990 by announcing substantial investment in the reopening of its historic Superior Mine.[45]

OTHER COMPANIES

To round out the picture, we need to summarize the experience of three other copper companies, two of them historically important and one rising to prominence after the Second World War. All were out of the copper business before the end of the 1980s debacle.

Calumet and Hecla

Calumet and Hecla enjoyed renewed vigor during the war years. It prospered well from its acquisition of the Wolverine Tube Company, which at the time plied the company with profits, payroll, and executive talent well in excess of any of the other areas of the diversified business. The acquisition in 1953 of 7 percent of Calumet and Hecla stock by C. C. Jung and his group of financial specialists brought significant changes in the strategic management of the company.[46] Under the new influence, executive offices were moved from Boston to Chicago, leaving behind the family domination represented by the sons of Agassiz and Shaw. The new C & H leadership instituted positive diversification efforts into timber, sawmills, and plastics that boosted employment figures to levels not seen by the company in nearly thirty years. With more than 5,000 people employed and the company's overall performance and outlook improved, the attention of various conglomerates was soon drawn to Calumet and Hecla. The end for the historic company came, as it had for other copper pioneers, from oil interests. An offer of $123.5 million by Universal Oil Products Company was accepted, and Calumet and Hecla became yet another copper subsidiary for yet another oil conglomerate.

The takeover occurred during the long 1967 copper strike. As it dragged on, Universal responded by allowing the mines to flood, writing them off as a $13 million loss. Another historic copper company thereby passed on, but there was still life in the initial Michigan Copper Range properties, where the White Pine operation was a profitable mine with 1,000 employees in 1988.

AMAX

The independent investment in and profit from the Climax molybdenum mine culminated with American Metal merging with Climax as American Metals Climax, shortened to AMAX in 1974.[47] By 1952 the earlier investments made by American Metal in African copper and other minerals were paying off handsomely. American Metal's investments in O'Okiep and Tsumeb, which it shared with Newmont, collectively produced almost as much in profits as its northern Rhodesian property and required a much smaller investment.

Thanks to its African and Climax profits, the growth of AMAX was sizable, rapid, and quite diverse. From 1957 to 1963 AMAX grew in size by two-thirds while other copper companies were going through a period of stagnation. Although AMAX produced only one-third the copper of Kennecott, by 1974 it was close to the size of Kennecott in its total assets. The key to AMAX's success was its well-managed diversification efforts, focusing on potash, oil, coal, aluminum, iron ore, and nickel. While its aluminum venture was basically a failure and its nickel diversification was less than successful, AMAX's ventures into iron ore and coal were sufficiently profitable to make up those shortfalls.

As AMAX was learning from its diversification experience, it was facing challenges on another front. Like Anaconda and Kennecott, AMAX confronted the prospect of expropriation; but to its advantage, the threat to AMAX was in Africa. Because the new African governments lacked managerial expertise they could not pursue immediate and complete expropriation. The transition was a gradual one, with AMAX staying on for a time as consultant and management agent.

To insure itself against losses in African output during its gradual withdrawal, AMAX turned to supplementing its domestic copper operation. The company joined in a fifty-fifty venture with Anaconda to harvest the low-grade ore remaining at Twin Buttes, Arizona—a losing proposition, as it later turned out. It attempted to acquire the Copper Range Company but was prevented from doing so by the Justice Department. Painful housecleaning was forced on the firm during the depressed mining years of the early 1980s: the great AMAX molybdenum mine at Climax, Colorado, was closed; lead, nickel, potash, and phosphate operations were idled or sold. By 1990 AMAX was no longer part of the U.S. copper scene.

Duval Corporation

Duval is a relatively young company in terms of copper involvement. Although it was chartered in Texas in 1926 as the Duval Sulphur Company and expanded into potash in 1930, its entry into copper did not come until 1959, with the acquisition of the Esperanza property in Arizona and option rights (which it eventually exercised) on the Mineral Park ore body, also in Arizona.

In 1965 Duval bid on and was awarded an $83 million advance from the

General Services Administration to develop its Sierrita deposit, located close to the Esperanza Mine. This undertaking was to be the lowest-grade ore development attempted up to that time. Profit potential in this mine was limited by the government's contractual right to one-half the production at one-half the market price. By 1974 Duval had become the fifth largest copper-mining firm in capacity. Molybdenum recovery from its Sierrita and Mineral Park mines was a major factor in its profitability.

Duval's concerted involvement in copper was to continue only until 1986. Although its operations at Esperanza and Mineral Park had been closed for several years, Duval kept the Sierrita in full operation as its principal copper-producing facility. In the early 1970s, though, Duval became a subsidiary of Pennzoil United. In the copper crisis of the 1980s, Pennzoil sold Duval's three Arizona copper properties to the Cyprus Minerals Corporation, facilitating the latter's drive to become number two in the industry.

SUMMARY

In 1946 the United States was dominant in the world copper industry. Since the dominant firms in the U.S. industry were Anaconda and Kennecott, both of which had substantial foreign interests, those two firms dominated the industry worldwide. ASARCO was important in the United States primarily as a processor of other firms' metals, although it was a large producer outside this country. Phelps Dodge was a distant third in U.S. production and a significant but not a major force on the world scene. Beyond those four were numerous small producers of little moment. The world's copper resources were almost entirely in private hands, except in the USSR. Copper was unchallenged, except for steel, as an industrial metal. U.S. production was diversified over Montana, Arizona, New Mexico, Utah, and Michigan, whereas world production was relatively concentrated in the United States, Chile, and Peru.

Forty-four years later, the scene had radically changed. Anaconda and the original independent Kennecott were no more. Phelps Dodge had fought its way to the top, but Cyprus Minerals had suddenly emerged in second place (Table 6.1). In contrast with the tradition of American leadership, British-controlled RTZ Minerals, with most of its other interests in the third world, had become number three in the U.S. copper industry. Number four, Magma, had come from dependent starvation to

TABLE 6.1 Major U.S. copper mines by ownership and capacity, 1990

Rank	Company	Mine	State	Capacity (thousands of tons per year)
1	Phelps Dodge	Morenci/Metcalf	Arizona	172
		Chino	New Mexico	95
		Tyrone	New Mexico	92
2	Cyprus Minerals	Sierrita/Esperanza	Arizona	91
		Bagdad	Arizona	47
		Inspiration	Arizona	33
		Casa Grande	Arizona	11
3	RTZ Minerals	Bingham Canyon	Utah	200
4	Magma	San Manuel	Arizona	108
		Pinto Valley/ Miami Superior	Arizona	64
5	ASARCO	Ray	Arizona	74
		Mission Complex	Arizona	36
		Troy	Montana	18
		Silver Bell	Arizona	21
6	Montana Resources	Continental (Butte)	Montana	89
7	Copper Range	White Pine	Michigan	51

SOURCE: U.S. Congress, Office of Technology Assessment, *Copper: Technology and Competitiveness* (Washington, D.C.: Government Printing Office, September 1988), p. 202, and supplementary information.

autonomous growth. Number five, ASARCO, was a processor that had become a miner as well. Numbers six and seven, Montana Resources and Copper Range, were newcomers with less than five years' experience in copper. Of the U.S. copper firms, only Phelps Dodge and ASARCO had any significant foreign interests. Numbers three, six, and seven were single-mine interests insofar as their participation in the American copper industry was concerned. There were no noticeable copper producers beyond number seven.

Yet all of these firms had attained their advanced positions by acts of marked industrial courage. They had ridden out a series of disastrous events. They had borrowed and invested when the returns were doubtful and alternative uses of capital resources had appeared much more promising. They had ruthlessly cast aside historical properties which had become a drain on resources and managerial energy. They had been equally relentless in actions necessary to cut labor costs. Jobs had been slashed in dependent communities, but the remaining employment was far above what it would have been if they had not survived. Despite wage cuts, they had made what was still a relatively high-wage U.S. industry into a low-cost producer in a world setting.

In the doing, the United States had lost its dominant position in the world copper market but had stayed a close second in world production. Maintaining that position was not an accomplishment of government policy. It was the achievement of seven autonomous private firms functioning in a world industry where all of their competitors enjoyed state protection, and in most cases state ownership and operation.

It remains to be seen what world events and company labor policies contributed to this industrial survival.

CHAPTER 7

THE PRODUCT MARKET IN
THE POSTWAR ERA

ALL THAT COULD BE SEEN in the copper industry from the vantage point of 1946 was onward and upward. The civilian shortages of a depression and a war needed to be made up. In addition, the United States had passed its Critical Materials Stockpiling Act of 1946 as an early response to the emerging cold war. The law authorized a copper stock level of 1.13 million tons initially, then raised it to 1.9 million tons in 1950, before a reduction to 1.0 million tons in 1952.[1] The actual stockpiles of copper reached only 0.54 million tons in 1951 and 1.04 million tons by 1960, but the latter figure was still equivalent to only one year's total production of U.S. mines.

THE KOREAN PERIOD

The government-driven expansion of the American copper industry was accelerated by the Defense Production Act of 1950, a response to the Korean conflict. Under this measure loans, purchase contracts, and tax amortization benefits were offered for new or expanded copper-mining enterprises.[2] Many of the fifty-five projects undertaken between 1950 and

1956 were marginal in that they could not survive with the return of a competitive market.

Prices had been rather tightly controlled by most governments during the immediate post–World War II period, but the British government finally allowed resumption of trading on the London Metal Exchange in 1953, in effect reestablishing the world's free market for copper. Prices rose sharply from what would have been about $1.00 to $1.50 per pound in 1983 terms (Figure 7.1). Meanwhile, nondefense demand had been growing with the renewal of housing and civilian industrial and commer-

FIGURE 7.1 **Copper Prices (1983 dollars)**
on the London Metal Exchange

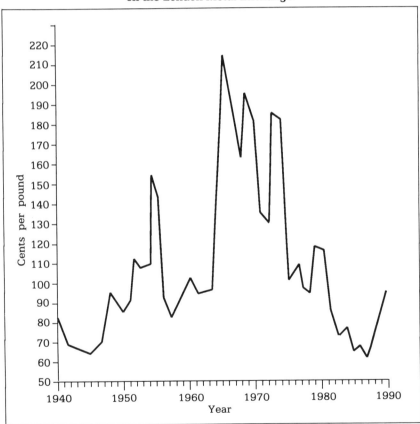

SOURCE: Kenji Takeuchi, John E. Strongman, Shunichi Maeda, and C. Suan Tan, *The World Copper Industry: Its Changing Structure and Future Prospects* (Washington, D.C.: World Bank, 1987), p. 10; and authors' calculations.

cial production. The automobile industry, among others, was booming, and a nascent copper-demanding electronics industry was emerging. Even so, the government subsidies of 1950–1956 had created overcapacity once the Korean conflict had ceased, a situation that was exacerbated by expansion of copper production in Africa and South America. Nevertheless, developments under way did not stop merely because world copper prices fell sharply after 1953. The total mine capacity in the market economies grew 6.7 percent per year between 1956 and 1961, while consumption rose only 3.4 percent per year during the same period.[3]

Despite falling profits, the surge of copper expansion continued (see Figure 7.2). The long strike in the copper industry in 1959 cost 300,000

FIGURE 7.2 **Copper-Mine Capacity and Production in the Market Economies,1960-1986**

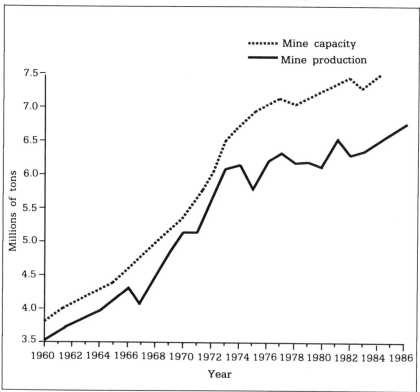

SOURCE: Kenji Takeuchi, John E. Strongman, Shunichi Maeda, and C. Suan Tan, *The World Copper Industry: Its Changing Structure and Future Prospects* (Washington, D.C.: World Bank, 1987), p. 55.

tons in production, but a half-million tons of new annual worldwide mining capacity came on line during the same period. Thus in 1960, although consumption rose nearly 9 percent, world production rose by 17 percent. Prices, of course, responded accordingly. Hoping to stem the price decline, major producers in Zaire, Zambia, Canada, and the United States announced a 10 percent production cutback in 1960; Peruvian and Chilean mines followed the next year.[4] A further cut of 15 percent was announced in 1963. Foreign producers purchased copper on the London market in an attempt to stabilize prices. Nevertheless, the average return on investment remained attractive, as shown by the U.S. figures in Table 7.1.[5]

VIETNAM TO OPEC

By 1963 conditions were accumulating for a new boom in the copper industry. Industrial production was growing rapidly throughout the developed and newly industrializing world. The developed nations were experiencing a communications expansion and the United States would accelerate military production during 1965–1972 because of the Vietnam war. World copper consumption grew, on the average, 4.8 percent per year from 1963 to 1973. Although copper-mining capacity was increasing rapidly as well, a series of strikes, civil disturbances, and producer policies

TABLE 7.1 **Average return on investment, major U.S. copper companies, 1950–1956 and 1957–1963**

	Percent return	
Company	1950–1956	1957–1963
Phelps Dodge	19.0	9.6
Newmont	17.4	12.1
AMAX	16.7	15.0
Kennecott	16.6	8.4
ASARCO	13.6	6.9
Anaconda	8.0	5.0

SOURCE: Kenji Takeuchi, John E. Strongman, Shunichi Maeda, and C. Suan Tan, *The World Copper Industry: Its Changing Structure and Future Prospects* (Washington, D.C.: World Bank, 1987), p. 21.

NOTE: Newmont, AMAX, and ASARCO are diversified companies; contributions of copper toward their revenues are only part of their total earnings.

prevented full utilization. Mine capacity, which had grown at 6.7 percent per year during the years 1956–1960 expanded only 2.4 percent per annum between 1960 and 1965.[6] Zaire experienced civil disturbances during 1963–1965. Zambia confronted transportation difficulties and fuel shortages consequent to the Rhodesian declaration of independence. A traffic embargo followed in the early 1970s. The political unrest discouraged expansion in both African countries. Major strikes occurred in Chile in 1965, in Australia in 1964 and 1965, and for nearly nine months in the United States in 1967–1968. Accumulated stocks were depleted quickly, and the U.S. government reserve was drawn down from over 1 million tons in 1963 to 250,000 tons in 1967. Directly contracted relationships between producers and consumers further reduced the supplies available on the open market and contributed to the soaring LME price (Figure 7.1).

As usually happens, the boom of the 1960s carried within itself the seeds of its own destruction. Accelerating inflation and slowing productivity growth were the prime portents. U.S. consumer prices, which had risen at 2 percent per year from 1960 to 1968, rose 5 percent per year from 1968 to 1973.[7] For the Organization for Economic Cooperation and Development (OECD) group of developed nations, the comparable trends were 2.7 percent and 5.6 percent respectively. Real gross domestic product (GDP) per person employed in the United States grew at 2.6 percent per year during 1960–1968 but slowed to 1.3 percent per annum for 1968–1973. The OECD figures dropped only 4.0 percent and 3.6 percent respectively. U.S. balance-of-payments deficits rose from zero in 1964 to over $10 billion by 1972, ultimately forcing a devaluation of the dollar.

A resultant sharp, short world recession in 1970–1971 was followed by an extraordinary boom in 1972–1973, with OECD growth in GDP reaching 5.4 percent in the first year and 6 percent in the second.[8] But that proved to be the last gasp of a thirty-year period of sustained growth. The Organization of Petroleum Exporting Countries (OPEC) quadrupling of oil prices in 1973 was enough to push the already shaky world economy into a lengthy period of stagflation—slow growth accompanied by rapid inflation. The 1974–1975 recession in the United States turned out to be the deepest since the 1930s. The recovery beginning in 1976 was not complete before the second oil price shock of 1979–1980 brought about a tripling of petroleum prices. Another round of virulent inflation began, which was stifled by a recession in 1981–1983 that was even deeper than that of the previous decade. Thus the GDP growth rate of the industrial market economies declined from 4.9 percent per year during 1960–1973 to 2.8 percent in 1973–1980 and 1.1 percent in 1980–1983. Copper prices turned sharply downward, bottoming out at 58 cents per pound in October 1984; but they were measured in historically inflated terms. From the autumn of 1983 to the summer of 1987, their real value was at 1930s levels. Then, with little warning, prices turned suddenly upward.

INDUSTRY ORGANIZATION

The 1960s and 1970s were periods of substantial change in the ownership of the copper industry, in many cases changes which appear to be reversing themselves at the start of the 1990s. Until the early 1960s, the bulk of the world's copper production was in the hands of a few large multinational private firms, most of them integrated across mining, smelting, and refining. Subsequently, the industry worldwide has become more diversified by increased state ownership or control, acquisition of copper companies by multinational energy firms, and the growing importance of nonintegrated mining companies.

The nationalization trend began in Zaire in 1967, spread to Zambia and Chile in 1969 and 1971, and to Peru in 1974. Mexico joined the trend in 1980, not by expropriation but by initiation of a joint public-private enterprise.[9] That year the twelve large state-owned mines in Africa and Latin America were the source of 37 percent of the noncommunist world's total copper production.[10] In 1981, 62 percent of the mining, 73 percent of the smelting, and 77 percent of the refining capacity in developing countries was in government hands.[11] Comparable figures for the developed countries were 35 percent, 30 percent, and 24 percent. The U.S. capacity shown in Figure 7.3 was, of course, totally private.

The matter of state ownership is significant. The state-owned mines all have a tax or currency-creation source for purchase of properties and equipment, or for production cost subsidization; moreover, they often have political motives for maintaining production and employment despite operating losses. Their access to loans from international development agencies also provides them the opportunity to expand at exactly those times when private firms are having the most difficulty in obtaining expansion capital. Thus, the trend toward state ownership appears to have spent itself for the moment. In fact, in 1988 Mexico reversed its policies and is today pursuing privatization of its copper industry.[12] The African

FIGURE 7.3 **The U.S. Copper Industry in 1986**
(production numbers in 1000 metric tons)

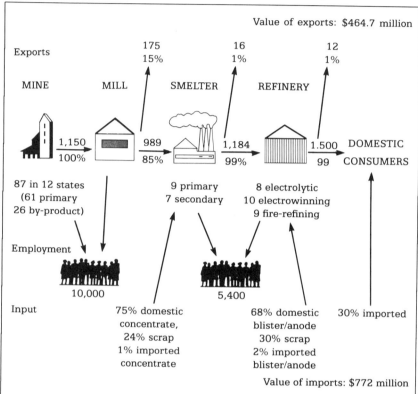

SOURCE: U.S. Congress, Office of Technology Assessment, *Copper: Technology and Compet-itiveness* (Washington, D.C.: Government Printing Office, September 1988), p. 12.

producers are of declining importance. The future of state ownership is largely in the hands of the Chilean and Peruvian governments.

High oil prices were the principal factor in the acquisition of copper mines by energy companies (Table 7.2). Awash with cash from the 1973–1974 and 1979 surges of oil prices, these companies were looking for opportunities for diversification. They were familiar with minerals extraction, although they did not foresee the coming collapse in price. The result was major acquisitions in the United States, Canada, Peru, and Australia. Grass-roots exploration; purchase of unexplored, undeveloped, or proven ore bodies; and acquisition of companies already producing were all involved. The oil companies' owners were a significant source of moderniza-

TABLE 7.2 Major acquisitions of copper-producing companies and properties by energy companies, 1963–1982

Year	Acquiring company	Acquired company
1963	Cities Service	Tennessee Copper
1963	Cities Service	Miami Copper
1968	Pennzoil	Duval
1968	Universal Oil Products	Calumet and Hecla
1974	Shell	Billiton
1977	ARCO	Anaconda
1977	Louisiana	Copper Range
1978	Exxon	Disputada
1979	Hudson Bay	Inspiration
1979	AMOCO	Cyprus
1980	Superior Oil	Falconbridge
1980	British Petroleum	Selection Trust
1981	SOHIO	Kennecott
1982	Occidental	Cities Service

SOURCE: Kenji Takeuchi, John E. Strongman, Shunichi Maeda, and C. Suan Tan, *The World Copper Industry: Its Changing Structure and Future Prospects* (Washington, D.C.: World Bank, 1987), p. 84.

tion capital, which could not at that time have been generated within the copper industry. This acquisition era did not survive the early 1980s, however. The oil companies had bought in just when overcapacity and slower industrial growth were driving prices downward. Then, when oil prices tumbled as well, they reversed themselves and began rapidly divesting themselves of copper properties or abandoning them. By 1990 that part of the copper industry which had been petroleum-owned was largely back in the hands of traditional mining firms.

Since the multinational copper companies of the 1960s had most of their smelting and refining capacity in developed countries, nationalization of the mines by less-developed countries reduced integration to that degree. The flip side of this trend was development of new smelting and refining capacity in Japan and West Germany (Figures 7.4 and 7.5). In each case, the expansion was fostered by the governments during the 1960s and 1970s, out of concern for their lack of domestic copper production. Given the necessity for adequate and dependable supplies of feedstock for efficient operation of smelters and refineries, these companies provided attractive financing arrangements and long-term purchase contracts to capital-short nations, thereby contributing significantly to the overcapacity

FIGURE 7.4 **Primary Smelter Production: 1970, 1980, 1986**

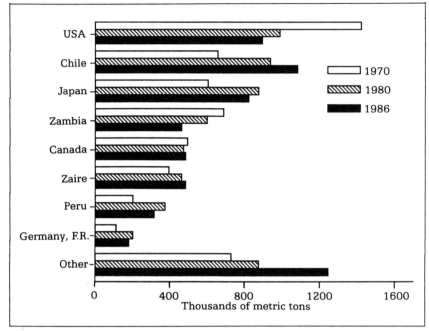

SOURCE: U.S. Congress, Office of Technology Assessment, *Copper: Technology and Competitiveness* (Washington, D.C.: Government Printing Office, September 1988), p. 71.

which emerged in copper mining in the mid-1970s. In January 1989 came the announcement that Mitsubishi would build a 250-million-ton copper smelter on the Houston ship canal at Texas City, Texas.[13] The source of its feedstock and the destination of the anode bars were not included in that announcement. In any case, the project has been stalled for more than two years while environmental questions are being resolved.

CONSUMPTION TRENDS

These strong cyclic stagflation movements of the 1970s and 1980s took the copper industry for a roller coaster ride. Consumption in the non-communist world shot up between 1970 and 1973, plunged in 1975, only to rise to a new peak in 1979 (Table 7.3). When consumption again declined in the worldwide recession of 1980–1982, accompanied by high inflation and interest rates, exchange rates unfavorable to the United States

FIGURE 7.5 **Primary Refinery Production, 1986**

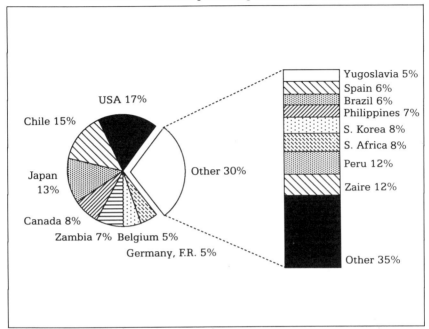

SOURCE: U.S. Congress, Office of Technology Assessment, *Copper: Technology and Competitiveness* (Washington, D.C.: Government Printing Office, September 1988), p. 71.

and massive losses to U.S. producers led them to abandon marginal facilities, at the same time undertaking measures to reduce production costs drastically. Almost immediately, however, consumption began to rise again, exceeding the 1979 peak in 1984 and then continuing upward, though at a slower pace, to unprecedented heights as of 1990.

The experience illustrates the risks of investment decisions in such a volatile market. Obviously, more is involved than overall economic growth trends and the vagaries of the business cycle. Intransigent and probably irreversible trends affect both the consumption and the production of copper. The share of value added in industry, particularly in manufacturing, as a percentage of GDP in industrial countries has been steadily declining, whereas the share of services has increased—and services, by and large, do not use copper. Copper consumption per capita in the developed countries is no greater now than it was in 1929. The intensity of copper use per million U.S. dollars of GDP (measured in constant 1980 dollars) in industrial countries, which had increased from

TABLE 7.3 Refined copper consumption by country or region, 1970–1988

Country or region	Consumption (thousands of metric tons)									
	1970	1973	1975	1979	1981	1982	1984	1986	1987[a]	1988[a]
Industrial countries	5,387	6,331	4,801	6,535	6,147	5,671	6,333	6,244	6,429	6,592
North America	2,005	2,386	1,574	2,468	2,271	1,823	2,272	2,321	2,405	2,420
United States	1,860	2,221	1,397	2,165	2,030	1,664	2,041	2,095	2,173	2,180
Canada	145	164	177	303	242	159	231	226	232	240
EEC-9	2,045	2,180	1,967	2,337	2,166	2,145	2,227	2,363	2,392	2,460
Japan	821	1,202	828	1,330	1,254	1,243	1,368	1,219	1,284	1,356
Developing countries	636	905	969	1,378	1,494	1,410	1,663	1,925	2,026	2,098
Asia	302	418	425	610	735	651	927	1,095	1,173	1,217
China	208	287	300	360	330	288	393	608	660	670
Latin America	179	268	306	469	432	445	396	467	471	494
Africa	48	87	86	97	116	103	109	106	91	97
Southern Europe	108	131	151	182	212	212	232	253	291	290
Industrial plus developing[b]	6,023	7,236	5,770	7,904	7,641	7,174	7,981	8,168	8,455	8,690

SOURCE: World Bank, "World Bank Predictions," 1988, p. 3 (mimeographed draft).

[a] Estimated.
[b] Market economies only.

2,441 pounds in 1960 to 2,480 pounds in 1965, decreased to 1,642 pounds in 1983.[14] The intensity of copper use is increasing in the developing countries, but not at a pace to offset the decline in the industrial countries. And the use in developing countries stagnated during the early 1980s because of the decline in their rates of growth. The same is true, of course, of all major industrial metals (Table 7.4). In addition, the changing industrial mix from the "smokestack" to the "high tech" industries is moving use away from the "old" metals such as copper, iron ore, lead, zinc, and tin toward such "new" materials as beryllium, tantalum, silicon, zerconium, titanium, lithium, and platinum.

Substitution for copper by other materials has also taken its toll.[15] Aluminum has come into competitive use as an electrical and thermal conductor because for the same degree of conductivity it is lighter than copper. Development of competitively priced superconducting materials may be an impressive threat to copper, if formidable technical obstacles can be overcome. Plastics have proved adequate and cheaper for many piping uses. Optical fiber cables are just beginning to replace copper in telecommunications and now pose a serious threat. Material-saving technological changes such as miniaturization have reduced the amount of copper required in its remaining applications.

Not that copper use is about to be eliminated. Copper is one of the most versatile of metals, with superior electrical and high thermal conductivity, strong resistance to corrosion and to bacteria, high strength, ductility, malleability, and pleasing color. Those attributes guarantee it a solid base of future use. Expansion of electronics and computerization continues to be promising. But copper's known uses have been fully exploited, and substantial new uses are not apparent. The end uses of copper in the United States are shown in Figure 7.6.

Yet in the midst of gloomy predictions based on these factors, copper consumption in 1986 exploded with a 4.7 percent increase, followed by slower but persistently upward growth rates for the remainder of the decade. Involved was sharply increased production of metal-intensive capital goods, but it is too early to predict whether the post-1973 decline in the metal intensity of output has been reversed. In the United States, depreciation of the dollar generated new export demand, which required new investment in capital goods after a long lag. The turnaround in machine-tool production was especially impressive. As a result of the renewed emphasis on capital goods, copper consumption grew at almost the same rate as in the overall economies of the developed countries during

TABLE 7.4 **World consumption of selected major metals, and industrial production and real GDP in industrial countries, 1961 to 1988[a]**

Metal	Consumption[b]							Growth rate[c]		
	1961	1970	1973	1982	1983	1984	1988	1961–73	1973–84	1984–88
Aluminum, primary	3,471	8,149	11,182	10,906	12,074	12,652	19,842	9.1	1.4	14.2
Copper, refined	4,219	6,023	7,215	7,065	6,820	7,551	8,265	3.9	1.2	2.4
Lead, refined	2,507	3,486	3,797	4,033	3,810	3,959	4,326	3.1	−0.2	2.3
Zinc, refined	2,688	4,368	4,829	4,491	4,582	4,713	5,235	4.5	−0.3	2.8
Tin	169	185	200	153	141	154		1.4	−2.4	
Nickel	223	444	502	422	498	581		7.0	1.3	
Steel	262	441	488	460	473	647		5.3	−2.6	
Industrial production index[d]	56.7	90.9	98.6	118.2	125.9	135.1		4.7	2.9	
Real GDP[e]	3,499	5,422	5,954	7,525	7,885	8,248		4.5	3.0	

SOURCE: Kenji Takeuchi, John E. Strongman, Shunichi Maeda, and C. Suan Tan, *The World Copper Industry: Its Changing Structure and Future Prospects* (Washington, D.C.: World Bank, 1987), p. 41.

[a] Excludes centrally planned economies.

[b] Includes secondary metal, unless otherwise noted. In thousands of metric tons, except that steel is in millions of metric tons.

[c] Least-squares trend growth rates for aluminum, copper, lead, and zinc; end-point growth rates for tin, nickel, and steel.

[d] 1975 = 100.

[e] In billions of U.S. dollars at 1980 prices and exchange rates.

FIGURE 7.6 **U.S. Copper Consumption
by End-Use Sector, 1986**

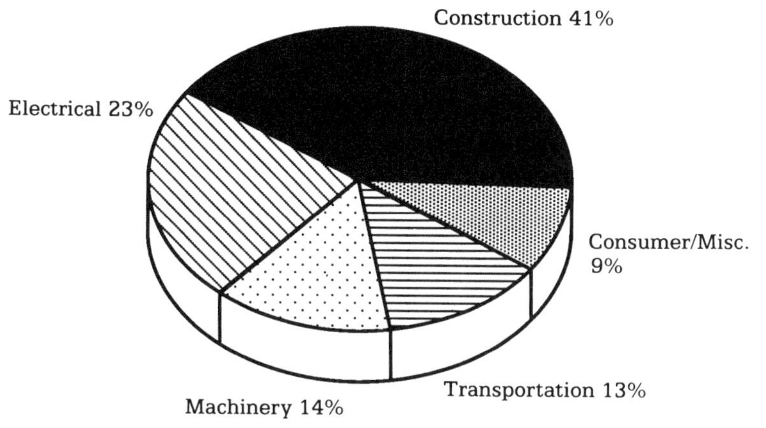

Construction 41%

Electrical 23%

Consumer/Misc.
9%

Transportation 13%

Machinery 14%

SOURCE: U.S. Congress, Office of Technology Assessment, *Copper: Technology and Competitiveness* (Washington, D.C.: Government Printing Office, September 1988), p. 11.

1986–1990. Also, it grew at double the overall economic growth rate in the developing and newly industrializing countries.

In this confusing picture the World Bank predicts an average growth in world copper consumption of 1.9 percent per year for the remainder of the century. That is above the 1.1 percent trend rate of the 1973–1983 period, but well below the 4.7 percent per annum of 1950–1973.[16]

SUPPLY TRENDS

The alert reader will have noted the substantial gap between the mine production trends of Figure 7.2 and the consumption figures of Table 7.3. The difference is the reprocessing of scrap copper, shown for the United States in Figure 7.7. This phenomenon is limited to developed nations, the others having no significant amount of scrap available. Consumption trends for the U.S. copper industry have been and will be dependent on worldwide capacity and output and the relative success of various countries in winning their share of that market. Even though Chile has moved

FIGURE 7.7 **U.S. Copper Production and Consumption, 1975-89**
(secondary production is from scrap)

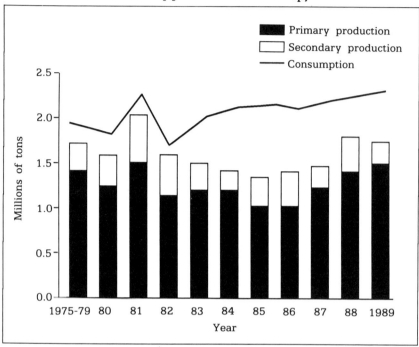

SOURCE: U.S. Congress, Office of Technology Assessment, *Copper: Technology and Competitiveness* (Washington, D.C.: Government Printing Office, September 1988), p. 11.

into first place among copper producers, the United States has never been far behind (Table 7.5). Its relative decline has been due in part to its responsiveness to market conditions. As noted earlier, when fixed foreign-exchange commitments confront falling prices in producing countries characterized by government ownership or control of productive capacity, the pressure is to expand output to stabilize external income rather than to contract in face of declining profits. This tendency is effectuated by international agencies such as the World Bank, Export Import Bank, and International Monetary Fund, which lend to developing countries on the basis of "need." By contrast, producers in the developed countries have great trouble obtaining private development capital, in part because of these very policies. Thus, with capacity utilization averaging only 86.6 percent in the market economies during 1975–1983 (compared to 93.5 percent for 1960–1974),[17] capacity continued to increase markedly in the developing countries while being cut back by the industrial nations (Table 7.6). If it had not been for serious political difficulties in the African copper-producing nations, the dichotomy would have been even more dramatic.

The low-capacity utilization of the 1970s and early 1980s (Figure 7.2) signaled to the U.S. industry the need for drastic action. Nearly thirty mines were closed temporarily or permanently between March 1981 and January 1983. Employment fell by 41 percent in the U.S. copper industry during that period. Between 1980 and 1986, 760,000 tons of copper-mining capacity (11 percent of the total for the world's market economies) were eliminated.[18] Another 240,000 tons of capacity were taken out of commission for modernization. The closures were heavily concentrated in the United States and Canada. Thus, while Chile increased its production 15 percent in 1982, U.S. mine output plunged 26 percent.[19] As a result, the industrial market economies experienced a net capacity decline of 595,000 tons while the capacity of the developing countries increased by 217,000 tons. Whereas net imports were 6 percent of U.S. consumption in 1981, they had soared to 27 percent in 1987.

By 1988 the world copper industry was again operating at near capacity, with production distributed as in Figure 7.8. Market economy stocks declined by nearly 400,000 tons in 1987 alone.[20] During the boom U.S. firms increased capacity through improved technology and in addition opened some new mines. The outlook to the end of the century, however, is for further capacity decline in the U.S. and Canada (Table 7.7). In comparison, new projects are coming on line in Australia, New Guinea, and Zaire and are under consideration in Chile.[21] A persistent Zambian decline has been temporarily arrested through World Bank assistance, but over the long run the nation faces a fall in both ore reserves and ore grade. With secondary sources (scrap) providing over 15 percent of the total copper supply in 1986 and projected at 16.2 percent by the year 2000, the world faces no copper shortage. The challenge will be to make production costs low enough for each country to compete with the others and for copper to compete with its potential substitutes.

PRODUCTION COSTS

Because copper is a homogeneous product, competition in the world copper industry boils down to a battle of cost containment. Once overcapacity

TABLE 7.5 Copper ore production, by principal country or economic region

Country or region	Actual (thousands of metric tons)					Growth rate[a] (% per annum)		
	1969–71	1979–81	1986	1987[b]	1961–86	1970–86	1987–2000
Industrial	2,435	2,528	2,361	2,390	1.2	–1.0	–1.3
North America	2,042	2,069	1,891	1,995	0.9	–1.4	–1.7
United States	1,447	1,388	1,147	1,275	0.2	–2.1	–0.8
Canada	595	681	743	720	2.3	–0.1	–3.6
Oceania	155	237	245	223	4.7	2.2	3.5
Australia	155	237	245	223	4.7	2.2	3.5
Nonmarket	1,095	1,486	1,609	1,630	3.9	1.9	1.8
USSR	930	1,037	1,030	1,040	2.2	0.0	1.5
Eastern Europe	165	450	579	590	11.0	7.3	2.2
Developing	2,712	3,916	4,488	4,521	3.6	3.0	2.5
Asia	298	641	817	835	8.3	6.3	3.6
China	110	166	200	210	4.0	3.4	7.4
Philippines	163	302	217	214	7.4	1.8	1.2

Africa	1,281	1,348	1,327	1,289	1.4	-0.1	-1.2
Zambia	685	591	513	509	-0.6	-2.0	-4.0
Zaire	386	455	503	499	2.7	1.1	0.9
Latin America	984	1,619	2,018	2,027	4.1	5.1	3.2
Chile	694	1,071	1,400	1,375	4.0	4.7	3.7
Mexico	63	171	182	206	6.6	8.9	2.1
Peru	204	364	397	406	3.8	5.0	-0.1
Oceania	0	161	179	218	0.0	0.0	4.8
Papua New Guinea	0	161	179	218	0.0	0.0	4.8
Southern Europe	150	147	149	152	1.0	-0.5	6.6
World	6,242	7,931	8,459	8,541	2.8	1.5	1.4

SOURCE: World Bank, "World Bank Predictions," 1988, p. 10 (mimeographed draft).

[a] Least-squares trend for historical periods 1961–1986.
[b] Estimated.

TABLE 7.6 Copper-mining capacity at beginning of year, 1970–1983 (thousands of metric tons per year)

Country or region	1970	1974	1977	1980	1983	Net increase	
						1974–77	1977–83
United States	1,569	1,715	1,787	1,701	1,716	73	−71
Canada	621	930	898	880	907	−32	9
Australia	136	227	249	245	263	23	14
West Europe	122	172	195	195	187	23	−8
Japan	127	91	82	68	59	−9	−23
Total industrial	2,576	3,134	3,211	3,089	3,133	77	−79
Mexico	64	82	100	272	272	18	172
Chile	744	862	907	1,075	1,184	45	277
Peru	218	222	376	399	404	154	27
Other Latin American	33	23	23	18	54	0	32
Zambia	758	771	771	635	608	0	−163
Zaire	363	522	567	499	526	45	−41
South Africa	132	191	181	218	222	−9	41
Namibia	33	36	54	41	52	18	−3
Other Africa	35	77	82	73	91	5	9

Philippines	136	227	259	372	353	32	94
Indonesia	0	45	64	64	73	18	9
Malaysia	0	30	27	27	27	-3	0
Other Asia	12	27	50	45	64	23	14
Papua New Guinea	0	181	181	172	185	0	4
Yugoslavia	91	132	154	145	168	23	14
Other Southern Europe	79	52	50	32	36	-2	-14
Total developing[a]	2,695	3,479	3,847	4,087	4,318	367	472
Market economies	5,271	6,613	7,058	7,176	7,451	445	393
China[b]	120	150	170	177	187	20	17
World (excluding centrally planned economies)	5,391	6,763	7,228	7,353	7,638	465	410

SOURCE: Kenji Takeuchi, John E. Strongman, Shunichi Maeda, and C. Suan Tan, *The World Copper Industry: Its Changing Structure and Future Prospects* (Washington, D.C.: World Bank, 1987), p. 87.

[a] Excluding China and centrally planned economies in Asia.
[b] Including other nonmarket economies in Asia.

FIGURE 7.8 **Copper Production in Market Economies, 1988**

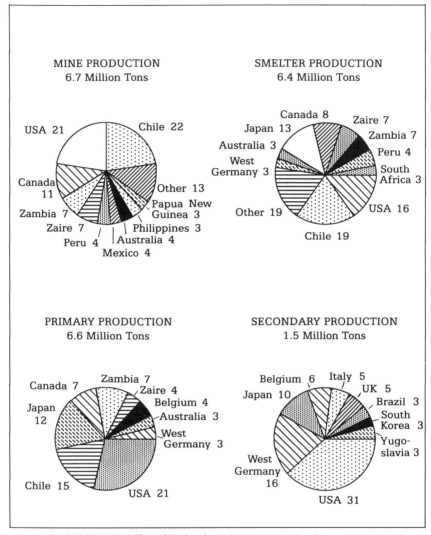

SOURCE: U.S. Congress, Office of Technology Assessment, "Nonferrous Metals: Industry Structure," background paper (Washington, D.C.: Government Printing Office, September 1990), p. 13.

TABLE 7.7 **Projected mine capacities of the major copper-producing countries, 1988–2000, in thousands of tons of copper in concentrates and leach output**

Country or region	1988	1989	1990	1995	2000
Zambia	510	500	490	420	300
Zaire	500	500	490	530	600
South Africa	198	186	180	186	181
Other Africa	107	99	89	48	40
Australia	270	300	310	330	350
Papua New Guinea	250	300	300	320	350
Philippines	220	190	190	200	200
Indonesia	107	115	150	150	150
Other Asia and Middle East	243	244	247	260	278
United States	1,590	1,620	1,680	1,500	1,450
Canada	800	800	780	710	650
Chile	1,510	1,630	1,700	2,100	2,350
Peru	400	380	370	390	420
Mexico	280	290	290	320	350
Brazil	54	60	85	130	150
Other Latin America	3	5	10	19	19
Portugal	20	85	110	130	130
Yugoslavia	128	130	140	150	150
Other Western Europe	142	140	138	130	120
Total market economies	7,332	7,574	7,749	8,023	8,238

SOURCE: World Bank, International Economics Department.

emerged, the interplay of seven cost factors determined winners and losers: labor costs, pollution-control standards and costs, energy costs, interest costs, inflation, exchange rates, and coproduct and by-product credits. Most of these cost forces are beyond the control of any individual company or even the industry as a whole. For the most part they are extraneous determinants which the successful firm must somehow offset internally. To do so, the producers have only technology, labor productivity, and economies of scale as potential offsetting factors.

Labor Costs

Widely differing rates of inflation, fluctuating exchange rates, and the lack of statistical data services in several countries make it extremely difficult to get a fix on comparative labor costs in the copper-producing countries. Because of working conditions, geographic isolation, skill requirements, and a tendency toward unionization, miners are among the highest-paid workers in all parts of the world. On the average, the differential compared to industrial pay is about 65 percent in Chile, Peru, Mexico, and South Africa and 40 percent in the United States.[22] These are premiums above sharply different bases, however. Table 7.8 provides hourly wage rate comparisons for the various countries involved in copper production in 1980 and 1985. Total compensation for the United States and Canada would include another 40 percent or so in supplementary benefits, which are less or nonexistent in the other countries. At the time of this writing the gap between American and other rates has closed somewhat, because of negotiated wage concessions, the fall in value of the U.S. dollar, and rising wages in Japan. Nevertheless, there remains a substantial U.S. wage premium to be overcome by higher labor productivity and lessened cost of other factors.

TABLE 7.8 **Worldwide copper industry wage rates (nominal U.S. currency)**

Country	Wage rate (dollars per hour)	
	1980	1985
Developed		
United States	11.90	16.00[a]
Canada	9.60	11.70
Australia	10.00	9.80
Japan	5.30	6.40
Less developed		
Mexico	2.70	1.80
Chile	2.70	1.60
Philippines	1.90	1.50
Peru	0.90	0.70
Zambia	2.40	0.60

SOURCE: U.S. Congress, Office of Technolgy Assessment, *Copper: Technology and Competitiveness* (Washington, D.C.: Government Printing Office, September 1988) p. 204.

[a] U.S. wage rates declined 20–25 percent in 1986 as a result of union decertification and contract concessions.

Pollution Control

No other nation has imposed on its copper industry pollution-control standards as stringent as those of the United States. The impact, primarily on the smelting phase of production, was even greater than it might otherwise have been because the standards were imposed primarily during a time when world copper prices were already falling and U.S. firms were under heavy pressure from other rising costs. The industry invested over $2 billion in controlling air pollution between 1970 and 1981, with continuing additions to production costs of 10 to 15 cents per pound.[23] The effect on production costs varied widely from company to company, but the widespread consequences are illustrated by the fact that during the 1980s ASARCO costs for reducing emissions at the Hayden smelter were $132 million. Expenditures for the same purpose at Ajo were $45 million, compared to $150 million at Morenci, $150 million at Magma, and $102 million each for Inspiration Consolidated Copper Company and Kennecott Copper (the latter dividing expenditures between its Garfield and Chino smelters). Nevertheless, by closing outmoded smelters, remodeling where possible, and replacing where not, copper smelters reduced their sulfur dioxide emissions by three-fourths, achieving a capture rate of 90 percent.

Energy Costs

Copper mining, smelting, and refining are energy-intensive activities. In addition to their direct impact, multiplying energy costs struck all suppliers to the copper industry. Oil prices are fairly comparable for all copper producers; electricity, which is a more important energy source for the industry, varies widely in cost, depending mostly on the availability of hydroelectric power. The U.S. copper industry is positioned in about the middle among its competitors in energy costs.

Inflation, Interest, and Exchange Rates

Although all copper producers were confronted by rising inflation and fluctuating interest and exchange rates, the impacts differed widely by nation and by company.

Energy costs were the principal worldwide factor in the pervasive inflation of the 1970s and early 1980s. (National policies, particularly in some

less developed countries, were independent causes.) Expectations of inflation, along with internal economic and political conditions of risk, in turn
were major factors in determining interest rates. Some of the third world
copper producers, which might have expected exorbitant interest rates in
light of objective conditions, were aided by subsidized loans from international agencies, as we have seen.

While domestic mines struggled with maintaining a debt-to-equity ratio
sufficiently low to allow attainment of funding at already high interest
rates, third world countries could obtain significant sums of money for
little or no interest, and with debt-to-equity ratios nearing unity.[24] This
subsidized third world borrowing helped Chile, Zambia, and Zaire,
among others, to expand their copper operations and scale of productions
as well as to increase efficiency, while U.S. producers were being restricted
in such efforts by high interest rates and drains on capital caused by
pollution control and high energy costs.

The rates of exchange among international currencies responded to the
differentials in inflation and interest rates, exacerbated by domestic economic policies and balance-of-payments phenomena. Although the U.S.
inflation experience was generally more modest than that of its copper
competitors, the combination of federal budget deficits, credit restraints,
and interest rates, its attractiveness as a safe haven for international money
flows, and a growing balance-of-payments deficit, all feeding upon one
another, resulted in an appreciation of the U.S. dollar relative to other
international currencies during the early 1980s. That and devaluations in
the currencies of some other copper producers put this country at a
disadvantage as a world source of copper. The result was to draw into the
United States large increases in copper imports from Canada, Chile, and
Peru. Decline in the value of the dollar starting in 1987 began to improve
the U.S. competitive position vis-à-vis the currencies of all but Mexico and
the Philippines, neither of which are important competitors in the U.S.
copper market.[25]

Chapter 2 noted the contribution of coproducts or by-products to the
returns of copper-producing firms. But the prices of these metals are
generally as volatile as those of copper. The prices of most by-products
rose during the late 1970s, then plunged more rapidly than copper prices
from 1980 to 1984.[26] Nevertheless, throughout the period by-product
credits were significant factors in lowering the copper production costs in
Sweden, Canada, Mexico, New Guinea, Peru, and Zaire. At the same time,
the United States, Chile, Indonesia, and Zambia suffered from relatively
low by-product credits.

Cost-Reduction Efforts

Under pressures for survival, the 1980s was a period of strenuous efforts at cost reduction by almost all the major copper producers. Traditionally, the industry had rested on its cyclic nature, trusting that its losses in periods of slack demand and low prices would be made up at the top of the business cycle. The long depression in copper prices, however, sent the survivors scrambling for permanently lowered cost structures. Table 7.9 shows comparative costs by nation for various years between 1975 and 1985. Given that the average annual price on the London Metal Exchange in 1984 was 62.6 cents, the cost challenge to the United States is obvious. It was against this cost structure and price relationship that the competing countries struggled through the mid-1980s.

Most of the cost savings of the industrial countries have come from internal improvements in labor costs, technology, and productivity, whereas exchange-rate adjustments have dominated the cost changes among developing countries. The competitive status of the United States has further improved as a result of the relative decline in the value of the dollar. Productivity gains in Chile have been largely wiped out by deterioration in the ore grade and an increase in the stripping ratio. Zambia

TABLE 7.9 **Production costs for major nonsocialist copper-producing countries (cents per pound of refined copper, nominal U.S. currency)**

Country	1975	1980	1984	1985
Papua New Guinea	23.8	17.9	32.4	43.2
Indonesia	35.5	33.3	46.0	49.7
Chile	47.2	56.7	48.8	42.2
Peru	51.1	41.2	56.8	41.2
Zaire	55.1	51.1	45.2	39.8
Zambia	61.6	84.3	66.0	55.8
Mexico	27.3	42.1	37.9	79.5
Australia	38.3	27.6	63.8	51.9
South Africa	41.3	42.7	45.6	28.6
United States	61.6	73.4	78.1	65.3
Canada	28.4	−9.6[a]	56.1	42.3
Philippines	38.1	57.3	55.5	85.9
Average	48.8	50.0	56.9	50.6

SOURCE: U.S. Congress, Office of Technology Assessment, *Copper: Technology and Competitiveness* (Washington, D.C.: Government Printing Office, September 1988), p. 197.

[a] Negative costs because of coproducts/by-products credits.

moved from the highest-cost to the lowest-cost producer through a combination of exchange-rate adjustments and productivity improvements, despite small declines in the ore grade. Australia achieved most of its cost improvements through by-product credits.

Cost savings in the United States have been attained by closure of high-cost mines, productivity improvements through modernization of equipment and mining techniques, enhancement of ore grades by exploitation of better deposits, and lowering of labor costs. Overhead costs have been cut, primarily via computerization and a drastic thinning of management and staff ranks. Several U.S. producers have abandoned high-cost smelting and refining, relying on favorable custom-smelting rates offered by Japanese smelters with a shortage of feedstock. (The cost-reduction efforts of specific firms were described in Chapter 6.) A technological change of particular note has been the application of leaching, solvent-extraction, and electrowinning techniques to newly mined ores, in situ ore bodies, tailings, and ore dumps. In consequence, SX-EW accounted for 13 percent of total U.S. production in 1987 and 23 percent in 1988.[27]

These changes, which have allowed U.S. mines to maintain production while drastically slashing employment, are reflected in the productivity trends shown in Figure 7.9. For the market economies as a whole, average direct costs are estimated to have fallen from 63 cents per pound in 1981

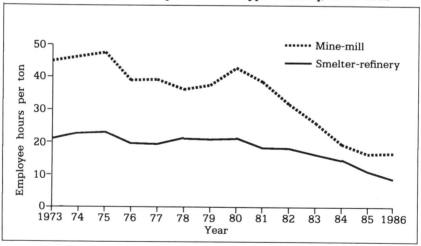

FIGURE 7.9 **Productivity in the U.S. Copper Industry, 1973–1986**

SOURCE: U.S. Congress, Office of Technology Assessment, *Copper: Technology and Competitiveness* (Washington, D.C.: Government Printing Office, September 1988), p. 16.

to 45 cents in 1986, and average total costs from 82 cents per pound to 66 cents per pound during those same years.[28] Within that context, the U.S. industry overall is now a low-cost, extremely profitable producer (Figure 7.10).

PRICE TRENDS

To understand the intense volatility of copper prices (see Figure 7.1), we need to keep in mind that the demand for copper is price inelastic. That is, in the short run at least, price has little impact on the quantity bought, but the quantity required has a multiplied impact on the price. As noted earlier, there are substitutes for copper in most uses. Still, copper is an

FIGURE 7.10 **Average net operating costs for major copper-producing nations, 1986, compared to mine product. Net costs equal gross mining, milling, and smelting or refining charges, including transportation, minus by-product credits. The average total cost is compared to mine output only, because while some countries (for example, Peru) have very little smelting or refining capacity, the charges are attributed to the country in which the ore is mined.**

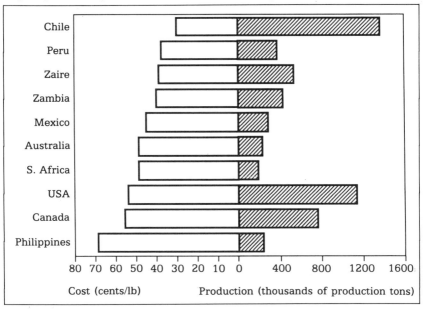

SOURCE: U.S. Congress, Office of Technology Assessment, *Copper: Technology and Competitiveness* (Washington, D.C.: Government Printing Office, September 1988), p. 16.

intermediate good used in the production of a variety of final products and is a relatively minor contributor to the total production cost of most of those products. In the short run, a manufacturer of automobiles, computers, or electrical apparatus for commercial construction will not shut down assembly lines and undertake research and development in search of a substitute because the price of copper has increased. Rather, the user will bid for the needed share of current stocks while pursuing longer-run substitution if continued high prices are expected. Conversely, there will not be an immediate and substantial shift to copper when its price declines.

As noted in Chapter 4, within the gyrations typical of inelastic demand, the long-run trend of copper prices had been steadily downward throughout the period before and even during the Second World War. The end of price controls, the demands of postwar world reconstruction, and shortages of civilian goods, along with the national defense stockpiling of the cold war and the Korean conflict, all worked to drive prices sharply upward. The slow economic growth of the 1950s, accompanied by rapid capacity expansion in the industry, diminished prices. This period was followed by another international economic boom during the 1960s, at the same time that copper supplies were interrupted by strikes, political unrest, and expropriation. Next was the worldwide slowdown in economic growth engendered primarily by sharply rising energy costs during the 1970s. This long decline took world copper prices below costs of production for many producers, particularly those in the United States, who were forced to take the difficult decisions of the 1980s. The choice was to cut costs or to close. U.S. producers pursued both courses simultaneously.

When the industrial world began to recover from the deep recession of the early 1980s, its demands confronted reduced supplies and capacity. As already noted, the LME prices began at a low of 57.7 cents per pound in October 1984, hovered at around 59 cents in November 1986 (Table 7.10), then leaped upward to $1.30 by the end of 1987, and, with considerable fluctuation between $1.00 and $1.59, averaged $1.18 for 1988 and $1.29 for 1989, dropping back to $1.20 for 1990.

This volatile price behavior was the backdrop before which the collective bargaining drama that we shall examine in Chapter 9 was performed. Low prices and large losses compelled some painful decisions. For many of the petroleum firms which had bought into copper as an outlet for their swollen cash flows of the 1970s, the message seemed to be "get out." For those with a long-term commitment to the industry, the signal was differ-

TABLE 7.10 **Monthly copper prices on the London Metal Exchange, 1983–1990 (U.S. cents per pound)**

Month	1983	1984	1985	1986	1987	1988	1989	1990
January	71.3	62.4	61.7	64.3	61.1	120.8	117.9	107.3
February	74.7	64.8	63.0	63.7	62.6	105.7	140.4	107.0
March	72.5	68.1	63.0	65.5	66.5	107.0	150.0	119.1
April	76.0	69.5	68.1	65.0	67.3	103.7	141.4	121.8
May	80.1	64.4	69.4	64.4	69.0	111.0	124.2	124.3
June	77.2	61.9	65.0	64.1	71.3	115.2	115.4	117.2
July	77.3	60.4	66.9	61.0	76.9	100.4	113.6	121.9
August	74.4	60.7	64.4	59.1	79.7	99.8	125.2	131.5
September	70.8	58.7	62.0	61.1	82.1	110.5	130.8	137.5
October	65.1	57.7	62.8	59.7	89.2	133.3	129.7	124.4
November	63.0	61.0	62.1	59.1	114.5	149.9	120.6	117.3
December	64.2	59.9	63.1	60.6	130.1	158.7	109.7	112.7
Average	72.2	62.6	64.9	62.3	80.8	118.0	128.9	120.2

SOURCE: *Metals Week,* Grade A monthly average settlement price.

ent: invest, cut costs, and then compete. As a result, employers fought with their unions for labor-cost concessions, only to have prices and profits soar almost before the ink was dry on the final settlements. Nevertheless, the companies persevered in their cost-cutting technological and labor-relations innovations—determined to compete, whatever the future might hold. And the unions did not fight those changes as vigorously as might have been expected, whether from bargaining weakness or out of the same concern for the industry's future.

To project that future, we need some cautionary perspectives:

1. The high prices of 1987–1990 were nominally unprecedented, but not in real terms. Deflated, they were substantially below those of previous booms (Table 7.11).

2. The high prices emanated from a sudden recovery of world demand at a time of reduced production and productive capacity. Continued low world production is attributable to conditions abroad, which cannot be depended on to persist. For the United States, recovery from the 1981–1982 recession ended in the final quarter of 1990. The pertinent question is how low the price will fall in the 1991 downturn.

3. Over the long term, experience has shown that high prices for copper call forth both expanded supplies and a shift to substitutes. Together these forces work to dampen a further rise.

The most hopeful development for the long-run health of the U.S. copper industry is its aggressive investment and cost cutting, which have restored its historical status as *the* low-cost producer on the world scene. The industry can make money at the 60 to 80 cents per pound constant-dollar range, but there is no guarantee that volatile and inelastic demand will not again depress prices below the minimum of that range.

TABLE 7.11 **Copper prices, 1950–1989ª (dollars per pound)**

| Year | Nominal price | Real price | |
		MUVᵇ	US GNPᶜ
1950	0.246	1.042	
1951	.304	1.112	
1952	.358	1.250	
1953	.332	1.194	1.448
1954	.343	1.262	1.459
1955	.484	1.748	1.994
1956	.453	1.579	1.806
1957	.303	1.033	1.164
1958	.273	0.915	1.027
1959	.328	1.115	1.204
1960	.339	1.129	1.224
1961	.317	1.029	1.133
1962	.322	1.035	1.128
1963	.323	1.058	1.116
1964	.484	1.559	1.644
1965	.645	2.062	2.136
1966	.765	2.362	2.448
1967	.569	1.737	1.768
1968	.621	1.912	1.840
1969	.733	2.144	2.062
1970	.707	1.917	1.881
1971	.540	1.410	1.361
1972	.536	1.283	1.289
1973	.893	1.846	2.017
1974	1.030	1.747	2.134
1975	0.619	0.943	1.167
1976	.701	1.055	1.243
1977	.655	0.898	1.089
1978	.684	0.814	1.059
1979	.993	1.044	1.413

TABLE 7.11 (continued)

Year	Nominal price	Real price MUV[b]	Real price US GNP[c]
1980	1.091	1.046	1.423
1981	0.871	0.831	1.037
1982	.740	.716	0.828
1983	.796	.791	.858
1984	.689	.696	.714
1985	.709	.709	.709
1986	.687	.581	.674
1987	.892	.686	.849
1988	1.180	.907	1.123
1989	1.289	N.A.	1.021

SOURCE: World Bank, unpublished data; 1989 from *Metals Week*.

[a] London Metal Exchange, cash, wirebars to the end of August 1981; from September 1981 to June 1986, high-grade cathodes replaced wirebars; from July 1986 on, Grade A (which includes high-grade cathodes and high-grade wirebars) replaced high-grade cathodes.
[b] Deflated by Manufacturing Unit Value (MUV) index.
[c] Deflated by U.S. GNP deflator.

CHAPTER 8

UNIONISM, COLLECTIVE BARGAINING, AND THE LABOR MARKET, 1946–1966

IN 1946 UP TO 125,000 WORKERS were engaged in the extraction, process-ing, and fabrication of nonferrous metals. Of this group the International Union of Mine, Mill and Smelter Workers claimed approximately 75,000 persons.[1] The dominant organization in numbers, it was far from domi-nant in bargaining power because it had to share representation with an unusually large array of other unions. It is essential to become familiar with this peculiar bargaining system, and with the underlying factors that brought it about, to understand labor-management relations in the indus-try over the following twenty years.

THE PROBLEM OF STRUCTURE IN NONFERROUS COLLECTIVE BARGAINING

The Emergence of Multiple Unionism and Pluralistic Bargaining

At the end of World War II, the nonferrous metals industry had an extremely complex structure of collective bargaining, more like that of the railroads than of automobiles or basic steel. All the major producers except Kennecott had been organized, and Kennecott was about to be. But instead of a single great industrial union, such as the United Automobile Workers or the United Steelworkers, nonferrous had more than twenty-five recognized labor organizations. The preponderance were craft unions engaged in maintenance, repair, and construction, or in the operation of industrial railroads on the larger mining properties. The basic characteristic of these unions, as with craft unions everywhere, was that each organization controlled and represented a distinct and specific occupation—electrician, machinist, pipe fitter, or brakeman.

One union in the industry conformed to the industrial rather than the occupational type: the Mine, Mill and Smelter Workers, which acquired that name in 1916 as successor to the Western Federation of Miners. Like its colorful forebear, Mine Mill was a genuine industrial union from the start, as represented by its historic jurisdictional claim, amended slightly in 1936, to organize and represent "all persons working in and around all mines (except coal mines), mills, smelters, refineries . . . open pits . . . power shovels . . . and reduction plants."[2] This broad formulation of its jurisdictional territory is concerned solely with processes and technical functions in the extractive branch of the industry. It says nothing about specific occupations. What it does do is lay claim to all jobs within this industrial domain. In other words, the *product*—the extraction of nonferrous metals—defines the union's jurisdiction, not some specific occupation.

In the history of the nonferrous industry, as Chapter 5 shows in more detail, local craft unions had begun to appear by the 1890s, when the Western Federation of Miners was formed as an industrial union and potential rival. Through the years the crafts functioned in the mining camps as friendly societies or social clubs—organized, but usually not recognized by the employers. Recognition typically came with the enactment of the Wagner Act in 1935, which authorized the National Labor Relations Board to establish bargaining units, conduct representation elections, and direct employers to bargain collectively with the unions that won these elections.

Mine Mill, of course, gained recognition in the same way. Inasmuch as it had to share representation rights with the craft groups, it could not enjoy the unitary and all-embracing bargaining status acquired by the USW in steel or the UAW in automobiles. There the board had rejected the jurisdictional claims of the crafts and designated plant-wide or company-wide bargaining units for representation by a single industrial union. Because Mine Mill had to share representation with many different crafts, it wound up with what are technically known as *residual* or *production and maintenance* bargaining units, typically confined to production jobs in mining and mucking underground, in the crushing plants and concentrators, and in the smelters and refineries. Many, if not most, of these jobs were semiskilled or common labor, although some, such as miner or crane operator, were highly skilled but had no craft organization.

In a word, the nonferrous industry became a classic case of multiple-union representation for collective bargaining, partly with a base in Mine Mill as an industrial union and partly with a base made up of many craft unions, with each union negotiating on its own behalf. The bargaining, local and decentralized, was also highly competitive and unstable, with endless jockeying of the different unions for leadership in designing the pattern for settlement. Strikes became the rule rather than the exception.

The Problem of Bargaining Structure in Nonferrous

Since 1935 federal labor law concerning union representation of employees has been regulated by the dictum of "unions of their own choosing." In essence this expression means that employees are to decide whether they wish to be represented by a union for purposes of collective bargaining, and if they do, which union is to represent them—the principle of self-determination. A second principle is that of bargaining effectiveness. It is less easily understood, but can be said to mean that the right to be represented by a union presumes that the organization will be able to achieve agreements with management that are acceptable to a majority of the employees in the bargaining unit. Obviously what is "acceptable" is imprecise, but at the least it means that the majority deems itself better off with the bargain struck for it than if its members had to bargain for themselves, without a union. More broadly, bargaining effectiveness includes the notion that union representation will be available to all groups in a given work force who desire to have it.

When the principles of self-determination and bargaining effectiveness are involved in practice, conflict between them is apt to follow. Self-determination can bring about a splintering of the work force into a large number of small craft unions, which in turn denies bargaining effectiveness to groups of lesser skill for whom no craft organization exists. The same outcome can create difficulties for the employer as well, in the form of rigid and costly work-separation rules.

At the same time, increased bargaining effectiveness calls for large consolidated bargaining units which merge craft occupations with those involving semiskilled and unskilled groups. Pushed far enough, these massive units can wipe out the right of self-determination. This dichotomy was at the core of the acrimonious dispute over craft versus industrial unionism in the 1930s. The two principles cannot be reconciled; they can only be compromised. For example, craft workers could be allowed to vote on whether they wished to be represented by an appropriate craft union or, in a different context, whether they wished to sever their group from a large industrial unit, to substitute a craft union for their representation.[3]

In nonferrous production, several factors in the history of the industry (examined later) usually led to multiple-union structure for representation: the maintenance and construction crafts; the railroad brotherhoods; a residual industrial unit of production workers for whom craft representation was not feasible. Initially at least, the outcome was decentralized local bargaining between the employer and the individual unions in each of the three groups. Moreover, in some cases the scope of collective bargaining for all three groups was confined to a given property, although an employer with multiple-plant operations remained free to adopt a coordinated strategy for all of his properties together.

In the early years after the war, the craft unions in the nonferrous mines found this arrangement generally satisfactory, because it granted them full exercise of their right of self-determination and also full advantage of what Alfred Marshall called "the importance of being unimportant," that is, the right to exact substantially higher wages and benefits because of the scarcity and nonreplaceability of their members, whose wages represented a small proportion of total costs. Nonetheless, the employers certainly did not mind the ensuing localized nature of collective bargaining, or the endemic negotiating weakness of the lesser skilled group—although they found onerous the restrictive work rules imposed by the craft unions.

The real opponents of these unusual bargaining arrangements, therefore, were the leaders of Mine Mill and, by 1950, of the United Steelworkers. This circumstance did not occur by chance and should occasion no surprise. Both organizations were industrial unions. Accordingly, their preoccupation lay with increased bargaining effectiveness, rather than with full self-determination. Mine Mill had begun looking favorably at company-wide bargaining as early as its 1940 convention. By 1946 it had formulated a comprehensive scheme for centralized bargaining demands and strategy on an industry-wide basis.[4] The Steelworkers, of course, had independently developed a similar outlook with the formation of their predecessor, the Steel Workers Organizing Committee (SWOC), in 1936.

To these two industrial unions, the structural problem was what each of them came to describe as a "fragmentation" of collective bargaining, by which they meant a dissipation of bargaining strength brought about by the splitting up of the nonferrous work force among more than twenty-five international unions. To them the problem was to consolidate under one leadership the divided bargaining efforts of these many labor organizations. The solution to this structural problem, they contended, demanded at the very least the cooperation of the already existent craft unions in a joint effort, despite their tradition of independence and self-determination. To the employers, fragmentation as such was less a problem than a bargaining advantage, granted the peculiar difficulties associated with craft representation.

The most important conflict in nonferrous mining between industrial and craft unions has already been illustrated by two important events in Chapter 5: (1) the opposition of the crafts to readmission of the Western Federation of Miners to the AFL in 1910–1911, and (2) the three-and-a-half-month strike against Anaconda called by the Metal Trades Department, successfully concluded at the national level without giving Mine Mill a voice in the negotiations. The national AFL later came under harsh attack by John L. Lewis, who correctly perceived the underlying threat to all industrial unions in the dominant role of John P. Frey, head of the Metal Trades Department, in negotiating the entire agreement without the knowledge or consent of the sole industrial union involved, Mine Mill.

Factors Responsible for the Nonferrous Bargaining Structure

Unionism in the nonferrous industry already had a long history by late 1935, when Lewis launched the Committee for Industrial Organization to introduce industrial unionism to steel and automobiles, where there had been little precedent of any unionism at all. The CIO conception, as Lloyd Ulman has noted, was to "organize from the top down" by means of committees that would press the NLRB to design large industrial bargaining units, where single-union representation would be the outcome of successful elections. In nonferrous, however, things had been the other way around: unionism had been introduced by self-organization "from the ground up" over more than forty years before the CIO had come into being. Self-determination at the local level had been the guiding principle, and there had been no NLRB protection to aid these voluntary private undertakings. The inevitable result was a diverse type of union structure, in which the craft principle would predominate. At the same time, the Western Federation of Miners (and its successor, Mine Mill) kept the principle of industrial unionism visible and active throughout the period.

In any event, the inheritance of the nonferrous industry in 1946 was the complex system of decentralized collective bargaining earlier described. No one designed this system in the sense that the original CIO designed its version of industrial unionism. Rather, it was the product of a particular history, in a particular environment.

For example, in 1937 the NLRB handed down its "Globe Doctrine," in a somewhat belated response to numerous complaints that the board had been favoring industrial over craft unionism, establishing bargaining units that provided for single-union representation only in mass-production industries. To deal with the issue, the board decided that both craft and production-worker groups should choose for themselves between craft and industrial union representation. This acknowledgment of the principle of self-determination had the effect of extending the protections of the new Wagner Act to all of the existing unions in nonferrous. More particularly, it enabled the numerous craft organizations in the industry to win certification as bargaining agents through representation elections, which in turn would bind the employers in the industry to recognize and bargain with these unions if they had not voluntarily done so earlier. In short, Globe reinforced the already established diverse and decentralized structure of nonferrous unionism from 1937 on, with many representation elections occurring with the rapid expansion of the industry after 1940.

Geography and technology were also important in the formation and shaping of the nonferrous bargaining system. The industry is characterized by geographic dispersion, with mines and smelters usually in the West, refineries in the West or Southwest, and fabricating and reclaiming plants scattered among the East, Midwest, Southwest, and West. Accompanying this dispersion of activities is a wide range of metal products—copper, lead, zinc, silver, gold, nickel, titanium, and uranium, as well as others. Each metal requires specialized smelting and refining facilities, while their respective ore deposits are scattered in widely differing locations. Taken together, the many employers and the vast geographic spread of their diverse operations have also contributed to the initial decentralization of collective bargaining and to the difficulties the unions had in establishing uniformity of wages and benefits.

Furthermore, on the mining and smelting side in particular, economically efficient activities have dictated that production be conducted where nature has placed the ore, to take advantage of significant weight losses in processing. As a rule, the ores are found in remote places. In consequence, labor markets are typically small, restricted, and almost entirely dependent on a single employer. Given the lengthy tradition of frontier conflict within the industry, its isolated mining camps have made for hard and bitter strikes, until recently occurring with each new contract negotiation.

Another element significant for the shaping of the nonferrous bargaining system involved the takeover of control of the national leadership of Mine Mill by a faction affiliated with the Communist Party of the United States. As noted earlier, communist domination began in the years just before World War II, when Reid Robinson was president of the union. It continued throughout the period until Mine Mill was absorbed by the United Steelworkers in 1967. Control by the communist faction had many debilitating consequences for the organization. It created bitter internal dissension, followed by numerous secession movements. By 1950 it led to expulsion of the union from the CIO. In turn, this action encouraged raiding and defections, particularly in the fabricating branch of the industry. From 1955 on, the Mine Mill leadership was under constant legal attack by the federal government, which sapped the union's finances, distracted its officers' attention from union interests and objectives, and discredited and isolated the organization to the point where it became incapable of providing bargaining leadership or even of negotiating effectively on behalf of its members. Undoubtedly these adverse developments prepared the way for eventual takeover by the USW, which in turn introduced a radical new departure in the bargaining system of the nonferrous industry.

Finally—and indeed partly because of the advent of communist control of Mine Mill—the United Steelworkers itself began to play an increasingly powerful role in nonferrous labor relations. With Mine Mill's expulsion in February 1950, it had been widely expected that the national CIO would charter a new rival union to challenge for representation rights throughout the industry. This expectation did not materialize, because Philip Murray, who was head of the USW and also president of the CIO, had at the very least reached an understanding (if not a formal agreement) with Walter Reuther of the United Automobile Workers, whereby the USW was to occupy Mine Mill's territory in mining, smelting, and refining, while the UAW would take the fabricating plants. This settlement called for a program of promoting secessions and undertaking aggressive raiding, an effort in which the UAW was markedly successful, while the USW was not.

But the Steelworkers were ultimately to profit from the government's continuing prosecutions of the Mine Mill leadership, which extended over more than a decade. When they finally ended in June 1966, with no convictions, the way was cleared for the merger of 1967. In the end, therefore, the large jurisdictional ambitions of the USW were fulfilled; it was to emerge as the dominant union in nonferrous, and to introduce an approach to collective bargaining that, somewhat ironically, was to carry forward the basic ideas that Mine Mill had worked out twenty years before.

BARGAINING DEVELOPMENTS AND RELATIONS

The Diversity of Company-Union Bargaining Models

At one end of the spectrum of different bargaining systems at the level of the individual companies is ASARCO, which had begun collective bargaining in the latter half of the 1930s. Until the mid-1950s ASARCO was not primarily a domestic mining company. Rather, it was the operator of more than twenty smelters and refineries, extending from Tacoma to Baltimore, that treated a broad array of metals mined by other firms.

Because smelting and refining call primarily for unskilled and semiskilled labor, the operations of the company held little attraction for the AFL crafts, but did have strong appeal for Mine Mill—because the latter was an industrial union. Thus, with the minor exception of the electricians, ASARCO's plants had been organized by Mine Mill alone, in allembracing plant-wide production units. At the start, negotiations were conducted exclusively on a local basis, although the bargaining parties on each side were affiliated respectively with an interplant national union and a multiplant company. Because of this very fact, by the mid-1950s the parties had transformed their bargaining system to a company-wide negotiation over major economic matters, supplemented by plant bargaining for local matters. This arrangement was to become permanent. It also conformed well to the CIO conception of industrial unionism, precisely because of its company-wide bilateral nature and the presence of only one national union.

At Phelps Dodge unionism had made no effective appearance until 1942, when the NLRB conducted a series of Globe elections. These were held on a craft-by-craft basis, including the company's industrial railroads. In addition, the board designed a "residual" unit for production workers who had no recognized craft union and were employed in the open pits, concentrating plants and smelters in the company's western operations. Many of these employees were Spanish speaking or American Indian, lacking comparable education and skills. Mine Mill understood their problems and handicaps. An industrial union, it easily became their representative for collective bargaining.

In 1942 Phelps Dodge had properties at Morenci, Ajo, Bisbee, and Douglas in Arizona, and refineries at El Paso, Texas, and Laurel Hill, New York. This dispersion of activities, together with the parallel dispersion of organizing efforts by more than twenty unions, made for local elections concerning union representation. As a result, PD developed a property-by-property system of negotiation, typically with separate groups—the AFL for metal trades, the railroad brotherhoods, and Mine Mill for production workers. Circumstances as well as distance isolated the two refineries, along with the company's several subsidiary fabricating plants, from local bargaining at the western mining properties. This extreme decentralization of bargaining units and negotiations was not unwelcome to PD: it was the next best thing to having no unions at all.

From the beginning of bargaining relations at Phelps Dodge, Mine Mill was able to achieve joint bargaining about economic issues and other matters that could be made uniform concerning the properties belonging to the company's western mining operations. These settlements necessarily excluded Ajo, where Mine Mill had lost a representation election to the Chemical Workers. Thus Ajo tended to be independent of the pattern at the other locations, where Mine Mill settlements both influenced and were influenced by craft settlements, except for purely local union issues. At all properties, as in Kennecott, the railroad brotherhoods bargained separately.

This brings us to Kennecott. Until his retirement in 1942, Daniel C. Jackling had determined the company's labor policies. Not surprisingly, throughout his career he was adamantly opposed to unions, very much in the tradition of mining entrepreneurs throughout the industry in those times.[5] Within a year of Jackling's departure, the NLRB ordered the disestablishment of company unions at Utah Copper. While the board's decision was on appeal by Kennecott, it ordered representation elections, following this action by issuing certifications for the AFL crafts, the railroad trainmen, and a production-worker unit for the pit and concentration plants. This residual unit was successfully claimed by Mine Mill, which already had ASARCO's Garfield smelter serving Kennecott's Utah copper operations.[6] Ultimately, the company lost its appeal and was compelled to recognize and bargain collectively with the three groups of unions. During 1944–1948, unionization was extended in roughly the same pattern to Kennecott's Nevada, Ray, and Chino divisions.

Initially Kennecott bargained only on a local basis, union by union. Gradually the unions began to coordinate bargaining on the local level, although here the railroad brotherhoods remained strongly independent. Eventually the company was to develop a two-tier system of negotiations, company-wide for economic matters (wages and wage-related benefits) and local for local issues. By contrast, Phelps Dodge successfully fought off company-wide bargaining, although it was dealing with almost the same tripartite group of union organizations.

During the period around the end of World War II, most of the smaller copper mines, such as Inspiration and Miami, were also organized, as were properties developed after 1950, such as ASARCO's Silverbell and Mission mines and Duval's (now Cyprus Minerals') mines at Sierrita, Mineral Park, and Esperanza. During 1956–1957 Magma brought its new San Manuel property into production. It was organized along the same structural lines as Kennecott and Phelps Dodge, with a metal trades group belonging to the AFL (by now AFL-CIO) crafts, a railroad operating craft (now the United Transportation Union), and an industrial unit (Mine Mill) for the underground mine and smelter. One year later the NLRB held elections and certified unions in a similar pattern for Magma's underground mine and smelter at Superior.

Because the three big copper companies all had fabricating subsidiaries in the East and Midwest, and ASARCO also had such a subsidiary (although it was still primarily a nonferrous smelting and refining company), the unionization of the work force took the same geographic path. The typical division between the specialized crafts and the production workers usually emerged, with the production workers attracted to industrial unionism and thus to Mine Mill. One of the central locations on the fabricating side was Brass Valley, near Waterbury, Connecticut. Others were Baltimore, Perth Amboy, Yonkers, and Fort Wayne. In all of these locations, and others too numerous to mention, unionism usually was introduced through organization drives, representation elections, and NLRB certifications. The period of greatest activity in organizing extended from 1937 to 1950.

Mine Mill and the Communist Issue

Communist control of Mine Mill's national leadership had emerged by 1940 and was consolidated by the addition of the National Association of Die Casting Workers after protracted controversy between 1942 and 1944. In this way Mine Mill acquired Albert Skinner and Irving Dichter as members. Skinner was to become the last president of the organization on June 22, 1963, and Dichter also would be a future officer. Both were strong and intelligent, and both became associated with the communist faction after the merger.

There was trouble within the faction during the later war years, including the defection of Ken Eckert, who had been an active and prominent participant.[7] Apparently, too, the communist group, whose leader at that time was Maurice Travis, had become increasingly disaffected with Reid Robinson as national president, despite his long-time acceptance of the party line and its discipline.

In November 1946 the faction removed Robinson, replacing him with Travis as president. Travis, who later publicly admitted to membership in the Communist Party, held office for less than a year, although he remained on the executive board. His successor, John Clark, was not a communist but rather a man of modest abilities, easily manipulated, and inclined to be vacillating—in short, a natural choice through which the party group could continue to exert control.

A few months later, in June 1947, Congress passed the Taft-Hartley Act, extensively amending the Wagner Act. Included in the new law was Section 9(h), whose purpose was to weaken unions under communist control. The method employed was the noncommunist affidavit, which had to be filed with the NLRB by the officers of any local and its parent national union, as a condition precedent to their use of the services of the board in matters of complaints by employers against unfair labor practices,[8] or in questions concerning representation in collective bargaining. The oath required that the affiant declare (1) that he was not a member of the Communist Party, (2) that he was not "affiliated" with that party, and (3) that he was neither a member of nor supported any organization that advocated the forcible or illegal overthrow of the government of the United States. Thus any union official who was a communist was confronted with a hard choice. He could subscribe to the affidavit anyway and risk criminal charges by the federal government, or he could refuse to take the oath, which thereupon would deprive his union of the protections and assistance of the labor-management relations law.[9]

In what was to prove a fateful step, the Mine Mill leaders chose not to file the affidavits. The immediate consequences were to open the union to raiding by its jurisdictional rivals, to encourage certain employers to refuse to continue bargaining relations, and to deny the union any opportunity to participate in representation elections. Beyond these severe handicaps, the decision created a serious split within Mine Mill from the top down, isolating it even further from the national leadership of the CIO. Before long it began to suffer losses of membership and increasingly straitened finances.[10]

During 1946–1949 the issue of communist control of several CIO unions began to come to a head, forcing Philip Murray to address the problem. It was a monumental task, for several reasons. Any attack on a member union for any reason would violate the sacred tradition of autonomy and self-determination in policy making. If the attack were based only on support for the Communist Party, the executive board of the CIO could be charged with attempting to impose its own political orthodoxy, by denying freedom of thought to its opponents. In truth, the real issue was not personal liberty but the power to control a labor organization.

The CIO executive board approached its problem from the standpoint of traditional American trade unionism: each member national union is autonomous and has exclusive control of its own internal affairs, with due regard for its obligations to the federation, as prescribed by the CIO constitution. In this view, it was intolerable that an outside organization, such as the Communist Party, with external and conflicting interests that included commitments and even subjection to a foreign government, should exert control over the internal affairs of a member union of the CIO. In such circumstances, appeals to the principles of autonomy and personal liberty serve simply as a cover for domination by an outside body whose aims and activities are in blatant conflict with those of the CIO and, indeed, with independent unionism itself.

On the one side, the interests of the CIO were those of an association of business unions committed to collective bargaining within a system of private enterprise. On the other, the interests of the American Communist Party were those of the foreign power that controlled the party and that was governed by totalitarian principles functioning within a system of state socialism. As a particularly malignant attack on free-trade unionism, this deep and pervasive conflict of interests made communist domination of a member union wholly incompatible with the control and policies of the CIO itself.

At the CIO convention in 1949, Murray brought the fight, which had been brewing for years, into the open. He obtained an amendment to the constitution of the organization that made any member of "the Communist Party, any fascist organization, or other totalitarian movement" ineligible to serve as an officer or member of the executive board.[11] Backed by this statement of principle, the executive board then could bring charges of communist domination against eleven of its member unions.

This was the substance of the charges against Mine Mill, along with the ten other organizations. In the Mine Mill case, the board appointed a hearing committee consisting of Jacob Potofsky (Amalgamated Clothing Workers), Joseph P. Curran (National Maritime Union), and Emil Mazey (United Automobile Workers). The charge laid before the committee declared that the aims and activities of the union were "consistently directed toward the achievement of the program or the purposes of the Communist Party rather than the objectives and policies set forth in the Constitution of the CIO." At the hearing, in which the union was given a full and fair opportunity to cross-examine adverse witnesses and to present testimony and exhibits of its own, the CIO submitted two categories of evidence: first, an abundant and detailed showing of a one-to-one correspondence over many years between positions taken by Mine Mill spokesmen and official union publications on the one side and by the Communist Party through its spokesmen and official publications on the other. Second, two former officials of the union, Homer Wilson and Ken Eckert, the latter a party member at one time, presented detailed testimony describing episodes in which officials of the party met with Mine Mill officers and board members to give them instructions and to formulate union policies. The union defense refused the opportunity to cross-examine either of these important witnesses.

Following the hearings, the special CIO committee decided unanimously that Mine Mill was under Communist Party control. On February 15, 1950, the union was expelled from the CIO.[12] Mine Mill had now become a pariah organization in the American labor movement.

As noted earlier, there was some expectation that after the expulsion the CIO would charter a new union in the mining, smelting, and metal-fabricating field. There was precedent for such a step but it was not followed. Probably the reason lay in the jurisdictional interests of Philip Murray and Walter Reuther. Murray was president of the Steelworkers (as well as the CIO), while Reuther headed the Automobile Workers. These two powerful organizations were already at hand to begin raiding Mine Mill. The USW could aim at nonferrous mining, smelting, and refining, while the UAW could go after the brass foundries, die casting, and metals fabrication. This is exactly what happened, except that the UAW was far more successful in the endeavor than the USW. In fact, the Steelworkers accomplished very little in the fifteen years that followed Mine Mill's expulsion.

In 1949 ASARCO's Garfield smelter was taken out of Mine Mill and put into the International Union of Marine and Shipbuilding Workers, in a local secession movement that ultimately led to capture of the smelter by the Steelworkers. Other than this single plant, all the rest of ASARCO's fourteen far-flung properties, from Tacoma through Omaha to Baltimore and Perth Amboy, stayed with Mine Mill.

At Kennecott, which completed a new refinery at Garfield in 1951, the USW defeated Mine Mill in a de novo certification election. But this was a rare victory, for Mine Mill successfully held out in election challenges at the Arthur and Magna concentrators and at the Bingham pit. The union also retained its hold at Kennecott's Ozark Lead properties in Missouri and at the Ray and Chino divisions.

The Steelworkers made two unsuccessful attempts to capture locals at Butte, Great Falls, and Anaconda. According to Vernon Jensen, their initial efforts in 1950 were badly planned, between a failure to cultivate local leaders and an unconvincing approach to the membership. There was also the formidable opposition of the Anaconda Company itself, which for reasons of its own preferred Mine Mill as a bargaining representative.[13] In 1954 the USW made a second attempt on Anaconda. This time the local leadership of Mine Mill was conducting an internal struggle against the Travis group in the national office. A tentative deal was arranged to have the locals affiliate with the Steelworkers. But Mine Mill's national leadership fought back vigorously, for Butte was one of its most vital bastions. In March 1954 Mine Mill swamped the USW in the NLRB elections.[14]

The story at Phelps Dodge was somewhat different. At the new Ajo smelter in 1951 the USW defeated Mine Mill in a de novo election. Mine Mill never did gain a foothold at this important property. A year later a group of AFL crafts known as the Nonferrous Metals Council won representation rights against Mine Mill in an election involving the new Lavender pit at the Copper Queen branch in Bisbee. However, the union held on at the underground mine and concentrator at the Copper Queen.

At this time Orville Larson had been a vice president of Mine Mill for nearly ten years. He was a highly competent official, well regarded by both labor and management in Arizona, and had stayed independent of the controlling communist faction in the union. Larson continued to direct Arizona affairs for Mine Mill until 1961, representing an organization then in steady decline because of defensive lawsuits and weakening finances. In that year he finally resigned to take the post of international representative of the United Steelworkers in the rather obscure location of Globe, Arizona. He was instructed to report directly to national headquarters in Pittsburgh, while his mission was to conduct a raiding operation against Mine Mill.

His efforts proved unsuccessful, with one exception. He was able to capture the Douglas smelter from his old union in a representation election in early 1962 that reflected his high standing with the rank and file.

Elsewhere in the nonferrous industry, Mine Mill had held up rather well, winning elections in the Coeur d'Alene silver and lead district of Idaho and in the tristate lead area around southwest Missouri. In Brass Valley and other parts of fabrication, the UAW and other organizations made serious inroads, while the USW won a major victory at Sudbury, Ontario, in the nickel branch of the industry.[15]

With its defeat at the Douglas Reduction Works in 1962, Mine Mill was about to make its last stand. The reason lay not in successful raiding by its rivals but in growing internal weakness. Behind this decline was a series of costly federal lawsuits against the leadership, all involving the communist issue. In addition to draining the union's treasury, these proceedings absorbed the time and energy of the officers, leaving the organization practically leaderless for several years.

One line of government attack began in the 1950s with an order of the Subversive Activities Control Board declaring that Mine Mill was communist infiltrated. On November 1, 1965, the U.S. Court of Appeals in Washington, D.C., remanded this order on a finding that it was based on "stale evidence" gathered during 1952–1955. With this action, the proceeding was terminated.[16]

The second prong of the government's attack was directed at the noncommunist affidavits required of union officers every twelve months. On February 3, 1955, the NLRB upheld the findings of its hearing officer in a case involving Precision Scientific Company. The hearing officer claimed that the affidavit of Maurice Travis, secretary-treasurer of Mine Mill, was false on its face. He publicly explained that, although he had quit the party, he continued to believe in the principles of communism and in the Communist Party—an admission that was hopelessly inconsistent with the affidavit to which he had subscribed. The board's finding thus deprived the union of the protections of the National Labor Relations Act.[17] In December 1956 the U.S. Supreme Court ruled that the NLRB could not deny Mine Mill its right to the protection of the Taft-Hartley Act, declaring that "Section 9(h) is for the protection of unions as well as for the detection of Communists." Only the guilty officers were subject to the penalties in the section. Eventually, in 1961, Travis' conviction was voided by the Supreme Court because of a question of whether the original trial had been conducted in the proper court.

In November 1957 the government obtained an indictment of fourteen Mine Mill officials, charging them with a conspiracy to defraud the United States by filing false noncommunist affidavits.[18] Nine of the defendants were convicted by a jury in trial court, but this verdict was overturned by the Court of Appeals, 10th Circuit, because the trial judge had allowed inadmissible hearsay to become part of the record. At the same time, the Appellate Court declared that there was sufficient evidence to support the indictment as well as the finding of the jury that the defendants "were members or affiliated with the Communist Party." The court ordered new trials for seven of the nine defendants.[19]

This case—the Dennis case—was retried, and six of the defendants were again convicted. The decision of the trial court was affirmed by the U.S. Court of Appeals, 10th Circuit.[20] This time the defendants appealed to the United States Supreme Court on a variety of grounds. The Court reversed the decision, with a remand, on the sole technical basis that the defendants had been refused opportunity to cross-examine certain witnesses at a grand jury proceeding. This decision, which came down on June 20, 1966, did not address the evidence in the case.[21]

The remand would have required a third trial of the matter, but at this point the government dropped its case. The probable reasons are that the affidavit provision had been repealed in 1959, making the issue moot, while the evidence itself had become stale over the several years that the case had been in court.

One of the codefendants in the Dennis case was Albert C. Skinner, who had taken over as the last president of Mine Mill on June 22, 1963, replacing John Clark. Skinner had come to Mine Mill from the Die Casters in 1942. By the early 1950s he was assigned to the defense of the Mine Mill locals against USW raids at Kennecott's Utah Copper Division, where he proved to be an intelligent and resourceful leader and negotiator.

With the decision of the Supreme Court in June 1966, the Steelworkers' leadership concluded that there was no future in further attempts to raid

Mine Mill. On the contrary, now that it was public knowledge that the Mine Mill leadership had been set free from the taint of continuing litigation, the USW might absorb the organization without incurring the opprobrium of seeming to tolerate communists. Exploratory talks were promising. On August 29, 1966, the two unions agreed to a mutual assistance pact, looking toward a formal merger. Significantly, a joint statement signed by Skinner and by I. W. Abel, new president of the Steelworkers, expressed concern about the "fragmentation" of collective bargaining in the nonferrous industry. The agreement contained three provisions:

1. Each organization would respect the other's bargaining certifications and contractual relations.
2. Both unions would "continue their efforts, together with all other unions in the industry, to develop a *common program* for the achievement of collective bargaining with the employers." (Emphasis added.)
3. Both unions would work for better legislation.[22]

At the Steelworkers' convention in September 1966, a set of merger proposals was approved. They provided that Mine Mill would become a USW affiliate on February 1, 1967, and that Mine Mill locals would become USW locals on the following July 1. Early in January 1967, the executive board of Mine Mill unanimously recommended approval of these arrangements and called a special convention in Tucson for January 16–18. At Mine Mill's last convention, Abel of the USW addressed the meeting. On January 17 the merger proposals were approved. The Steelworkers promptly issued temporary charters to sixty-five Mine Mill locals, then took over as chief negotiator for the combined organizations. After three-quarters of a century of turbulent and colorful history, one-third of it as the Western Federation of Miners and the rest as Mine Mill, the unique union of nonferrous miners had ceased to exist.[23]

One question remains to be answered. Why did the Steelworkers achieve so little success in their long effort to raid Mine Mill after 1949? Certainly it was not for lack of resources or power. A major part of the answer is that Mine Mill was an unusual union. Its foundation was a militantly devoted rank and file, whose history reached back to 1893 and the turbulent times of the Western Federation of Miners. Its people lived in the rough and remote mining camps of the American West. The environment and the times demanded strength and self-reliance for the endless struggles against equally aggressive and tough employers. Thus the members developed a stalwart and unyielding loyalty to their union. It became a central part of their lives, not a mere membership card.

Furthermore, Mine Mill was an industrial union; indeed, it was one of the first. It was open to all of those with little or no skill; it was not limited to a particular occupation; and it was employee conscious rather than job conscious. Given the chance, it would have elected to become a single industry-wide union, from the mine to the fabricating plant, instead of a "residual" organization, surrounded by more than a dozen narrow craft unions, as circumstances compelled it to be.

Nonetheless, the openness of its outlook toward access to membership gave the union a strong appeal. In the copper region of the Southwest, most of the members were Hispanic in origin. Limited in skills and educational preparation, excluded from the traditional crafts, discriminated against in many different ways, these people found their only opportunity in the mines and smelters, as lowly production workers. Mine Mill gladly accepted them and took pains to develop them as shop stewards, local officials, and even higher officers. Organizational commitment naturally followed. It was the same in Montana, with the Irish, the Slavs, and the Cornish. The union gave them dignity and independence. It was their organization and they would not readily abandon it. Above all else, it was a miners' union—rather than a union of steelworkers, in which it would be a minority interest.

Despite the long and bitter conflict over communist penetration and control at the top, Mine Mill continued to command the loyalty of its members. Secessions were extremely rare on the mining side of the nonferrous industry. They were more common in the eastern fabricating plants, where the circumstances were quite different.

Another factor was the approach taken by the Steelworkers union. It lacked sustained commitment. It did not involve a well-planned campaign. It showed little sophistication in addressing the rank and file. And it was opportunistic. In consequence, it met with failure.

Finally, the attitude of the mining companies was a factor. Except for Kennecott, the firms inclined to Mine Mill rather than the Steelworkers. Partly, this preference reflected self-interest. As Mine Mill's strength slowly eroded after its expulsion, its ability to strike, and above all to lead, steadily declined. It had become a "left-wing company union," as one of its officials ruefully admitted. But beyond this, the mine operators fully appreciated the Steelworkers' great strength, and they were wholly aware of the union's enormous bargaining gains in basic steel. Why court disaster, they asked themselves?

Kennecott was the exception. From 1949 on it gave indications that it hoped to see the USW win out over Mine Mill. Probably the ideological factor was of some importance. Of greater impact was the influence of Charles R. Cox, president of Kennecott during the critical period from 1950 to 1962, who took a direct and continuing interest in labor policy. Cox had come to the company after many years in the basic steel industry, last as president of Carnegie-Illinois. He was on good terms with president David J. McDonald and other USW leaders, and through direct experience had come to hold the union's approach to collective bargaining in high regard. As a result, Kennecott's labor policies gradually assumed the characteristics of those of employers in basic steel—a fact that was not lost on the other copper companies.

To sum up, then, Mine Mill's rank and file gave it a strong will to live and to most of the nonferrous industry it was, faute de mieux, the preferred alternative in labor relations. In the end, therefore, the only way the USW could establish itself and assume leadership was to take over Mine Mill, which it did in 1967.

Negotiations and Strikes

We have seen that, from its inception, copper bargaining was highly decentralized and localized. First, it was local, or plant by plant. Second, each plant had multiple union representation (typically by craft specialties), plus the railroad operating groups, plus a residual unit for the employees in the mine-haulage-crusher-concentrator-refinery group. With open-pit mines, the excavation or shovel jobs might belong to the Operating Engineers, assisted by laborers from Mine Mill, while haulage went to the brotherhoods if by rail or the Teamsters if by truck. From the crushing plant through the refinery, the production jobs belonged to Mine Mill, while the crafts performed maintenance and repairs.

Before 1956 collective bargaining was based on a tripartite structure involving the AFL crafts, the brotherhoods, and Mine Mill for the production group—all confined to the plant level. Even so, the three groups did not bargain as a unit. Although there was some leadership, it was shifting and tenuous from year to year. Contracts were made either for a single year or for two years with a wage reopener after the first. A strike usually followed each expiration. Although the industry was a unit in a sense, and had been so regulated by the Nonferrous Metals Commission (a dependent unit of the National War Labor Board) and later by the Wage Stabilization Board, the lack of system and cohesion in the bargaining made for diversity in wages, occupational structure, and work rules. These were the national consequences of decentralization.

Naturally, these bargaining arrangements were a source of dissatisfaction and frustration for Mine Mill, and later for the Steelworkers, because they were industrial unions with an interest in interplant and intercompany patterns and comparisons. At ASARCO in the early fifties, where except for the Garfield smelter all properties had been organized by Mine Mill, "strangers" began appearing at local bargaining sessions—in the person of national officers and local representatives from other ASARCO plants. Before long it was apparent that the union was selecting a "target" plant and, upon obtaining an acceptable settlement, extending the "pattern" to the other properties. In this way standardized wage increases could be obtained without changing contract language or basic local differences. By 1956 both management and union recognized the advantages of centralizing the bargaining for all but the recycling (scrap) plants. In consequence, the ASARCO–Mine Mill Council came into existence. A two-tier negotiation system was introduced, with one set of negotiation sessions for company-wide matters and another for local problems at each plant.

The evolution at ASARCO was comparatively easy because only one industrial union was involved, and that union—for its own reasons—badly wanted centralization.

At Kennecott a similar outcome was achieved, even though a tripartite structure of multiple union representation existed at the company's four principal mining divisions. In short, it proved possible to get all groups at all locations to bargain centrally over general economic matters, and then locally over local matters. The company was favorable to this approach, thanks to its president at the time. Charles Cox, influenced by his long experience with the USW in basic steel, saw advantages to the company in the nationalization or standardization of wages and working conditions among the several plants. Greater efficiency in bargaining might have been another influence.

Phelps Dodge was a different case. It, too, had the tripartite structure at its main properties at Morenci, Ajo, and Bisbee-Douglas. But its two refineries were not part of its Western Mining Operations. They were far distant from the company's mines; they were operated by a subsidiary, Phelps Dodge Refining Company; and, from the start, their labor relations were conducted separately from those of the parent company.

Up to this point Phelps Dodge's pattern was quite similar to Kennecott's, save for the special position of the refineries. But unlike Kennecott, PD had no desire to move toward centralized company-wide bargaining or uniform contracts across the properties. It preferred to make separate settlements with each of the tripartite groups at each of its branches, although it would go along with standard increases across the properties. The results were local strikes and some diversity in agreements. During the 1959 bargaining the company was surprised to see a Mine Mill representative from the El Paso refinery show up at negotiations on one of the western mining properties. Its prompt response was to inform him that he was there as a guest of the unions, in the capacity of an observer, and that there would be no discussion of El Paso matters.

The year 1956 marked an important turning point in bargaining history. For the first time ASARCO became the lead company. For the first time the industry witnessed a long-term contract, won by ASARCO for a three-year term without a strike. In that year Phelps Dodge also won a three-year settlement, but not without a lengthy and violent strike at Morenci. And in 1956 ASARCO went over to its two-tier company-wide bargaining system, while PD obtained long-term contracts on its preferred property-by-property basis.

Three years later, in 1959, strikes were the rule. At Morenci, Phelps Dodge took a strike by Mine Mill that lasted from August until the following February, shutting down the entire property. Just as operations were being resumed, the railroad brotherhoods, who so far had not participated in negotiations, submitted a list of strong demands, including acceptance of national railroad rules for application to PD's extensive local industrial railroad. When Phelps Dodge rejected the proposal, the brotherhoods abruptly struck the property, which had only just reopened. Management made the unusual decision to continue operating, believing that the new strike was illegal because the brotherhoods had failed to give statutory notice of the labor dispute to the Arizona Industrial Commission. On the same reasoning the company concluded that the railroad unionists now ceased to be employees, and it began hiring replacements. The NLRB subsequently ruled that the strike was legal in that notice to the commission would have constituted an idle act, since that body had no mediation machinery. The board then ordered PD to put the strikers on a special preferential reserve list for new hires as attrition occurred. Nonetheless, PD's replacement policy proved effective and the brotherhoods never regained their previous influence at Morenci.

At the end of this negotiating round virtually all the companies settled for three-year contracts; the exception was ASARCO, which accepted a two-year term.

The negotiations in 1962 were made noteworthy by the appearance of Orville Larson in his new capacity as USW negotiator at Phelps Dodge. At these meetings Sylvain Schnaittacher, speaking for Mine Mill, took the Phelps Dodge spokesman aside to suggest that his union, which was now under raiding pressure at the Douglas Reduction Works, might be interested in a two-year "early-bird" settlement at all PD properties, which would protect Mine Mill's threatened representation rights at Douglas as an incidental part of the bargain. The company promptly agreed, and the two sides held off signing to avoid any charge of making a "premature" contract during the legally required open period. Nonetheless, the Steelworkers attacked the agreement before the NLRB, which ruled that the Douglas contract was in fact premature. It thereupon ordered a representation election at the Douglas smelter, and the Steelworkers succeeded in ousting Mine Mill.

By 1964 all of the major producers had contracts expiring simultaneously. At Phelps Dodge it was evident that something new and important was going on when all of the unions except Mine Mill jointly appeared, represented by one spokesman. Their demand was for a common settlement, the very idea that Mine Mill had been urging since 1939. In this negotiation Mine Mill stood alone, with Irving Dichter as its spokesman. After a token strike it settled along with the others. Only Kennecott had a strike. In the end, with minor exceptions, the copper companies all had three-year contracts with simultaneous expiration dates of July 1, 1967.

Clearly, increased centralization of bargaining and uniformity of increases in wages and benefits were emerging from what had been a highly decentralized system. The door was slowly opening to a form of coalition bargaining.[24]

How the Steelworkers Overcame Fragmentation

The leaders of Mine Mill were aware of bargaining vulnerability as early as 1939.[25] The chief difficulty at that time was that large sections of the industry were nonunion. The splitting up of the work force in plants that had been organized was a further weakening agent. The union chose to concentrate for the time being on the five largest employers in the industry, with the ultimate aim of achieving company-wide bargaining. In the meantime, the war stimulated a rapid increase in union membership, which in turn obscured the underlying problem of continued bargaining fragility.

In 1946 the question was again prominent. It was addressed at the union's convention that fall, with the presentation of an elaborate diagram outlining the leadership's view of the "ideal bargaining structure" for the nonferrous industry. Its dominant theme was centralization—of bargaining strategy for the union and, in time, of joint bargaining with the employers.[26]

The scheme envisaged three main components for bargaining—die casting, extraction (mining, smelting, and refining), and brass foundries. Although the concept of distinguishing, however roughly, the different product markets was novel and important, no other branches of fabrication, such as wire and cable plants, were recognized. Thus copper was separated from lead-zinc, and other lesser metals. Furthermore, the scheme called for isolating the major mining companies for separate negotiations. This approach was notable for its recognition of the notion of company-wide bargaining, and even more, for its identification of the longer-run principles of pattern-following and, as the ultimate goal, industry-wide bargaining.

Another basic element in the Mine Mill scheme was a series of chronological proposals for: (1) a national wage policy committee to frame the broad demands for each contract round; (2) an extractive industry conference for interpreting and applying those demands in the main branches of the nonferrous industry (copper, lead-zinc, casting, and brass production); (3) at the next level below the conference, separate bargaining committees for each of the principal employers.[27] Most important of all, the arrangement allowed the extractive conference to review and approve or reject negotiated settlements reached at the individual company level. By this device the framers of the scheme at least foreshadowed the basic idea of *coordinating* the company settlements *to enforce a common pattern*, an idea that was not to come into practice until 1967.[28]

Over the intervening twenty-one years, Mine Mill was never able to carry out this quite sophisticated scheme for a centralized bargaining strategy. The most it could do was struggle for a rough kind of pattern-following, working where possible with the other unions, property by property and then company by company, as in 1951, 1959, and 1964. In short, the Mine Mill leadership, standing alone, could not overcome the inherent limitations of decentralized bargaining.

Some fundamental changes were to occur starting March 14–16, 1967, in Salt Lake City. There the newly merged Mine Mill and United Steel-workers brought delegates from their combined 200 locals together with representatives of some twenty-six other nonferrous unions.[29] Their immediate task was to formulate bargaining proposals for negotiations affecting 45,000 employees and about 100 employers, whose agreements would expire on or about July 1. Their larger assignment was to design an effective strategy for achieving the results of industry-wide bargaining within the continuing context of the decentralized system that legally still remained in effect.

Under USW leadership the nonferrous meeting produced a lengthy and detailed list of contract goals for the forthcoming bargaining. Among those objectives was one concerned with "Master Agreements and Termination Dates," which read as follows:

> The major companies in this industry still operate with separate collective bargaining agreements at each location. Many agreements even have different termination dates. This antiquated system has long since been abandoned by most major companies and unions. This should be done in nonferrous also. Certain of the nonferrous companies have negotiated single economic settlements for most plants for several years. They should now convert these half-way arrangements to full Company-Wide Master Agreements including coverage of all subsidiary units. This would facilitate both negotiations and contract administration. All agreements in each company and in the industry should bear a common termination date and should provide for automatic inclusion of newly certified or recognized units.[30]

This statement contained three primary concepts: (1) all contracts should have the same termination date; (2) each employer should negotiate a complete company-wide master agreement; and (3) the company-wide agreement should include all subsidiaries of the parent concern.

The first concept was intended to increase negotiating and strike effectiveness. It would compel the employer to confront parallel and uniform demands at all of his properties. At the same time it would deny him the possibility of substituting among plants if a strike should occur at some of them but not others. In short, he would face a total shutdown. The same would hold for competing producers. Thus, a coalition of unions could legally impose an industry-wide strike simply by breaking off negotiations simultaneously.

The second notion—a single company-wide contract—would simplify negotiations by bringing all unions together under one agreement. This would promote uniformity, while also lending the strength of the entire group to the weaker locals. Finally, the third concept would extend the master agreement of each company to its subsidiaries. This would incorporate in the main agreement fabricating plants, brass foundries, and specialized mining activities such as lead-zinc. In this way the power of the union combination would be extended downward and outward, from the mine all the way to the manufacturing plant.[31]

It should be evident that this contract proposal ultimately contemplated one of two possible routes to uniform wages and benefits throughout the nonferrous industry. One would involve industry standardization through pattern-following, via a series of parallel negotiations among the companies. The other envisaged a single massive negotiation, with all employers in the same room, aimed at either a joint industry-wide contract or a set of parallel company-wide agreements. As matters later worked out, pattern-following was to prevail, but only partially.

How then did the Steelworkers reach the objective of centralized bargaining under unitary control? Essentially, by the formation of a coalition of some twenty-five unions that agreed to act as a unit and to "coordinate" their bargaining with the nonferrous employers. To achieve this agreement, the USW had to make it enticing enough to the many craft internationals to induce them to abandon their hitherto cherished traditions of independence and autonomy. It was not an insurmountable obstacle. In the first place, the Steelworkers could provide the technical resources— research experts and skilled negotiators—and the funds to conduct massive negotiations and to lead a lengthy strike. Second, it could hold out the promise of much larger prospective gains in wages and benefits through the introduction of a more powerful system of bargaining, granted that in fact these gains might turn out to be less than the crafts could have obtained for themselves. And in the third place, the USW could offer a national industry conference as a means for receiving and carefully considering the specific demands of the participating international unions. In turn, each craft would be assured that its particular needs would be carefully addressed in the formulation of bargaining demands. The crafts had everything to gain and seemingly little to lose by joining the coalition under the leadership of the Steelworkers.

The first step in the formation of the coalition was to bind the unions to act jointly through a new bargaining institution, the national Nonferrous Industry Conference. The second was to oblige them to submit their demands to the conference for review and formulation. The third was to induce these internationals to consent to the appointment of a single spokesman for the conference—who was to be Joseph P. Molony, a vice president of the Steelworkers. Subsequently, in a subtle demonstration of that union's ultimate power to conduct the negotiations, Molony formed a Nonferrous Industry Coordinating and Steering Committee (CSC) to determine and execute bargaining strategy on behalf of the conference.

To conduct negotiations, the CSC adopted three working principles, to which all of the participating internationals agreed: (1) no single organization could strike without prior sanction of the CSC; (2) no organization could finally settle its dispute with an employer without approval of the CSC; and (3) no organization could end a strike and return to work except after approval by the CSC. Technically, the conference had to approve these decisions by its vital subcommittee.

In this way the USW created a coalition, or union of unions, under its own leadership to supersede the traditional decentralized bargaining system of the industry. It also achieved effective coordination as the essential modus operandi for the coalition. Here the key elements were CSC approval of the strike, the settlement, and the return to work. On the union side, therefore, a single consolidated negotiating system had been brought about. Or, put a little differently, a single central bargaining unit had been inserted between the many local units and the nonferrous employers—and most important, without these employers' consent. The rules of the game had been changed dramatically. By creation of one of the most complex bargaining cartels probably ever devised, the USW would soon launch the longest major industry-wide strike in American labor history.

The Industrial Union Department of the AFL-CIO already had been studying the problem of decentralized bargaining for some time, under the leadership of Richard T. Leonard.[32] In addition, Otis Brubaker, research director of the USW, had a hand in the work. And it is plausible that Skinner and Dichter, the two former Mine Mill officers who had joined the USW with the merger, also made a contribution. After all, they had struggled with the problem of localized multiple-union bargaining for a quarter-century and had developed a fairly good approximation to the coalition idea as early as 1946.

In any case, the result was a subtle and sophisticated conception of centralized collective bargaining that was to prevail in the nonferrous industry for the next twenty years.

CHAPTER 9

COLLECTIVE BARGAINING
DEVELOPMENTS AND
NEGOTIATIONS, 1967–1990

THE MERGER OF Mine Mill into the United Steelworkers was concluded in January 1967, at Mine Mill's last convention, although formal completion was delayed until early July. The momentous decision in Tucson freed the leadership of both organizations to work out the details of the system of coalition bargaining they had agreed to introduce into the nonferrous industry.

THE GREAT STRIKE

The Bargaining Situation

The basic objective of the newly united organizations was to bring about a drastic shift in bargaining power in favor of twenty-six unions, acting as a unit, at the expense of the nonferrous employers, particularly those in copper. To reach this goal required a massive expansion of the traditional scope of negotiations, whose boundaries until that time had been confined to the "appropriate" craft and production units designated by the NLRB following the certification elections conducted years before.[1]

A redrawing or consolidation of those boundaries was not in fact the aim of the coalition. The actual goal was to attain industry-wide uniformity in wages, economic benefits, and work practices throughout all plants of all companies in the industry. The centralization of bargaining was a preliminary means to this ultimate end. The standardization of contracts industry-wide is not at all the same as industry-wide bargaining, although the two are easily confused. Industry-wide bargaining requires that employers negotiate jointly as a group, usually through a committee.[2] When a settlement is reached, its terms may be incorporated in each employer's contract or, less likely, all of the employers sign a common master agreement.

By contrast, uniformity among separate employer contracts in an industry does not require this extreme degree of centralization, and for the same reason it is easier to achieve. The union or coalition of unions sets its negotiating goals, selects a target company, and works for a settlement with this employer, possibly after calling a strike. The unions then make this settlement the industry pattern and proceed to enforce the pattern settlement either by threatening or by continuing strikes against the other employers until they fall in line. This method was the choice of the USW coalition in 1967.

Within two months of taking control of Mine Mill, the USW met in conference with thirteen other national nonferrous unions at Salt Lake City. From the start, the Steelworkers' leadership dominated the meetings. The Nonferrous Industry Conference (NIC) was their creation—an organization to receive, consider, and approve bargaining demands from the individual unions and their locals. Molony, designated to serve as chairman, became the key man in the forthcoming negotiations. Finally, the "1967 Nonferrous Bargaining Policy Goals" was a USW document, on which only the Steelworker delegates could vote.

This declaration of policy is the key to the whole USW approach to enlarging the scope of bargaining in the nonferrous industry, and thus to an explanation of the long strike that was soon to follow. The first objective was to achieve "full company-wide master agreements including coverage of all subsidiary units." The second was common termination dates for "all agreements in each company and in the industry." And the third was "one industry-wide wage scale in nonferrous."

The concept of a company-wide master agreement was entirely foreign

Joseph Patrick Molony (1906–1977). Molony came
to this country from Ireland in 1925, working first as a
railroad laborer and then on the ore docks of Republic
Steel in Buffalo. A man of natural intelligence, a leader,
and an orator, he became an organizer for SWOC in
1936 and headed the Little Steel strike in 1937. From
1942 to 1965 he was a regional director and member
of the executive board of USW. Elected international
vice president in 1965, he retired in 1973. With the
merger of the Mine Mill into USW in 1967, Molony
became principal architect of the large coalition of
nonferrous unions and its chief negotiator and spokesman during the eight-month strike in 1967–68. (*Photo
courtesy of Historical Collections and Labor Archives, Penn
State and the United Steelworkers of America.*)

Albert Chester Skinner (1908–1985). Skinner came
to the International Union of Mine, Mill and Smelter
Workers as part of the merger with the Die Casting
Workers in 1944. After many years of staff work with
the national office, in 1962 he became the last president of Mine Mill. When that union was absorbed by
the USW in 1967, Skinner was asked by Joseph P.
Molony, head of the new nonferrous union coalition,
to join the strategically decisive Coordinating and
Steering Committee. Subsequent to the long strike in
1967–68, Skinner became chief safety officer of
USW in Utah. (*Photo courtesy of Historical Collections
and Labor Archives, Penn State and the United Steelworkers of America.*)

to the industry. To illustrate, at that time Kennecott Copper Corporation bargained centrally and jointly with its several unions to achieve new contracts that were separate for each of its four copper mining and smelting operations. More important, the orbit of these negotiations did not include the company's Tintic Division in Utah, which produced lead, zinc, and silver. Nor did it include its Ozark Lead subsidiary in Missouri, its Chase Brass and Copper fabricating subsidiary in Ohio, or its Kennecott Refining Corporation subsidiary in Baltimore. By contrast, the inclusion of every one of these plants in a company-wide bargaining unit was a mandatory objective for the bargaining strategy of the USW coalition.

To elaborate the problem further, consider Phelps Dodge Corporation, whose Western Operations then included mines and smelters at four locations in Arizona. The corporation was also parent of Phelps Dodge Refining Corporation, which refined copper in El Paso and in Laurel Hill, and had always bargained separately, with different representatives and bargaining units, from Western Operations. Through Phelps Dodge Industries, PD also owned Phelps Dodge Copper Products Corporation, which had a telephone wire and cable plant in Fordyce, Arkansas; four wire and cable plants in Yonkers (Habirshaw Division), and still other plants elsewhere. This firm had always bargained independently and through its own representatives, with separate units and contracts, on a plant-by-plant basis. Furthermore, Phelps Dodge as a whole was strictly a domestic copper producer, except for by-products.

For yet another special situation, consider ASARCO. In 1967 it was relatively small in copper mining but large in copper smelting and refining. It was the nation's largest producer of silver, which it mined along with lead in Idaho. It also mined lead and zinc in Missouri. It had smelters for these different metals in widely scattered places such as East Helena, Omaha, El Paso, Corpus Christi, and Amarillo. It had major refineries in Baltimore and Perth Amboy. Finally, ASARCO had two domestic subsidiaries, Revere Copper and Brass, an eastern fabricator, and Federated Metals, a scrap-reclaiming concern with plants in San Francisco; Los Angeles; Sand Springs, Oklahoma; Whiting, Indiana; and Newark, New Jersey. At that time bargaining had already been centralized with Mine Mill through the ASARCO Council, which included plants producing almost the whole array of major nonferrous metals. Although the bargaining was centralized for economic matters, the properties still had separate contracts, and there were local negotiations as well. For plants outside the council, separate local agreements were the rule.

Anaconda, by contrast, had a less complex structure than the other principal producers. Its copper operations were based on the mines at Butte, the smelter at Anaconda, the refinery at Great Falls, and the fabricating plants of the company's subsidiary, American Brass, largely located in the Brass Valley area of Connecticut but also spread across the entire country.

These four companies illustrate the diverse collection of activities then known as the nonferrous metals industry. Led by the United Steelworkers, the objective of the coalition was to obtain uniformity of wages and benefits in the industry by broadening the orbit of the traditional pattern of collective bargaining. To quote vice president Molony's statement six months after the strike had begun:

> The unions want equal pay for equal work in the industry. They want common levels of pensions, insurance, job security, paid holidays, shift differentials, etc. . . . We do want and expect to be able to achieve basically common economic settlements with each company for all properties of that company whose agreements have expired or which are without agreements.[3]

To achieve these goals required a strategy. The one adopted by the Steelworkers' coalition was to some extent flexible and pragmatic, hence tinged with some ambiguity. The aim, as should now be clear, was uniformity and standardization, particularly in economic matters. This goal implies, but does not require, industry-wide bargaining in the strict sense of joint negotiations with all of the employers together in the same room.[4] Instead, from the start of negotiations in early 1967 the coalition began insisting on the NIC demand for *company-wide master agreements*— including subsidiaries—*with simultaneous expiration dates* for all contracts. Taken together, these two conditions would be enough to standardize wages and working conditions across product lines, say, copper, lead, zinc, and silver—and along the whole technological sequence from the mines to the fabricating and reclaiming plants.

These initial demands of the USW coalition contained the potential for industry-wide bargaining, if not in 1967 then in a later round. The reasons are obvious: parallel expiration dates would permit an industry-wide strike; the "coordination" of final settlements, by putting the coalition in a position to play the companies off against one another (in what would be an indirect form of industry-wide negotiations), could still yield the uniformity of contract provisions the unions were seeking.[5] At some point, direct joint bargaining with all employers together might come about. Indeed, there was always a remote chance, even in 1967, that it would emerge from the crisis atmosphere of a long strike finally on the verge of settlement.

In any case, the USW coalition was not aiming at formal industry-wide bargaining at that time. It began by insisting strongly that it wanted company-wide *master* agreements, simultaneous expiration dates for all contracts and uniformity of wages, benefits, and other conditions of employment at all plants in the industry. Strictly interpreted, a "master agreement" at a company means a single contract, embracing all subsidiaries, all plants, and all product lines. Coupled with identical expiration dates for all such master agreements, the coalition could call an industry-wide strike and then impose the pattern, step by step.

The evidence suggests that the employers did not fully comprehend the coalition's demands at the outset, although they soon realized that what they were actually facing was a demand not really for wages or benefits, but for a greatly enlarged scope of negotiations. Thus their first response was insistence that the bargaining be confined to the established limits derived from the underlying designated bargaining units, or to boundaries that later would be enlarged by mutual consent. This defensive strategy necessarily was rigid and technical. It also enjoyed substantial legal support.

Perhaps more by instinct than from formal deliberation, the approach of the nonferrous employers rested on three fundamental rules of procedure:

1. At no time shall a single employer join with other employers in joint bargaining with the USW coalition on any substantive matter—*the no-coalition rule.*
2. At no time shall a single employer engage in joint bargaining with the USW coalition for all of its subsidiaries—*the no-master-contract rule.*
3. All settlements reached by a given employer, including those at subsidiaries, must incorporate the previously observed jurisdictional limits—*the established-scope rule.*

The first rule precluded the possibility of industry-wide bargaining. The second rule eliminated the possibility of a master company-wide contract and prevented the elimination of previously established negotiating boundaries for particular units and subsidiaries within the parent company. And the third rule reinforced the second, by excluding the possibility of any settlement that would alter previously established boundaries.

Within this framework the employers entered the bargaining in 1967. Given the fundamental incompatibility of their limits and the coalition's ambitions concerning those limits, the outcome was inevitable: there could be no bargaining of substance between the two sides.

The Course of Bargaining during 1967

In the spring of 1967 the NIC appointed a series of bargaining committees, one for each company. Irving Dichter became head of the ASARCO group, and Orville Larson received the same assignment at Phelps Dodge. Soon after the strike began on July 15, Molony made himself chairman of the Nonferrous Industry Coordinating and Steering Committee (CSC). Significantly, Albert C. Skinner and Otis Brubaker were among the seven members. It is worth noting also that all of the negotiating committees were headed by Steelworkers, that the all-important steering committee was also headed by a Steelworker, and that some of the Steelworker participants were former Mine Mill leaders.

A taste of events to come was provided on February 16, 1967, when Phelps Dodge representatives from Western Operations met with Steelworker representatives, headed by Larson. Representatives of other unions at the Arizona operations were also present. The topic was comparative fringe benefits. At some point in the discussion, a pension expert for USW asked for data on employees at the El Paso refinery, which was not part of Western Operations. Speaking for PD, W. J. Uren, director of labor relations, replied that the desired information could be obtained only from Phelps Dodge Refining Corporation.

Having in mind Larson's statement that the unions would bargain only as a unit, with himself as spokesman, PD's attorney for Western Operations, John F. Boland, Jr., announced that the discussions could not go forward without certain written stipulations: (1) that each union present would consent to be represented by the bargaining committee and its sole spokesman, Larson; (2) that the refineries at El Paso and Laurel Hill would not be recognized in these discussions and that PD would not at this time negotiate concerning them; (3) that the negotiations would cover only established separate units and their contracts; and (4) that PD reserved the right to resume direct one-on-one bargaining with any of the units.

Meanwhile, letters from Pittsburgh began reaching the companies, all containing the identical list of demands contained in the NIC document of

March 1967, now irreverently known among the employer negotiators as "heaven in '67." On April 14 Molony and Skinner wrote to Robert G. Page, chairman of PD, asking that negotiations cover the entire company and its subsidiaries, with all PD unions represented and participating.

On May 10 and 31 the joint union committee, with its fifty-four representatives—including three from the El Paso refinery—met with the company. Phelps Dodge stated its willingness to go forward, subject to the protective conditions just noted. At the May 31 meeting Uren inquired of Larson and his colleague Sylvain Schnaittacher what they meant by the word "company" in these negotiations. They replied that it embraced all operations of Phelps Dodge—for example, Western Operations, the refinery at El Paso, the MacKenzie-Walton fabricating plant at Providence, and any other property owned by PD or its subsidiaries.

These meetings were fruitless: the company rejected the coalition's initial list of demands and the unions had nothing further to propose. On July 15 the strike began. All of the major companies were involved, for all had received the same demands, and all confronted the same challenge: to consent to negotiate over a company-wide master agreement or to take a strike.

What occurred was an industry-wide strike, fabricating plants included, over a subtle and highly abstract issue: the scope and structure of contract negotiations. In such a context, the plebian question of a wage increase could not even be reached, let alone considered.

Just before the strike began, on June 22, PD met again with the joint union bargaining committee. Larson again brought up the USW request for company-wide bargaining. PD again rejected it, countering with its first money offer. There was no response. No further meetings occurred until October 11–12, when the strike was already nearly three months old. At that time Larson introduced Edgar H. Ball, Jr., the USW representative at the Fordyce, Arkansas, cable plant, where the USW had recently been certified as bargaining agent. The joint union committee finally made its first counterproposal. Containing no mention of the earlier demand for a company-wide master contract, it had two requests: (1) that issues outstanding at Phelps Dodge and Phelps Dodge Refining would be "satisfactorily resolved *with all unions and simultaneously concluded*"; and (2) that agreements would be "satisfactorily and *simultaneously* concluded" at the Fordyce plant (emphasis added). Fordyce, Larson explained, was a substitution for MacKenzie-Walton, which had been sold in the meantime.

Both counterproposals were rejected by the company. If they had not been, the coalition would have got its foot in the door to company-wide bargaining, because acceptance would have meant implicit acceptance of joint bargaining by PD for Western Operations, the refining company and the products company together, at all plants. Thus PD rejected the proposal.

Nonetheless, the coalition's new offer did constitute a nominal retreat from its original demand for a company-wide agreement, including subsidiaries. The Fabian tactic of advancing one small step at a time had simply been substituted, while the original demand was left on the table.

Two months passed without any progress. Then, on December 12, Phelps Dodge made a new money offer, to which the coalition's response was a reiteration of its October 12 proposal. Another meeting was arranged for January 3–5, 1968. Molony joined Larson for the Steelworkers, and Walter C. Lawson, PD vice president and head of Western Operations, joined Uren on the company side. A substantial advance toward agreement on the economic issues was lost when the USW insisted once more on collateral settlements at El Paso and Fordyce.[6]

The foregoing profile of the Phelps Dodge negotiations between May 1967 and January 1968 is typical in its essentials of the experience of the other major copper companies. All of them were financially strong at the time and all were determined, from the top down, to resist the coalition's demand for a change in the bargaining structure. On the union side, the steering committee was waiting for defections from the employer ranks, although only one had occurred, during the preceding October. Tiny Pima Mining Company had settled for a money increase of 6 percent, but it was not representative enough to allow the coalition to establish its pattern for a general settlement. And so the stalemate wore on.

The Taylor Panel

By the start of 1968, inventories of copper and other nonferrous metals were starting to run low in the midst of the Vietnam conflict. Accordingly, Secretary of Labor W. Willard Wirtz and Secretary of Commerce Smith on January 24 established a special panel to investigate the industry's dispute and recommend means of settlement. George W. Taylor of the University of Pennsylvania was appointed chairman; Monsignor George Higgins, chairman of the National Catholic Welfare Conference, and George Reedy, former White House press secretary, were named members. Their brief was to mediate the dispute, and if they were unable to do so, to submit their recommendations for settlement. We should note that the panel approach was severely attacked by the industry as having no basis in law, as serving the union's underlying goal throughout the strike, and as an inferior alternative to the board of inquiry procedure under Taft-Hartley.[7]

Acting with unusual celerity, the panel scheduled sessions for January 30 and February 1, at which it would meet jointly with Molony and his coordinating and steering committee and with the four principal copper concerns. Its task was to ask two fundamental questions of each of the parties: (1) Is the demand for company-wide bargaining an impediment to settlement; and (2) What procedural steps might expedite a solution?

Spokesmen for the various companies agreed firmly that the union's steering committee should drop its demand for company-wide bargaining and return to negotiating on the basis of the original units. In putting forward this view, Lawson contended that unless the committee dropped its demand unconditionally he could see no end to the strike. Edmund J. Flynn, industrial relations counselor at Kennecott's Western Mining Division, termed the demand illegal and described it as a "power play" aimed at enabling "the Steelworkers to control bargaining throughout Kennecott and ultimately throughout the nonferrous industry." John Will, director of labor relations at Anaconda, told the panel that substantive negotiations could not even begin until the steering committee withdrew its company-wide demand.

Speaking for the unions, chairman Molony agreed with the witnesses for the employers that the demand for a change in the bargaining structure was the real barrier to settlement—but for a different reason: the companies wanted to retain the advantages they had enjoyed with fragmented bargaining. This, he said, was the real source of the impasse. The unions had never sought industry-wide bargaining. At the outset of the dispute, Molony insisted, they had sought company-wide bargaining with master contracts but had now dropped the idea of single master agreements. The two main issues remaining, Molony added, were common contract termination dates within each company and extension of the eventual economic settlement to all properties of the companies.[8]

The panel's effort at mediation inevitably ended in failure. So the body turned to the task of preparing its findings and recommendations. It began by describing the source of the dispute as a very complex issue of bargaining structure. Rejecting industry-wide bargaining as a solution, the panel instead proposed what it considered to be a more rational reformulation of existing negotiating boundaries, but one that was more limited than the coalition's company-wide demand. In the panel's conception, there would be three separate components for bargaining: (1) mining, smelting, and refining; (2) manufacturing or fabrication; and (3) lead-zinc-silver.

This tripartite scheme was ideal for ASARCO, for it would separate its lead-zinc, scrap-recovery, and fabricating operations from copper mining, smelting, and refining. At the same time, its unitary USW-ASARCO council would be divided according to product line and stage of production, which was highly attractive to the company. By contrast, the panel's approach did nothing positive for Phelps Dodge, for that company had no lead-zinc-silver production, its fabrication component was already separate, and it would now have to enlarge the sphere of Western Operations to include its copper refineries, which were separate for bargaining and administrative purposes. For Anaconda, the tripartite scheme was compatible with its existing bargaining structure. Kennecott, too, saw no significant problems: it already bargained centrally for the four properties in its Western Mining Division, which included its Garfield refinery; its fabricating plants in Ohio were already separate; and its lead-zinc operations in Utah and Missouri would fit nicely into the proposed arrangement. Similarly, the scheme would cause no problems for the smaller producers because many were specialists in copper, lead-zinc, or silver, and typically they were not integrated from mine to factory.

For the USW coalition, the panel proposal was decidedly a mixed bag and of no real help to its cause. True, it would put Phelps Dodge's two refineries in its Western Operations group. But it would preserve separation by property, by product, and by technological stage of production. There would be no company-wide bargaining, and there was no recommendation for common termination dates. In short, the steering committee's whole redesign of the bargaining structure was rejected, although that redesign was the sole rationale for the strike.

Settlement of the Strike

The strike dragged on into its eighth month. In early March President Lyndon B. Johnson summoned the parties to Washington with the request that they remain there until they had reached a settlement. All sides were now under increasing pressure: the administration, because of the copper shortage; the employers, because their company losses were beginning to mount; and the steering committee, because the rank and file were becoming restive about a long dispute whose issues most of them had never understood anyway.

After making a procedural agreement with the USW coalition that

negotiations for contracts at the refineries and fabricating plants would be
conducted concurrently but separately, Phelps Dodge resumed bargaining
for Western Operations on March 5. On March 8 a settlement was reached
for the Arizona properties: hourly wage rates would be raised an average
of 19.1 cents immediately, plus 16.4 cents on July 1, 1969, and 18.3 cents
on July 1, 1970, for a total of 54 cents. The total increase was 17.1 percent
over the midpoint of the Arizona scale, or an average of 5.2 percent yearly
over the 39½ months until the expiration of the new contract. It was not
an impressive annual rate of increase, given the inflationary context at the
time and the high costs of a strike of this extreme length.

What followed the oral settlement was highly significant. That same
afternoon John Coulter, negotiator for Phelps Dodge Refining Corporation, and Orville Larson, for the coalition at PD, reached a separate
settlement for the refinery at El Paso. Larson subsequently told Boland
rather casually that both settlements would have to go to the "steering
committee" (CSC) for approval.[9] According to Boland, this was the first
time he had learned of the CSC arrangement. The next morning he raised
the matter with Molony, who confirmed Larson's statement and added
that CSC would withhold approval of the two agreements until settlements had been reached for Fordyce and Yonkers. Boland protested, with
some heat, that this procedure constituted injection of an extraneous *ex
post* demand by a different set of union representatives, which in his
opinion was contrary to the obligation to bargain in good faith under the
Taft-Hartley law. Molony then explained that the settlement at Western
Operations was "pattern-setting," and that under the Steelworkers' constitution it had to be approved by the Nonferrous Industry Conference of the
coalition.

An entire week went by. Each day NIC spokesmen, who were staying at
the Willard Hotel, would inform Phelps Dodge representatives that the
two settlements had been neither approved nor rejected, for the reason
that no settlement had been reached at Fordyce and Yonkers. In particular,
the spokesmen for the coalition would emphasize that no expiration date
of June 30 had yet been agreed upon for these manufacturing plants, to
match the date agreed upon for mining and refining. Beyond any doubt,
the coalition was still striving for simultaneous dates of expiration at all
properties of Phelps Dodge Corporation.

In an effort to bring about consummation of the two pending settlements for mining and refining, Boland finally took the problem to W.
Willard Wirtz, the secretary of labor. At this meeting, Boland urged Wirtz

to get Arnold Ordman, general counsel for the NLRB, to move immediately for a "10(j)" injunction under Taft-Hartley which, if successful, would have yielded a court order directing the coalition to comply with section 8(b)(3) of the act. In turn this action would have sprung loose the two delayed settlements.[10]

Acting with remarkable speed, on the very next day the steering committee gained the necessary consent of the NIC for approval of both agreements which, significantly, was granted without concurring agreements for the fabricating plants. Shortly afterward, fabricating settlements were reached independently by different negotiators on each side. Equally significant, the fabricating plants gained smaller increases than those accepted for mining. Even more, the date of March 24, 1971, was agreed on for contract expirations at the four Yonkers plants and for the first contract at Fordyce. Thus the coalition sacrificed simultaneity of expiration dates, which had been one of its key initial demands. The strike had now been settled for all branches of Phelps Dodge, although operations could not be resumed until after March 22.

ASARCO also settled during this period, but with the interesting feature that the wage increases in copper exceeded those in lead-zinc-silver, while the latter were higher than those at the recycling plants. In short, the coalition had abandoned the goals of wage uniformity and equal absolute increases across the entire company. Equally important, ASARCO won a diverse set of contract termination dates: for copper, June 30, 1971; for the recycling plants, September 30, 1971; and for lead-zinc-silver, December 31, 1971.

At Anaconda, the settlements followed the PD pattern: 55-cent increases at mines and related facilities in Montana, Nevada (Yerington), and Arizona (Twin Buttes). Termination dates varied between thirty-nine and forty-two months (June 30 and September 30, 1971).

Kennecott settled on about the same basis, with smaller increases at its lead-zinc operations and at its Ohio fabricating plants. Helped by principles recommended by the Taylor panel, Kennecott had succeeded in preserving both established negotiating boundaries and separate contracts.[11]

Observations Concerning the Strike

The first question to be asked is, What brought about the longest major strike in American industrial history? The short answer must be, The demand of the coalition for company-wide bargaining with simultaneous settlements at all properties concerned. The NLRB so concluded on August 19, 1970, when it ruled in the Phelps Dodge case that this demand was unlawful. Here it should be added that the Federal Court of Appeals, 3rd Circuit, in Philadelphia subsequently decided that the board was wrong, largely because the judicial panel had no expertise in collective bargaining, hence no grasp of the issues in the case. When the U.S. Supreme Court later denied certiorari, it left the legal standing of coordinated bargaining in limbo, where it remains today.

In declaring that

> the integrity of a bargaining unit, whether established by certification or by voluntary agreement of the parties, cannot as here be unilaterally attacked,

the board had reached the heart of the issue.[12] For in fact the USW coalition had tried through an eight-month strike to expand the orbit of negotiations to encompass the full range of each of the companies' widespread activities, despite the long-established existence of legally created but decentralized bargaining units. To accomplish this end, the coalition had established two bargaining institutions: the Nonferrous Industry Conference, with delegates from all the unions, whose functions were to frame demands and to vote on any pattern-setting agreement; and the Nonferrous Industry Coordinating and Steering Committee, which had only seven members, led by Molony and including Brubaker and Skinner. The function of the steering committee was to serve as a command post for managing negotiations with each employer; for conducting a joint strike of the unions against all of the employers; for timing the final approval of already negotiated settlements; and through such timing for determination of when the strikers could return to work. Even more important, the steering committee could select the settlement that it wished to establish as "the" pattern, recommend it to the conference, and make sure that the delegates accepted it.

Viewed in greater detail, the steering committee had several basic responsibilities, all of them vital to the conduct of the strike. First, it decided on the acceptability of any settlement emerging from the local bargaining committees—to ensure uniform adherence to the pattern. Second, by guidance and by the power to withhold approval of any agreement, the committee could make sure that the settlements were simultaneous. Third, by exercise of the same power it could hold out for equalizing the occupational wage structure for all operations (entry rates and skill ranges) with the mining level, which had always been highest. Fourth, the committee could insist on parallel expiration dates for all contracts. And finally, the committee could insist on equal absolute increases, in cents per hour, at all properties of all the nonferrous companies, on top of the equalizing increases.

By tabling a specific settlement already agreed upon to obtain acceptable settlements elsewhere in each employer's operations, the committee sought to extend the terms of the initial agreement, essentially by refusing to consummate that agreement in the service of its larger, freely acknowledged purpose of winning uniform economic terms throughout the corporation. Having already negotiated through to settlement at a given segment of his operations, the employer found himself compelled to bargain all over again for the same segment at the steering committee level, over new and extraneous demands, with different union representatives who had not participated in the original bargaining. Here, then, is the core of the explanation for this long and frustrating strike.

What did the coalition gain from settlement of the long dispute? Its most significant achievement—and undoubtedly it was a most impressive one—was its now-demonstrated ability to hold together, without defections or open internal conflict, throughout a very difficult strike. In fact, the task required persuading twenty-six national unions and literally dozens of locals to unite, formulate a mutually acceptable set of demands, follow a common course of strike action, and maintain a central authority for joint control over the entire course of the long dispute. Undoubtedly the United Steelworkers made the largest contribution—in leadership and ideas and resources.

When it comes to the actual gain from bargaining during 1967–1968, the outcome is much less impressive. The wage and benefit improvements were not remarkable for those years. The wage differentials between mining and fabricating activities and among product lines were reinforced, not eliminated. Thus the industry-wide wage uniformity proclaimed in Salt Lake City as a basic bargaining goal for 1967 remained a distant objective. Moreover, there was no notable progress toward common dates for contract terminations. In short, the major accomplishment of the whole undertaking was the formation of the coalition itself, which, by showing its staying power, was to provide the basis for pattern-bargaining in copper mining, smelting, and refining for four more rounds of negotiations to come over the next twelve years.

NEGOTIATIONS AND OTHER DEVELOPMENTS

The Early Seventies

There were some elements that were familiar and some that were new in the 1971 negotiations. The union coalition was again very much in evidence, with the Steelworkers dominating and with Joseph P. Molony still chairman. The organizational setup was the same: the conference, made up of delegates from the locals and responsible both for formulating bargaining goals and for final approval of pattern-setting agreements recommended by the steering committee; the coordinating and steering committee, which managed all negotiations and approved all settlements; and finally, the bargaining committees at the various companies, which transmitted tentative settlements to the steering committee for final action.

What was different in 1971 was that the bargaining was confined to the extractive side of copper—rather than covering the whole of nonferrous, from the mines to the metal manufacturing plants. There were two basic reasons for this change. First, as noted earlier, the coalition had settled the 1968 strike on terms that separated contract expiration dates by metal and by technological stage. An enormous concession, this agreement constituted nothing less than abandonment of the whole USW approach to collective bargaining in the industry. That approach, it will be recalled, was based on the idea that basic steel and nonferrous were analogous industries. By conceding this differentiation of termination dates, the coalition was at least tacitly accepting the principle that nonferrous was neither a cohesive nor a homogeneous industry. There was no other way the coalition could get a settlement in 1968, and by March an increasingly restive and discontented rank and file had made settlement imperative. But this is not to say that the USW leadership had actually given up its ultimate goal of uniformity in wages and benefits throughout the nonferrous industry. On the contrary, this objective was deferred temporarily in 1971, only to be reasserted vigorously by USW president Abel in 1974.

Second, the coalition's approach in 1971 was not to demand company-wide bargaining, but rather to concentrate on copper, and within copper on mining, smelting, and refining, not fabrication. With this shift in strategy, the basic principles of the steering committee were to engage in parallel but separate negotiations with some ten employers; to choose a target company, as the process of discovery through negotiation revealed where the best offers were to be found; to recommend the best tentative settlement for approval by the conference; and then to make that settlement the pattern to be held before the other companies as the standard they were expected to accept if they wished to avoid a strike. Details and local deviations could be filled in later. Alternatively, the recalcitrant employer (in this period usually Phelps Dodge or ASARCO) would be faced with a strike and shutdown while competitors who had yielded could go on producing, taking over the laggard's market share as well.

To recapitulate, in 1971 the USW coalition had gone over to the UAW system of pattern-following bargaining. Furthermore, it did so where this technique had the best chance of success—in the extractive phase of copper production, where perfect substitutability prevailed among the finished copper products turned out by the various companies, and at a time when profitability was unusually great.

When the conference met in Salt Lake City in the spring of 1971, it decided to make automatic cost-of-living adjustments (COLAs) its principal bargaining demand for that round. What was contemplated was a mechanism that tied a cents-per-hour wage increase to a given number of points of increase in the official Bureau of Labor Statistics consumer price index. Each quarter the supplement would be calculated, and each year the total supplement would be "rolled in" to the hourly base rates. The proposal was timely because accelerating inflation had been under way since 1965. As conceived, however, money wages would be tied to the level of consumer prices, regardless of movements in the price of copper or of conditions in the copper labor markets.

By midnight of June 30, 30,000 employees went on strike. More would follow as contracts were to expire at ANAMAX and White Pine at the end of July. With the onset of the strike, Molony told the press that pending offers of 85.3 cents over three years failed to meet "critical needs" and were "significantly inferior" to settlements in aluminum. In this instance, the pattern sought by the coalition was being influenced by wage concessions in a quite different industry, but one in which the Steelworkers had partial representation.

On July 19 Magma Copper made itself the tentative leader by offering an "uncapped" (no upper limit) COLA clause and an added increase in basic rates of 92 cents per hour over the next three years. Anaconda followed the next day, and the steering committee said that it would pass on both settlements by July 24. Meanwhile, by the next day the committee had in hand final offers from Kennecott and Phelps Dodge, which also included COLA clauses. Up to July 20 ASARCO had been vigorously resisting this provision. Phelps Dodge had also fought the COLA concept, finally trying to temper it by proposing that the price of copper be incorporated in the formula. Over the next week, settlements that included an uncapped COLA provision were approved by the coalition for Magma, Anaconda, Kennecott, and Phelps Dodge. By the end of August, the smaller companies were in the fold, but Anaconda stayed on strike until late September because of a stubborn dispute over the revision of some craft work rules.[13]

The COLA clause was the central issue in the 1971 dispute. There was more to it than the clause itself: Molony was extremely anxious to win this objective in order to use it as a bargaining chip in forthcoming negotiations in big steel, which had abandoned its COLA provision some years earlier when inflation had ceased to be a serious issue. Thus the coalition had made nonferrous its target industry in 1971, just as it had used aluminum to the same effect in the same year to jack up the wage offers of the copper companies. More important, the COLA provision, which was to take effect on July 1, 1972, would prove to be the primary source of money wage inflation over the next decade. Ultimately it would produce a "scissors" crisis, in which hourly wages were soaring at the same time that the price of copper was plunging to depths below average variable cost of production.

In March 1974, the conference met in Tucson, where it reasserted vigorously its 1967 goal of wage uniformity throughout the nonferrous industry: "We call for the installation of a common job classification system in the nonferrous industry, which uses the same wages and salary rates for the same job classes. We seek a common wage scale throughout the industry that reflects equal pay for equal work."[14]

Because the content of the jobs in the occupational structure of the industry (skill, effort, responsibility, working conditions) varied enormously from the mines to the concentrators, smelters, refineries, fabricating plants, foundries, and scrap plants, the only way to obtain the desired uniformity—equal pay for equal work—was to get the employers to agree to a uniform system of job evaluation, so that divergent jobs could be evaluated and then grouped and assigned correlated standard pay rates. Such a system had been introduced by United States Steel in 1945 and became a joint union-management tool—the Cooperative Wage Survey (CWS) manual system—for the company's steel plants. In Charles Cox's time as head of Kennecott, the system had been adopted in that company, despite stout resistance from Mine Mill. But the rest of the copper producers were strongly opposed. Accordingly, president Abel of the Steelworkers conceded in 1974 that the goal of a common, industry-wide wage structure was unlikely to be attained in 1974, although he had hopes for 1977.

The conference also declared that its bargaining objectives in 1974 included "very substantial wage and salary increases" to correct for inflation and to allow for "wide profit margins" and improved labor productivity.[15]

For this round Anaconda became the lead company with a total money offer of 61 cents per hour (28 cents in the first year, 16 in the second, 17 in the third). The offer came on June 26, before any strike. A coalition spokesman, not disclosing the amount at the time because, he said, it awaited approval by the steering committee, went on to note that it might not be sufficient to avoid a strike. Kennecott, Phelps Dodge, and ASARCO, he claimed, had made wage proposals not "anything like" Anaconda's, although its proposal fell short of USW settlements in aluminum, containers, and basic steel. Once more the unions were appealing to interindustry comparisons. Also, they were emphasizing total money settlements rather than the more subtle problems of uniformity in wage structure. Finally, as a result of the 1968 concessions, the negotiations were concerned solely with the extractive side of copper.

On July 1 the steering committee extended copper expiration dates to midnight of July 14. At the same time it approved the Anaconda deal, declaring that the other employers would have to "meet the money value" of that offer. There is reason to believe that the committee was maneuvering to make Kennecott the pattern-setter this time, for it already paid the highest hourly wages (in part because of the operation of the CWS evaluation system).

On July 15 ASARCO, Phelps Dodge, Magma, and Inspiration all went on strike. At this time the Anaconda settlement had a total value—including benefits—of $3.10 per hour, of which wage rates and adjustments in classification constituted 86.4 cents. Kennecott also weighed in at $3.10 hourly, but with 79 cents for wage rates. At the end of July, Phelps Dodge, ASARCO, Magma, Miami, and Inspiration were all on strike, to be joined the next day by ANAMAX.

Settlements at the major companies—ASARCO, Phelps Dodge, and Magma—finally were reached between August 15 and 20. ASARCO agreed to pay an immediate increase of 85 cents—just below Anaconda's

86.5 cents—while Phelps Dodge settled for 83.5 cents. Soon afterward Inspiration, Miami, and White Pine reached agreements for similar amounts.

The Job Discrimination Case at Inspiration

Union-management relations in southwestern copper mining in the 1970s were not confined to triennial bouts of bargaining over wages and benefits. In 1973 the two sides found themselves in the unusual positions of joint defendants in a job discrimination case brought by the federal government against them as the outcome of a proceeding commenced by the Equal Employment Opportunity Commission in 1966.[16]

Actually, the great significance of the case is that the whole industry was on trial. First, the practices found to be in violation of Title VII of the Civil Rights Act of 1964 and charged against Inspiration and its unions were the same practices hitherto followed by Kennecott, Magma, Phelps Dodge, and other copper producers as well as the copper unions. Second, the union locals also charged with these practices were affiliates of national unions typically involved at other companies through other locals: Boilermakers, Carpenters, Pipefitters, Operating Engineers, Electricians, United Transportation Union, Machinists, Steelworkers, and Teamsters. In other words, Inspiration had the tripartite setup typical of unions found in most of the nonferrous industry.

The raw materials of the case consisted of a labor force that the court classified as "Anglos," Mexican-Americans, and American Indians;[17] and a collection of unions composed of shop and railroad crafts, and two residual production units belonging to the Steelworkers and the Teamsters. These last units were organized as industrial unions and involved the concentrator, leaching plant, and smelter. All of these bargaining units had emerged from Globe elections conducted by the NLRB in 1942–1943.

The central problem in the case was *access* to jobs, more specifically, access to certain jobs, restriction of access to certain jobs, and denial of access to certain jobs—all on the basis not primarily of qualifications, but rather according to the presence or absence of certain traits peculiar to each of the three groups. The ruling criteria were first language, physical characteristics, and line of geographic origin or descent. In brief, an ethnic survey of the Inspiration work force disclosed that the unattractive, lower-paid, and relatively unskilled smelter and leaching plant jobs were predominantly held by Mexican-Americans and American Indians, while the more attractive, better-paid, and more skilled craft and railroad jobs were held primarily by Anglos. At the apprentice level, of fifty-seven accepted applicants, one was Mexican and one was Indian. As for the alternative route upward—from laborer to helper to journeyman craftsman—Anglos could move up to helper and then to journeyman, whereas members of the other two categories could not.

Thus the distribution of the work force was the result of certain practices that controlled access or rejection. For example, the court found that no employee had a right to transfer jobs from one jurisdiction to another except by joint permission of the employer and the affected unions. Further, the court concluded that the company had denied all transfers to the craft or railroad units; that it had refused in specific cases to allow members of the excluded groups to move into the machine shops or into crane operator jobs; and that it also had blocked all transfers to craft jobs from those in the Steelworker units. Moreover, the court held, the company used a qualifications test that the court found not to be job related, hence irrelevant to a determination of actual qualifications. Finally, the court found that for both hires and transfers Mexican-Americans were routinely assigned to jobs in the Mine Mill, USW, and Teamsters units, while Anglos were more likely to go into the craft units.

Accordingly, the court concluded that the employer had engaged in a pattern or practice of job discrimination with respect to transfers between bargaining units and access to apprenticeship programs. To end this set of practices, the court ordered both the company and its codefendant unions to open up the transfer and apprenticeship systems on equal terms for all three groups. Thus the "affected class" (Mexican-Americans and American Indians) was no longer to be required to meet higher standards, for age or high school education, than had to be met by the Anglo group. Educational requirements were to be uniform for new hires; any entrance tests had to be strictly job related and also be acceptable to the court. For transfers, members of the affected class were to be allowed to use plant seniority in making bids, because otherwise they would be unable even to qualify under occupational seniority assigned in the desired job. They were also accorded "rate retention" in making transfers where the new job paid less than the old one. Finally, the court protected the requirement that all candidates for hire, transfer, or apprenticeship must be qualified for the assignment, in the interests of business efficiency. But the determination of qualifications now had to be job related and uniformly applied for all groups.

This pathbreaking decision revolutionized personnel practices in copper and beyond copper, throughout the mining industry, in those regions where racial or ethnic discrimination had been a routine practice for many years.

The Late Seventies

From the 1971 negotiations on, the notions of target companies, pattern-setting, and pattern-following all became characteristic of each three-year bargaining round, with the USW steering committee in control. In 1971 Magma was the first employer to yield on COLA, followed within twenty-four hours by Anaconda. Then the pattern was accepted by the other copper firms. In 1974 the basic issue was the size of the total money offer. This time Anaconda set the pattern, with Kennecott close behind. By 1977 Kennecott had emerged as the wage leader and target company—a role that it continued to hold through the 1983 round.

It was also during the 1974–1977 period that Frank S. McKee became chief negotiator for the USW coalition. McKee had begun his career as a steelworker in Tacoma, then later became director of district 38 of the USW in Southern California. Still later he became secretary-treasurer of the national union, while continuing to serve as chief negotiator in copper. As a bargainer, McKee soon won a reputation as intelligent, resolute, and unyielding—traits that were to produce handsome returns for the unions during the first years of his tenure, but that later were to end in disaster.

At midnight of June 30, 1977, labor agreements expired at seven of the copper producers and a strike began. According to the coalition leadership, there was no alternative because no pattern-setting agreement had been reached. Then on July 2 Kennecott made its offer, accompanied by a parallel overture from Magma. In essence, the Kennecott proposal included an increase of 85 cents an hour over the next three years, mostly as a general increase, with the balance allocated to adjustment of pay differentials; revision of the CWS manual; and improvements in sick leave, pension, and unemployment benefits. In return, the company dropped some minor requests for concessions, agreed to leave the COLA formula intact at 1 cent per hour for each 0.3 point rise in the Consumer Price Index, to be applied quarterly, with annual roll-ins of the cumulative total to be applied to all wage-related money benefits. The company also agreed to roll in to hourly rates immediately 38 cents in accumulated upward adjustments. Local issues delayed the end of the Kennecott strike until after July

19. Ten days later Anaconda and Cities Service (formerly Miami Copper) settled on the Kennecott pattern.

By contrast, Phelps Dodge, ASARCO, and three smaller producers continued to hold out. Phelps Dodge's basic objective was to rid itself of the COLA premium, which it had opposed from its inception in 1971. PD had proposed that the formula be changed to include the price of copper. On August 8 the company settled on Kennecott's terms, with retention of the COLA formula, for its employees in Arizona and Texas. The other employers stayed out some weeks longer.[18]

With the 1980 negotiations, the copper industry once more wound up on strike—its sixth in succession from 1964. Two months earlier the coalition conference had announced that it expected to get a large increase in wages because of the high level of profits in the industry. But this time the opposition of the employers was unusually strong, because the demand for copper had begun to decline. A lengthy and substantial drop in price was in the offing, both occasioned in part by the strong deflationary policy adopted by the Federal Reserve in 1979.

From the USW standpoint, no prestrike offers were acceptable because they fell well short of those already received in aluminum and basic steel—a comparison that had now become routine. On the employers' side, there was general agreement that part of the COLA adjustment (29 cents) should be diverted to pay for other benefits, as the Steelworkers had already agreed to do in basic steel. Furthermore, Phelps Dodge had initiated a demand that the COLA system be dropped entirely. On these issues, a strike—and a long one at that—became inevitable.

As matters worked out, the Kennecott settlement again became the pattern, but only after a seventy-one-day strike. Phelps Dodge held out another three weeks in a vain effort to resist the growing cost-price squeeze, but finally settled on October 3, on the hope that the rate of inflation would decline while the price of copper would recover. ASARCO was the last to reach agreement, on November 10. In the outcome, the USW had saved the COLA formula while successfully fighting off the companies' proposal to divert COLA payments to money benefits.[19] The price of these successes would turn out to be extremely high: a disastrous strike at Phelps Dodge in 1983.

The 1980 round was the last of four similar negotiations after the end of the big strike in 1968. Over the next three years the bargaining situation was to undergo drastic change, to reflect the sharply deteriorating condition of the copper industry.

Another view of bench-mining and rail operations at Bingham Canyon. (*Photo courtesy of Kennecott Corporation and Alexis C. Fernandez.*)

Headframe of the Anaconda Mine. The Anaconda was the greatest of the American underground copper mines and the most productive of the many mines at Butte, known as "the richest hill on earth." (*Photo courtesy of the American Heritage Center, University of Wyoming, and Dr. Charles C. Daly.*)

A recent view of the Phelps Dodge Reduction Works at Morenci, Arizona, looking northeast. In the left foreground are the crushing plant, ball mill and flotation plant; in the upper right center is the older Morenci concentrator; and on the right the now-closed Morenci smelter. (*Photo courtesy of Phelps Dodge Morenci, Inc.*)

COLLAPSE OF THE PATTERN SYSTEM

The Scissors Crisis of 1980

Starting in 1980, American copper suffered its most extreme economic contraction since the early 1930s. It was the result of a conjuncture of three adverse forces: rapid wage inflation, domestic recession in demand under the deflationary monetary policy introduced by the Federal Reserve, and a surge of copper imports stimulated in part by a substantial rise in the exchange value of the dollar.

Although these events have already been described from the price side, it is important to combine price and wage developments to illustrate the scissors effect shown in Figure 9.1. If we look at price first, its traditionally notorious instability shows up initially in a declining phase during 1974 to 1978; a sharp rise from 1978 through 1979; and a very sharp decline beginning in 1980 and continuing through 1986. In money values, the domestic producers' price of cathodes (the COMEX price plus a supplement of 5 cents) started from a low of 51.2 cents a pound in 1972 (annual average). In February 1980 it reached its peak at $1.329, plunging by the following December to 88.10 cents. By 1986 the average annual price was only 66.05 cents. Thus between 1980 and 1986 (annual averages), the price of the product of the industry dropped 35 percent.

If we turn now to wages, the money value of the average annual starting rate displays a steep and unbroken ascent from 1972 through 1986, for a simple average yearly rate of advance of 12.4 percent. Through 1983 the average annual rate of increase was an incredible 13.9 percent—while the price of copper had a net advance of only 4.5 percent yearly in the same period. In short, the wage rate was rising three times as fast as the product price during these difficult years. Also, it should be noted, the entry rate serves here only as a proxy for all straight-time occupational wage rates. There is reason to believe that relative skill rate differentials were being compressed during this period, because negotiated increases were fixed in flat cents per hour, as were the rolled-in increases under the COLA mechanism.

COLA was the principal factor in the upward march of basic rates after 1972, as can be illustrated by the entry rate: excluding COLA supplements, it rose 60 percent through 1983, or 5.5 percent yearly. By contrast, the starting rate *including* COLA adjustments jumped 153.5 percent in the

FIGURE 9.1 **Comparitive Behavior of Cathode Price and Straight-Time Entry Rate, Including Cost-of-Living Adjustment, 1972– 1986**

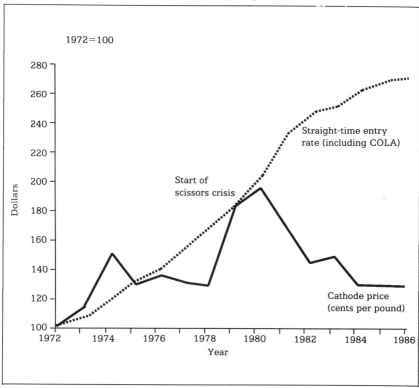

SOURCE: Prices from U.S. Department of the Interior, Bureau of Mines, *Minerals Yearbook*, various issues, 1973–1986; wage data from Magma Copper Company, Phelps Dodge Corporation, and Kennecott Corporation.

same period, or more than 13.9 percent yearly. Stated another way, by 1983 COLA supplements represented over one-third of the base entry rate. Last, it should be noted that through the annual roll-ins the COLA supplements entered all of the occupational rates and through these all of the wage-related benefits such as overtime, vacation pay, and sick-leave pay. There can be no doubt, therefore, that gross hourly labor costs rose even faster than the base starting rate through these years.

If we refer back to Figure 9.1, it is obvious that labor costs were running ahead of product price from 1975 and that after 1979 the gap between them became enormous as prices began to plunge while wages continued to soar upward. The only offset available to producers was increased labor productivity. But it was impossible to match the growing gap by this means.

The price-wage scissors was only one component of the economic problems of the industry after the close of the seventies. Chapter 7 has already detailed the impact on U.S. copper production of the combination of national and international recession, perverse exchange rates, and rising imports during the early and mid-1980s. Of special significance to the present discussion is the employment impact (Table 9.1). Even between 1972 and 1979, when the copper market was still buoyant, total employment in both extraction and fabrication dropped by 9,300 jobs, or 12 percent. In the main, this decline reflected technological improvements and closures of inefficient mines and plants rather than contraction of production. By 1979 the Federal Reserve had introduced its deflationary policy, whose joint consequences were a protracted sharp drop in the demand for copper and in the price of copper, while at the same time the external value of the dollar began a six-year rise that sucked in a large increase in copper imports. With copper wages continuing to rise with the tie (through COLA) to the advancing level of consumer prices, the scissors crisis began its extended harsh domination of the domestic branch of the industry.

Between 1979 and 1983 total employment fell by 14,400 persons in extraction (-43 percent) and 9,200 (-26.5 percent) in fabrication. Although employment was divided about equally between the two branches,

TABLE 9.1 **Employment in extraction and fabrication of domestic copper, 1972–1986**

Year	Extraction[a]		Fabrication[b]	
	No. employees	No. production workers	No. employees	No. production workers
1972 (May)	38,200	N.A.	39,100	N.A.
1979	33,300	25,600	34,700	27,200
1980	30,000	23,000	30,800	23,100
1981	36,300	28,000	29,300	21,900
1983	18,900	13,500	25,500	18,700
1986	11,400	8,800	23,000	17,800

SOURCE: U.S. Department of Labor, Bureau of Labor Statistics, *Supplement to Employment and Earnings, United States, 1909–1984* (July 1987); other occasional issues.

[a] Mining, smelting, and refining of copper ores.
[b] Rolling and drawing of cathode copper.

the contraction was substantially less in fabrication because imported cathodes could be substituted for domestic, an option obviously unavailable to the extractive side. Note also that the impact of the contraction during 1979–1983 was relatively greater for production workers alone than for all categories together.

What we have, then, in this difficult period is an exceedingly steep and unbroken rise in wages, a steep decline in product price (from 1980), and a very severe contraction in employment. Together these three strong movements were to constitute the setting for labor-management negotiations in 1983. To set the stage for these decisive events, it is worth repeating from Chapter 7 the impact of the contraction on the economic position of the employers.

Anaconda suffered a loss of $332 million in 1982, with unit costs of copper production running at nearly double the market price. Within a year the company closed its Berkeley pit at Butte and allowed the flooding of its underground mines. Soon afterward, the business was permanently liquidated after a century of operations. Kennecott reported losses of $189 million in 1982 and $91 million in 1983. In these years the company laid off 3,000 employees and temporarily suspended operations at Ray and Chino. For 1982 ASARCO reported a loss of $38 million. It cut employment 24 percent at its Mission Mine and closed Silver Bell excepting for leaching. Phelps Dodge reported a loss of $74 million in the same year. On April 17, 1982, it closed down all of its mining operations and began living off its substantial inventories. In October the company resumed mining at its Morenci-Metcalf complex, following with Ajo in February 1983, and Tyrone in May. In 1983 the company lost $63.5 million and its cash flow was negative.

It was the same story at Magma, Duval, Inspiration, White Pine, and the other smaller producers. Thus while the country had resumed overall economic expansion, the copper industry was barely surviving in conditions of deep depression. In this unhappy context it entered negotiations for new labor contracts in the spring of 1983.

The Phelps Dodge Strike

From the standpoint of the leadership of the USW coalition, the requisite basic strategy for the 1983 negotiations was comparatively simple. No concessions were to be granted in wage rates or in wage-related benefits. McKee and his associates were, of course, fully aware of the economic distress of the copper industry, for they had watched the long procession of layoffs and closures of properties over the preceding years. But they could see no benefit to their members from concessions to the employers. Instead, they held firmly to the classic union tradition of no cuts in money wages. According to this tradition, general reductions in wages would only reduce purchasing power, hence do no good for employment. Special cuts for the weaker companies would undermine the entire wage pattern of the industry, again without benefit to employment. Why sacrifice a uniform structure of money wages that had been painfully built up through a series of hard strikes over a long period of time?

In short, then, the industry pattern of wages and benefits had to be defended at all costs. Therefore, no concessions. Yet the economic predicament was desperate enough to require some gesture of recognition. Thus it was decided to offer a cap on all occupational wage rates for the coming three years, provided that the employers agreed to keep the COLA mechanism intact. In this way, the roll-ins would continue to add to basic rates each year, while the employees would get the interim pay supplements each quarter. The cap could at most only slow the rate of increase in basic rates. Even in these dismal circumstances, then, hourly labor costs would continue to rise.

On the employers' side, the basic problem was perceived to be COLA, the primary factor in the inflation of labor costs, which in turn were about 42 percent of all costs. The employers were not united, however, on how hard to push to get rid of COLA, or about possible relief from fluctuating copper prices.

In 1982 the price of wirebar copper had averaged 74.3 cents per pound. In 1983 it began creeping upward, starting at 80.2 cents in January and peaking for the year in May at 85.6 cents. If an employer were optimistic about a continuing rise over the longer term, he could find the combination offer of a wage cap with a retained COLA clause rather attractive, simply because revenue per pound might rise faster than cost per pound, which would afford some relief from the four-year scissors problem.

For an employer who foresaw no extended rise in price, there was no prospect at all for relief. His losses would continue and probably even increase, and his cash position would only worsen. His alternatives were equally bleak: accept the offer and wait for bankruptcy; reject the offer, take a strike, and shut down; or reject the offer, take the strike, and try to continue operating.

In mid-April 1983 Frank McKee, head of the Steelworkers' coalition of unions, and Judd Cool, chief negotiator at Kennecott, dropped a bomb-shell on the industry by suddenly announcing that they had reached agreement on a new three-year contract to take effect July 1. Its major provisions held all basic rates at present levels. The COLA mechanism was kept intact, however, with its quarterly supplements to take-home pay still to be set by the formula of 1 cent for each 0.3 point rise in the Consumers Price Index, and with annual roll-ins of these increments into basic rates. Thus the upward thrust of wage costs was not eliminated. The coalition did make minor concessions in certain benefits that were unique to Kennecott—paid sick-leave days were reduced and a $7,500 cap was placed on lump-sum benefits for retirement, death, and disability pay-ments.[20] What was important to Kennecott management was the union's agreement to eliminate an employment security plan introduced in the early 1960s.[21] That plan had guaranteed continued employment to workers displaced by modernization or implementation of new technolo-gies, which Kennecott was contemplating at the time and later carried out.

This settlement was made some ten weeks before the Kennecott con-tract expiration dates. Because it was privately negotiated between Cool and McKee, it took the other employers by surprise. Nor was their evident discomfiture lessened by the coalition's public claim that it expected the new agreements to set the pattern for the entire extraction branch of the copper industry. Toward the end of June, Magma and ASARCO accepted the Kennecott pattern and several smaller companies followed. Only Phelps Dodge and Duval held out.

During the preceding twelve months, Phelps Dodge had gone through an economic convulsion of protracted shutdowns and heavy layoffs. Its chairman, George B. Munroe, had toured the company's mining camps in an attempt to set forth the company's plight to its employees, their fami-lies, and anyone else who would listen, apparently in hopes of preparing the way for contract concessions in 1983. In January of that year, top management began reviewing its bargaining options against a backdrop of growing losses, a serious cash drain, and a stringent program of cost cutting from which the unionized employees were contractually exempt. Phelps Dodge had recognized already that it would be perilous to negoti-ate from the assumption of an impending permanent recovery of copper prices—as the Kennecott negotiators had—the more so because at the time PD was purely a copper producer, with no parent oil company to provide further infusions of cash if prices failed to recover (Kennecott by this time was a subsidiary of SOHIO).[22]

Accordingly, the problem for PD defined itself: an imperative need for a prompt and substantial reduction in labor costs. As Munroe and Richard T. Moolick, president of the corporation, viewed the problem, the heart of the trouble was twofold: the inflationary labor-cost effects of the COLA mechanism and the uneconomically high level of occupational base rates, in particular at the lower end.[23]

Munroe and Moolick decided to adopt three bargaining demands, which were to be laid before the union coalition during the forthcoming negotiations covering the Arizona properties: (1) total elimination of the COLA system; (2) introduction of a dual scale of pay rates that would be lower for all new hires and new promotions at all levels, but unchanged for all present incumbents; and (3) a proportionately greater cut in the rate for new hires at the laborer (unskilled) level, to restore skill differentials that had been uneconomically compressed by COLA increments and past general settlements.

In undertaking this strategy, PD management entertained no real hope that the coalition would settle for anything close to these concessions. Rather, it assumed that a strike on July 1 was certain, because it had no expectation that the coalition would depart from the target company-pattern system it had been following since 1967. Thus the ultimate choice lay between closing down and attempting to operate. Financially, closure would only increase losses, while by playing the pattern-following game one more time the company would lose its market share and its regular customers, only to end the agony by having to settle on terms that it had found unacceptable from the start. One alternative remained: to break out of captivity to the pattern system by pressing its own demands to impasse, accepting a strike, and attempting to operate.

Once this strategy was chosen, the problem became that of preparation for one of the most difficult of all strikes, as PD itself had ample reason to know from its experience with continuing operations during the rail brotherhoods' strike at Morenci in 1959. Available manpower and manpower requirements had to be carefully estimated and a production schedule worked out. Operating personnel had to be trained and assigned. Security arrangements had to be made to protect lives, property, access to and egress from the plants. The risks of violence had to be faced and controlled. Court papers had to be drafted in case the dispute got out of hand and threatened to destroy civil order.

All of these preparations were predicated on a worst-case scenario: PD standing alone. In the midst of this planning, PD management was undoubtedly disturbed and probably angered by the surprise announcement of the early Kennecott settlement, which the coalition promptly proclaimed to be the new industry pattern, to be imposed on an entire group of employers whose economic positions (including Kennecott's) were already desperate by any measure.

Phelps Dodge's response was not long in forthcoming. It demanded a termination of the COLA system and was told by the unions that all companies must conform to the Kennecott pattern, hence the COLA must be left untouched. Stalemate followed. Then, just before July 1, the company added a second proposal: a two-tier wage structure, with exemption for present incumbents and a larger cut at the lower end of the occupational range. The company's two demands ran head-on against the pattern. Impasse had now arrived. On June 30 the Federal Mediation Service brought Frank McKee and Robert Petris, representing the coalition, together with John F. Boland, Jr., and M. P. Scanlon, for the employer. Nothing was gained from this meeting; both sides held firmly to their respective positions. On the same day PD representatives told the unions' bargaining committee for the Arizona properties that if a strike took place the company intended to operate, and when it did it would put its last offer into effect. As July 1 began, the midnight shift failed to appear. The strike was on.

Phelps Dodge's decision to operate was a step that had rarely been taken by American management during the postwar years, although it began to occur more frequently with the advent of concessionary bargaining in the deflationary period of the early 1980s. To say the least, it was highly controversial and produced much hostile criticism—and not from union spokesmen alone. One view was the rather trite contention that the conflict represented a failure of communications, while another claimed that the company's underlying purpose was not a settlement or relief from labor costs but old-fashioned union busting.

There is scant reason to accept an explanation that appeals to bad communications, for it lacks any basis in fact. Both sides were fully acquainted with each other's bargaining goals and limits for more than two months before the strike. From mid-April on, there was never any question that Phelps Dodge was adamantly opposed to the terms of the Kennecott deal and was determined to get substantial relief from its burden of labor costs. It was equally obvious and in fact was also public knowledge that the USW coalition had deliberately chosen Kennecott as the target company and had made its settlement with that company the pattern to which the other employers would be held under threat of strike. And it was even more obvious to any careful observer that this designated pattern provided no relief from labor costs beyond the token concession of a three-year cap on basic rates. Even that very modest boon was rendered negligible by its ironclad tie to the continuance of COLA. Both sides understood all this full well. Thus the dispute was not the product of any misunderstanding.

If the company's real purpose had been union busting, then clearly the coalition had at hand an entirely adequate means to thwart it. It merely needed to consent to bargain directly about PD's claimed needs rather than insisting with undeviating rigidity that the Kennecott terms had already been established and must be accepted by all of the other employers. Through that intransigence the unions were actually challenging Phelps Dodge with a hard and narrow choice: follow the pattern or take a strike. It was the sixth time this sequence had been played out since the formation of the coalition in 1967—as a means, some would say, to box in a recalcitrant employer with contract terms negotiated elsewhere and immune from the give-and-take of direct bargaining with that same unwilling employer.

And so, on this occasion again, a strike was precipitated, in full expectation of its usual consummation—surrender on the target company's terms. Only this time the outcome was very different, because of PD's decision to operate. The challenge issued to the company by the coalition placed the union's whole system of collective representation at risk, for under these new conditions there was a real prospect that the strike could be lost.

With the start of the strike Phelps Dodge scheduled a two-shift operation of twelve hours daily for each shift, seven days a week. The work force initially was composed of supervisors, nonunion employees, and union employees who either had been on layoff or had refused to go on strike. By early August this force of between 800 and 900 men and women was close to exhaustion from the demanding schedule. On August 8 the company began preparations at Morenci to hire new people at the gate, to fill out its complement, and to replace permanently all strikers who refused to return to work.

The potential for violence, which had been present from the start of the strike, now began to rise dangerously. At the same time it had long been obvious that the sheriff's deputies and the local courts were both inadequate and unwilling to protect civil order and civil rights in Morenci,

Douglas, and Ajo. On August 9 Governor Bruce Babbitt flew to Morenci, where he met with company and union officials and by exercise of pressure compelled the company to shut down operations at Morenci for ten days. According to the *Daily Labor Report* (August 10, 1983), PD's reluctant decision to close down came

> after a group of hundreds of angry strikers displaying baseball bats, steel clubs, shovels and other implements had claimed it would assault police barricades on Highway 666, enter the mine and take out nonstriking workers by force.

The company told the governor, however, that it intended to resume operations after the truce had expired. The governor then sent in the National Guard to restore order and when the ten days were up, PD restarted production and began hiring at the gate.

Each new hire was given a written statement informing the individual that he or she was a new employee and a permanent replacement for a striker and could not be displaced by a striker if or when the strike was ended. The work force was quickly built up to the desired level. Over the next several months the unions filed various charges of unfair labor practices with the NLRB, all of which were eventually dismissed. Picketing continued as the strike remained technically in effect for over two more years. After July 1, 1984, while the strike was still running, petitions for the decertification of all the unions at the Arizona properties began circulating. The elections that eventually followed all went against the unions. In Arizona, Phelps Dodge became a nonunion company for the first time since 1942.

There is no question that an employer has a legal right to continue production once a strike has been called against him. He also has a collateral right to hire replacements for the employees on strike. At the same time, employees have the right to engage in a lawful strike and to pursue "protected" activities in behalf of their cause—for example, peaceful picketing and nonthreatening expressions of opinion, or conveyance of information through signs, pamphlets, or by word of mouth.[24] There are other activities on behalf of the strikers' cause that are not protected by law, but on the contrary are proscribed because they involve coercive interference with, or deprivation of, the rights and liberties of others—nonstrikers, supervisors, owners, or innocent bystanders. Among these are threats and intimidation, obstruction of ingress to and egress from work sites, physical harm to persons, damage to property, and the carrying of weapons or intimidating implements.[25] A legal cause may be pursued only by lawful means, so that the rights and freedoms of others may also be fully protected.[26]

From the first day of the Phelps Dodge strike, the dispute was characterized by a bitter confrontation, exacerbated by mass picketing and substantial and growing resort to proscribed activities by strikers and numerous outsiders. This already high level of social conflict in three small and isolated mining camps—Morenci, Douglas, and Ajo—reached its climax on August 8, when the company began preparations to hire replacements at the gate. There were open threats to kill nonstrikers and their families, to seize the plants, and to forcibly evict those working inside. This was the dangerous situation that compelled a reluctant Governor Babbitt to send in the National Guard to reestablish public order. His action accomplished its purpose. With resumption of operations, the company was soon able to recruit additional replacements. It then became clear that the strike had been lost.[27]

In retrospect, two factors explain the unions' defeat. Once government intervention had restored order and thereby terminated the illegal activities, it became obvious that the strike lacked popular support. It was a cause that could not be sustained by peaceful persuasion. A majority of Phelps Dodge employees had been on layoff for many months because of the badly depressed copper market. Having just been recalled a few months before July 1, they had little enthusiasm for a strike that brought a renewed period of idleness as the price of an attempt to extend the settlement terms reached at Kennecott two and a half months before. The coalition leaders gambled that past history would be repeated, but this time they lost everything.

Another aspect of unionism at PD concerns the Tyrone branch in New Mexico. There a group of four unions, acting as a unit known as the Pact, had narrowly won a representation election in 1968. The date is significant because the adoption of the routine three-year contract put the Tyrone expiration dates one year later than for the Arizona operations—and not by accident, company spokesmen contend. In consequence, with any strike against the Arizona properties, PD could keep production going at Tyrone. A few years later this advantage was augmented by the opening of the Hidalgo smelter at Playas, in west central New Mexico. Utilizing the new Finnish flash-furnace system and meeting all environmental requirements, it is the company's primary smelter for Tyrone and all Arizona operations. Its remote location has been enough of an obstacle to prevent union organization.

In spring 1984 the labor agreement at Tyrone came up for renewal. It contained a long-established "me too" clause that declared that economic terms and conditions agreed upon for the Arizona operations would also apply at Tyrone. With the advent of the 1983 strike, PD abolished COLA and adopted the two-tier wage system at its Arizona operations. With the "me too" clause, it now had precedent to introduce similar proposals at Tyrone. They were accepted by the Pact group, which also made other concessions in its sustained effort to avoid a highly inconvenient strike on the property at that time.

In mid-1984 the United Steelworkers conducted a presidential election to replace the late Lloyd McBride. One of the candidates was Lynn Williams; the other, Frank McKee. After a bitterly fought contest, Williams won. In November McKee gave up his posts in the union, including chairmanship of the USW copper coalition. Subsequently, Williams replaced him with Edgar H. Ball, Jr., who had originally come into prominence in 1967 as union negotiator at PD's cable plant at Fordyce, Arkansas.

There was a final, ironic twist to the now-historic negotiations in 1983. Early in 1984, while McKee was still in charge, Kennecott and Magma launched an appeal to the coalition to reopen negotiations because of the worsened economic position of the copper industry. The price of domestic wirebar, for example, had dropped from 85.63 cents in May 1983 to 68.79 cents in January 1984.[28] ASARCO declined to participate, which was just as well because the request was flatly rejected. Thus the Kennecott pattern had been protected at the very site at which it had originated.

Negotiations in 1986

The setting for collective bargaining in 1986 was drastically different from 1983 in several respects. In becoming nonunion, Phelps Dodge presented the coalition for the first time with the problem of incomplete organization of employees in the extractive branch of the industry. No longer could the pattern-following technique be relied on to "keep wages out of competition," because one of the largest employers was now immune to the pressure. The approach had to be company by company, and it would be crippled from the start by the competitive power of the big nonunion producer. Furthermore, PD had demonstrated that it was possible to take a strike, continue operating, and win—if careful arrangements were made and an experienced, out-of-work labor force was available. This lesson was not lost on Kennecott, Magma, and Inspiration, all of whom now began planning to take the same route.

On the union side, the coalition remained intact and still under the highly centralized dominance of the Steelworkers. But there were two decisive differences. The coalition no longer enjoyed complete control of all the producers in copper extraction and it had a new chairman. Edgar Ball had indicated a possibly seismic change in strategy by observing at the outset of negotiations in mid-February 1986, "I think with the present condition of the industry we've got to look at each situation on its own merits."[29] It was notable enough to concede recognition of the industry's plight, which was now in its sixth year. It was even more significant to suggest a case-by-case approach; for if this statement meant anything, it meant that the time had come at last to turn to separate company bargaining. That alone could provide the responsiveness to local needs and conditions, and the flexibility to the negotiators, to allow realistic settlements in a long-troubled industry.

The continuing distress was the principal constant carried over from the past into 1986. For the preceding three years the average price of domestic copper had held at about 66 cents a pound, about half the peak of $1.33 in February 1980. No sustained recovery of price was to occur until the spring of 1987. This very fact speaks simply but eloquently to the underlying cause of the industry's protracted troubles, from labor relations to profitability.

The negotiations in 1986 had been preceded in January 1985 by a second abortive interim meeting with the coalition, at the request of Magma, Kennecott, Inspiration, and ASARCO. These companies had sought the meeting in hopes of gaining some relief from their economic plight. A proffered cut of $2.50 per labor hour was rejected by Kennecott, which had a long list of other requests for specific types of relief, and the meetings collapsed.

At that point the previously acquiescent pattern-setter, Kennecott, became a hard bargainer. What had been happening at its flagship Bingham Canyon Mine in Utah was typical. Employment had fallen from almost 8,000 in 1970 to less than 5,000 in 1982. Another 2,000 were laid off in 1983. Claiming a loss of $25 million per quarter in 1984, Kennecott demanded that the union accept a $6 per hour wage and benefit cut. When the union did not respond in time, the mine was closed in March 1985.

Some of its smaller operations had already been idled because of the inclement conditions. Total employment had fallen from about 12,000 at the time British Petroleum's SOHIO subsidiary took over to 2,000 as the end of the 1983 agreement neared.

In January 1986 Newmont Mining asked the unions for a $6 hourly cut in wages and benefits and a two-tier pension and insurance plan for its Magma and Pinto Valley subsidiaries. Kennecott followed with a massive claim for an hourly cut of approximately $8, or one-third of the gross hourly labor cost of $24. The $24 hourly wage came to over $45,000 per employee per year, by far the highest in the industry (Magma's gross hourly labor cost was about $19.80; ASARCO's $20). Of the $6 hourly cut that Newmont sought for Magma, two-thirds would have been wage rates. The coalition rejected these requests. When no further progress was made, Kennecott, Magma, and Inspiration began their planning for a strike with continued operations. Kennecott also offered to spend $400 million to modernize its closed Utah facilities if the employees would meet its concession demands. It later added the offer of a $1,000 bonus to the 130 people working during the shutdown and the first 1,878 people on the recall list, in return for a favorable ratification vote.

When negotiations resumed in June, it was apparent that the unions wished to avoid a strike—they had been badly hurt by their trial of strength at Phelps Dodge and were fully aware of the companies' preparations to continue operating. Governor Babbitt, wanting no strike for his own reasons, again involved himself as a mediator in some of the talks.

Magma and Pinto Valley reached agreements at the end of the month that cut costs by 20 percent ($4) for about 3,000 employees and eliminated COLA provisions. ASARCO settled a few days later, after intensive bargaining that yielded about 20 percent in pay cuts across the board, with an accompanying guarantee of later restoration. The COLA clause was suspended for the next three years, but not eliminated. Kennecott gained removal of its COLA provisions, a four-year contract that constituted further insurance against a future return to pattern-bargaining, and a reduction of occupational pay rates that was proportionately larger at the lower end of the scale, as well as substantial work-rule concessions. For the first time Kennecott also won a master agreement covering all of the unions in the coalition, accompanied by supplemental agreements for special concerns, rather than separate agreements with each organization. Kennecott paid the promised bonuses and undertook the promised modernization, selling its Ray mines to ASARCO and its Chino properties to

Phelps Dodge to pay in part for the Bingham investment. Magma, too, won pay cuts that were graduated downward, while its COLA system was replaced with a bonus pay arrangement that was uniform across the board and was to be triggered by two factors: attainment of designated productivity goals and prevailing copper prices of 75 cents a pound or more.

As had happened in basic steel itself in 1986, and for the same underlying reasons, the copper bargaining this time involved no target company and no industry-wide pattern. On the contrary, the negotiations were decentralized, responsive to local conditions, and flexible. One element of the former system was retained, the practice of final approval by the Nonferrous Industry Conference. Still, a new start had been made and new institutions had begun to emerge.

THE TURN OF THE DECADE

With the 1986 concessions, Phelps Dodge found itself with higher wage rates in its nonunion and Tyrone operations than those paid by its unionized competitors and its own newly purchased Chino complex. But, at least in the short run, with rising prices and profits this did not matter. The company had promised to share good times with its employees through bonuses tied to the price of copper. Some of the smaller firms had done the same. As they did so, Kennecott and other unionized firms found it necessary to follow along to avoid unrest. (Kennecott had suggested during the 1986 negotiations that it would be willing to do so, even though it would accept no contractual obligation in the matter.)

Employer intransigence continued, as demonstrated in 1988, when Cyprus purchased the Inspiration Consolidated Copper Company's properties. It refused to recognize Inspiration's labor agreements, arguing that it had purchased the assets, not the company. Cyprus maintained the existing wages and added periodic bonuses, but it ignored work rules and it integrated operations across craft lines.[30] Six of the ten unions affected filed unfair labor practice charges; the other four filed recognition petitions with the NLRB, seeking elections to restore their representation status. The company compromised with the International Brotherhood of Electrical Workers by agreeing to contract out all of its electrical work, except routine maintenance, to IBEW-organized contractors who would give hiring preference to any electrician who wanted to leave the company's employ.[31] The other unions thereupon dropped their unfair labor practice charges and coalesced around a joint representation election, a gamble which they lost when the employees voted 392 to 204 for non-union status.[32]

Magma and its unions experienced early conflict when bonuses were denied for the last quarter of 1988 and the first half of 1989, despite high prices and profits. Production targets had not been achieved because of startup problems with new equipment, even though the employees had averaged $11,000 in bonuses for the earlier 1986–1988 period.[33] That issue still rankled when the Magma and ASARCO contracts neared their June 1, 1989, terminations. As provided in the 1986 agreement, ASARCO employees had recovered through periodic increases about half of their previous wage concessions. Nevertheless, with rising wages and profits, the unions expressed determination to recover what they had given up in 1986. The companies argued that they had not yet recovered from their pre-1987 losses. They threatened to operate and to replace strikers during any stoppage. Magma filed a unit-clarification petition with the NLRB that threatened the status of the craft unions. Despite the initial posturing on both sides, ASARCO's settlement came easily, considering its low-cost position and the fact that half of the wage concessions had already been restored. The new agreement restored the remainder and added improved insurance provisions. It even returned some but not all of the unions' cherished work rules and safety provisions.[34]

Magma carried a high debt load because of its spinoff from Newmont and its expansion and modernization program, and it also had some high-cost properties. Its potential gain from the higher prices had been limited in that it had sold forward much of its future output to obtain badly needed financing. After the company moved in house trailers, began obvious preparations to house and feed replacement workers, and hired security guards, the unions relented and accepted $1.50 per hour spread over three years (compared to ASARCO's $1.85), and additional wage increases tied to further copper price increases. The previous dual price and production-based bonus was eliminated. Instead, base rates would rise by 0.6 percent for each 5-cent increment in price between 95 cents and $1.70 per pound. (In 1990 Magma added another complication for future negotiations by reopening its Superior underground mine with a completely nonunion work force of 270 working in a team environment.)[35]

These settlements left Kennecott, ASARCO (Ray), and Phelps Dodge (Chino) for negotiations in 1990 and PD (Tyrone) for 1991. Entering the 1990 negotiations, one of the union negotiators commented, "We've shared the pain; now we want to share the gain." In the interim Kennecott had paid $8,000 apiece in bonuses to Bingham Canyon employees, including the 1986 ratification bonus, and Phelps Dodge and ASARCO had paid similar amounts at the Chino and Ray operations. The basic union demands were for restoration of the 1986 wage concessions, and replacement of some of the work rules and insurance provisions taken away at that time. The crafts felt most strongly about the work rules, but all of the employees were anxious for the companies to pick up health care and hospitalization expenses, which had been shifted to the employees in 1986. The unions showed early strength when Chino employees voted to reject a lower company offer nine months before the contract termination.[36] The companies postured with NLRB unit-clarification petitions, various manifestations of intent to replace and operate, and, at Chino, an employee decertification petition.[37] The Phelps Dodge/Chino negotiations took place in Las Cruces, New Mexico; the ASARCO/Ray exercise, in Phoenix. Not wanting to return to the Arizona scene of their 1986 mortification, the Salt Lake–based Kennecott unions opted for the neutral ground of Seattle. The relevant Steelworkers district director, rather than the International's nonferrous coordinating committee chairman, was the chief negotiator in each case, a sharp departure from the arrangement which had prevailed since 1967.

The Kennecott settlement was reached first. Bargaining began early with local representatives given one month to pursue local issues. When they made little progress, the United Steelworkers district director, one craft union representative, and the company human resources director set themselves up as an oversight committee to either push to completion or wash out the remaining local issues. In less than a week of bargaining, the parties settled the major economic issues. A $3,000 ratification bonus was a carrot. A 23 percent first-year wage increase, followed by across-the-board 25-cent-per-hour increase in each of the subsequent years, would bring the average hourly rate in 1992 to just a few cents less than it had been before the 1985 shutdown, but with no COLA renewal and no accommodation for the intervening inflation. Kennecott's relatively generous health-care plan had been downgraded in 1986 to require employee premium contributions, a $350-per-person and $700-per-family deductible, and 80/20 copayment. The copayment remained, but the company agreed to pick up the total premium with $100 and $350 deductibles, respectively. Pension improvements were granted, a concession eased by the fact that as a condition of sale BP Minerals America had retained responsibility for all previous retirees. Special concessions were made to some of the crafts and some seniority provisions were restored, but the company took a hard line on job assignments.

Though the company had been given a free hand in assigning people across classification and craft lines by the 1986 master agreement, most of the unions in the coalition agreed that it had not abused the privilege. For example, where an assigned crane operator might have waited all shift for some use of the crane, now the crane would remain unmanned until needed, at which time someone on a crew with something to lift would enter and operate it. The company has never assigned a Steelworker to operate a shovel that has been traditionally manned by an Operating Engineer, for instance.

At any rate, the interunion jurisdiction question is almost irrelevant except in the mine, which is staffed by 250 Steelworkers, 140 Machinists, 70 Electricians, 60 Operating Engineers, and 40 members of the United Transportation Union. The Steelworkers, "wall to wall" in the concentrator and smelter, share the refinery only with a few Electricians. The historical situation has been reversed, with the crafts now needing the bargaining power of semiskilled workers more than the latter need them. The master agreement, with its supplements, involves eight international and thirteen local unions, but the master agreement is clearly a company/ Steelworkers creation. The unions were unsuccessful in gaining the desired limitations on contracting out but, all in all, they were relieved to come off as well as they did.[38]

With Kennecott settling on May 22, the Chino agreement followed quickly on June 12.[39] The settlements were distinctly related, though not identical. There was no ratification bonus at Chino. The first- and second-year wage increases were the same, but a $400 lump-sum bonus was substituted for a wage increase the third year. The medical deductibles were reduced only to $200 and $400 for individual and family, respectively, but a vision-care plan and improved dental care were added. There were no pension improvements and there was no mention of work-rule restorations. Clearly, Phelps Dodge employees at Chino were no more anxious to take on their employer than were Kennecott employees at the Bingham Canyon complex. That more than passivity was involved is indicated by the spate of decertification elections pending at Chino. The only one completed at this writing, that of the Pipefitters, went to the union by a very narrow margin.[40]

Not so with the Ray employees of ASARCO. The company had previously restored $1 per hour and now offered to add the Kennecott $2 first-year and 25-cent second- and third-year increase, plus health and pension improvements. Money did not turn out to be a problem, but the percentage distribution of the first-year increase, which would have given more per hour to the higher paid, did create an issue over which the employees struck, leaving other benefit and work-rule issues unresolved.[41] After a three-week shutdown, sweeteners in the form of vision care, orthodontics, and a 401(k) savings plan were enough to sell the previous wage and benefit offer and even save flexibility in work assignments.[42]

The 1991 negotiations at Tyrone will complete the round; that is, unless the decertification petition filed by a number of Tyrone employees in August 1990 results in elimination of union bargaining rights before the contract expiration date.[43] But one fact seems apparent: at least for now, pattern-bargaining is dead. Management eschews it, and none of the unions appears inclined to give battle to restore it. Contract provisions have commonality where conditions are similar, but the differences in levels are substantial. The pay rates at ASARCO's Ray operation average more than $1 an hour across the various classifications above those of the other unionized firms. Rates are equivalent between Kennecott and PD's Chino, but the latter did not receive the settlement bonus and the lump-sum third-year payment will not equal Kennecott's automatic third-year advance. Kennecott's health and pension benefits also are more generous. Magma's rates average about the same as those of Kennecott and Chino, although there are substantial differences for individual classifications; but the equality is an accident of the current copper prices. Magma rates can vary by approximately 75 cents per hour, depending upon price. All of those pay differences have come about in just one set of decentralized negotiations, and parallel differences have emerged in work rules. To add to those cross-company differences, nonunion Morenci still pays more and Cyprus Minerals less than the union operations. Sporadic payment of bonuses by the various companies, union and nonunion, make it exceedingly difficult to compare annual incomes.

The economic provisions will continue to be related across companies which, after all, are competitors in the same product market, thus confronting identical market conditions. But at least for the foreseeable future those provisions, both economic and work practices, will reflect the differing geological and technological conditions under which copper is produced. The union coalition remains firm, with no signs of defection. The membership is less firm, however, with decertification petitions almost epidemic, particularly among the crafts. The coalition is even more dominated by the Steelworker majority than in the past. But it is a more chastened USW, willing to concede bargaining leadership to the locals, who after all are familiar with conditions affecting the various properties. District and local leaders, too, remain committed to the welfare of their also-chastened members. Employers appear less likely to lapse into expediency, and union leaders and members seem more aware that their well-being depends first and foremost on the ability of the industry and their companies to compete in a world market. All of the companies seem determined to operate through any strike, with a few apparently ready to take action within the limits of the law to achieve nonunion status. How long the moderating effect of the 1980s will prevail remains to be seen.

CHAPTER 10

THE PAST AS PROLOGUE AND
INSTRUCTION

HISTORY IS BOTH the most reliable indicator of the future and the most instructive source of guidance for it. While many lessons could be drawn from the past 145 years, three stand out:

1. On the product-market side, U.S. firms that face reality, abandon expediency, invest in themselves, and keep faith with their industries can be world-class, low-cost producers.
2. On the labor-market side, industrial relations systems must be home grown and reflect the realities of the industry, the enterprise, and the workplace. They cannot be successfully imposed from other environments, regardless of their origin or success.
3. Neither product market nor labor market can afford to ignore the other. They are so intertwined that no enterprise or set of enterprises can survive and prosper without close attention to the realities and interactions of both.

The following summary of events and developments will highlight these lessons and help in projecting the outlook for the American copper industry and its product and labor markets.

THE INDUSTRY AND ITS PRODUCT MARKETS

Historical Profile

Before the beginning of mining on the Upper Michigan peninsula in 1845, little copper was produced in the United States and the sources were few and scattered. The Michigan developments were the real start of the industry. Much of the production consisted of native copper, the purity of which commanded a premium price on the market. Although the peninsula mining zone comprised many companies, the total area was small; the Calumet and Hecla Company and its predecessors dominated production. Moreover, by closing entry to new competitors, the company could easily form selling pools that were able to drive up the price of copper.

This price manipulation, and indeed the Michigan dominance of the industry, both ended with the discovery and development between 1880 and 1920 of the great western mines. Among the first of these properties was a group in the Morenci district—the Joy, Longfellow, Metcalf, Coronado, and Shannon mines.[1] Then followed the main sequence—the Copper Queen, the Anaconda group, Old Dominion, United Verde, Irish Mag, Bingham Canyon, Nevada Consolidated, Magma Superior, the Alaska group, Ray, Chino, Miami, Inspiration, United Verde Extension, Tyrone, and Ajo. Even this lengthy list understates the facts, because many important early properties lost their identities through absorption by others. Copper often was found adventitiously in the determined search for gold and silver. When the age of electrification began sharply boosting the demand for copper after 1880, it became appropriate to seek out the red metal itself.

In short, demand proved to be the active factor in promoting both the discovery and development of new mines and the reworking of old deposits. As a result, American copper production soared at a fabulous compound annual rate of over 11 percent from 1881 through 1912. The secular rate of increase began to slow down thereafter except for a brief interval in the 1920s. From 1920 on into the 1980s, only one great new mine was opened—Morenci in 1942—although a few medium-scale properties were developed between 1950 and 1975.[2]

A Mature Industry

In addition to the decline in the rate of discovery of new ore deposits, the response of mine production to temporary surges in demand began diminishing. In the First World War, output jumped 40.3 percent between 1916 and 1918, as against only 15.7 percent from 1941 to 1943. In fact, by 1940 a permanent and growing import surplus had emerged, which could be sustained because the domestic demand for copper continued to expand.

During the extended postwar period from 1946 through 1985, the long-term rate of increase in primary production of copper (excluding old scrap) slowed much more. The average annual refinery output during 1946–1950 from both domestic and foreign ores averaged 1,072,748 short tons, compared with 1,358,485 short tons for 1981–1985. The advance from the midpoint of the first period to that of the second was 26.6 percent, or only 0.76 percent yearly over the entire thirty-five-year period.[3]

Output became increasingly unstable after World War II. Major upswings took place during 1946–1950, 1954–1957, 1959–1966, and 1967–1972, with increases of, respectively, 41 percent, 20 percent, 55.7 percent, and 65 percent. Finally, during 1981–1985 primary production dropped by a calamitous 31.6 percent, as part of an industry-wide depression of nearly six years' duration that ended only in early 1987. This period was one of enormous financial losses, severe cuts in employment and production, and bitter labor disputes.

If we look at the main components of primary copper production in the United States, we find that in the five years between 1946 and 1950 average refined imports were 229,167 short tons yearly, as against 409,632 short tons during 1981–1985—a substantial increase of 78.7 percent. By contrast, average annual refined exports fell sharply between the two periods—from 125,051 short tons in 1946–1950 to only 56,474 tons during 1981–1985, a drop of 55 percent.

What was happening over these thirty-five years was that the domestic consumption of copper was running well ahead of domestic primary production, while the increasing shortfall was being covered by decreasing exports and rapidly growing imports. These interrelationships are reflected in the behavior of what the Bureau of Mines calls *apparent consumption*, a measure that combines refinery output with refined imports, net of refined exports plus any increases in stocks, for each year (military set-asides for the Office of Metal Reserves, a legacy of the early postwar years, must also be deducted, but these have not been important for many years). Annual changes in stocks are both short-term and self-limiting, hence exert no significant influence on the long-term trend of domestic consumption.

As to the relationship between imports and exports, the United States had reached its peak in exports of refined copper in 1928 and has had a growing import surplus since 1940.

During 1946–1950 apparent consumption increased rather substantially, to average 1,138,031 short tons per year. For 1981–1985, the average annual figure had expanded to 1,656,360 short tons, for an impressive gain of 45.5 percent over thirty-five years. This large relative increase compares with the advance of only 26.6 percent for domestic output of primary copper over the same period. At bottom, the gap between the two growth rates reflects the gradually expanding import surplus throughout the postwar years and, behind this, the steady if modest growth in aggregate domestic demand for copper. Furthermore, the gap underscores the very slow rate of increase in domestic primary production after World War II. Two principal factors account for this retardation: the apparent end of discoveries of major new domestic ore deposits and the gradual decline of average ore grade. More and more, the American producers have been compelled to turn to modern technologies to extract additional production from existing mines and reduction works. Outstanding among the innovations have been in situ and heap leaching, flash furnaces, portable crushers, and new modes of ore transport.

It should also be remembered that in the period before 1920 the United States was the world leader in copper production, and as such accounted for more than half of world output. Even with continued growth in domestic primary production, the nation now has fallen to a close second on the list, rebounding to 21 percent in 1988 behind Chile's 22 percent, after producing only 17.3 percent of total world output in 1986. In short, the mines of Africa, Chile, and Canada, more recently augmented by those at Bougainville Island in the western Pacific, Ok Tedi in Papua New Guinea, and Ertsberg (Copper Mountain) in West Irian (Indonesia), have shifted the production balance away from the United States—which, however, remains the world's largest consumer of copper.

A comparison of average yearly apparent consumption for 1946–1950 and 1981–1985 with resident population for the same periods reveals that population rose 63.6 percent over the thirty-five-year interval while apparent consumption grew by only 42.6 percent. Looked at in another way, average annual copper consumption per head fell from 18.54 pounds in 1946–1950 to 14.1 pounds during 1981–1985. What these two comparisons say is that the amount of copper employed in additional capital goods for replacement and expansion (direct consumption of copper by final users is very small) has been slowly declining per unit of new capital, an effect that has been offset mainly by the secular rate of increase in the production of capital goods over these thirty-five years. Capital goods have been slowly becoming less "copper intensive" over time, but not enough so to invoke a long-run absolute decline in apparent consumption of the metal.

Looking back now over the long history of this small but still important industry, we can say that with the slowdown in the rate of increase in primary copper production after 1912, and the parallel increases in the volatility of its price and in the instability of production from about the same date, American copper entered a period of gradually increasing maturity. Its advent was concealed or at least obscured by certain events that were strongly disruptive: World War I, the depression of 1919–1921, the boom of 1922–1929, the Great Depression, World War II, the Korean War, the most intensive phase of the war in Vietnam (1965–1972), the first oil shock (1973), the second oil shock (1979), and finally the severe deflationary recession that began in the fall of 1979 and ended in November 1982.

All of these events involved either surges or collapses in the demand for copper over relatively short periods. The shifts in demand associated with the outbreak and termination of wars—of which there were four, excluding delayed postwar slumps—typically involved sharp upswings and downswings in primary production because of the metal's array of vital military uses. It follows that there is no way to isolate unambiguously the influence of maturation in the declining rate of increase in the demand for copper. But if we take account of all of these ten major disturbances to the American economy together, apparent domestic consumption of copper rose at a simple annual average rate of only 1.2 percent over the thirty-five years in question. The contrast with the astonishing record achieved over the thirty years before 1912 points directly to maturation as a depressive influence. At its roots lie a secular shift in aggregate final demand away from hard goods and into services, and a growing importance of technical substitution of other metals and materials for copper—for example, plastic for pipe and tubing, aluminum for automobile radiators and high-tension cable, and fiber optics and short-wave radio for communication.

As matters stand today, American copper has certainly not become a declining industry. Rather, it is characterized by slowing growth in demand and increasing dependence on imports, a joint process that has been under way for the past four decades. Note should also be taken of the virtual stability in the long-term real price of copper over this lengthy period. If we ignore short-term movements, the clear long-term trend has involved a constant relationship—or constant terms of trade—between the prevailing money price of copper and the index of implicit price deflators for GNP.

Technological improvements, ore grade, scale effects, and the quality of labor and management relationships, all combined, have not been potent enough to bring about a lasting decline in the nominal price of copper relative to general price levels over these thirty-five years. This anomaly stands in sharp contrast to the pronounced and sustained fall in the real price of copper between 1890 and 1945, in the years of the industry's great expansion and technical improvements. Here again is a sign of maturation in the industry.

The Instability of Copper Prices

The long-term stability of copper prices is in sharp contrast to their short-run instability. The earliest significant price swing moved from 35.6 cents per pound (money price) in 1872, when the first Lake Pool was in force, to a low of 9.5 cents during the slump of 1894. The next upswing lifted price to 20.9 cents in 1907, which was followed by a fall to 13.3 cents in 1913. This was quickly succeeded by a surge to 29.2 cents in 1917, induced by soaring military requirements. Then followed a collapse to 12.7 cents in the depression of 1919–1921, after which the boom in the 1920s drove price back up to 18.2 cents by 1929. Next, the Depression pushed price down to its historic low of 5.7 cents in 1932. By 1941 recovery had lifted price to 11.9 cents, where it was kept by price control until 1946, when it rose to 14.4 cents. The next upswing took price to 43.5 cents in 1956; a six-year period of sustained weakness ended in 1962, at 30.8 cents. Another upswing followed, which advanced it to 58.2 cents in 1970. The first oil shock (1973) pulled price to 59.5 cents, but this movement was reversed in the following year. The next pronounced upswing began from 66.5 cents in 1978, moving successfully to 93.3 cents in 1979 and $1.024 in 1980. By the spring of that year the great slump in price had begun, carrying it precipitously downward from a peak of $1.12 to a low of 66 cents in 1986. From 1986 through 1990 the price of copper displayed sustained strength, which has carried it into a range of $1.10 to $1.50 per pound. Yet in constant dollar (real) terms, the price at the end of the 1980s was substantially below that at the decade's beginning.

It should by now be evident that, except for brief interludes of official control or of private manipulation, the price of copper has been extremely volatile throughout its modern history. In this respect its behavior has been similar to that of the basic agricultural commodities, except that copper has never enjoyed the benefits of price-raising federal intervention. Nor has the American branch of the industry had access to fresh investment capital from international agencies at subsidized low rates of interest; or, even more important, to special assistance from such agencies when earnings from exports have been unexpectedly depressed by declining copper prices. On the contrary, the American copper industry must sell its product unaided, in markets subject to worldwide competition from producers in several countries. This competition is made particularly acute by subsidized state enterprises, the intervention of international financing agencies, the persistent high level of interest rates in the United States, the comparatively high American wage level, and the special charges for mandatory pollution controls that, while admittedly necessary, are almost unique to the United States.

Why is the price of copper so volatile? In a superficial sense, the answer is that copper is sold under fully competitive circumstances in a world market in which the price is free to fluctuate on the exchanges. Self-interest leads traders on both sides of the market to bargain for prices that are thereby made uniform except for differences in transport costs and dates of delivery.

From the standpoint of conventional comparative statics, the copper market involves a demand that is highly price inelastic, particularly in the short run. The case is one of derived demand, in the sense that copper serves almost entirely as an intermediate good that typically is a minor component of various investment goods, particularly in manufacturing, construction, and transportation. As Alfred Marshall pointed out in 1890, a good that has a derived demand will have a "stiff and inelastic" demand function where (1) the good is essential in the sense that there is no close substitute available for it; (2) the price elasticity of demand of the final capital good in which the copper is embodied is low enough that a small change in its price will have little effect on the amount that can be sold; (3) the share of copper in the total cost of the final good is very low, so that a small change in the price of copper will have a negligible effect on the position of the supply curve of the final good; and (4) the supplies of the other goods and services ("inputs") employed to make the final good are zero-elastic in terms of changes in their prices, because they are mostly composed of fixed capital that is immobile in the short run—thus an increase in the price of copper will have little effect on the demand for copper and none on the quantities of these cooperating inputs.[4] In short, they can be "squeezed" through the ensuing depression of the demand functions for their services.

The demand for copper is derived; thus, it has little price elasticity in the short run because the four cumulative conditions just stated are typically present where copper is used in investment goods. Over longer periods of time conditions (1), (2), and (4) can change, primarily because buyers gain greater flexibility in substituting for or against copper. Accordingly, the demand function for copper becomes somewhat more price elastic over longer periods of time.

On the supply side, for very short time spans the supply of copper is virtually a stock rather than a flow. Hence it is close to zero-elastic as to price. For intermediate periods the supply will be more elastic because producers can vary output to some extent, even with fixed facilities, while the flows of copper imports and exports can also be altered to gain better returns. Over the longer term, somewhat greater flexibility may prevail. In the American case, however, there is an apparent lack of significant new deposits, while ore grade is decreasing. Producers have augmented long-run supply elasticity via technological innovations such as leaching and capital instruments of larger capacity, which permit more effective exploitation of existing mine and ore-reduction capacity, and by reworking old deposits and tailings for additional metallic recovery.

Given the relatively inelastic demand for copper for industrial uses, major shifts in supply will bring large changes in price and relatively small changes in quantity sold. Given a similar price inelasticity on the supply side, significant swings in demand will cause relatively large changes in price and relatively small changes in quantity. For lengthier periods of hypothetical time, the relative price changes tend to decrease and the changes in quantities exchanged tend to increase.

Thus this model from conventional economics fits the copper case quite well. At its core, the model says that the less the time available for the actors (producers, dealers, and users) to work out decisions in their own interest under the conditions prevailing, the less the flexibility in their adjustments. Large price swings and small quantity movements are the result.

There remains the more dynamic principle known as the magnification of derived demand, which was described in Chapter 3. In brief, the principle says that because copper is an intermediate good used in the production of new capital goods, it will be highly sensitive—in price and quantity—to changes in the rate of net new investment. For technical reasons, a given percentage increase (or decrease) in that rate will have a direct and magnified effect that will shift the demand for copper upward and outward (or inward and downward) by an even greater percentage. Thus, sudden changes in the rate of new investments, which long have been recognized as perhaps the dominant factor in overall business fluctuations, exert disproportionately larger effects in the same direction on the demand for copper.

For these reasons, then, copper extraction (and for that matter, fabrication as well) has been highly unstable with regard to price and production for some seventy-five years, although this fact did not become apparent until after the First World War.

INTERACTION OF LABOR AND PRODUCT MARKETS

At this point it will be productive to examine briefly another form of interrelationship between types of prices, the interconnection between the labor and product markets in the industry over the years. Between 1956 and 1983 there was a strike in the extractive branch of the industry during each of ten successive contract negotiations. All but two of these rounds (1962 and 1964) generated major strikes, of which two were lengthy and difficult but did not include all of the producers (1956 and 1959). Four that followed after 1964—1967–1968, 1971, 1980, and 1983—were industry-wide, lasted eight months in one case and at least two months in the others, and involved highly intractable issues.

Although it would be too much to claim that a strong and clearly defined statistical correlation can be shown between the behavior of the product market and contemporaneous or lagged events in the labor market during these six major negotiating rounds, there can be no doubt about their decisive parallelism. To illustrate, the strikes in 1956 occurred during a rather strong upswing of 20 percent in primary production. In 1959, lengthy stoppages took place at the outset of an extended expansion through 1966, whose cumulative magnitude was 55.7 percent. Then followed the very long shutdown of 1967–1968, which started with the onset of another upswing that reached 65 percent by 1972. Within that same expansion the unions won the extremely important COLA clause in

1971, with only brief strikes. In the 1980 round, the central issue was a substantial wage demand, which had been predicated on high profits that were realized in an expansion that had just begun to fail when negotiations started. Finally, 1983 is the one case in which conditions in the product market had sunk to depression levels with regard to price, production, and profits, and in which an irreconcilable conflict was joined between the unions and Phelps Dodge over the elimination of the COLA clause and the concession of a wage cut through introduction of a two-tier wage structure. On this occasion the strike concerned only one large employer. More important, the employer continued to operate throughout the strike and eventually gained a decertification of all unions at its Arizona properties and El Paso refinery after the dispute had lasted more than two years.

During the 1986 round of negotiations, with the looming threat of two important nonunion companies, there was no strike. As far as the product market was concerned, the industry found itself in the sixth straight year of an economic collapse in which primary production had fallen 31.6 percent, cathode price was down 50 percent, inventories were at record high levels, and all the surviving companies were awash in red ink. These difficulties had spread into the labor market, bringing in their train severe unemployment and a general mood of demoralization. In these circumstances wage concessions of about 20 percent were granted. During the 1989–1990 round the unions seemed timid, considering the high copper prices and the unprecedented profits most of the companies were enjoying; but the competition from nonunion firms had made them so.

How, then, should we interpret the relationship between events in the labor market and those in the product market?

The problem is not one of simple one-way causation. Forces acting on the product market (for example, shifts in demand) can and certainly do directly affect sales, production plans, employment, and the characteristics of union demands in contract negotiations. Factors influencing the labor market can affect the number and quality of workers available to employers, while wage settlements in other industries can shape the demands of unions and the framework for settlements.

But we are not dealing only with two-way causation, either. There are independent influences as well. For instance, the decision of the twenty-six nonferrous unions to form a bargaining coalition and to strike for enlargement of bargaining scope and for uniform settlements and simultaneous expiration dates cannot persuasively be explained by tight labor markets in 1967, or by brisk sales and rising prices of copper and lead. The origin and specific content of these formal demands derived from a technical theory of collective bargaining that had little to do with the economic characteristics of either the labor market or the product market in either the nonferrous or copper industries at that particular time. In short, we are confronted with a subtle problem of multiple causation not readily reducible to quantitative magnitudes or technical correlations. Yet external influences certainly shape the bargaining process and its outcome.

With these caveats in mind, let us undertake the more modest exercise of considering negotiating episodes in which influences in the product and labor markets indeed have played a significant part. In the period beginning with 1956, there have been nine different instances in which the labor and product markets in copper came into conflict with readily discernible consequences. Six of them involved hard and lengthy strikes, while one (1986) included no strikes at all but did reflect deep economic distress. Of the six strikes, the most severe was that of 1967–1968, when the central issue was the technical one of a reformation of negotiating scope for bargaining. To the cooperating unions the goal was not money—at least for the immediate round—but increased bargaining power, which, of course, greatly stiffened the resistance of the companies. More significant for present purposes, it was the exceptional economic strength of the contemporary product market, with its consequential effects on the labor market as well, that enlarged the gulf between the parties and in a loose sense "financed" a technical struggle over the design of bargaining arrangements. On the very same grounds, this particular struggle would have been inconceivable in 1983, for reasons that will become apparent.

The other prominent strikes of the period fall into two classes, one in which the product market was strong and expanding (1956, 1959, and 1971), and one in which expansion had already reached its terminus or changed into severe contraction (1980 and 1983). Finally, there is the special case of 1986. No strike took place; major wage concessions averaging 20 percent were agreed upon; four-year contracts became acceptable in certain "basket cases"; and the economic circumstances of the entire industry had become desperate. Four years later the unions were stymied in their attempts to recover lost ground by the looming presence of large nonunion producers.

The inference should be clear: in all of these episodes the condition of the product market was either one of great strength and buoyancy, or of such protracted weakness as to make the necessity for drastic measures obvious to the most obtuse or reluctant participant. In all instances the product market did make a difference, although it was not the sole factor at work. In the great strike of 1967, it was both permissive and supportive, but not really decisive. In 1971 it lent strength to the demand for a COLA provision. The origin of that demand was extraneous and political: the Steelworkers wished to establish a precedent in copper to justify the reinstatement of a COLA clause in basic steel. By contrast, in 1980, 1983, and 1986 the impact of the product market was strongly negative: it provoked firm employer resistance and hence lengthy strikes in 1980; in 1983 it caused the defection of Phelps Dodge from the pattern system and its determination to continue operations even when struck; and finally, in 1986, it triggered the universal demand of the remaining unionized employers for substantial wage concessions tailored to their own special circumstances.

SOME LESSONS FROM THE LABOR MARKET

That brings us to the primary labor-market lesson, the grave mistake of attempting to transfer to the nonferrous industry concepts of collective bargaining that seemingly had worked well in basic steel.

The Overcentralization of Collective Bargaining

The drive for centralized control of wage-making in nonferrous mining had two sources. One was Mine Mill, which for twenty years had struggled in vain to become the wage leader and thus to dominate the industry. The other was the United Steelworkers, which had introduced industry-wide bargaining to basic steel in the early 1950s and planned to expand the idea to nonferrous with the expected success of its raiding campaign against Mine Mill. With the merger of the two organizations in 1967, uniformity of wages and benefits throughout the nonferrous industry was proclaimed to be the top goal, with the new union coalition for coordinated bargaining as the means.

Well into the long strike which followed, Joseph P. Molony described the goal as including uniformity of wages and economic benefits throughout the nonferrous industry, for all extractive and reduction activities and for all fabrication of these many metals. Or, as Molony himself put the matter, the coalition sought "basically common economic settlements with each company for all properties of that company." In his declaration, we saw in Chapter 9 that Molony referred to "equal pay for equal work in the industry" and "common levels of pensions, insurance, job security, paid holidays, shift differentials." Clearly, the goal was not just equal pay for all jobs; it was equal pay for comparable jobs, with comparability to be established by past practice, by previously negotiated relationships, or by formal job evaluation under the Steelworkers' preferred CWS system adopted from the basic steel industry.

If we recall the discussion of clusters and contours in Chapter 1, the ruling idea of the coalition had to be that the job clusters of the nonferrous industry—from mining to fabrication—were standardized across the many different metals involved, and—far more important—that the producers of these metals shared a common product market within which they sold their output. From these mistaken assumptions, it followed that there existed a common wage contour that extended across all of the firms and throughout all the stages of production. Accordingly, uniformity was supposed to be the key to taking wages out of competition.

Behind all this thinking was the model of basic steel as that industry was largely structured at the time, characterized by a well-standardized and stable technology, a set array of standardized products, a few large producers guided by the administrative pricing policies of the United States Steel Corporation, and relative freedom from the threat of imports. From this ruling perception, highly centralized collective bargaining and uniform contracts naturally followed. Such an arrangement simply expressed the traditional industrial unionism of the CIO—comparable pay for comparable work in all plants, and parallel absolute increases with each successive contract round.

Acting on the premise that nonferrous was a cohesive and homogeneous industry like basic steel, Molony and his colleagues decided in 1967 to insist on a common set of bargaining demands, to achieve uniformity of wages and benefits throughout. They assumed that all nonferrous firms were competing in the same product markets and therefore should bargain along the same wage contour. That was a fatal mistake.[5]

If the goal is to raise wages, the problem of any union in a system of private enterprise is to "follow the product"—in other words, to organize all of the competing producers. If the union is to eliminate the weakening influence of competing nonunion sources of supply, it must attain full occupancy of its product market, whether it be cigars, steel, or copper. The union gains full occupancy by an indirect route, through a complete organization of the correlative labor markets for all competing firms in the product market in which its employers operate. By matching its organizational and contractual scope with the full range of the relevant product market, the union is able to pursue its pattern of standardization in wages and benefits with all of the competing employers. Because all of the producers must confront the same terms of settlement—the pattern—the effect is to reduce the amount of total job loss in each firm when wages, costs, and prices are forced up.[6] At the core of the approach, of course, is strike effectiveness, which is pushed to its ultimate limits when all firms have been organized and all are under contracts with simultaneous expiration dates.

In this analysis—which John R. Commons described as "taking wages out of competition"[7]—everything turns on the notion of *the product*. And it is precisely here that the problem of bargaining centralization in nonferrous turns out to be very different from that in basic steel. To begin with, "nonferrous" is simply a portmanteau concept for collecting under one rubric a group of more than ten different metals "other than iron"—metals used in a broad range of final products,[8] sold in many different primary markets, and derived for the most part from different ores found in different locations. Precious metals sometimes are extracted as by-products of the base metals, but otherwise virtually the only common factor among the nonferrous metals is that they are obtained by the same basic extractive technology.

In brief, the nonferrous metals are almost completely independent of one another for final uses. In economic terms they are neither substitutes nor complements, hence their cross-elasticities, practically speaking, are zero.[9] For example, other things remaining equal, if a 1 percent fall in the price of copper leaves the demand for lead unchanged, the cross-elasticity of demand for lead is zero, the demand for lead is unaffected because the two metals are not substitutes. They are independent commodities. And the same relationship holds, pair by pair, for all the other metals in the nonferrous group.

As a practical consequence, the producers and the unions in the copper industry have no reason to fear a drop in the price of nickel or silver, for neither change will cause a diversion of sales from copper to nickel or silver and therefore a drop in copper revenues or employment. On the same principle, the copper unions need not fear a significant shift by metal buyers from copper to nickel if the price of copper should rise following successful negotiation of new labor agreements that provide higher wages and benefits. And so it goes for copper against all the other nonferrous metals.

The economic independence of the nonferrous metals from one another has strong implications for the labor market as well. Because copper workers turn out a product that has no close metallic substitutes for its main uses, the wage and price policies of the copper industry have no economic importance for nickel or silver workers. In the product market, these different labor groups do not compete against one another.[10]

Certain factors of labor supply also promote the economic independence of the copper workers from the others. The labor markets in nonferrous are widely scattered geographically. Distance makes migration costly; it also deprives workers of the market information that induces them to move. Obviously, the factor of distance is strongest between mining, which is typically in the West, and fabrication, which is usually in the Midwest or East. But even among the mining centers themselves, distance has some importance. Finally, there are sharp differences in the nature and range of the occupational skills required at the extraction versus the fabrication end of the business. These, too, contribute to the independence of the various nonferrous labor markets as they do to their product markets.

Within each metal industry there is another significant contrast, especially with the basic steel industry. In steel the various occupations are essentially integrated. Within each department of a steel mill, the various classifications move upward in a logical sequence separated by relatively small skill increments. Through on-the-job experience it is possible to move according to seniority from the least skilled to the most skilled classification. Even the maintenance crafts are selected by seniority from less skilled applicants and trained through an in-plant apprentice program. In the copper industry, on the other hand, even without the differences in union affiliation there are substantial discontinuities in technology and skill requirements that tend to lock workers into boxes instead of putting them on ladders.

So far, then, the drift of our argument is that it is possible for a single industrial union, or a mixed coalition of unions, to raise wages and benefits in some given important branch of metal production (once it has been fully organized) without extending the scope of bargaining to the remainder of the nonferrous industry. Put alternatively, there is simply no need to strive for uniformity of wages and benefits across the whole industry unless the ruling purpose involves other reasons, perhaps political or organizational.

To conclude, then, the eight-month effort of the nonferrous coalition to compel a unilateral extension of negotiating scope to the entire industry was both futile and unnecessary and, as it turned out, a failure as well. The price of zinc has nothing to do with the price of copper. The wages of silver and lead miners in northern Idaho have nothing to do with the wages of production workers in a copper wire and cable plant in Yonkers. Indeed, since 1940 the real competitive problem for copper—unlike basic steel—has been between domestic and foreign sources. During the entire period after World War II the United States has run an import surplus in copper. It is in this international rivalry among sources that the cross-elasticity of demand reaches very high values. Moreover, the coalition of American copper unions has been wholly impotent with respect to this international competition because it could not extend the zone of copper bargaining to include the miners in Chile and Peru, or in Zaire and Zambia.

The Inflexibility of Pattern-Bargaining

In the 1971 bargaining round, the coalition leadership abandoned its 1967 strategy and chose to pursue wage uniformity through pattern-following, while confining the scope of negotiations to the production side of copper, exclusive of fabrication. Although it continued to hold out the hope of eventual uniformity throughout nonferrous, the fact is that it has made no move in that direction in more than two decades.

After the debacle imposed by the employers' determined and unbending resistance in 1967–1968, the coalition leadership searched for a more workable negotiating contour. The fact that acceptable contracts were achieved over the four subsequent rounds of negotiations indicated to the unions that they were now bargaining on the right contour. Even more significant, these agreements all preserved the old NLRB-designated units, with which the employers were required by law to bargain. That meant that the unions were able to pursue their endless quest for uniformity without at the same time assuming the impossible burden of attempting to compel the companies to bargain over wider boundaries. Not until 1983 was the copper contour called into question.

What is the meaning of wage uniformity? In its simplest form the same job pays the same rate and benefits at any place of employment in a given industry. Basically, the notion is one of fairness as perceived by the industrial worker. It is a variant of the concept of equality, for compensation within an occupation. No doubt, too, equal pay for equal work is a powerful slogan that union leaders take seriously. Dave Beck, late head of the Western Conference of Teamsters and subsequently of the entire union, once defended the concept by observing that he could travel between Seattle and Spokane by any one of three different railroads at the same fare for the same class of service. What was good for business ought to be good for the labor market, he reasoned.

A more subtle version, briefly considered in Chapter 1, is that in a given industry there will be a similarity of job clusters, hence an implicit occupational wage structure across firms. If the equal pay principle is applied to the key job in each of the clusters, then the satellite jobs can be tied to the key rate through customary differentials, bargaining, or job evaluation, and wage uniformity will exist in the industry. Wages will be equal for all comparable jobs, while differentials for the satellite jobs will be standardized through collective bargaining. In consequence, runs this reasoning, wages in the industry will be "taken out of competition." If the union does not fight to equalize wages upward, competition will equalize them downward, to the lowest common denominator.

What this means is that if pay rates and benefits for comparable key and satellite jobs are standardized across firms through uniform contracts, then by definition there can be no deviation in rates to account for differences in production costs. Conversely, if in fact there do exist variances in average labor costs per unit of output, then these must be attributable to differences in the productive efficiencies of the resources employed in the competing firms—managerial skills, capital equipment, or labor. It follows, then, that the correction or leveling out of these differences in average cost is accomplished by raising resource productivities and emphatically not by cutting wages. Wages have already been taken out of competition; to manipulate them to improve narrow profit margins would be to reinsert labor as a factor affecting the competition among firms in the industry, at the expense of the more efficient firms and their employees.

This argument helps to explain what union leaders mean when they speak of "no cuts" or "no concessions," even to save an enterprise from failing. Once a standard pattern has been set, the granting of concessions will upset the associated cost structure, at the expense of the most efficient. Saving one firm in an industry, the least efficient, is unlikely to affect the total consumption of the product of that industry, and therefore the total number of jobs generated within it. This matter was actually fought out in the upper reaches of the Steelworkers hierarchy in 1982–1983, in the midst of a severe recession in basic steel. The advocates of concessions, who included president Lloyd McBride, based their case on the need to save jobs, whereas the opponents, who notably included Frank W. McKee, international secretary and head of the copper coalition from 1977, argued that concessions would help only the weakest producers at the expense of the strongest.[11] Edmund Ayoub, a talented economist and adviser to McBride, took the case one step further, contending that there existed substantial excess capacity in the steel industry that should be eliminated by in effect squeezing out the least efficient firms.[12] Doubtless Ayoub was influenced by his sophisticated perception that for a decade the rate of increase in money wages in steel had been outrunning the rate of gain in labor productivity, which he attributed to low operating rates, too many marginal plants, outmoded technology, and poor local labor-management relations.

Ayoub's longer-run goal for steel was a creative proposal for the USW and the companies, in which productivity would be improved by an exchange of obsolete work practices for assurance from the companies of substantial investments to modernize facilities. Unfortunately, the bargain was never struck. The debate remained mired in the muddy issue of whether to offer a general wage cut, perhaps augmented by a temporary suspension of COLA adjustments.

The copper industry was in almost exactly the same predicament in the same years. But in this instance McKee was the chief bargainer—and with a great deal of autonomy, which was the USW tradition. Soon after the death of McBride in November 1983, McKee, who would soon become a candidate to replace him, wrote to all USW locals to announce that he was "openly declaring war on concessions, vacillation, timidity, discrimination and apathy in the union."[13] The announcement of this uncompromising version of the no-cuts doctrine followed by only six months the copper coalition's attempt to force Phelps Dodge to accept the Kennecott contract. There the principle had been rigorously applied in the midst of the worst depression in the industry since the early 1930s. It will be recalled that the attempt ended in failure, along with a strike, continued operations, and ultimate decertification of the unions on most of that company's properties. McKee's hard-line position was a prime source of contention between Lynn Williams and himself as they competed for the USW presidency between 1983 and 1985. When Williams took office in 1986, this intransigence was also the cause of his replacing McKee with the more flexible Edgar Ball to conduct the concession bargaining necessary in copper during that year, as it was in steel.[14]

As these two cases illustrate, the fundamental policy issue confronting unions and management in industries such as steel or copper turns on their answers to two fundamental questions: First, shall there be centralization or decentralization of the wage-making authority in the industry; and, second, shall the ultimate objective for wage policy in the industry be uniformity or diversity in wages and benefits? Within this framework of choice, it should be obvious that wage uniformity requires centralization of wage-setting while wage diversity calls for decentralization.

Centralized wage-setting in an industry creates a twofold problem. It calls for regulation at a distance, both in the formulation of the rules and in their implementation; and the results are insensitivity to local problems and needs and inflexibility in negotiation. Both deficiencies operate to stifle much of the creative potential of collective bargaining as a problem-solving institution. The bargainers lack both the time and the expertise to acquire familiarity with divergent local situations. Setting their own objectives, they proceed to impose them from afar in the determined pursuit of uniformity. The benefits of uniformity may outweigh the costs of inflexibility when the underlying forces are homogeneous, but not when they are characterized by a basic diversity.

For an industry with the stability and homogeneity of basic steel in, say, 1960, centralized bargaining and uniform contracts posed no obvious difficulties, although some formidable problems lay just below the surface. By 1984 the entire system had disintegrated, not so much because of the previous insistence on uniformity, but because the height the uniformly imposed wage and benefit structure had reached was no longer realistic in the face of foreign and mini-mill competition. Decentralization was essential to make concessions achievable. For the union in particular, it was a case of shifting to a new negotiating policy by diversifying it over a whole range of plants where the alternative was extinction.

In copper the crisis had been reached a year earlier. The diversity in the industry was geologically based and not amenable to solution by forcing the high-cost firms to adopt the efficiencies of the low-cost firms. Even the technology, in most cases, was dictated by the geology. A Phelps Dodge could live with a Kennecott pattern only as long as there was strong demand and a permissive price structure. As prices fell, it was necessary to respond to the realities of local cost. Nevertheless, unlike steel the following year, the challenge was met not with flexibility but with an obdurate response. In the outcome, the unions lost their bargaining rights entirely in about half of the industry. Ironically, unyielding defense of the industry pattern was the very cause of the collapse of pattern-bargaining in copper.

The Outlook for Labor Relations

At the outset of negotiations in 1983, the unions enjoyed almost 100 percent occupancy of the labor markets in copper mining, smelting, and refining. That was their summit. Economic distress, strikes, technological changes, restructuring, and major changes of ownership were to alter the entire setting over the rest of the decade.

First, all labor organizations were decertified as bargaining agents at the Phelps Dodge properties in Arizona—Ajo, Bisbee, Douglas, and Morenci—and also at the refinery at El Paso, Texas. Soon after, decertifications occurred at the Duval mines at Sierrita and Esperanza, Arizona. Then, largely nonunion Cyprus Minerals Corporation began a series of copper-mining acquisitions that included Duval; the nonunion Old Dick Mine at Bagdad, Arizona; the ANAMAX (Twin Buttes) Mine jointly owned by Anaconda and AMAX; Noranda's Lakeshore Mine near Casa Grande, Arizona; and, finally, in 1988, the Inspiration Consolidated Mine and production facilities in the Globe-Miami district. Meanwhile, Kennecott closed its Nevada operations and sold Chino to Phelps Dodge and Ray to ASARCO. Kennecott itself later continued to operate only at Bingham Canyon, now as simply "Kennecott Corporation," a wholly owned subsidiary of RTZ Minerals, Ltd., of London.

From the labor-management aspect, the most important fact is that Phelps Dodge is now the largest producer in the United States, while Cyprus Minerals is second. All of PD's properties presently operating in Arizona are nonunion, as are all of the Cyprus operations. Finally, the Dennis Washington interests in Montana have reopened Anaconda's old Berkeley pits at Butte, also on a nonunion basis. Accordingly, at least one-half of U.S. extractive capacity today is nonunion. After some four decades, the industry once again is characterized by incomplete labor organization, with all of the handicaps this implies for pattern-bargaining and wage uniformity.

The properties that remain unionized are ASARCO (Mission, Ray, Hayden, and El Paso), Magma (San Manuel, Superior, and Pinto Valley), RTZ Minerals (Bingham Canyon), PD (Tyrone and Chino, New Mexico), and White Pine (Michigan). Contractual relationships on these properties are characterized by a variation in wages and work rules as well as in termination dates. The simultaneity sought in 1967 and almost fully achieved in copper extraction is gone. In consequence, the 1989–1990 collective bargaining round occurred in a three-vector context: some negotiations in 1989, some in 1990, and a large fraction of mine capacity—involving the two biggest producers—with no labor negotiations at all. Within the unionized sector, some firms granted wage rate increases and some put part of the pay in bonuses not to be factored into the rates. ASARCO now has higher pay rates than the other firms, which are for the most part uniform in pay but not in benefits. All of the 1989–1990 contracts were negotiated with full awareness of what was going on elsewhere, but all of the negotiations were conducted independently. District officials participated with local officers in negotiations without the national unions present, although the latter approved the settlements after the fact. Decentralization was paramount.

Of course, employees at all of the nonunion entities retain the right to opt for unionization and may do so in the future, depending on how they feel their employers have treated them. But so far the pressures seem to be in the direction of further decertification. The nonunion employees are in the driver's seat. One can say that the union coalition is bargaining for them, because nonunion employers dare not let their conditions lapse if they want to avoid reunionization. And in fact they have not fallen behind. Yet the employees avoid dues and union obligations. Any attempt to restore the pattern system seems totally unlikely. The size of the nonunion sector, together with the divergence of expiration dates on the organized properties, deny any possibility of an industry-wide strike. Thus, there is no way to establish a pattern.

The divided situation prevented the unions from fully recovering their 1986 concessions, despite the favorable demand and profit situation. If those conditions continue, the possibilities for recertification of disgruntled employees should keep employers sharing with their nonunion employees. Wage and benefit levels, therefore, should reflect the industry's progress. Information sharing among union locals will prevent wide departures in the economic settlement levels, but should not impede consideration of local issues to the degree national dominance once did. One round is not enough to be sure, but probably the most important implication of the present situation is that both sides will be able to engage in bargaining about their own problems and interests, unhampered by the rigidity and inflexibility that prevailed in 1983.

THE FUTURE OF THE COPPER INDUSTRY

In 1985 the U.S. Bureau of Mines forecast a rate of annual output growth for the U.S. copper industry of between 2.9 percent and 4.5 percent per year, for the remainder of the century.[15] Subsequent events have made that projection highly unlikely. The future of the U.S. copper industry depends on world conditions of supply and demand for copper products and the ability of U.S. firms to compete for their share of this potential business.

The World Outlook

Two opposing views prevail concerning the future of the world copper industry, along with certain nuances that lie in between. The pessimistic view regards copper as a technologically obsolete metal that is about to be overwhelmed by substitutes. The industry is said to be in fundamental decline, saved temporarily by a stimulus of high prices that cannot last. True, there has been a sharp reduction in production costs to levels of 40–60 cents a pound, but by creating large profit margins all this saving will do is call forth a brief surge of output. Prices will then collapse. The continued high prices since the 1987 recovery can easily be explained as the result of temporary influences joined in an unusual combination: a fall in world production because of labor disturbances and technical difficulties in Africa, South America, and the Far East; and a transitory jump in world demand occasioned by the exhaustion of large inventories which were involuntarily built up during the slump of 1980–1986, as well as by military uncertainties in the Middle East.

The evidence advanced to support the claim that current copper prices cannot last stresses the frequent occurrence of the peculiar phenomenon of "backwardation" in the price structure for copper on the COMEX commodity exchange. When it occurs, the spot price for immediate deliveries runs higher than prices for future deliveries on forward contracts for specified months, despite the fact that future deliveries involve costs of carrying and storing the metal in the meantime. The argument runs that sellers are selling forward because they expect a collapse in price. To take advantage of this situation, they divert copper from spot sales, which decreases currently available supply and thereby drives up current prices. By the same action, future prices are depressed—hence the backwardation. The recurrence of this phenomenon has to mean that prices prevailing since the recovery that began in the spring of 1987 are being undermined by longer-term developments in supply and demand, which will again point them substantially downward.[16]

There is another way, however, to interpret the phenomenon of backwardation. It is that the copper market has been unusually tight ever since the price recovery began in 1987—not because copper is being diverted to forward sales, but because the current demand for copper has been persistently increasing. Also, imports have been cut by strikes and foreign disturbances. The resulting upward pressure on spot prices distorts the time structure; the spot price exceeds futures prices, notwithstanding the costs of carrying inventories. The result is backwardation rather than a "contango," where future prices exceed the spot price, rising with the length of the future period. Over the past twenty-five years, however, a contango has prevailed about 70 percent of the time.

The argument for pessimism appeals to an expected permanent world-wide contraction in demand because of the belief that copper is facing displacement across the whole range of its traditional uses. But the evidence is far from impressive. It involves the introduction of aluminum on high-tension power lines, which began many years ago; the advent of plastic pipe; the substitution of fiber optics for communications (which has much more recency and importance, although it, too, is not yet decisive); and the recurring rumors of developments in superconductors, which so far have not included a practical technology for their production and use. A more reasonable view of the future for copper would declare that the American branch of the industry has long since reached the slow-growth characteristics of a mature industry, but that absolute decline has yet to come.

The case for optimism is that demand has not yet entered a secular decline. To be sure, the metal will continue to display its traditional cyclic instability, because of its peculiar characteristics as an intermediate good. But this attribute should not be confused with a long-term downward trend. Copper retains its very useful intrinsic features. If it continues to be efficiently produced and priced, it can continue to compete in many uses. As for the supply side, there is no vast unsold stock of the red metal in the hands of refiners, dealers, traders, and users. It was this very overhang of supply, in fact, that depressed prices from 1980 on for seven very difficult years. Indeed, it was the absorption of this excess supply that finally restored money price to levels at which producers again could earn competitive profits. Granted that several new mines are under development in Chile, Brazil, Mexico, Australia, Papua New Guinea, and Portugal, it will be another three to five years before most of them will be fully on line.[17] Moreover, other contemporary influences are working to depress world supply.

One of them is that some of the overseas mines have incurred a substantial fall in ore grade by their earlier resort to extraction of the richest ores to stave off a fall in earnings during the long years of low prices, as Simon D. Strauss of ASARCO has recently noted.[18] Another element is that the mines of Zambia and Zaire, in particular, have been undermaintained for years because of foreign-exchange difficulties. Further, these properties lack extensive reserves. Those third world nations that are currently under-going industrialization may well increase their consumption at a higher annual rate than will prevail in the fully industrialized countries, because their pattern of production will necessarily be more copper intensive.[19] Under what may or may not prove to be short-run restraints, Bougainville has been shut down by domestic unrest, and Philippine production is similarly threatened. Anti-inflationary policies of the new Peruvian regime have been met by widespread strikes, and both of Chile's principal mines are suffering serious technical problems.[20] Theft and scandal overwhelmed and closed Mexico's Cananea Mine; privatization may restore it to produc-tion, but not without difficulty and time lag.[21]

The World Bank weighs in on the optimistic side by projecting a 1.9 percent per annum growth in copper consumption for the years 1990–2000,[22] up from a 1.3 percent per annum forecast made in 1986.[23] It predicts that the production response to that consumption demand will reflect the pattern that was shown in Table 7.5: a slow but steady decline for copper production in the United States and Peru, and a more rapid decline for Canada and Zaire, with all other copper producers on the increase. In this scenario Chile and the United States remain first and second, but with a widening gap between them and previously minor countries playing a larger part.

The U.S. Role

The World Bank prediction for the United States is based on the assump-tion that all of the viable copper deposits that can be competitively devel-oped are already known and in production. Accordingly, mine capacity can only decline over the long run (as indicated in Table 7.7). Increased competitiveness of the U.S. mines is based on improved technology and management rather than on discovery of richer or more workable ore bodies. The projection reflects the belief that the U.S. industry will remain a vigorous competitor, keeping its production costs low in the face of the substantial wage differential.

In the United States over the postwar years, primary production (which excludes scrap) rose at an average annual rate of only 0.76 percent, which compares with an annual rate of increase in apparent consumption of 1.22 percent per year. Thus copper imports have been supporting American copper consumption for a long time. As domestic output slows its rate of increase, as is reasonable to expect, foreign suppliers will fill the gap.

The severe problems experienced by the American copper industry over the past two decades did not have their origin either in excess imports or in adverse technical substitution. They came from an acceleration of inflation, the insertion of a credit squeeze from 1979, and the cumulative acceptance of an unsustainably high level of labor costs. All of these turned the U.S. industry into the world's leading high-cost producer.[24] The deliberate adoption of a policy of tight money in late 1979 eventually cut the inflation rate, but the consequences for copper were strongly adverse: a collapse of output and price, a surge of imports, a huge accumulation of inventories, and an undeniable challenge to get control of runaway labor costs.

At the same time, the seven lean years that followed 1980 revealed that the people in American copper had a strong will to survive. They succeeded in slashing costs to about 50 cents a pound by rationalization and innovations that have drastically reorganized the process of production, and thereby have ended the industry's traditional labor-intensive status. The United States is again an efficient competitor in the world market. If price holds between 90 cents and $1.10 for the longer term, a far more conservative expectation than the World Bank projection of Table 10.1, U.S. copper should enjoy an assured future as well as adequate capability for meeting its traditional challenge of cyclic setbacks.

In retrospect, everything that was done to slash production costs during the 1980s could have been done in the 1970s or even the 1960s. There have been no technological breakthroughs. Every technology recently installed has been available for decades. Every mistake contributing to

TABLE 10.1 Projected copper prices, 1990–2000[a]

Year	Current dollars	1988 U.S. dollars per ton	
		MUV[b]	US GNP[c]
1990	0.825	0.544	0.670
1995	1.225	0.677	0.779
2000	1.450	0.640	0.705

SOURCE: World Bank, International Economics Department.

[a] These projections were made by the World Bank staff in early 1988. The actual average LMS price for 1990 turned out to be 1.202. Over the long run, the validity of the projections will depend on fulfillment of the bank's optimistic expectations of capacity expansion accompanied by modest consumption growth.

[b] Deflated by Manufacturing Unit Value (MUV) index.

[c] Deflated by U.S. GNP deflator.

excessive labor costs made by either management or labor was not only foreseeable but actually foreseen by some. Without an imminent threat to survival, however, expediency prevailed. Management was unwilling to forgo short-run profit for long-run well-being. Steelworker leaders were convinced that the steel formula was invincible and so failed to consider its consequences for the copper industry. Labor leaders, whether from steel or copper, were unwilling politically to say no to available short-run gains for their membership in favor of long-run job preservation. But these are common human tendencies. Both industry and labor leadership deserve commendation for facing up to reality when the only other option was demise of the industry. Can the experience offer hope for greater foresight and fortitude in the future?

Unless and until the lessons are forgotten, greater management vigilance is probable. The unions are chastened but still strong and capable of protecting and pursuing the well-being of their members. Nonunion competition is a two-edged sword, as long as bargaining rights are guaranteed by law. It restrains the unions, but it also forces nonunion employers to consider the interests of their employees. For the nation as a whole, the message is that American industry can survive and prosper without resorting to third world wages and working conditions, if and as long as there is concerted willingness to accept and respond to the realities of the product market and the labor market, and their technological implications.

NOTES
INDEX

NOTES

1. The Copper Industry and Its Industrial Relations

1. Garth L. Mangum and Stephen L. Mangum, "Steel on the Industrial Staircase: A Conceptual Model for Early Warning to Other Industries and Nations," *Economic Development Quarterly* (February 1988): 31–32.

2. Vernon H. Jensen, *Heritage of Conflict: Labor Relations in the Nonferrous Metals Industry up to 1930* (Ithaca: Cornell University Press, 1950); idem, *Nonferrous Metals Industry Unionism, 1932–1954: A Story of Leadership Controversy* (Ithaca: Cornell Studies in Industrial and Labor Relations, New York State School of Industrial and Labor Relations, 1954).

3. C. Harry Benedict, *Red Metal: The Calumet and Hecla Story* (Ann Arbor: University of Michigan Press, 1952); William B. Gates, Jr., *Michigan Copper and Boston Dollars: An Economic History of the Michigan Copper Mining Industry* (Cambridge, Mass.: Harvard University Press, 1951).

4. Arthur B. Parsons, *The Porphyry Coppers* (New York: American Institute of Mining and Petroleum Engineers, 1933).

5. Orris C. Herfindahl, *Copper Costs and Prices: 1870–1957*, published for Resources for the Future, Inc. (Baltimore: Johns Hopkins University Press, 1959); Raymond F. Mikesell, *The World Copper Industry: Structure and Economic Analysis*, published for Resources for the Future, Inc. (Baltimore: Johns Hopkins University Press, 1979); Thomas R. Navin, *Copper Mining and Management* (Tucson: University of Arizona Press, 1978).

6. Leonard J. Arrington and Gary B. Hansen, *The Richest Hole on Earth: A History of the Bingham Copper Mine* (Salt Lake City: Utah State University Press, October 1963), monograph series, vol. 11:1; Robert Glass Cleland, *A History of Phelps-Dodge, 1834–1950* (New York: Knopf, 1952); Isaac F. Marcosson, *Anaconda* (New York: Dodd, Mead, 1957); idem., *Metal Magic: The*

Story of the American Smelting and Refining Company (New York: Farrar, Straus, 1949); Ira B. Joralemon, *Copper: The Encompassing Story of Mankind's First Metal* (Berkeley: Howell-North, 1973).

7. John P. Hoerr, *And The Wolf Finally Came: The Decline of the American Steel Industry* (Pittsburgh: University of Pittsburgh Press, 1988).
8. Until its absorption of the aluminum workers in the middle of the Second World War, the United Steelworkers (then under the presidency of Philip Murray) adhered to the principle of one union to each industry—in that case, steel.
9. Hoerr, op. cit., p. 405.
10. John T. Dunlop, "The Task of Contemporary Wage Theory," in John T. Dunlop, ed., *The Theory of Wage Determination*, proceedings of a conference held by the International Economic Association (New York: St. Martin's Press, 1957), pp. 3–30. (Also published under the same title in George W. Taylor and Frank C. Pierson, eds., *New Concepts in Wage Determination* (New York: McGraw-Hill, 1957), pp. 117–139).
11. Dunlop, op. cit., p. 16.
12. George H. Hildebrand has explored this problem at length in "External Influences and the Determination of the Internal Wage Structure," in J. L. Meij, ed., *Internal Wage Structure* (Amsterdam: North-Holland, 1963), pp. 260–299.
13. Dunlop, op. cit., p. 17.
14. For a contemporary view of the matter, see Richard B. Freeman, *Labor Markets in Action: Essays in Empirical Economics* (Cambridge, Mass.: Harvard University Press, 1989), p. 205.
15. Dunlop, op. cit., pp. 18–19.

2. Geography, Geology, and Technology

1. Ira B. Joralemon, *Copper: The Encompassing Story of Mankind's First Metal* (Berkeley: Howell-North, 1973), pp. 255–256.
2. Ibid., pp. 245–249, 253–269.
3. Ibid., pp. 143–165.
4. Ibid., pp. 350–356.
5. The town was named for an early explorer, Robert Kennicott.
6. Joralemon, op. cit., pp. 367–371.
7. Ibid., p. 375.
8. Ibid., pp. 273–289.
9. Walter S. White, "The Native-Copper Deposits of Northern Michigan," in John D. Ridge, ed., *Ore Deposits of the United States, 1933–1967* (New York: American Institute of Mining, Metallurgical, and Petroleum Engineers, 1968), vol. 1, pp. 303–325. See figure 1, p. 305.

10. Ibid., pp. 314–315.
11. Taken from White's assessment of competing theories of ore genesis; ibid., pp. 321–322.
12. Isaac F. Marcosson, *Anaconda* (New York: Dodd, Mead, 1957), pp. 21–29.
13. Charles Meyer, Edward P. Shea, Charles C. Goddard, Jr., et al., "Ore Deposits at Butte, Montana," in Ridge, op. cit., vol. 2, pp. 1375–1415. Data from p. 1376.
14. Ibid., pp. 1376–78.
15. Ibid., pp. 1381–91.
16. Ibid., pp. 1413–15.
17. Arthur B. Parsons, *The Porphyry Coppers* (New York: American Institute of Mining and Petroleum Engineers, 1933), p. 338; Charles A. Anderson, "Arizona and Adjacent New Mexico," in Ridge, op. cit., vol. 2, p. 1172.
18. Parsons, op. cit., p. 339.
19. Anderson, op. cit., p. 1165.
20. Ibid., p. 1173.
21. Ibid.
22. Parsons, op. cit., p. 343.
23. Anderson, op. cit., p. 1178.
24. Parsons, op. cit., pp. 340–341.
25. Anderson, op. cit., p. 1187.
26. C. E. Julihn, "Copper: An Example of Changing Technology and the Utilization of Low-Grade Ores," in F. G. Tyron and E. C. Eckel, eds., *Mineral Economics*; lectures under the auspices of the Brookings Institution (New York: McGraw-Hill, 1932), p. 123.
27. Ibid. The square set was a box frame of 12″ × 12″ timbers. It was first introduced on the Comstock lode by Philip Deidesheimer in the early 1860s.
28. Ibid., pp. 125–126.
29. Parsons, op. cit., pp. 431–432, 463–465, 466–471, 473.
30. Julihn, op. cit., pp. 121–122.
31. Parsons, op. cit., pp. 393–400.
32. Orris C. Herfindahl, *Copper Costs and Prices: 1870–1957*, published for Resources for the Future, Inc. (Baltimore: Johns Hopkins University Press, 1959), p. 213. By 1950 the figure had reached 74 percent. In 1907 open pits accounted for only 1.8 percent of primary output.
33. Ibid., p. 76.
34. Ibid., pp. 441–445, 446–454.
35. Ibid., pp. 442–444.
36. Julihn, op. cit., p. 129.
37. Parsons, op. cit., pp. 53–54.
38. The basic work on the psychology of the act of innovation is Abbott Payson

Usher, *A History of Mechanical Inventions* (Cambridge, Mass.: Harvard University Press, rev. ed., 1954), pp. 60–72.

39. Herfindahl, op. cit., pp. 201–202, 206–207.

40. The technologies and processes described in the remainder of this chapter are summarized from Thomas R. Navin, *Copper Mining and Management* (Tucson: University of Arizona Press, 1978), pp. 15–79, 97–109; U.S. Congress, Office of Technology Assessment, *Copper: Technology and Competitiveness* (Washington, D.C.: Government Printing Office, September 1988), pp. 103–147.

3. Emergence of the Copper Industry

1. C. Harry Benedict, *Red Metal: The Calumet and Hecla Story* (Ann Arbor: University of Michigan Press, 1952), p. 18; William B. Gates, Jr., *Michigan Copper and Boston Dollars: An Economic History of the Michigan Copper Mining Industry* (Cambridge, Mass.: Harvard University Press, 1951), pp. 1–29.

2. Benedict, op. cit., pp. 1–5; Ira B. Joralemon, *Copper: The Encompassing Story of Mankind's First Metal* (Berkeley: Howell-North, 1973), p. 52.

3. Joralemon, op. cit., pp. 56–57.

4. Benedict, op. cit., pp. 33–35.

5. Ibid., p. 40.

6. Ibid., pp. 44–45, 60.

7. Ibid., p. 58.

8. Ibid., pp. 65–73.

9. Ibid., pp. 148–150.

10. Ibid., pp. 77–79.

11. Ibid., pp. 170–174, 184.

12. Ibid., pp. 175–178.

13. Ibid., pp. 177–180.

14. Ibid., p. 191.

15. Ibid., pp. 136–140.

16. *Moody's Manual of Investments, American and Foreign, 1947* (New York: Moody's Investors Service, 1947).

17. *Wall Street Journal*, February 23, 1968.

18. Ibid., April 4 and April 10, 1968.

19. Isaac F. Marcosson, *Anaconda* (New York: Dodd, Mead, 1957), pp. 20–25, 31–32.

20. Joralemon, op. cit., p. 73.

21. Marcosson, op. cit., p. 32; Joralemon, op. cit., pp. 79–81.

22. Marcosson, op. cit., pp. 44–45; Joralemon, op. cit., p. 82; Yvonne Levy, "Copper: Red Metal in Flux," *Monthly Review Supplement* (San Francisco: Federal Reserve Bank, 1968), p. 7.

23. Levy, op. cit., p. 8.
24. Marcosson, op. cit., p. 57; Levy, op. cit., pp. 8–9.
25. Marcosson, op. cit., pp. 57–58.
26. Ibid., p. 88.
27. Ibid., pp. 90–91.
28. Ibid., pp. 93–95.
29. Ibid., p. 113.
30. Ibid., pp. 112–113.
31. Ibid., pp. 132–133.
32. Ibid., pp. 138–140.
33. Ibid., pp. 211–214.
34. Ibid., pp. 194–199.
35. Ibid., pp. 255–259.
36. Ibid., pp. 168–171; 183–186.
37. *Moody's Manual of Investments, 1947*.
38. Ibid.
39. Isaac F. Marcosson, *Metal Magic: The Story of the American Smelting and Refining Company* (New York: Farrar, Straus, 1949), pp. 25–30.
40. Ibid., pp. 30–31.
41. Ibid., pp. 36–43.
42. Ibid., pp. 45–53.
43. John H. Davis, *The Guggenheims: An American Epic* (New York: William Morrow, 1978), p. 73.
44. Marcosson, *Metal Magic*, pp. 60–64.
45. Ibid., pp. 68–69.
46. Ibid., pp. 75–80.
47. Ibid., pp. 84, 91.
48. Arthur B. Parsons, *The Porphyry Coppers* (New York: American Institute of Mining and Petroleum Engineers, 1933), p. 148.
49. Ibid., pp. 142–156.
50. Ibid., pp. 256–264.
51. Marcosson, *Metal Magic*, pp. 200–201.
52. Ibid., p. 87; Parsons, op. cit., p. 70.
53. Parsons, op. cit., pp. 72–73; Marcosson, *Metal Magic*, p. 88.
54. Parsons, op. cit., pp. 74–75.
55. Ibid., p. 75; Marcosson, *Metal Magic*, p. 88.
56. Parsons, op. cit., pp. 118, 120.
57. Ibid., p. 125.
58. Ibid., p. 126.
59. Ibid., p. 129.
60. Ibid., p. 130.
61. Ibid., pp. 208–212.

62. Ibid., pp. 185–186, 191.
63. Ibid., pp. 195–196.
64. Ibid., p. 196.
65. Ibid., pp. 197–198.
66. Lone E. Janson, *The Copper Spike* (Anchorage: Alaska Northwest Publishing Company, 1975), p. 16.
67. Ibid., pp. 16–19; Davis, op. cit., pp. 101–102.
68. Janson, op. cit., pp. 52–54, 109–117.
69. Ibid., p. 145.
70. U.S. Federal Trade Commission, *Report on the Copper Industry, Part 1*, "The Copper Industry of the United States and International Copper Cartels" (Washington, D.C.: Government Printing Office, 1947), pp. 135–136.
71. Marcosson, *Metal Magic*, p. 112.
72. Ibid., pp. 126–128, 131.
73. Ibid., pp. 166–167.
74. *Moody's Manual of Investments, 1947.*
75. Leonard J. Arrington and Gary B. Hansen, *The Richest Hole on Earth: A History of the Bingham Copper Mine* (Salt Lake City: Utah State University Press, October 1963), monograph series, vol. 11:1, p. 68; *Moody's Manual of Investments, 1947.*
76. Arrington and Hansen, op. cit., pp. 68–69.
77. Parsons, op. cit., p. 52.
78. Arrington and Hansen, op. cit., p. 32; John Hays Hammond, *The Autobiography of John Hays Hammond* (New York: Farrar and Rinehart, 1935), vol. 2, p. 516.
79. Arrington and Hansen, op. cit., p. 32n7; Hammond, op. cit., p. 516.
80. Parsons, op. cit., p. 66.
81. Ibid., p. 67.
82. Ibid., p. 68.
83. Ibid., pp. 68–69.
84. Ibid., pp. 431–432.
85. Ibid., pp. 442–443.
86. Arrington and Hansen, op. cit., pp. 70–71.
87. Arrington and Hansen, op. cit., p. 79; *Moody's Manual of Investments, 1947.*
88. Robert Glass Cleland, *A History of Phelps Dodge, 1834–1950* (New York: Knopf, 1952), pp. 3–5.
89. Ibid., pp. 7, 17.
90. As reported in *Phelps Dodge: A Copper Centennial, 1881–1981*, p. 6. This volume was a supplement to the trade journal *Pay Dirt*, published monthly in Bisbee, Arizona, and concerned with affairs of the mining industry. See also Cleland, op. cit., pp. 91–98.
91. *Pay Dirt*, op. cit., p. 7; Cleland, op. cit., pp. 99–102.

92. Cleland, op. cit., p. 107.
93. Ibid., pp. 140–149.
94. Ibid., pp. 130–132.
95. Ibid., pp. 151–157, 193–194.
96. Parsons, op. cit., p. 111.
97. Ibid., pp. 78–79.
98. Federal Trade Commission, op. cit., p. 144; Cleland, op. cit., pp. 220–225.
99. Cleland, op. cit., pp. 246–254; *Pay Dirt*, op. cit., pp. 51–55.
100. *Moody's Manual of Investments, 1947*.
101. Parsons, op. cit., pp. 161–183; Arthur B. Parsons, *The Porphyry Coppers in 1956* (New York: American Institute of Mining, Metallurgical, and Petroleum Engineers, 1957), pp. 96–109.
102. Robert H. Ramsey, *Men and Mines of Newmont: A Fifty-Year History* (New York: Octagon Books, 1973), pp. 28–29, 52, 147–153.
103. Parsons, *The Porphyry Coppers*, pp. 226–250; idem, *The Porphyry Coppers in 1956*, pp. 137–147; Joralemon, op. cit., pp. 241–243.
104. Ramsey, op. cit., pp. 13–35, 36–38, 178–198.
105. Parsons, *The Porphyry Coppers*, pp. 225–255.

4. The Copper Market to the End of World War II

1. U.S. Federal Trade Commission, *Report on the Copper Industry, Part 1*, "The Copper Industry of the United States and International Copper Cartels" (Washington, D.C.: Government Printing Office, 1947), pp. 30–31. These figures include a small amount of secondary copper and make no allowance for changes in stocks or net imports. Data from U.S. Department of the Interior, Bureau of Mines, permit extension of the series through 1946.
2. Ibid., p. 66. These per capita figures are based on "apparent consumption" divided by population. Apparent consumption is the algebraic sum of primary production plus scrap, plus withdrawals less additions to stocks, plus imports less exports.
3. Apparent consumption for 1946 is based on U.S. Department of the Interior, Bureau of Mincs, *Minerals Yearbook, 1946* (Washington, D.C.: Government Printing Office, 1948), p. 459. Per capita consumption is calculated from population figures estimated for 1945 and 1946.
4. It should not be assumed that the mines opened in this period were all open pit, or all concerned with porphyry ores. Four were open-pit operations; five were underground, of which two involved block caving.
5. "Kennicott" was the original spelling, which was changed in 1915 with the formation of Kennecott Copper Corporation.
6. Orris C. Herfindahl, *Copper Costs and Prices: 1870–1957*, published for Resources for the Future, Inc. (Baltimore: Johns Hopkins University

Press, 1959), p. 159, presents a compilation based on official American data.

7. The properties of both Zaire (formerly the Congo) and Zambia (formerly Northern Rhodesia) are now state-owned enterprises. The same is true in Chile. In South Africa the O'Okiep Mine was started in 1937, Tsumeb in 1947, and Palabora in 1966. See Robert H. Ramsey, *Men and Mines of Newmont: A Fifty-Year History* (New York: Octagon Books, 1973), pp. 79, 126–127, 238.

8. Data from Bureau of Mines, and from Federal Trade Commission, op. cit., p. 66.

9. The Bureau of Mines includes copper obtained from imported ores and from copper matte in its series for total supply, which increases the figure by about 15 percent. Most of these imports came from mines owned by Anaconda and Kennecott in Chile and by ASARCO in Mexico.

10. Data for apparent consumption, supply, imports, and exports are for 1908–1941 from Federal Trade Commission, op. cit., p. 66; for 1942–1946 calculated from Department of the Interior, op. cit., p. 459. In this context "demand" and "supply" refer not to the functional relationships between prices and quantities of theoretical economics, but to actual transactions.

11. Federal Trade Commission, op. cit., pp. 57–60. The "miscellaneous" category represented 19.9 percent in 1920 and 14.7 percent in 1940. We have reassigned building construction, ship building, and manufactures for exports to capital goods, and automobiles to consumer goods.

12. The *Engineering and Mining Journal* has been publishing daily average transaction prices since 1866 (Federal Trade Commission, op. cit., p. 85).

13. For further discussion, see Federal Trade Commission, op. cit., pp. 80–84; Herfindahl, op. cit., pp. 182–185; and Raymond F. Mikesell, *The World Copper Industry: Structure and Economic Analysis* (Baltimore: Johns Hopkins University Press, 1979), pp. 80–85, 365–366.

14. In the long run there is, of course, a link between COMEX and LME prices. But as Herfindahl (op. cit., pp. 187–195) points out, the link is quite slack in short periods because of uncertainty regarding future price movements and because of buyers' preferences for established ties to domestic producers, to ensure a place in the queue. Time and transfer costs are also key factors in separating the two markets.

15. Federal Trade Commission, op. cit., pp. 30–31. During World War II Alfred Marshall's "particular expenses" curve was applied to price control in copper, through payment of bonus premiums to high-cost marginal mines. These properties could therefore sell at the ceiling price.

16. For the data and their sources, see Figure 4.4.

17. William B. Gates, Jr., *Michigan Copper and Boston Dollars: An Economic History*

of the Michigan Copper Mining Industry (Cambridge, Mass.: Harvard University Press, 1951), pp. 42–48, 53.

18. Ibid., p. 64.
19. Ibid., pp. 78–80.
20. Federal Trade Commission, op. cit., pp. 184–185; Herfindahl, op. cit., pp. 73–76.
21. Gates, op. cit., pp. 85–86.
22. Ibid., pp. 71, 86–87.
23. Herfindahl, op. cit., pp. 80–82; Federal Trade Commission, op. cit., pp. 185–186.
24. Federal Trade Commission, op. cit., pp. 85–87, 186.
25. Herfindahl, op. cit., pp. 92–106.
26. Ibid., pp. 107–110.
27. Federal Trade Commission, op. cit., p. 83.
28. The argument is from Paul M. Sweezy, "Demand under Conditions of Oligopoly," *Journal of Political Economy* 47 (August 1939): 568–571. The Sweezy case requires small numbers, barriers to entry, and does not explain how the price was determined in the first place.
29. Herfindahl, op. cit., pp. 196–197, 231–233; and Mikesell, op. cit., pp. 366–367, reach similar conclusions.

5. The Roots of Copper Industry Unionism

1. Richard E. Lingenfelter, *The Hardrock Miners: A History of the Mining Labor Movement in the American West, 1863–1893* (Berkeley: University of California Press, 1974), pp. 3–30.
2. Vernon H. Jensen, *Heritage of Conflict: Labor Relations in the Nonferrous Metals Industry up to 1930* (Ithaca: Cornell University Press, 1950), p. 1.
3. Ibid., pp. 11–18; Alan Derickson, *Workers' Health, Workers' Democracy, the Western Miners' Struggle, 1891–1925* (Ithaca: Cornell University Press, 1988).
4. John R. Commons et al., *History of Labor in the United States* (New York: Augustus M. Kelley, 1966), vol. 1, pp. 83–87, 124–125, 578–580; vol. 2, p. 501.
5. Jensen, op. cit., pp. 11–15.
6. Ibid., pp. 13–15, 22–24, 32–37, 42–52.
7. Ibid., pp. 96–115.
8. Lloyd Ulman, *Rise of the National Trade Union* (Cambridge, Mass.: Harvard University Press, 1955), p. 49.
9. Jensen, op. cit., pp. 54–55; Lingenfelter, op. cit., p. 27.
10. Jensen, op. cit., pp. 58–59.

11. Ibid., p. 59; Selig Perlman and Philip Taft, *History of Labor in the United States, 1896–1932* (New York: Augustus M. Kelley, 1966), vol. 4, p. 214.
12. Philip Taft, *The AFofL in the Time of Gompers* (New York: Harper, 1957), pp. 150–152.
13. Jensen, op. cit., pp. 58–59.
14. Taft, op. cit., p. 152.
15. Jensen, op. cit., p. 62.
16. Ibid., pp. 152–153, 160; Perlman and Taft, op. cit., pp. 215–216.
17. Taft, op. cit., p. 155; Perlman and Taft, op. cit., pp. 216–217.
18. Jensen, op. cit., pp. 90–95.
19. Perlman and Taft, op. cit., p. 189.
20. Jensen, op. cit., pp. 118–159.
21. Ibid., p. 163.
22. Paul F. Brissenden, *The I.W.W.: A Study of American Syndicalism* (New York: Russell and Russell, 1920, 1957), pp. 57–59.
23. Quoted in Jensen, op. cit., p. 164.
24. Brissenden, op. cit., pp. 68–69.
25. Ibid., pp. 74–76.
26. Harry A. Millis and Royal E. Montgomery, *Organized Labor* (New York: McGraw-Hill, 1945), pp. 118–119.
27. Jensen, op. cit., pp. 202–204.
28. Harry Orchard, *The Confessions and Autobiography of Harry Orchard* (New York: McClure, 1907), pp. 206–223.
29. Melvyn Dubofsky, *We Shall Be All: A History of the Industrial Workers of the World* (Chicago: Quadrangle Books, 1969), pp. 96–104.
30. Brissenden, op. cit., pp. 136–140.
31. Dubofsky, op. cit., pp. 108–113.
32. Jensen, op. cit., p. 179.
33. Ibid., pp. 192–193.
34. Dubofsky, op. cit., pp. 360–361.
35. Jensen, op. cit., p. 195.
36. Dubofsky, op. cit., pp. 120–125.
37. Brissenden, op. cit., p. 80.
38. Jensen, op. cit., p. 196.
39. Ibid., p. 239.
40. Ibid., p. 246.
41. Ibid., pp. 246–248; Dubofsky, op. cit., pp. 319–331.
42. Lingenfelter, op. cit., pp. 128–156.
43. Jerry W. Calvert, *The Gibraltar: Socialism and Labor in Butte, Montana, 1875–1920* (Helena: Montana Historical Society Press, 1988), pp. 15–18.
44. Isaac F. Marcosson, *Anaconda* (New York: Dodd, Mead, 1957), pp. 118–126.

45. Calvert, op. cit., pp. 74–75.
46. Ibid., p. 26.
47. Ibid., p. 72.
48. Ibid., p. 52.
49. Ibid., p. 78; Jensen, op. cit., p. 323.
50. Jensen, op. cit., p. 306.
51. Calvert, op. cit., pp. 81–86.
52. Dubofsky, op. cit., pp. 303–305.
53. Calvert, op. cit., pp. 88–90.
54. Dubofsky, op. cit., pp. 366–368.
55. Ibid., pp. 391–392, 421, 450–451.
56. J. Kenneth Davies, *Deseret's Sons of Toil* (Salt Lake City: Olympus, 1977), pp. 23–26.
57. Jensen, op. cit., p. 259.
58. Ibid., p. 262.
59. Ibid., pp. 266–269.
60. Ibid., pp. 273–288.
61. William B. Gates, Jr., *Michigan Copper and Boston Dollars: An Economic History of the Michigan Copper Mining Industry* (Cambridge, Mass.: Harvard University Press, 1951), p. 114.
62. Ibid., p. 113.
63. Ibid., pp. 129, 133.
64. Ibid., p. 135.
65. Jensen, op. cit., p. 346.
66. Ibid., pp. 367–368.
67. Dubofsky, op. cit., pp. 370–375.
68. Ibid., p. 384; Jensen, op. cit., p. 400.
69. Jensen, op. cit., pp. 404–406; Dubofsky, op. cit., pp. 385–390.
70. Jensen, op. cit., p. 370.
71. Ibid., p. 377.
72. Ibid., p. 431.
73. Ibid., p. 452.
74. Ibid., p. 464.
75. Vernon H. Jensen, *Nonferrous Metals Industry Unionism, 1932–1954: A Study of Leadership Controversy* (Ithaca: Cornell Studies in Industrial and Labor Relations, New York State School of Industrial and Labor Relations, 1954), p. 5.
76. Ibid., p. 10.
77. Ibid., pp. 36–44.
78. Ibid., pp. 13–17.
79. Philip Taft, *The AF of L from the Death of Gompers to the Merger* (New York: Harper, 1959), pp. 142–144; Walter Galenson, *CIO Challenge to the AF of L* (Cambridge, Mass.: Harvard University Press, 1960), p. 4.

80. Jensen, *Nonferrous Metals*, p. 27.
81. Ibid., pp. 38–45.
82. Gates, op. cit., pp. 171–172.
83. Jensen, *Nonferrous Metals*, p. 280.
84. Ibid., pp. 49–50.
85. Galenson, op. cit., p. 208.
86. Jensen, *Nonferrous Metals*, pp. 88–96.
87. Ibid., pp. 125–137.
88. Ibid., pp. 183–185.

6. Changing Industry Structure, 1946–1990

1. Thomas R. Navin, *Copper Mining and Management* (Tucson: University of Arizona Press, 1978), pp. 215–217.
2. Ibid., pp. 218–221.
3. Ibid., pp. 222–225.
4. "Newspaper Says Montana's Mining Industry Is Rebounding," *Pay Dirt*, July 1988, p. 18A.
5. "Copper Prices Make Dennis Washington's Gamble Pay Off," *Pay Dirt*, July 1988, p. 30A.
6. "New Butte Mining Expanding Work in Old Underground Area," *Pay Dirt*, December 1989, p. 8A; "Teamwork Brings Success in Butte," *Pay Dirt*, May 1990, p. 5B.
7. Navin, op. cit., pp. 264–267.
8. Ibid., pp. 268–270.
9. Ibid., p. 272.
10. Ibid., p. 266.
11. Ibid., p. 272.
12. Garth Mangum and Camille Guth, "The Future of Utah Copper," *Utah Business and Economic Review* (January–February 1987): 15–17.
13. "Kennecott, Once Mighty Name in Copper, Fades into History," *Pay Dirt*, October 1987, pp. 11B–13B.
14. "Base Metals Turn to Gold," *Economist*, January 14, 1989, p. 62.
15. Ira B. Joralemon, *Copper: The Encompassing Story of Mankind's First Metal* (Berkeley: Howell-North, 1973), pp. 375–377.
16. "RTZ's Lord Clitheroe Assures Utah That All Will Go Smoothly," *Pay Dirt*, April 1989, pp. 20A–21A; U.S. Congress, Office of Technology Assessment, *Nonferrous Metals: Industry Structure* (Washington, D.C.: Government Printing Office, September 1990).
17. "Expansion to Up Copper Output by 35,000 Tons," *Pay Dirt*, January 1990, pp. 4A–5A.
18. "A Model of Efficiency for Copper Mines," *Salt Lake Tribune*, February 19,

1989, p. 6G; "Frank Joklik Named Copper Man of the Year," *Pay Dirt*, March 1989, p. 5B.

19. RTZ Corporation PLC, *Annual Report and Accounts, 1989*, p. 56.

20. Navin, op. cit., pp. 235–237.

21. "PD's Douglas Smelter Has Six More Months of Life—Maybe," *Pay Dirt*, August 1986, pp. 7A–9A.

22. Navin, op. cit., p. 237.

23. "Phelps Dodge Splits Activities into Two Divisions," *Pay Dirt*, October 1988, p. 2A.

24. "Phelps Dodge Appears Determined to Remain No. 1 in Copper," *Pay Dirt*, May 1987, pp. 18A–19A.

25. "Phelps Dodge Reports Higher Profits for 1986," *Pay Dirt*, March 1987, pp. 14A–15A.

26. "Phelps Dodge Pushing Ahead on Many Fronts," *Pay Dirt*, November 1987, p. 6A; "Phelps Dodge Sets Profit Record," *Pay Dirt*, February 1989, p. 6B; "Phelps Dodge Plans Hefty Investments," *Pay Dirt*, June 1989, p. 8B; "Phelps Dodge Earnings Up Sharply," *Pay Dirt*, August 1989, p. 6B; "Phelps Dodge Net Sets More Records," *Pay Dirt*, November 1989, p. 7B; "Earnings Decline at Phelps Dodge," *Pay Dirt*, May 1990, p. 6B.

27. Navin, op. cit., pp. 247–251.

28. "ASARCO Signs Agreement Buying Ray Mine for $72 Million," *Pay Dirt*, November 1986, p. 10A; "Mission, Ray Expansion to Assure Copper Feed," *Pay Dirt*, March 1989, pp. 5A–6A.

29. "ASARCO Turns the Corner, Chairman Tells Stockholders," *Pay Dirt*, May 1987, p. 11B; "ASARCO Expanding Its Copper Production," *Pay Dirt*, March 1989, pp. 4A–7A.

30. Joralemon, op. cit., pp. 3–11.

31. Navin, op. cit., p. 317–320.

32. "Cyprus Minerals Has Had Remarkable Growth in Three Years," *Pay Dirt*, June 1988, p. 5A.

33. "Lakeshore Will Give Cyprus Cathode Production," *Pay Dirt*, July 1987, pp. 4A–5A; "New Operation to Double Arizona Gold Production," *Pay Dirt*, November 1987, p. 5A.

34. "Cyprus Minerals Moving Its Beryllium at Texas Project," *Pay Dirt*, November 1986, p. 10A; "Cyprus Minerals Acquires Domestic, Spanish Talc Properties," *Pay Dirt*, October 1988, p. 15A; "Cyprus Makes Deal for Foote Minerals," *Pay Dirt*, January 1988, p. 7A.

35. "Cyprus Gets Inspiration for $125 Million in Cash," *Pay Dirt*, June 1988, pp. 4A–5A.

36. Navin, op. cit., p. 302.

37. "Cypress Gets Inspiration for $125 Million in Cash," *Pay Dirt*, June 1988, p. 4A.

38. "Cyprus Plans to Buy Copper Refinery," *Pay Dirt*, March 1989, p. 3A.
39. "Cyprus Posts Record '89 Earnings," *Pay Dirt*, February 1990, p. 7A.
40. "Cyprus Completes Inspiration Deal, Renounces Labor Pacts," *Pay Dirt*, June 1988, p. 7A; "Unions File Unfair Labor Practices Charges against Cyprus," *Pay Dirt*, August 1988, p. 3A.
41. Navin, op. cit., pp. 298–300.
42. Ibid., pp. 291–296.
43. "Newmont Gold Reports Increased Production, Higher Earnings," *Pay Dirt*, November 1986, p. 15A.
44. "To Install Flash Furnace at San Manuel Smelter," *Pay Dirt*, October 1986, p. 5A; "Magma Spinoff Will Get Newmont out of Domestic Copper," *Pay Dirt*, October 1986, p. 4A.
45. "Old Superior Is Being Reborn," *Pay Dirt*, March 1990, pp. 4A–6A; "Magma Restarts Mine after Eight-Year Hiatus," *Pay Dirt*, November 1990, pp. 4A–5A.
46. Navin, op. cit., p. 201.
47. Ibid., pp. 278–284.

7. The Product Market in the Postwar Era

1. Kenji Takeuchi, John E. Strongman, Shunichi Maeda, and C. Suan Tan, *The World Copper Industry: Its Changing Structure and Future Prospects* (Washington, D.C.: World Bank, 1987), p. 19.
2. Ibid., p. 20.
3. Ibid.
4. Ibid., p. 22.
5. Thomas R. Navin, *Copper Mining and Management* (Tucson: University of Arizona Press, 1978), pp. 155–159.
6. Takeuchi et al., op. cit., p. 23.
7. Ibid., pp. 25, 29.
8. Ibid., pp. 29–31.
9. U.S. Congress, Office of Technology Assessment, *Copper: Technology and Competitiveness* (Washington, D.C.: Government Printing Office, September 1988), p. 52.
10. Takeuchi et al., op. cit., p. 80.
11. Office of Technology Assessment, op. cit., p. 51.
12. Ibid.
13. "Mitsubishi Metals," *New York Times*, January 17, 1989.
14. Takeuchi et al., op. cit., pp. 40–45.
15. Ibid., pp. 45–52.
16. World Bank, "World Bank Predictions," 1988, p. 3 (mimeographed draft).

17. Takeuchi et al., op. cit., p. 54.
18. World Bank, op. cit., pp. 4–5.
19. Office of Technology Assessment, op. cit., pp. 17, 39.
20. World Bank, op. cit., p. 10.
21. Ibid., pp. 7–10.
22. Office of Technology Assessment, op. cit., p. 193.
23. Ibid., pp. 118–170.
24. Takeuchi et al., op. cit., p. 62.
25. Office of Technology Assessment, op. cit., p. 214.
26. World Bank, op. cit., pp. 6–10.
27. Ibid., pp. 5–6.
28. Ibid., p. 6.

8. Unionism, Collective Bargaining, and the Labor Market, 1946–1966

1. Vernon H. Jensen, *Nonferrous Metals Industry Unionism, 1932–1954: A Story of Leadership Controversy* (Ithaca: Cornell Studies in Industrial and Labor Relations, New York State School of Industrial and Labor Relations, 1954), p. 281. Jensen estimated this figure by dividing total annual income by the monthly per capita charge times 12.
2. Ibid., p. 28.
3. This was the basic approach adopted by the NLRB in *Globe Machine and Stamping Company*, 1A LRRM, pp. 122–127 (1937).
4. International Union of Mine, Mill and Smelter Workers, *Proceedings, Forty-Second Annual Convention* (1946), p. 136; Jensen, op. cit., pp. 133–136.
5. Jensen, op. cit., pp. 210–212; Leonard J. Arrington and Gary B. Hansen, *The Richest Hole on Earth: A History of the Bingham Copper Mine* (Salt Lake City: Utah State University Press, October 1963), monograph series, vol. 11:1, pp. 81–82.
6. In late 1958 Kennecott bought the Garfield smelter from ASARCO, taking control early in 1959.
7. Dichter, Skinner, and Eckert all supported the communist position during the lengthy dispute over admission of the Die Casting Association. Jensen, op. cit., pp. 82, 128.
8. Interestingly, employers were not required to file such affidavits as a condition for using the services of the board.
9. This provision of Taft-Hartley was repealed by an amendment in the Landrum-Griffin Act in 1959.
10. Mine Mill exacerbated its conflict with the CIO leaders by its active support of Henry A. Wallace's independent Progressive Party in the 1948 presidential election. As Wallace later discovered with some chagrin, this party turned out to be controlled by communists.

11. Congress of Industrial Organizations, *Proceedings, Eleventh Constitutional Convention* (1949), p. 240; Jensen, op. cit., p. 253.

12. U.S. Senate, *Report of the Subcommittee on Labor-Management Relations of the Committee on Labor and Public Welfare*, "Communist Domination of Certain Unions," Senate Document no. 89, 82nd Cong., 1st sess.; Jensen, op. cit., pp. 260–267; Max M. Kampelman, *The Communist Party vs. the CIO: A Study in Power Politics* (New York: Frederick A. Praeger, 1957), pp. 175–194.

13. Jensen, op. cit., p. 278.

14. Ibid., pp. 286–293.

15. As recently as 1989 there was still a single Mine Mill local at the Falconbridge Nickel property in Ontario.

16. *International Union of Mine, Mill and Smelter Workers v. Subversive Activities Control Board*, USCA, DC, no. 17135, November 3, 1965; *Daily Labor Report* 213, November 2, 1965.

17. *Decision of the National Labor Relations Board in the Matter of Maurice E. Travis*, February 3, 1955.

18. The history of the case is both interesting and complex. The original indictment in Denver named Albert Pezzati, Raymond Dennis, Irving Dichter, Graham Dolan, James Durkin, Asbury Howard, Alton Lawrence, Jack C. Marcotti, Chase J. Powers, Harold Sanderson, Albert C. Skinner, Maurice E. Travis, Jesse R. Van Camp, and Charles Wilson. In the nine-year course of the proceedings, Pezzati left the country, while Dolan, Durkin, Howard, Lawrence, Marcotti, and Powers were dropped from the indictment for various reasons. During the shrinkage in the number of defendants from fourteen to ten and finally to seven, the group became known as the "Denver Ten."

    The original federal indictment came in 1957, for a conspiracy to defraud the Unied States in signing and filing the noncommunist affidavits then required by section 9(h) of Taft-Hartley. A motion to dismiss the indictment was denied in Federal Court, District of Colorado, 160 F. Supp. 787 (decided March 27, 1958). The case then went through two trials, two appeals to Federal Appellate Court, and two remands—including a decision by the Supreme Court of the United States to remand on a technicality in which the Court did not address the substantive evidence.

19. *Raymond Dennis et al. v. United States*, 302 F. 2d 5 (decided March 5, 1962; rehearing denied April 11, 1962); remanded for retrial on a technical error.

20. On retrial, a second conviction was obtained, which was upheld on appeal. 346 F. 2d 10 (decided April 26, 1965).

21. U.S. Supreme Court, 384 U.S. 855 (decided June 20, 1966).

22. *Daily Labor Report* 168, August 29, 1966.

23. *Daily Labor Report* 8, January 12, 1967; 49, March 13, 1967. As of the latter date, Mine Mill had 28,000 American and 14,000 Canadian members; all American nonferrous unions together had about 45,000 members.

Although the formal completion of the merger was set for July 1, consummation was delayed for several more days. See United Steelworkers of America and the International Union of Mine, Mill and Smelter Workers, *Agreement of Affiliation of United Steelworkers of America and the International Union of Mine, Mill and Smelter Workers,* dated November 18, 1966, which includes the following attachments: Exhibit A, seniority list for Mine Mill personnel; Summary of the Agreement of Affiliation and Merger, dated November 18, 1966, signed by Bernard Kleiman, general counsel, USW, and Nathan Witt, general counsel, IUMMSW.

24. The foregoing section is based in part on interviews in 1986 with John Corbett, John F. Boland, Jr., M. P. Scanlon, and Ralph B. Sievwright.

25. See Philip Taft, "The Problem of Structure in American Labor," *American Economic Review,* 27 (March 1937): 4–16; Jensen, op. cit., p. 48.

26. Recall that ASARCO plants were already being unionized by Mine Mill in 1939. At this company alone—for some reason—fragmentation never occurred. Instead, Mine Mill became sole bargaining agent for the entire work force at each property except the Garfield smelter.

27. The scheme did not address the question of multiple unionism, which was at the core of the fragmentation problem. Casting was not a part of nonferrous, either.

28. The role of the locals in this arrangement is somewhat obscure. They were to send delegates to the wage policy committee and to the company bargaining committees. But the overall scheme was so highly centralized that the national office staff would have been able to exert actual control.

29. The other unions were Electrical Workers, Electricians, Machinists, Teamsters, Auto Workers, Operating Engineers, Laborers, Trainmen, Conductors, Firemen, Railway Carmen, Boilermakers, Carpenters, Painters, Plumbers and Pipe Fitters, Office Employees, Pattern Makers, Sheet Metal Workers, Switchmen, Bricklayers, Chemical Workers, Structural Iron Workers, Locomotive Engineers, Molders, Independent Office Employees, and Shipbuilders.

30. *Daily Labor Report* 58, F-1-4, March 24, 1967.

31. William N. Chernish, *Coalition Bargaining: A Study of Union Tactics and Public Policy* (Philadelphia: University of Pennsylvania Press, 1969), pp. 5–6, 27–28, 179–182; George H. Hildebrand, "Cloudy Future for Coalition Bargaining," *Harvard Business Review* (November-December 1968): 114–128.

32. Chernish, op. cit., p. 185.

9. Collective Bargaining Developments and Negotiations, 1967–1990

1. Negotiations beyond the limits of the original units had already emerged for mutual convenience (for example, the ASARCO–Mine Mill Council and the numerous metal trades councils at various properties). These developments

were the product of mutual consent, however, and fell far short of the USW goals of 1967.

2. This system prevailed in big steel from 1956 to 1984, when the employers' committee was dissolved.

3. From an official statement of the USW position presented to a special federal review panel by vice president Joseph P. Molony, *Daily Labor Report* 21, January 30, 1968.

4. Later Molony admitted that the coalition initially had proposed that all companies meet together with the unions in a single city to make it "easier for us to negotiate simultaneously." The employers promptly rejected the idea.

5. To accomplish this goal, the coalition could hold off final approval of all settlements while insisting that the other employers match the terms granted by the most liberal one—a version of the "most favored nation" principle.

6. This sequence of events is based primarily on the Decision and Order, National Labor Relations Board (August 19, 1970); and Trial Examiner's Decision, Matter between Phelps Dodge Corporation, charging party, and G. B. Curry, president, International Union of Operating Engineers, Local no. 428, et al., *Decisions and Orders of the National Labor Relations Board*, 184, at 976, June 30, 1970–August 19, 1970 (Washington, D.C.: Government Printing Office, 1974).

7. *Daily Labor Report* 21, January 30, 1968. In fact, the industry was by no means anxious to invoke Taft-Hartley. Rather, it hoped to have the coalition and its members found guilty of an unfair labor practice for their alleged refusal to bargain in good faith. At the time, both Kennecott and Phelps Dodge were charging parties in separate proceedings before the NLRB.

8. *Daily Labor Report* 20, January 29, 1968; 21, January 30, 1968; 22, January 31, 1968; 23, February 1, 1968.

9. Interview with John F. Boland, Jr., November 24, 1986. In his corroborative account of these events, Martin S. Bennett, trial examiner in the Phelps Dodge case before the NLRB, stated that Molony was the person who first told Boland of necessary approval by the steering committee. Bennett also referred to "approval by the NIC," the Nonferrous Industry Conference. In fact, the Coordinating and Steering Committee had the actual control; the NIC merely ratified its actions. Cf. *Decisions and Orders of the National Labor Relations Board*, at 986.

10. Phelps Dodge filed charges against the union coalition for its Western Operations on February 28 and June 17, 1968. On July 10, 1969, the trial examiner handed down his decision, supporting the company's complaint that the respondent unions had violated section 8(b)(3) of the Labor-Management Relations Act by seeking unilaterally to impose company-wide bargaining; by making the Arizona settlement conditional on NIC approval; and by refusing to execute the Arizona agreement, although it had been reduced to writing,

until settlements were reached at other units of the company. On August 19, 1970, the NLRB sustained these findings and recommendations.

Kennecott Copper Corporation filed similar charges against its segment of the coalition on October 19, 1967.

11. *Daily Labor Report* 55, March 19, 1968; 59, March 25, 1968; 60, March 26, 1968.

12. *Decisions and Orders of the National Labor Relations Board*, at 977. The board cited the following leading case on behalf of its position: Douds v. International Longshoremen's Association, 241 F. 2d 278, 282–283 (C.A.2).

13. *Daily Labor Report* 127, July 1, 1971; 138, July 19, 1971; 139, July 20, 1971; 144, July 27, 1971; 145, July 28, 1971; 176, September 10, 1971; 185, September 23, 1971.

14. *Daily Labor Report* 142, July 23, 1974.

15. *Daily Labor Report* 124, June 26, 1974.

16. Commerce Clearing House (CCH), Employment Practices Decisions, *U.S. v. Inspiration Consolidated Copper Company*, 6 EPD 8918; United States District Court, District of Arizona; no. 70–91 Globe; April 9 and September 25, 1973.

17. These three ethnic categories were devised by the court, but without quotation marks for the "Anglo." Presumably, that term was intended to refer rather broadly to Caucasians of northern European, Irish, and British stock and "Mexican-American" to Spanish-speaking persons primarily of Mexican origin or descent.

18. *Daily Labor Report* 128, July 1, 1977; 129, July 5, 1977; 142, July 22, 1977; 147, July 29, 1977; 153, August 8, 1977.

19. *Daily Labor Report* 127, June 30, 1980; 128, July 1, 1980.

20. *Daily Labor Report* 75, April 18, 1983.

21. Garth Mangum and Camille Guth, "The Future of Utah Copper," *Utah Business and Economic Review* (January-February 1987): 18.

22. The Standard Oil Company of Ohio (SOHIO), its successor (the Standard Oil Company), and the latter's eventual sole owner (British Petroleum Company) had been pumping large sums into the support of Kennecott, which had experienced a cumulative loss of over $600 million by 1986. ARCO had done the same thing with Anaconda until it abandoned mining in 1983. Magma drew support for its operating losses from its parent, Newmont Mining. ASARCO was able to save itself during these dreary years because it was a diversified metals producer, not solely dependent on copper mining.

23. For American mining as a whole, the wage premium for unionized over nonunionized properties has been estimated at 60 percent—the highest for all primary industrial groups. See Peter Linneman and Michael L. Wachter, "Rising Union Premiums and the Declining Boundaries among Noncompeting Groups," *American Economic Review*, Papers and Proceedings, 76 (May 1986): 103–107.

24. The distinction between protected and proscribed strike-supporting activities was sharpened by the NLRB in *Clear Pine Mouldings, Inc.*, 268 NLRB no. 173 (decided February 22, 1984).

    May an employer who hires replacements during a strike legally offer them permanent jobs, as Phelps Dodge did in 1983? To do so would threaten the opportunity for strikers to return to their jobs once the dispute was settled. In turn this would constitute antiunion discrimination in violation of federal labor law, as the U.S. Supreme Court found in 1938 in *National Labor Relations Board v. Mackay Radio and Telegraph Co.*, 304 U.S. 333 (decided May 16, 1938). But in his majority opinion Justice Owen J. Roberts added a contradictory dictum that effectively set aside the protection against discrimination by holding that an employer "is not bound to discharge those hired to fill the places of strikers, upon the election of the latter to resume their employment, in order to create places for them." This finding is still the rule today. Thus the assurance of permanence remains legal. The promise made by Phelps Dodge in 1983 qualifies for this exemption, but more relevant is the fact that the PD strike was never settled or abandoned. Accordingly, the strikers never made an unconditional offer to return, and no technical possibility for discrimination could occur.

25. In the *Fansteel* case in 1939, the U.S. Supreme Court confronted the problem of the limits of protected strike activity. *Fansteel Metallurgical Corporation v. NLRB*, 306, U.S. 240, 1939.

26. A leading arbitration case that carefully distinguishes protected from proscribed strike activities is *Indiana Bell Telephone Co.*, 22 LA 567, 1954.

27. If the coalition leaders had abandoned the strike at this point, the strikers would have become eligible for reemployment in any vacancies extant or forthcoming, although their replacements had preferential standing at the time, as a condition of their initial employment. By continuing the strike for another two years, the leaders took the strikers past the July 1, 1984, first anniversary date, whereupon they lost all standing, including the right to vote in the later decertification elections.

28. U.S. Department of the Interior, Bureau of Mines, *Minerals Yearbook, 1983* and *1984*.

29. *Daily Labor Report* 29, February 12, 1986; 126, July 1, 1986; 140, July 22, 1986; interview with John R. Corbett, July 1986.

30. "IBEW Members to Have Representation Election at Miami," *Pay Dirt*, January 1989, p. 14A.

31. "Cyprus Miami and Electrical Union Reach Unusual Pact," *Pay Dirt*, March 1989, p. 8A.

32. "Cyprus Miami Workers to Hold Representation Vote April 27th," *Pay Dirt*, April 1989, p. 12A.

33. "Early Labor Contract Negotiations Break Off at Magma Copper," *Pay Dirt*, February 1989, p. 6A.

34. "Copper Strike Threat Vanishes as ASARCO, Magma Get Pacts," *Pay Dirt*, July 1989, pp. 3A–4A.
35. "Magma Kicks Off Innovative Labor Package at Superior," *Pay Dirt*, November 1990, pp. 8A–9A.
36. "Chino Union Members Reject Proposed Early Three-Year Pact," *Pay Dirt*, November 1989, p. 3A.
37. "Union Defectors Are Stirring the Pot at Chino," *Pay Dirt*, May 1990, p. 7A.
38. "Kennecott Gains Early Settlement," *Pay Dirt*, June 1990, pp. 8A–9A; confidential interviews with participants.
39. "New Labor Contract in Place at Chino Mines in New Mexico," *Pay Dirt*, July 1990, p. 8A.
40. "Chino Pipefitters Reverse Field, Vote to Retain Union," *Pay Dirt*, September 1990, p. 10A.
41. "Union Workers on Strike at ASARCO's Ray Unit in Arizona," *Pay Dirt*, July 1990, pp. 7A–8A.
42. "New Labor Contract in Place at ASARCO's Ray Mine in Arizona," *Pay Dirt*, August 1990, p. 3A.
43. "Tyrone Workers File Decertification Petition with NLRB," *Pay Dirt*, September 1990, p. 10A.

10. The Past as Prologue and Instruction

1. William C. Conger, "History of the Clifton-Morenci District," in Michael Canty and Michael N. Greeley, eds., *History of Mining in Arizona* (Tucson: Mining Club of the Southwest Foundation, 1987), pp. 99–128.
2. To some extent the Morenci and Metcalf pits were preceded by the older underground Joy, Longfellow, and Metcalf mines. In the main, however, the pits were based on the previously undeveloped Clay ore body, acquired in 1931.
3. All data concerning primary production and its components, apparent consumption and its components, and prices are taken from U.S. Department of the Interior, Bureau of Mines, *Minerals Yearbook*, various issues.
4. Alfred Marshall, *Principles of Economics* (London: Macmillan, 5th ed., 1907), vol. 1, pp. 384–386.
5. It is true that industry-wide uniformity might have been useful for political and organizing purposes.
6. On the lower elasticity of demand for labor at the industry level, see George H. Hildebrand, *American Unionism: A Historical and Analytical Survey* (Reading, Mass.: Addison-Wesley, 1969), pp. 66–74.
7. John R. Commons, "American Shoemakers," in *Labor and Administration, 1684–1895* (New York: Macmillan, 1913).
8. Thus lead is used in storage batteries and for solder; zinc, in galvanizing; silver, in photographic film; copper, in wire and tubing; gold, in jewelry and

for dental and monetary purposes; nickel, as an alloy and catalyst; and molybdenum, as a steel hardener.

9. The cross-elasticity of demand for lead, L, relative to the price of copper, C, may be expressed arithmetically as $(\Delta q_L/Q_L) \div (\Delta p_C/P_C)$, where the changes (Δ) are small.

10. It can be demonstrated that the craft unions in nonferrous might well have made larger gains by acting independently instead of joining a coalition, because the demand for skilled services is normally much less elastic than the demand for semiskilled and unskilled workers. The principal reason is that craft work is essential, has no close substitutes, and represents a very small percentage of total production cost.

11. John P. Hoerr, *And the Wolf Finally Came: The Decline of the American Steel Industry* (Pittsburgh: University of Pittsburgh Press, 1988), pp. 69, 344, 399.

12. Ibid., pp. 65–68, 72.

13. Ibid., p. 403.

14. Ibid., pp. 405–406, 516, 608–609.

15. Cited in Raymond L. Mikesell, *The Global Copper Industry, Problems and Prospects* (London: Croom Helm, 1988), p. 140.

16. Steven C. Leuthold, "Short Copper! Why the Red Metal Is Headed down the Tubes," *Barron's*, November 14, 1988. Two years later—on October 18, 1990—the price was $1.24 a pound.

17. U.S. Congress, Office of Technology Assessment, *Copper: Technology and Competitiveness* (Washington, D.C.: Government Printing Office, September 1988), pp. 74–75.

18. "Honoree Strauss Predicts No Steep Drop in Copper Prices," *Pay Dirt*, January 1989. Simon D. Strauss is a retired vice chairman of ASARCO.

19. Anthony G. B. Hayes, as quoted by Tim Metz, "Copper Stock Prices Are Expected to Climb, at Least Briefly, Following Rise in Metal's Price," *Wall Street Journal*, December 16, 1988.

20. Robert H. Woody, "Worldwide Turmoil Bodes Well for U.S. Copper Producers," *Salt Lake Tribune*, September 25, 1990.

21. "The Horrendous Problems at Cananea Have Very Deep Roots," *Pay Dirt*, September 1989, pp. 6B–7B; "Mexico Finally Sells Cananea," *Pay Dirt*, September 1990, pp. 6A–7A.

22. World Bank, "World Bank Predictions," 1988, p. 3 (mimeographed draft).

23. Kenji Takeuchi, John E. Strongman, Shunichi Maeda, and C. Suan Tan, *The World Copper Industry: Its Changing Structure and Future Prospects* (Washington, D.C.: World Bank, 1987), p. iii.

24. Richard de J. Osborne, chairman of ASARCO, as cited in Alecia Swasy, "Out of the Pits: Once Nearly Moribund U.S. Copper Industry Springs Back to Life," *Wall Street Journal*, December 16, 1988.

INDEX

WERTHEIM PUBLICATIONS IN INDUSTRIAL RELATIONS

Published by Harvard University Press

J. D. Houser, *What the Employer Thinks*, 1927
Wertheim Lectures on Industrial Relations, 1929
William Haber, *Industrial Relations in the Building Industry*, 1930
Johnson O'Connor, *Psychometrics*, 1934
Paul H. Norgren, *The Swedish Collective Bargaining System*, 1941
Leo C. Brown, S.J., *Union Policies in the Leather Industry*, 1947
Walter Galenson, *Labor in Norway*, 1949
Dorothea de Schweinitz, *Labor and Management in a Common Enterprise*, 1949
Ralph Altman, *Availability for Work: A Study in Unemployment Compensation*, 1950
John T. Dunlop and Arthur D. Hill, *The Wage Adjustment Board: Wartime Stabilization in the Building and Construction Industry*, 1950
Water Galenson, *The Danish System of Labor Relations: A Study in Industrial Peace*, 1952
Lloyd H. Fisher, *The Harvest Labor Market in California*, 1953
Donald J. White, *The New England Fishing Industry: A Study in Price and Wage Setting*, 1954
Val R. Lorwin, *The French Labor Movement*, 1954
Philip Taft, *The Structure and Government of Labor Unions*, 1954
George B. Baldwin, *Beyond Nationalization: The Labor Problems of British Coal*, 1955
Kenneth F. Walker, *Industrial Relations in Australia*, 1956
Charles A. Myers, *Labor Problems in the Industrialization of India*, 1958
Herbert J. Spiro, *The Politics of German Codetermination*, 1958
Mark W. Leiserson, *Wages and Economic Control in Norway, 1945–1957*, 1959
J. Pen, *The Wage Rate under Collective Bargaining*, 1959
Jack Stieber, *The Steel Industry Wage Structure: A Study of the Joint Union-Management Job Evaluation Program in the Basic Steel Industry*, 1959
Theodore V. Purcell, S.J., *Blue Collar Man: Patterns of Dual Allegiance, in Industry*, 1960
Carl Erik Knoellinger, *Labor in Finland*, 1960
Sumner H. Slichter, *Potentials of the American Economy, Selected Essays*, edited by John T. Dunlop, 1961
C. L. Christenson, *Economic Redevelopment in Bituminous Coal: The Special Case of Technological Advance in the United States Coal Mines, 1930–1960*, 1962
Daniel L. Horowitz, *The Italian Labor Movement*, 1963

Adolf Sturmthal, *Workers Councils: A Study of Workplace Organization on Both Sides of the Iron Curtain*, 1964

Vernon H. Jensen, *Hiring of Dock Workers and Employment Practices in the Ports of New York, Liverpool, London, Rotterdam, and Marseilles*, 1964

John L. Blackman, Jr., *Presidential Seizure in Labor Disputes*, 1957

Mary Lee Ingbar and Lester D. Taylor, *Hospital Costs in Massachusetts: An Economic Study*, 1968

Kenneth F. Walker, *Australian Industrial Relations Systems*, 1970

David Kuechle, *The Story of the Savannah: An Episode in Maritime Labor-Management Relations*, 1971

Studies in Labor-Management History

Lloyd Ulman, *The Rise of the National Trade Union: The Development and Significance of Its Structure, Governing Institutions, and Economic Policies*, second edition, 1955

Joseph P. Goldberg, *The Maritime Story: A Study in Labor-Management Relations, 1957*, 1958

Walter Galenson, *The CIO Challenge to the AFL: A History of the American Labor Movement, 1935–1941*, 1960

Morris A. Horowitz, *The New York Hotel Industry: A Labor Relations Study*, 1960

Mark Perlman, *The Machinists: A New Study in American Trade Unionism*, 1961

Fred C. Munson, *Labor Relations in the Lithographic Industry*, 1963

Garth L. Mangum, *The Operating Engineers: The Economic History of a Trade Union*, 1964

David Brody, *The Butcher Workmen: A Study of Unionization*, 1964

F. Ray Marshall, *Labor in the South*, 1967

Philip Taft, *Labor Politics American Style: The California State Federation of Labor*, 1968

Walter Galenson, *The United Brotherhood of Carpenters: The First Hundred Years*, 1983

Distributed by Harvard University Press

Martin Segal, *The Rise of the United Association: National Unionism in the Pipe Trades, 1884–1924*, 1969

Arch Fredric Blakey, *The Florida Phosphate Industry: A History of the Development and Use of a Vital Mineral*, 1973

George H. Hildebrand and Garth L. Mangum, *Capital and Labor in American Copper, 1845–1990; Linkages between Product and Labor Markets*, 1991